nova net Self Help

MBU 203 KF

Test
Pg 78, & 84

10TH EDITION

Principles of
COST
ACCOUNTING

Charles F. Nagy, PhD, CPA
**Emeritus Accounting Faculty
Cleveland State University
Cleveland, Ohio**

Edward J. VanDerbeck, MS, CPA
**Professor of Accounting
Xavier University
Cincinnati, Ohio**

Contributing Editor: Dr. Michael R. Ruble
Western Washington University

SOUTH-WESTERN College Publishing

An International Thomson Publishing Company

Acquisitions Editor: Gary Bauer
Developmental Editor: Tom Bormann
Production Editor: Shelley Brewer
Production House: Bookmark Media
Title Cover Designer: Michael H. Stratton
Cover Illustrator: Michael H. Stratton
Internal Illustrator: Joseph M. Devine
Manufacturing Coordinators: Karen Truman & Sue Disselkamp
Marketing Manager: Dreis Van Landuyt

AE68JA
Copyright © 1996
by South-Western College Publishing
Cincinnati, Ohio

Library of Congress Cataloging-in-Publication Data:

Nagy, Charles F.
      Principles of cost accounting / Charles F. Nagy, Edward J.
VanDerbeck ; contributing editor Michael R. Ruble. — 10th ed.
          p. cm.
      Includes index.
      ISBN 0-538-84403-5
      1. Cost accounting. I. Vanderbeck, Edward J. II. Ruble, Michael
R. III. Title.
HF5686.C8S352 1995   94-43247
657'.42—dc20   CIP

 2 3 4 5 6 7 8 9 D1 4 3 2 1 0 9 8 7
Printed in the United States of America

I(T)P
International Thomson Publishing
South-Western College Publishing is an ITP Company. The ITP trademark is used under license.

Preface

WHY STUDY COST ACCOUNTING

The tenth edition of *Principles of Cost Accounting* provides a thorough understanding of cost concepts, cost behavior, and cost accounting techniques as applied to manufacturing cost systems. Students learn how to: determine costs of products and services more accurately; use the knowledge of product and service costs to set selling prices, to bid on contracts, and to analyze the relative profitability of various products and services; use techniques to measure the performance of managers and subunits within an organization; design an accounting system to fit the production and distribution system of an organization; and use the accounting system as a tool to motivate managers towards the organization's goals.

TENTH EDITION FORMAT

1. Provides coverage for a one-quarter or one semester cost accounting course.

2. Presents the principles and procedures of job order costing, process costing, and standard costing in a logical and concise manner.

3. Discusses the special purpose reports and analytical techniques of managerial accounting.

4. Retains the ten-chapter format—a distinguishing feature of the text. The main thrust of the revision has been to produce a very readable and relevant text that covers the essentials of cost accounting, introduces real-world examples where appropriate, reinforces the discussion with demonstration problems, and offers students practice in mastering the topics with relevant end-of-chapter questions, exercises, and problems. Some problems are adapted to computer solution.

5. Integrates the uses of cost information with a discussion of cost accumulation systems and procedure, while offering practice material that closely resembles the chapter presentation.

TENTH EDITION FEATURES

The tenth edition includes several features to facilitate the learning process for the student and enhance the teachability of the text for the instructor.

APPENDICES

Appendix 2A illustrates Just-In-Time (JIT) inventory systems; Appendix 9A illustrates four-variance and three-variance methods of analysis.

DEMONSTRATION PROBLEMS

A demonstration problem is included at the end of each chapter (except Chapters 5 and 10) with a step-by-step explanation of how to solve it. The demonstration problem is constructed from a difficult concept(s) in the chapter and reinforces the techniques and procedures discussed in the chapter. Some chapters contain a problem very similar to the demonstration problem; if this is the case, it is indicated at the end of the demonstration problem.

REAL-WORLD EXAMPLES

Real-world examples are predominantly excerpts from articles in journals authored and read by accounting practitioners explaining the latest in cost accounting techniques used to adapt to the rapid changes in manufacturing technology. Examples of topics include just-in-time inventory systems, world-class manufacturing, highly automated manufacturing systems where direct labor costs are insignificant, and cost allocation methods aimed at determining the "true" cost of a product or service.

NEW INTEGRATED LEARNING OBJECTIVES

Learning objectives begin each chapter. Each learning objective is indicated in the text where first discussed. All end-of-chapter exercises and problems are identified by learning objectives.

KEY TERMS

Key terms are highlighted as they are introduced and are listed, along with page references, at the end of each chapter. A comprehensive glossary has been added at the end of the book which provides definitions for all of the key terms.

END-OF-CHAPTER MATERIALS

The end-of-chapter questions, exercises, and problems have been carefully written and revised to reflect the coverage as it appears in the chapters. There has been a concerted effort to provide the instructor with a wide choice of subject matter and degree of difficulty when assigning end-of-chapter materials. Additionally, selected problems may be solved using spreadsheet software.

NEW DIRECTED ASSIGNMENTS

At specific points within each chapter, students are directed to appropriate end-of-chapter assignments. This allows students to work practice items without completing the entire chapter.

SUPPLEMENTARY MATERIALS

A complete package of supplementary materials is available with the tenth edition of *Principles of Cost Accounting* to assist both instructors and students. The package includes materials that have been carefully prepared and reviewed.

AVAILABLE TO INSTRUCTORS

Solutions Manual. This manual contains the answers to all end-of-chapter questions, exercises, and problems.

Solutions Transparencies. Transparencies of solutions for end-of-chapter exercises and problems are available.

Instructor's Manual. Part 1 provides summaries and outlines for each chapter to facilitate development of classroom presentations and homework assignments. Part 2 contains a test bank of multiple choice questions and problems for each chapter, accompanied by solutions. Part 3 contains end-of-chapter problem check figures that may be reproduced and distributed to students at the discretion of the instructor.

MicroExam 4.0 offers a microcomputer version for MS-DOS computers of the printed test bank in the Instructor's Manual. MicroExam enables the user to select, mix, edit, and add questions or problems to create the type of text or problem set needed.

Achievement Tests. Six preprinted tests consisting of objective questions and short problems are available to adopters. Each test covers one or two chapters of text material.

Practice Set Keys. Solutions for both the manual practice set, Mountain Oak Office Interiors (MOOI), and the computerized practice set, WEMAKE TOYS INC., are available to adopters.

Template Diskette. This spreadsheet template disk can be used for solving selected end-of-chapter problems. The diskette, which may be copied, is available upon adoption from South-Western College Publishing. An ![SS] icon identifies the exercises and problems.

AVAILABLE TO STUDENTS

Study Guide and Working Papers. This item includes both a study guide and working papers bound in a single volume, with perforated pages for easy removal. The study guide provides a review summary for each chapter and questions and problems to test comprehension of chapter material. Solutions for all questions and problems are included in a separate section at the end of the study guide. The working papers include printed forms for use in solving the problems at the end of each chapter of the textbook.

The Mountain Oak Office Interiors Practice Set. This job order practice set is designed for use with the textbook after Chapter 5 has been completed. The revised practice set has been shortened by minimizing repetitive transactions.

WEMAKE TOYS INC. by Stephen S. Hamilton. This job order practice set is available in both a manual and a computerized version for IBM microcomputers.

ACKNOWLEDGMENTS

We wish to thank the American Institute of Certified Public Accountants and the National Association of Accounting for their permission to use their materials in this publication. We thank the following faculty who reviewed the previous edition or manuscript for this edition and provided helpful suggestions.

Sherrie Dusch
Barnes Business College

Lawrence J. Eaton
Gateway Technical College—
Kenosha Campus

Sharon Johnson
Kansas City Kansas Community
College

William P. Schindler
Clark State Community College

David R. Swehla
Coastline Community College

We continued to welcome your comments and suggestions.

Charles F. Nagy
Edward J. VanDerbeck

Brief Contents

Contents

Introduction to Cost Accounting

LEARNING OBJECTIVES

After studying this chapter, you should be able to:

1. Explain the uses of cost accounting data
2. Describe the relationship of cost accounting to financial accounting
3. Identify the three basic elements of manufacturing costs
4. Distinguish between the two basic types of cost accounting systems

The importance of accounting information to the successful operation of a business, including specific cost data, has always been recognized. However, in the current global economic environment, such information is more crucial than ever. Automobiles from Japan, electronic equipment from Korea, shoes from Brazil, and clothing from China are just a few examples of foreign-made products that have provided stiff competition to U.S. manufacturers both at home and abroad. As a result of these pressures, companies today are placing more emphasis on controlling costs in an attempt to keep their products competitive. Cost accounting provides the detailed cost data that management needs to control current operations and plan for the future. As Figure 1-1 illustrates, cost accounting provides the information that allows management to allocate resources to the most efficient and profitable areas of operation.

All types of business entities—manufacturing, merchandising, and service businesses—require cost accounting information systems to account for their activities. Manufacturers convert purchased raw

FIGURE 1-1   Production Process for Goods and Services

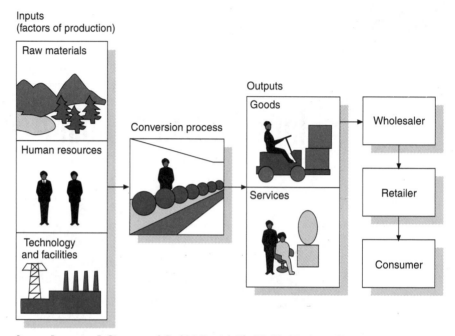

Source: Lawrence J. Gitman and Carl McDaniel, *The World of Business*, (Cincinnati, OH: South-Western Publishing Co., 1992).

materials into finished goods by using labor, technology, and facilities. **Merchandisers** purchase finished goods for resale. They may be **retailers**, who sell products to individuals for consumption, or **whole-salers**, who purchase goods from manufacturers and sell to retailers. **For-profit service businesses**, such as airlines, architects, and hair stylists, sell services rather than products. **Not-for-profit service agencies**, such as charities, governmental agencies, and some health care facilities provide services at little or no cost to the user.

The nature of the manufacturing process requires that the **accounting information systems** of manufacturers be designed to accumulate detailed cost data relating to the production process. Thus, it is common today for manufacturing companies of all sizes to have **cost accounting systems** that show the costs incurred and document where and how these expenditures were used. While the cost accounting principles and procedures discussed in the text emphasize manufacturers, many of the same principles apply to merchandising and service businesses. Cost accounting is now recognized as essential to the efficient operation of hospitals, social welfare agencies, and numerous other entities.

THE MANUFACTURING PROCESS

In many ways, the activities of a manufacturing organization are similar to those of a merchandising business. Both purchase, store, and sell goods; both must have efficient management and adequate sources of capital; both may employ hundreds or thousands of workers. The manufacturing process itself highlights the distinction between the two: merchandisers, such as Foot Locker, buy athletic footwear in marketable form to resell to their customers; manufacturers, such as Reebok, must make the goods they sell. Once the merchandising organization has acquired goods, it can perform the marketing function. The purchase of raw materials by a manufacturer, however, is only the beginning of a long, and sometimes complex, chain of events that results in a finished article for sale.

The manufacturing process involves the conversion of raw materials into finished goods through the use of labor and various other factory resources. The manufacturer must make a major investment in physical assets, such as factory buildings and specialized types of machinery and equipment. To carry out the manufacturing process, the manufacturer must purchase appropriate quantities of raw materials, supplies, and parts and build up a work force to convert these resources into finished goods.

In addition to the cost of materials and labor, the manufacturer incurs other expenses in the production process. Many of these costs, such as depreciation, taxes, insurance, and utilities, are similar to those incurred by a merchandising concern. Other costs, such as machine maintenance and repair, materials handling, and production setup, scheduling, and inspection, are unique to manufacturers. Once the goods have been manufactured and are ready for sale, the manufacturer performs basically the same functions as the merchandiser. The methods of accounting for sales, cost of goods sold, and selling and administrative expenses are similar to those of merchandisers. Service businesses, by comparison, have no inventories because the service is consumed at the time it is provided. Service businesses have revenue and operating expenses, but no cost of goods sold.

USES OF COST ACCOUNTING DATA

LEARNING OBJECTIVE
Explain the uses of cost accounting data

Principles of cost accounting have been developed that enable the manufacturer to process the many different costs associated with manufacturing and to provide built-in control features. The information produced by a cost accounting system provides a basis for determining product costs and selling prices, and it helps management to plan and control operations.

DETERMINING PRODUCT COSTS AND PRICING

Cost accounting procedures provide the means to gather the data needed to determine product costs and thus to generate meaningful financial statements and other reports relevant to management. Cost procedures must be designed to permit the determination of **unit costs** as well as total product costs. For example, the fact that a manufacturer spent $10,000 for labor in a certain month is not, in itself, meaningful; but if this labor produced 5,000 finished units, the fact that the cost of labor was $2 per unit is significant. This figure can be compared to the unit labor cost of other periods and, to some extent, competitors.

Unit cost information is also useful in making a variety of important marketing decisions:

1.   **Determining the selling price of a product.** Knowing the cost of manufacturing a unit of product aids in setting the selling price. This price should be high enough to cover the cost of producing the item, including the marketing and administrative expenses attributable to it, and to provide a profit. The real-world example on the following page illustrates this.

2.   **Meeting competition.** If a product is being undersold by a competitor, detailed information regarding unit costs can be used to determine whether the problem can be resolved by reducing the selling price, by reducing manufacturing costs, or by eliminating the product.

3.   **Bidding on contracts.** Many manufacturers must submit competitive bids in order to be awarded contracts. An analysis of the unit costs relating to the manufacture of a particular product is of great importance in determining the bid price.

4.   **Analyzing profitability.** Unit cost information enables management to determine the amount of profit that each product earns and possibly eliminate the least profitable products, thereby concentrating its efforts on those most profitable. It is not uncommon, however, for some companies to retain a certain line of goods yielding a very low profit, or even a loss, in order to maintain the product variety that will attract those customers who also purchase the more profitable items.

PLANNING AND CONTROL

The ultimate value of cost accounting lies in the use of the data accumulated and reported. One of the most important functions of cost accounting is to develop information that management can use to plan and control operations.

REAL-WORLD EXAMPLE

"THE $7 ASPIRIN"

The practice of *cost shifting* is explained in an article in *Management Accounting*, which discusses product costs and pricing in a service industry.

In response to a reader who wrote in to complain about being charged $7 for a single aspirin tablet during a hospital stay, Ann Landers responded that the charge included several elements in addition to the cost of the aspirin, including the prescribing physician's time, the administering nurse's time, the medical records department's efforts, and a surcharge for the hospital's unreimbursed Medicare patient charges. This practice of passing on unreimbursed charges such as Medicare to other areas of patient care is known as *cost shifting*.

A cost accountant who saw Ms. Landers' column added a number of other costs that were shifted to the cost of the aspirin. These included the cost of unreimbursed hospital care provided to indigent and impoverished patients, the uncollectible accounts receivable of the hospital, the cost of malpractice insurance, underutilized bed capacity, and hospital administrative and operating costs. After various costs are shifted from other products to the aspirin, the aspirin tablet now has a cost basis of $3.50. Add profit, and presto—the $7 aspirin.

David W. McFadden, "The Legacy of the $7 Aspirin," *Management Accounting*, April 1990, pp. 38–41.

Planning is the process of establishing objectives or goals for the firm and determining the means by which the firm will attain them. Effective planning is facilitated by the following:

1. **Clearly defined objectives of the manufacturing operation.** These objectives may be expressed in the number of units to be produced, the quality desired, the estimated cost per unit, or the timing necessary to meet customer demand without carrying excessive inventories.

2. **A production plan that will assist and guide the company in reaching its objectives**. This detailed plan includes a description of the necessary manufacturing operations to be performed, a projection of personnel needs for the period, and the coordination of the timely acquisition of materials and facilities.

Cost accounting enhances the planning process by providing historical costs that serve as a basis for future projections. Management can analyze the data to estimate future costs and operating results and to make decisions regarding the acquisition of additional facilities, changes in marketing strategies, and the availability of capital.

The word "control" is used in many different ways, but from the viewpoint of the manufacturing concern, **control** is the process of monitoring the company's operations and determining whether the objectives identified in the planning process are being accomplished. Effective control is achieved through the following ways:

1. Assigning responsibility
2. Periodically measuring and comparing results
3. Taking necessary corrective action

Assigning Responsibility. Responsibility should be assigned for each detail of the production plan. All managers and supervisors should know precisely what their responsibilities are in terms of efficiency, operations, production, and costs. The key to proper control involves the use of responsibility accounting and cost centers.

The essence of **responsibility accounting** is the assignment of accountability for costs or production results to those individuals who have the most authority to influence them. It involves an information system that traces the data to the responsible managers.

A **cost center** is a unit of activity within the factory to which costs may be practically and equitably assigned. A cost center may be a department or a group of workers; it could represent one job, one process, or one machine. The criteria for a cost center are (1) a reasonable basis on which manufacturing costs can be allocated and (2) a person who has control over and is accountable for many of the costs charged to that center.

With responsibility accounting, the manager of a cost center is accountable only for those costs that the manager controls. For example, labor and materials costs will be charged to the cost center, but the manager may be responsible only for the quantity of materials used and the number of labor hours worked. This manager would probably not be accountable for the unit cost of raw materials or the hourly rate paid to employees. These expenses are normally beyond the manager's control and are the responsibility of the purchasing and personnel departments. The manager may be responsible for the cost of machinery maintenance and repair due to misuse in the cost center, but he or she would not be responsible for the costs of depreciation, taxes, and insurance on the machinery if the decision to purchase the machinery was made at a higher level in the organization. If production in the cost center for a given period is lower than planned, this could be due to poor supervision, which is the manager's responsibility; however, if less-skilled workers are being hired, this is usually beyond the manager's control.

Cost and production reports for a cost center reflect all cost and production data identified with that center. In a responsibility accounting system, the specific data for which the manager is responsible would be highlighted or segregated to evaluate that manager's performance and initiate action to correct deficiencies. Quite often, however, both a cost and production report and a separate performance report will be prepared for a cost center; the **performance report** will include only those costs and production data that the center's manager can control.

These reports must be furnished at regular intervals (monthly, weekly, or daily) on a timely basis. To provide the maximum benefit, the reports should be available as soon as possible after the end of the period being reported. Reports not produced in a timely fashion are not effective as a control device.

Periodically Measuring and Comparing Results. Actual operating reports should be measured periodically and compared with the objectives established in the planning process. This analysis, which may be made monthly, weekly, daily, or even hourly in the case of production and scrap reports, is a major part of cost control because it compares current performance with the overall plan. The actual dollars, units produced, hours worked, or materials used are compared with the **budget**, which is management's operating plan expressed in quantitative terms (units and dollars). This comparison is a primary feature of cost analysis. The number of dollars expended or the quantity of units produced have little significance until compared with the budgeted amounts. Actual results of prior periods may also be compared to highlight meaningful trends.

Taking Necessary Corrective Action. The reports produced by the measurement and analysis of operating results may identify problem areas and deviations from the plan. Appropriate corrective action should be implemented where necessary. A significant variation from the plan is a signal for attention. An investigation may reveal a weakness to be corrected or a strength to be better utilized.

Management wants to know not only the results of operations, but how the results—whether favorable or unfavorable—compare with the plan, why things happened, and who was responsible. Management must be prepared to improve existing conditions; otherwise, the periodic measurement of activity has little value. Accountants can be key players in this endeavor as the following real-world example "Not Just Bean Counters Anymore" illustrates.

NOT JUST BEAN COUNTERS ANYMORE

Once upon a time South Central Bell, like so many other companies, had an accounting department that paid the bills, kept the records, and prepared the financial statements each month. Period. The other departments did the work, ran the company, and made the decisions. The accounting department kept score.

Not any more. When a corporate reorganization presented the opportunity to "show their stuff," South Central Bell's management accountants accepted the challenge and shed the backroom scorekeeping image forever.

How did we do it? By showing how management accountants can be value-added business partners and integral parts of the management team. To do this we had to step out of the traditional role of compilers (accurate and controlled transaction processors) and take on the roles of interpreter, adviser, and partner. We had to understand what the numbers mean, relate the numbers to business activity, and recommend alternative courses of action. Finally, we had to evaluate alternatives and make decisions to maximize business efficiency.

Steven R. Harrison, "Not Just Bean Counters Anymore," *Management Accounting*, March 1993, pp. 29–32.

RELATIONSHIP OF COST ACCOUNTING TO FINANCIAL ACCOUNTING

LEARNING OBJECTIVE
Describe the relationship of cost accounting to financial accounting

The objective of accounting is to accumulate financial information for use in making economic decisions. **Financial accounting** focuses on gathering information to be used in preparing financial statements that meet the needs of investors, creditors, and other external users of financial information. The statements include a balance sheet, income statement, retained earnings statement, and statement of cash flows. Although these financial statements are useful to management as well as external users, additional reports, schedules, and analyses are required for internal use in planning and control. Management spends most of its time evaluating the problems and opportunities of individual departments and divisions of the company rather than looking at the entire company at once. As a result, the external financial statements for the whole company are of little help to management in making these day-to-day decisions. Cost accounting provides the additional information required for these special reports to management and also provides data necessary to prepare the financial statements. For example, cost accounting procedures are necessary to determine: whether to make or buy a product component; the cost of goods sold on the income statement; and the valuation of inventories on the balance sheet.

COST OF GOODS SOLD

Merchandising concerns compute cost of goods sold as follows:

Beginning merchandise inventory
Plus **purchases** (merchandise)

Merchandise available for sale
Less ending merchandise inventory

Cost of goods sold

The amount of purchases represents the cost of goods acquired during the period for resale.

Because the manufacturing concern makes rather than buys the products it has available for sale, the term "finished goods inventory" replaces "merchandise inventory" and the term "cost of goods manufactured" replaces "purchases" in determining the cost of goods sold:

Beginning finished goods inventory
Plus **cost of goods manufactured**

Finished goods available for sale
Less ending finished goods inventory

Cost of goods sold

The cost of goods manufactured amount is supported by a schedule detailing the costs of materials, labor, and the expenses of maintaining and operating a factory.

The format of the income statement for a manufacturer is not significantly different from that of a merchandiser. However, the cost accounting procedures involved in gathering the data for determining the cost of goods manufactured are considerably more complex than the recording of merchandise purchased in its finished form. These procedures are introduced in this chapter and discussed in detail in subsequent chapters. The income statements for service businesses do not have a cost of goods sold section, because they provide a service rather than a product.

INVENTORIES

If a merchandiser has unsold items on hand at the end of an accounting period, the cost of the merchandise is reflected in the current asset section of the balance sheet in the following manner:

Finance Account

Current assets:
  Cash
  Accounts receivable
  Merchandise inventory

On the balance sheet of a manufacturing concern, the current asset section is expanded as follows:

Cost Accounting

Current assets:
  Cash
  Accounts receivable
  Inventories:
    Finished goods
    Work in process
    Materials

The balance of the **finished goods** account represents the total cost incurred in manufacturing goods completed but still on hand at the end of the period. The balance of the **work in process** account includes all manufacturing costs incurred to date for goods in various stages of production but not yet completed. The balance of the **materials** account represents the cost of all materials purchased and on hand to be used in the manufacturing process, including raw materials, prefabricated parts, and other factory materials and supplies. Raw materials for one company are often the finished product of another company. For example, rolled steel to be used in the production of automobiles would be the final product of the steel mill. Prefabricated parts would include units, such as electric motors, assembled by another manufacturer to be used in the manufacture of a product such as office machines. Other materials and supplies might include screws, nails, rivets, lubricants, and solvents.

Service entities do not have inventories on their balance sheets because they provide a service rather than a product. A summary comparison of manufacturing, merchandising, and service businesses appears on the following page.

Valuation of Inventories. Many procedures used to gather costs are unique to manufacturers. Manufacturers' inventories are valued for external financial reporting purposes using inventory costing methods—such as first-in, first-out (FIFO), last-in, first-out (LIFO), and moving average—which are also used by merchandisers. Most manufacturers maintain a perpetual **inventory system** that provides a continuous record of purchases, issues, and balances of all goods in stock. Generally these data are verified by periodic counts of selected items throughout the year. Under the perpetual system, inventory valuation data for financial state-

Business Sector	Examples	Product or Service	Inventory Account(s)
Service	Airlines, architects, hair stylists, sports franchises	Intangible benefits such as transportation, designs, grooming, entertainment	None
Merchandising	Athletic souvenirs, department stores, poster shops, wholesalers	Tangible products purchased from suppliers in finished form	Merchandise inventory
Manufacturing	Aircraft producers, athletic equipment makers, home builders, pharmaceutical producers	Physical products created by the application of labor and technology to raw materials	Finished goods, work in process, materials

ment purposes are available at any time, as distinguished from a **periodic inventory system** that requires estimating inventory during the year for interim statements and shutting down operations to count all inventory items at the end of the year.

In addition to providing inventory valuation data for the financial statements, the detailed cost data and perpetual inventory records provide the information necessary to control inventory levels, to ensure the timely availability of materials for production, and to detect pilferage, waste, and spoilage. Inventory valuation and control are discussed in detail in Chapter 2.

Inventory Ledgers. Generally both merchandisers and manufacturers maintain various subsidiary ledgers, such as that for accounts receivable. In addition, manufacturers usually maintain subsidiary ledgers for the general ledger inventory control accounts, Finished Goods, Work in Process, and Materials. These subsidiary ledgers are necessary for a perpetual inventory system and provide the detailed balances and information to support the balances in the control accounts.

Some manufacturers use a **factory ledger**, which contains all of the accounts relating to manufacturing, including the inventory accounts. This ledger, which is maintained at the factory, is tied in to the general ledger at the main office through a special account for the factory on the main office books and a special account for the main office on the factory books.

You should now be able to work the following: Questions 1–12.

ELEMENTS OF MANUFACTURING COST

Manufacturing or production costs are classified into three basic elements: (1) direct materials, (2) direct labor, and (3) factory overhead.

DIRECT MATERIALS

The costs of materials that become part of and can be readily identified with a certain manufactured product are classified as **direct materials** costs. Examples include lumber used in making furniture, fabric used in the production of clothing, iron ore used in the manufacture of steel products, and rubber used in the production of athletic shoes.

Many types of materials and supplies necessary for the manufacturing process either cannot be readily identified with any particular manufactured item or have a relatively insignificant cost. The costs of items such as sandpaper used in sanding furniture, lubricants used on machinery, and other items for general factory use are classified as **indirect materials** costs. Similarly classified are materials that actually become part of the finished product but whose costs are relatively insignificant, such as thread, screws, rivets, nails, and glue.

DIRECT LABOR

The cost of labor for those employees who work directly on the product manufactured, such as machine operators or assembly line workers, is classified as **direct labor** cost. The wages and salaries of employees who are required for the manufacturing process but who do not work directly on the units being manufactured are considered **indirect labor costs**. This classification includes the wages and salaries of department heads, inspectors, materials handlers, and maintenance personnel. Payroll related costs, such as payroll taxes, group insurance, sick pay, vacation and holiday pay, retirement program contributions, and other fringe benefits, even for the direct laborers, also are usually treated as indirect costs.

FACTORY OVERHEAD

Factory overhead is known by various names—factory burden, manufacturing expenses, indirect costs, manufacturing overhead, and factory expenses—and includes all costs related to the manufacturing of a product except direct materials and direct labor. Thus factory overhead includes indirect materials, indirect labor, and other manufacturing expenses, such as depreciation on the factory building and machinery and equipment, supplies, heat, light, power, maintenance, insurance, taxes, and payroll related costs. As factories have become more automated, factory overhead as a percentage of total manufacturing cost has increased dramatically.

SUMMARY OF MANUFACTURING COSTS

The costs of direct materials and direct labor are sometimes combined and described as the **prime cost** of manufacturing a product. Prime cost plus factory overhead equals total cost of manufacturing. Direct labor cost and factory overhead, which are necessary to convert the direct materials into finished goods, can be combined and described as **conversion cost**. These manufacturing costs are illustrated in Figure 1-2.

Marketing or selling expenses, general administrative costs, and other nonfactory expenditures are not included in the costs of manufacturing. However, some costs incurred by a manufacturer may benefit both factory and nonfactory operations. Examples include depreciation, insurance, and property taxes on a building that houses both the factory and the administrative offices. In this situation, an allocation of cost must be made to each business function.

FLOW OF COSTS

All three elements of manufacturing cost flow through the work in process inventory account. The cost of direct materials and direct labor used in production are charged (debited) directly to Work in Process. All other factory costs—indirect labor, indirect materials, and other factory expenses—are charged to the factory overhead account and later transferred to Work in Process. When goods are completed, the total costs incurred in producing the goods are transferred from Work in Process to the finished goods inventory account. When goods are sold, the costs incurred to manufacture the goods are transferred from Finished Goods to Cost of Goods Sold. Figure 1-3 illustrates the flow of manufacturing costs.

FIGURE 1-2   Prime Cost and Conversion Cost

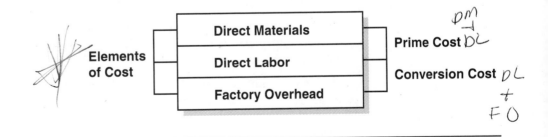

FIGURE 1-3   Flow of Costs

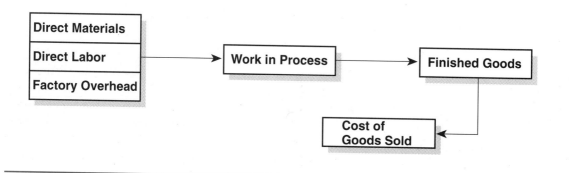

ILLUSTRATION OF ACCOUNTING FOR MANUFACTURING COSTS

Cost accounting procedures are used to accumulate and allocate all elements of manufacturing cost in a manner that will produce meaningful data for the internal use of management and for the preparation of external financial statements. The following example illustrates basic cost accounting procedures, utilizing the terminology and principles that were discussed previously.

The Eastern Furniture Company, a small, newly organized corporation, manufactures wicker furniture—both tables and chairs. The firm sells products directly to retailers. The basic steps in the company's production process are as follows:

1. Pieces of rattan, a natural fiber grown in the Orient, are purchased in precut specifications. The pieces are assembled to form the frame of the table or chair in the Assembly Department.

2. The legs and back uprights of the chair and the legs and outline of the tabletop are then wrapped in binding cane in the Wrapping Department.

3. The seat and back of the chair and the tabletop are now ready to be woven into place in the Weaving Department where the chair or table is finished.

The beginning balance sheet for the company on January 1 of the current year is presented as follows:

Eastern Furniture Company
Balance Sheet
January 1, 19—

Assets		Liabilities and Stockholders' Equity	
Cash	$ 40,000	Liabilities	$ -0-
Building	250,000	Capital stock	$365,000
Machinery and equipment	75,000	Total liabilities and	
Total assets	$365,000	stockholders' equity	$365,000

Assume, for the purpose of simplification, that in January the company makes only one style of table and no chairs. During January the following transactions are completed and recorded, in summary form:

1. Materials (rattan, binding cane, nails, tacks, staples, glue, and solvents) are purchased on account at a cost of $25,000.

Materials	25,000	
Accounts Payable		25,000

The cost of materials purchased is charged to the inventory control account, Materials. This treatment is based on the assumption that the company uses a perpetual inventory system.

2. During the month, direct materials (rattan, binding cane) costing $20,000 and indirect materials (nails, tacks, staples, glue, and solvents for cleaning) costing $995 are issued to the factory.

Work in Process (Direct Materials)	20,000	
Factory Overhead (Indirect Materials)	995	
Materials		20,995

Direct materials issued are charged directly to the work in process control account, but the indirect materials are charged to the factory overhead account. The factory overhead account will be used to accumulate various factory expenses that will later be transferred to Work in Process.

3. Total gross wages and salaries earned for the month were factory employees working on the product, $10,000; factory supervision, maintenance, and custodial employees, $3,500; and sales and administrative employees, $6,500. The entries to record the payroll and the

payments to employees (ignoring payroll deductions) would be as follows:

Payroll	20,000	
Wages Payable		20,000
Wages Payable	20,000	
Cash		20,000

paid off

4. The entry to distribute the payroll to the appropriate accounts would be as follows:

Work in Process (Direct Labor)	10,000	
Factory Overhead (Indirect Labor)	3,500	
Selling and Administrative Expenses (Salaries)	6,500	
Payroll		20,000

The wages earned by employees working directly on the product are charged to Work in Process, while the salaries and wages of the factory supervisor and the maintenance and custodial personnel, who do not work directly on the product, are charged to Factory Overhead as indirect labor. The salaries of nonfactory employees are debited to a separate expense account.

In order to focus on specific cost accounting procedures as distinguished from general accounting procedures, the general ledger account Selling and Administrative Expenses will be used to accumulate all nonmanufacturing expenses. Usually, separate general ledger control accounts would be established for selling expenses and administrative expenses.

5. Depreciation expense for the building is 6% of cost per year. The sales and administrative offices occupy one-tenth of the total building, and the factory operation is contained in the other nine-tenths. The expense for one month is recorded as follows:

Factory Overhead (Depr. of Building)	1,125	
Selling and Administrative Expenses (Depr. of Building)	125	
Accumulated Depr.—Building		1,250

($250,000 × .06 × 1/12 = $1,250; $1,250 × .90 = $1,125; $1,250 × .10 = $125)

The cost accounting principle illustrated here is that only those costs directly related to production should be charged to Factory Overhead. Depreciation on the portion of the building used as office space is an administrative expense and should not be treated as an element of product cost.

6. Depreciation expense for machinery and equipment is 20% of cost per year.

Dep EX

```
Factory Overhead (Depr. of Machinery and Equipment)  .    1,250
    Accumulated Depr.—Machinery and Equipment  . . .              1,250
```

($75,000 × .20 × 1/12 = $1,250)

All machinery and equipment is used in the factory for production purposes, so the depreciation expense is properly charged to Factory Overhead.

7. The cost of heat, light, and power for the month was $1,500.

utilities =
```
Factory Overhead (Utilities) . . . . . . . . . . . . . .    1,350
Selling and Administrative Expenses (Utilities)  . . . . .     150
    Accounts Payable  . . . . . . . . . . . . . . . . .            1,500
```

Because one-tenth of the building is used for office purposes, 10% of the total utilities cost is allocated to Selling and Administrative Expenses.

8. Miscellaneous selling and administrative expenses for telephone, office supplies, travel, and rental of office furniture and equipment totaled $3,750.

```
Selling and Administrative Expenses . . . . . . . . . .    3,750
    Accounts Payable  . . . . . . . . . . . . . . . . .            3,750
```

Many other expenses may be incurred by a manufacturing organization, but for simplicity it is assumed that no other expenses were incurred during the month. After posting the journal entries to the appropriate ledger accounts, Factory Overhead will reflect the following debits:

Transaction	Description	Amount
2.	Indirect materials	$ 995
4.	Indirect labor	3,500
5.	Depr. of building	1,125
6.	Depr. of machinery and equipment	1,250
7.	Utilities	1,350
	Total	$8,220

9. The balance in Factory Overhead is transferred to Work in Process by the following entry:

```
Work in Process  . . . . . . . . . . . . . . . . . . .    8,220
    Factory Overhead  . . . . . . . . . . . . . . . . .            8,220
```

The three elements of manufacturing cost—direct materials, direct labor, and factory overhead—are now accumulated in Work in Process. The debits in the account are as follows:

Transaction	Description	Amount
2.	Direct materials	$20,000
4.	Direct labor	10,000
6.	Factory overhead	8,220
	Total	$38,220

10. Assuming that all goods started in process have been finished, the following entry transfers the cost of these goods from Work in Process to Finished Goods:

Finished Goods	38,220	
Work in Process		38,220

Assuming that 1,000 tables were produced during the month, the unit cost is $38.22 ($38,220/1,000). The unit cost for each element of manufacturing cost is calculated as follows:

	Total	Units Produced	Unit Cost
Direct materials	$20,000	1,000	$20.00
Direct labor	10,000	1,000	10.00
Factory overhead	8,220	1,000	8.22
	$38,220		$38.22

If the same type of table is produced in future periods, the unit costs of those periods can be compared with the unit costs determined in the preceding example. Any differences can be analyzed so that management might take appropriate action.

The unit cost also serves as a basis for establishing the selling price of the tables. After considering the anticipated selling and administrative expenses, management establishes a selling price that should provide a reasonable profit. The selling price may be determined by adding a **mark-on percentage**, which is a percentage of the manufacturing cost per unit. For example, if management decides that a 50% mark-on percentage is necessary to cover the product's share of selling and administrative expenses and to earn a satisfactory profit, the selling price per unit, rounded to the nearest cent, would be calculated as follows:

Manufacturing cost	$38.22
Mark-on percentage (50%)	19.11
Selling price	$57.33

In later periods, it might be found that this particular item cannot be sold at a price high enough to provide a reasonable profit. Through analysis of the unit costs, management might effect a cost-cutting measure or perhaps even discontinue production of the item.

From this example, it is apparent that, at any given time, the cost of each item in inventory is available. It should be reemphasized that one function of cost accounting is the accurate determination of the cost of manufacturing a unit of product. This knowledge of unit cost helps management to plan and control operations and to make marketing decisions.

To continue with the example, assume that the following transactions take place in January (in addition to those already recorded):

11. Invoices of $25,000, representing costs of materials, utilities, and selling and administrative expenses, are paid.

Accounts Payable	25,000	
Cash		25,000

12. A total of 800 tables are sold to retailers at a net price of $57.33 each.

Accounts Receivable (800 × $57.33)	45,864	
Sales		45,864
Cost of Goods Sold (800 × $38.22)	30,576	
Finished Goods		30,576

Because the unit cost of each item is known, the cost of goods sold can be determined without a physical inventory or cost estimate.

13. Cash totaling $33,000 is collected on accounts receivable.

Cash	33,000	
Accounts Receivable		33,000

The accounts in the general ledger will reflect the entries as follows:

Cash					Accounts Receivable			
1/1 Bal.	40,000	3.	20,000	12.	45,864	13.	33,000
13.	33,000	11.	25,000	*12,864*			
	73,000		*45,000*				
28,000							

Finished Goods			
10.	38,220	12.	30,576
	7,644		

Work in Process

2. Direct materials	20,000	10.		38,220
4. Direct labor	10,000			
9. Factory overhead	8,220			
	38,220			

Materials

1.	25,000	2.	20,995
	4,005		

Building

1/1 Bal.	250,000

Accumulated Depr.—Building Equipment

5.	1,250

Machinery and Equipment

1/1 Bal.	75,000

Accumulated Depr.—Machinery and Equipment

6.	1,250

Accounts Payable

11.	25,000	1.	25,000
		7.	1,500
		8.	3,750
			30,250
			5,250

Wages Payable

3.	20,000	3.	20,000

Payroll

3.	20,000	4.	20,000

Capital Stock

1/1 Bal.	365,000

Sales

	12.	45,864

Cost of Goods Sold

12.	30,576

Factory Overhead

2. Indirect materials	995	9.	8,220
4. Indirect labor	3,500		
5. Depr. of building	1,125		
6. Depr. of machinery & equip.	1,250		
7. Utilities	1,350		
	8,220		

Selling and Administrative Expenses	
4. Salaries	6,500
5. Depr. of building	125
7. Utilities	150
8. Other	3,750
	10,525

After calculating the balance of each general ledger account, the equality of the debits and credits is proven by preparing a trial balance, as follows.

Eastern Furniture Company
Trial Balance
January 31, 19—

Cash	$ 28,000	
Accounts Receivable	12,864	
Finished Goods	7,644	
Work in Process	-0-	
Materials	4,005	
Building	250,000	
Accumulated Depreciation—Building		$ 1,250
Machinery and Equipment	75,000	
Accumulated Depreciation—Machinery and Equipment		1,250
Accounts Payable		5,250
Payroll	-0-	
Capital Stock		365,000
Sales		45,864
Cost of Goods Sold	30,576	
Factory Overhead	-0-	
Selling and Administrative Expenses	10,525	
	$418,614	$418,614

Note that the finished goods control account reflects the cost of the 200 units still on hand—200 × $38.22 = $7,644.

From an analysis of the general ledger accounts and the trial balance, financial statements for the period are prepared as follows:

new

Must Know.

Eastern Furniture Company
Statement of Cost of Goods Manufactured
For the Month Ended January 31, 19—

Direct materials:		
Inventory, January 1	$ -0-	
Purchases	25,000	
Total cost of available materials	$25,000	
Less inventory, January 31	4,005	
Cost of materials used	$20,995	
Less indirect materials used	995	
Cost of direct materials used in production		$20,000
Direct labor		10,000
Factory overhead:		
Indirect materials	$ 995	
Indirect labor	3,500	
Depreciation of building	1,125	
Depreciation of machinery and equipment	1,250	
Utilities	1,350	
Total factory overhead		8,220
Cost of goods manufactured during the month		$38,220

must Know!

Eastern Furniture Company
Income Statement
For the Month Ended January 31, 19—

Net sales		$45,864
Cost of goods sold:		
Finished goods inventory, January 1	$ -0-	
new Add cost of goods manufactured	38,220	
Goods available for sale	$38,220	
Less finished goods inventory, January 31	7,644	30,576
Gross profit on sales		$15,288
Selling and administrative expenses		10,525
Net income		$ 4,763

*Must
Know*

Eastern Furniture Company
Balance Sheet
January 31, 19—

Assets

Current assets:

Cash			$ 28,000
Accounts receivable			12,864
Inventories:			
Finished goods		$ 7,644	
Work in process		-0-	
Materials		4,005	11,649
Total current assets			$ 52,513
Plant and equipment:			
Building	$250,000		
Less accumulated depreciation .	1,250	$248,750	
Machinery and equipment	$ 75,000		
Less accumulated depreciation .	1,250	73,750	
Total plant and equipment			322,500
Total assets			$375,013

Liabilities and Stockholders' Equity

Current liabilities:

Accounts payable			$ 5,250
Stockholders' equity:			
Capital stock		$365,000	
Retained earnings		4,763	
Total stockholders' equity			369,763
Total liabilities and stockholders' equity			$375,013

The figures in the cost of goods manufactured statement were obtained by analyzing the appropriate general ledger accounts. The materials inventory account had no beginning balance but has an ending balance of $4,005. The amount of purchases during the period was determined by analysis of the debits to the materials account. The cost of direct materials used of $20,000 and the direct labor cost of $10,000 were obtained from the work in process account. All other items in the statement of cost of goods manufactured represent factory overhead and are determined from the factory overhead account in the general ledger.

This discussion has presented a complete cycle in cost accounting procedures. Before proceeding, carefully review the basic elements of terminology and flow of costs. A firm grasp of the fundamentals already covered is necessary to comprehend the more complex material in subsequent chapters. Figure 1-4 presents a graphic illustration of the flow of

FIGURE 1-4   Flow of Costs

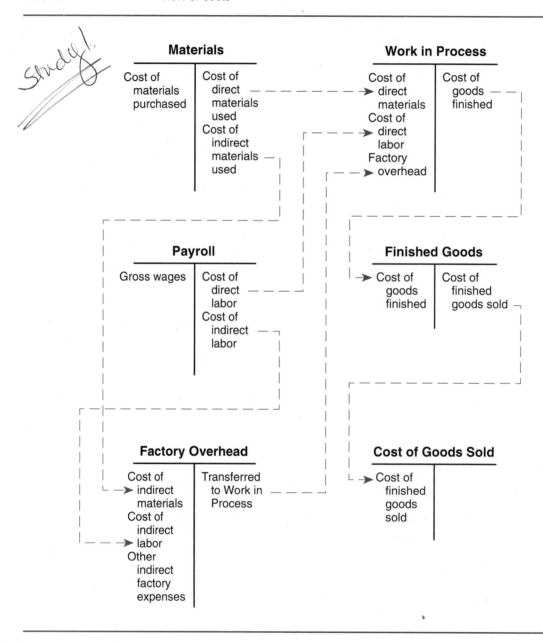

costs. You should study this illustration carefully, following each line to trace the flow of costs.

> **You should now be able to work the following: Questions 13–18; Exercises 1–4, 7; Problems 1, 5, 7.**

COST ACCOUNTING SYSTEMS

The previous example presented the basic foundation of a cost accounting system. In that illustration, costs were accumulated for one month. At the end of the month, the costs were divided by the total units produced to determine the unit cost. This accomplished one function of cost accounting: the determination of product costs—both total costs for the period and cost per unit. However, another important objective of a cost accounting system—cost control—could not be satisfactorily achieved using the described procedure. As was stated, unit costs could be compared with similar costs in future periods to determine if costs were increasing. Assuming that in a subsequent month the cost of direct labor had risen from $10.00 to $11.00 per unit, it is necessary to investigate and determine whether something can be done to correct the situation. The described accounting procedure restricts any investigation, because it is not known exactly where in the factory this increase has occurred. Labor costs went up; but did they go up because of a general rise in wages or because of inefficiency? Did labor costs increase throughout the manufacturing process or for a particular department or job? Answers to such questions are not readily available using the procedures described in the earlier example.

LEARNING OBJECTIVE
Distinguish between the two basic types of cost accounting systems

To provide management with the data needed for effective cost control, two basic types of cost accounting systems have been developed: the process cost system and the job-order cost system. Both systems are used to gather cost data and to allocate costs to goods manufactured. The selection of one method or the other depends on the type of manufacturing operation used by a given company. To determine the appropriate method, manufacturing operations are classified into two types: continuous or mass production and special order.

CONTINUOUS OR MASS PRODUCTION

This type of operation produces a continuous output of homogeneous products. Such an enterprise may produce a single product, such as an automobile, or many different products, such as soft drinks or pharmaceuticals. The factory generally is departmentally organized. Continuous or mass production industries include those manufacturing automobiles, tires, cement, chemicals, canned goods, lumber, paper, candy, foodstuffs, flour, glass, soap, toothpaste, chewing gum, petroleum products, textiles, plastics, and paints, and firms engaged in such processes as rubber compounding and vulcanizing. This type of manufacturing enterprise normally uses a **process cost system**.

Process cost accounting suits manufacturing situations in which all units of the final product are substantially identical. Finished units are placed in stock and removed as needed to fill customer orders. There are no separate jobs presenting substantially different characteristics; rather, the company (or a department within the company) produces large numbers of virtually identical items that are sold (or transferred to other departments) as orders are received. Process cost accounting techniques may be used by organizations that provide a service such as for determining the cost per X-ray in a hospital's X-ray department or the cost per passenger-mile for an airline. Chapters 6 and 7 cover process cost accounting.

SPECIAL ORDER

In this type of operation, the output consists of special or custom-made products; in other words, each product is made to order. An order may be an external or internal order for a predetermined quantity of products. Special order industries include those manufacturing or producing locomotives, ships, aircraft, machine tools, engines, structural steel, books and magazines, directories and catalogs, and specialty shops producing custom-made products such as clothing, shoes, hats, or custom-built homes. A **job-order cost system** is appropriate in these circumstances. Job-order cost accounting techniques may be used by service organizations such as accounting, architecture, and law firms to perform functions such as determining the cost to service a client. Figure 1-5 shows examples of the use of job-order cost and process cost systems in service, merchandising, and manufacturing businesses.

COMBINATION OF SYSTEMS

Some companies use both a job-order cost and a process cost system. For example, a company that manufactures goods on specific order but also produces, on a continuous basis, a number of small parts to be used in most job orders may benefit from combining the systems. The costs of making these small parts would be accumulated on a process cost basis, while the costs for each job would be gathered on a job cost sheet.

STANDARD COSTING

The job-order and process cost accounting systems are the principal systems used by manufacturing organizations. However, as useful as they

FIGURE 1-5   Uses of Cost Systems

Cost System	Service Business	Merchandising Business	Manufacturing Business
Job-Order	Architectural firm, executive recruiters	Lumber company, personal computer retailer	Custom homebuilder, printer
Process	Hospital x-ray department, hotel housekeeping	Newspaper publishing, agricultural wholesaler	Paper producer, brewery

are in providing cost data, these systems are still limited with regard to cost control. Although they make it possible to determine what a product actually costs, they provide no means to determine what the product should have cost. A standard cost accounting system, which is not a third system but may be used with either a job-order or a process cost system, is designed to furnish a measurement that will help management make decisions regarding the efficiency of operations.

Standard costs would be incurred under efficient operating conditions and are forecast before the manufacturing process begins. During operations, an organization compares the actual costs incurred with these predetermined standard costs. "Variances," or differences, are then calculated. These variances reveal which performances deviate from the standard, and thus they provide a basis on which management can take appropriate action to eliminate inefficient operating conditions. Standard cost accounting will be discussed in depth and illustrated in Chapters 8 and 9.

ILLUSTRATION OF JOB-ORDER COST SYSTEM

With a job-order cost system, costs are accumulated by job (or lot). One advantage of a job-order cost system is that the accumulation of costs for a particular job helps to determine its selling price. Or, if a job is done under contract with a set price, the profit or loss on the job can be readily determined by comparing the cost with the contract price. At the same time, costs that have been accumulated for a certain type of work will assist management in preparing bids for similar jobs in the future.

To illustrate the use of the job-order cost accounting system, assume that the Eastern Furniture Company accepts two orders to manufacture certain items during the month of February. These special orders are as follows:

1. From Wicker Warehouse: to manufacture 1,000 chairs to Wicker's specifications; contract price, $36,000.

2. From The Wicker Shop: to manufacture 500 tables to Wicker's specifications; contract price, $29,650.

After accepting these orders and planning the manufacturing requirements as to materials, labor, and overhead, the cost accounting department sets up a job cost sheet for each job. Figure 1-6 illustrates this form for the Wicker Warehouse order. All costs applicable to each job will be

FIGURE 1-6   Job Cost Sheet

CONRAD CANING COMPANY
Job Cost Sheet

Customer Name: Wicker Warehouse   Job No: 101

Address: 5525 Skyway Dr.   Date Started: 2/24

Houston, TX 77057

Quantity: 1,000   Date Completed: 2/28

Product: chairs

Description: 39" wicker

DIRECT MATERIALS			DIRECT LABOR			FACTORY OVERHEAD		
Date	Mat'l Req. No.	Amount	Date	Time Tkt. No.	Amount	Date	Basis Applied	Amount
2/24	5505	8,200	2/25	2101	2,500		60% of	
2/26	6211	4,000	2/27	2826	1,500		total	
			2/28	3902	2,000	2/28	over-head	5,007
Total		12,200			6,000			5,007

SUMMARY

				Remarks:
Direct materials	$12,200	Selling price	$36,000	
Direct labor	6,000	Mfg. cost	23,207	
Factory overhead	5,007	Gross profit	$12,793	
Total cost	$23,207			
Unit cost	$ 23.21			

accumulated on these forms. Job numbers 101 and 102, respectively, are assigned to these orders.

Transactions and journal entries for the month of February appear as follows. To highlight job-order cost accounting procedures, only those entries relating to the manufacture of goods will be illustrated. Routine entries, such as those for recording the purchase of materials, nonmanufacturing expenses, or payments to creditors, will be ignored, as these entries are made in the same way as previously illustrated, regardless of the cost system used.

1. Indirect materials with a cost of $2,620 are issued to the factory, and direct materials are issued as follows:

	Job 101	Job 102
Rattan	$11,000	$8,000
Binding Cane	1,200	1,000
	$12,200	$9,000

The entry at the end of the week to record the issues of materials appears as:

Work in Process—101	12,200	
Work in Process—102	9,000	
Factory Overhead (Indirect Materials)	2,620	
Materials		23,820

If the indirect materials could be directly traced to a specific job, the cost could be charged to that job; however, it is often difficult to determine which job benefited from the use of the various supplies. Thus, indirect materials costs are usually charged to Factory Overhead and later distributed among the various jobs.

2. Indirect labor costs of $2,180, and direct labor costs are incurred as follows:

	Job 101	Job 102
Direct Labor	$6,000	$3,750

The weekly entry to distribute these costs is recorded as follows:

Work in Process—101	6,000	
Work in Process—102	3,750	
Factory Overhead (Indirect Labor)	2,180	
Payroll		11,930

3. Monthly depreciation expense for the building is recorded as fol-
    lows:

    Factory Overhead (Depr. of Building)   1,125
    Selling and Administrative Expenses
    (Depr. of Building)   125
        Accumulated Depr.—Building   1,250

4. The entry to record monthly depreciation for machinery and equip-
    ment is recorded as follows:

    Factory Overhead (Depr. of Machinery
    and Equipment)   1,250
        Accumulated Depr.—Machinery
        and Equipment   1,250

5. The cost of utilities for the month of February is $1,300 and is
    recorded as follows:

    Factory Overhead (Utilities)   1,170
    Selling and Administrative Expenses (Utilities)   130
        Accounts Payable   1,300

6. Total charges to Factory Overhead for the month are shown as fol-
    lows:

    Indirect materials $2,620
    Indirect labor   2,180
    Depr. of building   1,125
    Depr. of machinery and equipment   1,250
    Utilities   1,170
    Total $8,345

    Assume that factory overhead is allocated as follows: 60% to Job 101,
    40% to Job 102.

Total Factory Overhead	60% Job 101	40% Job 102
$8,345	$5,007	$3,338

    The distribution of factory overhead would be recorded as follows:

    Work in Process—101   5,007
    Work in Process—102   3,338
        Factory Overhead   8,345

At the end of the month, the work in process and factory overhead accounts would appear as follows:

Work in Process—101		
1. Direct materials	12,200	
2. Direct labor	6,000	
6. Factory overhead	5,007	
	23,207	

Work in Process—102		
1. Direct materials	9,000	
2. Direct labor	3,750	
6. Factory overhead	3,338	
	16,088	

Factory Overhead			
1. Indirect materials	2,620	6. Transfer to Work in Process	8,345
2. Indirect labor	2,180		
3. Depr. of building	1,125		
4. Depr. of mach. and equip.	1,250		
5. Utilities	1,170		
	8,345		

The costs shown in the work in process accounts represent monthly totals (summary entries) for each element of manufacturing cost. These same costs are shown in more detail on job cost sheets such as the one illustrated previously.

7. Assuming both jobs were completed by the end of the month, the costs of the completed jobs would be transferred to the finished goods inventory control account:

Finished Goods	39,295	
Work in Process—101		23,207
Work in Process—102		16,088

8. When the goods are shipped and billed to the customers, the following entries are made to record the sales and the cost of the jobs:

*Add cost
from P8
28*

Accounts Receivable	65,650	
Sales		65,650

Cost of Goods Sold	39,295	
Finished Goods		39,295

The costs of producing the two jobs can be summarized as follows:

	Job 101 (1,000 Units)		Job 102 (500 Units)	
	Total Cost	Unit Cost	Total Cost	Unit Cost
Direct materials	$12,200	$12.20	$ 9,000	$18.00
Direct labor	6,000	6.00	3,750	7.50
Factory overhead	5,007	5.01	3,338	6.68
Total	$23,207	$23.21	$16,088	$32.18

The gross profit realized on each job is determined as follows:

	Job 101 (1,000 Units)		Job 102 (500 Units)	
	Total	Per Unit	Total	Per Unit
Selling price	$36,000	$36.00	$29,650	$59.30
Cost	23,207	23.21	16,088	32.18
Gross profit	$12,793	$12.79	$13,562	$27.12

The job cost sheets would reflect the previous information in more detail so that a short time after each job is completed, the gross profit can be determined. In addition, if management bids on similar jobs in the future, an accurate record of all costs would be available to assist management in determining contract prices.

WORK IN PROCESS CONTROL ACCOUNT

When jobs become too numerous to maintain a separate work in process account for each, a work in process control account in the general ledger will be used. In a job-order cost system, the details on the job cost sheets in the subsidiary job cost ledger support the balance in Work in Process in the general ledger.

WORK IN PROCESS IN THE MANUFACTURING STATEMENT

If there is work in process at the beginning and at the end of the month, it will be shown as follows in the statement of cost of goods manufactured for Galactic Manufacturing Company (note that this statement is more condensed than Figure 1-5 and reflects management's interest in summary data):

> **Galactic Manufacturing Company**
> **Statement of Cost of Goods Manufactured**
> **For the Month Ended June 30, 19—**[r]
>
> | | |
> |---|---:|
> | Direct materials used | $290,000 |
> | Direct labor | 240,000 |
> | Factory overhead | 130,000 |
> | Total manufacturing cost | $660,000 |
> | Add work in process inventory, June 1 | 85,000 |
> | | $745,000 |
> | Less work in process inventory, June 30 | 125,000 |
> | Cost of goods manufactured during the month | $620,000 |

The total manufacturing cost of $660,000 represents the cost of direct materials, direct labor, and factory overhead used during the month of June. Galactic Manufacturing incurred costs of $85,000 during the previous month for goods that were not completed at the end of that month. The total of $745,000, therefore, represents manufacturing cost that the company must account for. Work in Process at the end of June is $125,000, which represents the cost incurred to date for items that were not finished at the end of June. Therefore, the cost of goods completed in June, of which some were started in production the previous month, is $620,000. The work in process ledger account, in T-account form, would appear as follows at the end of the month:

Work in Process			
6/1 Balance	85,000	To Finished Goods	620,000
Direct materials	290,000		
Direct labor	240,000		
Factory overhead	130,000		
	745,000		
125,000			

If a job-order cost system is being used, the balance of $125,000 in the account represents the manufacturing cost incurred to date on jobs that have not yet been completed.

You should now be able to work the following: Questions 20–24; Exercises 5–6; Problems 2–4, 6.

KEY TERMS

Accounting information systems, p. 2
Budget, p. 7
Control, p. 6
Conversion costs, p. 13
Cost accounting, p. 1
Cost accounting systems, p. 2
Cost and production report, p. 7
Cost center, p. 6
Direct labor, p. 12
Direct materials, p. 12
Factory ledger, p. 11
Factory overhead, p. 12
Financial accounting, p. 8
Finished goods, p. 10
For-profit service businesses, p. 2
Indirect labor, p. 12
Indirect materials, p. 12
Job cost ledger, p. 32
Job cost sheet, p. 28
Job-order cost system, p. 26

Manufacturers, p. 1
Manufacturing (or production) costs, p. 12
Manufacturing process, p. 3
Mark-on percentage, p. 18
Materials, p. 10
Merchandisers, p. 2
Not-for-profit service agencies, p. 2
Performance report, p. 7
Periodic inventory system, p. 11
Perpetual inventory system, p. 10
Planning, p. 5
Prime cost, p. 13
Process cost system, p. 26
Responsibility accounting, p. 6
Standard cost accounting system, p. 27
Standard costs, p. 27
Unit costs, p. 4
Wholesalers, p. 2
Work in process, p. 10

SELF-STUDY PROBLEM

BASIC COST SYSTEM; JOURNAL ENTRIES; FINANCIAL STATEMENTS

 The post-closing trial balance of Jay Hawk Manufacturing Co. at September 30 is reproduced as follows.

Jay Hawk Manufacturing Co.
Post-Closing Trial Balance
September 30, 19—

Cash	15,000	
Accounts Receivable	18,000	
Finished Goods	25,000	
Work in Process	4,000	
Materials	8,000	
Building	156,000	
Accumulated Depreciation—Building		23,400
Factory Equipment	108,000	
Accumulated Depreciation—Factory Equipment		54,000
Office Equipment	12,000	
Accumulated Depreciation—Office Equipment		2,000
Accounts Payable		30,000
Capital Stock		175,000
Retained Earnings		61,600
	346,000	346,000

During the month of October, the following transactions took place:

a. Raw materials at a cost of $50,000 and general factory supplies costing $8,000 were purchased on account (materials and supplies are recorded in the materials account).
b. Raw materials to be used in production costing $41,000 and miscellaneous factory supplies costing $5,500 were issued.
c. Wages and salaries incurred for the month were as follows: factory wages (including $2,500 indirect labor), $34,000, and selling and administrative salaries, $5,000. (Ignore payroll withholdings and deductions.)
d. Depreciation was recorded for the month at an annual rate of 5% on the building and 20% on the factory equipment and office equipment. The sales and administrative staff uses approximately one fifth of the building for its offices.
e. During the month, various other expenses totaling $5,200 were incurred on account. The company has determined that one fourth of this amount is allocable to the office function.
f. Total factory overhead costs were transferred to Work in Process.
g. During the month, goods with a total cost of $79,000 were completed and transferred to the finished goods storeroom.
h. Sales for the month totaled $128,000 for goods costing $87,000. (Assume all sales were made on account.)
i. Accounts receivable in the amount of $105,000 were collected.
j. Accounts payable totaling $55,000 and wages payable totaling $39,000 were paid.

Required:

1. Prepare journal entries to record the transactions.
2. Set up T-accounts for all accounts listed in the September 30, 19—, Post-Closing Trial Balance and for Cost of Goods Sold, Factory Overhead, Selling and Administrative Expenses, Sales, and Wages Payable. Post the beginning trial balance and the journal entries prepared in Part 1 to the accounts and calculate the balances in the accounts on October 31.
3. Prepare a statement of cost of goods manufactured, an income statement, and a balance sheet.

SOLUTION TO SELF-STUDY PROBLEM

Suggestions:

Read the entire problem thoroughly, keeping in mind what you are required to do:

1. Journalize the transactions.
2. Post the beginning trial balance and the journal entries to the T-accounts that you set up and calculate the ending balance for each account.
3. Using the ending account balances, prepare a cost of goods manufactured statement, an income statement, and a balance sheet.

The specifics in the problem highlight the following facts:

1. The company is a manufacturer; therefore, three inventory accounts, Materials, Work in Process, and Finished Goods, will be used.
2. A temporary account, Factory Overhead, will be used to record all of the indirect materials, indirect labor, and other manufacturing expenses for the period.

Preparing the journal entries

a. & b. Note that there is only one inventory account for materials, which includes the cost of both direct and indirect materials. When the materials are issued into production, the direct materials are charged to Work in Process and the indirect materials are charged to Factory Overhead.

a.	Materials	58,000	
	Accounts Payable		58,000

b.	Work in Process	41,000	
	Factory Overhead (Indirect Materials)	5,500	
	Materials		46,500

c. The entry to record and distribute the payroll requires the use of the work in process account for the wages of employees who work directly on the product, the factory overhead account of the wages of employees who work in the factory but not directly on the product, and the selling and administrative expenses account for the wages of salespeople and administrative personnel.

c.	Work in Process	31,500	
	Factory Overhead (Indirect Labor)	2,500	
	Selling and Administrative Expenses (Salaries)	5,000	
	Wages Payable		39,000

d., e., and f. The depreciation on the building and equipment and the other expenses are divided between Factory Overhead and Selling and Administrative Expenses depending on the portion of the expense that relates to the factory and the portion that relates to the selling and administrative function. The balance in the Factory Overhead account at the end of the month is transferred to Work in Process.

d.	Factory Overhead (Depr. of Building)	520	
	Factory Overhead (Depr. of Factory Equipment)	1,800	
	Selling and Administrative Expenses (Depr. of Building)	130	
	Selling and Administrative Expenses (Depr. of Office Equipment)	200	
	Accumulated Depr.—Building		650
	Accumulated Depr.—Factory Equipment		1,800
	Accumulated Depr.—Office Equipment		200
e.	Factory Overhead (Miscellaneous)	3,900	
	Selling and Administrative Expenses (Miscellaneous)	1,300	
	Accounts Payable		5,200
f.	Work in Process	14,220	
	Factory Overhead		14,220

g., h., i., and j. When goods are completed, the cost of the goods is taken out of Work in Process and recorded in Finished Goods. When the completed goods are sold, the cost of these goods is removed from the finished goods inventory account and recorded in the cost of goods sold expense account, and the receivable and revenue are recorded for the amount of the sale.

g.	Finished Goods	79,000
	Work in Process	79,000
h.	Accounts Receivable	128,000
	Sales	128,000
	Cost of Goods Sold	87,000
	Finished Goods	87,000
i.	Cash	105,000
	Accounts Receivable	105,000
j.	Accounts Payable	55,000
	Wages Payable	39,000
	Cash	94,000

Posting the beginning trial balance and the journal entries to the T-accounts

Cash

9/30	15,000	j.	94,000
i.	105,000		
	120,000		
	26,000		

Accounts Receivable

9/30	18,000	i.	105,000
h.	128,000		
	146,000		
	41,000		

Finished Goods

9/30	25,000	h.	87,000
g.	79,000		
	104,000		
	17,000		

Work in Process

9/30	4,000	g.	79,000
b.	41,000		
c.	31,500		
f.	14,220		
	90,720		
	11,720		

Materials

9/30	8,000	b.	46,500
a.	58,000		
	66,000		
	19,500		

Building

9/30	156,000		

Accumulated Depr.—Building

		9/30	23,400
		d.	650
			24,050

Factory Equipment

9/30	108,000		

Accumulated Depr.—Factory Equipment				Office Equipment		
		9/30	54,000	9/30	12,000	
		d.	1,800			
			55,800			

Accumulated Depr.—Office Equipment				Accounts Payable		
		9/30	2,000	j.	55,000	9/30	30,000
		d.	200			a.	58,000
			2,200			e.	5,200

Wages Payable							93,200
j.	39,000	c.	39,000				38,200

Capital Stock				Retained Earnings		
		9/30	175,000			9/30	61,600

Sales				Cost of Goods Sold		
		h.	128,000	h.	87,000	

Factory Overhead				Selling and Administrative Expenses		
b.	5,500	f.	14,220	c.	5,000	
c.	2,500			d.	130	
d.	520			d.	200	
d.	1,800			e.	1,300	
e.	3,900				6,630	
	14,220					
-0-						

Preparing a Statement of Cost of Goods Manufactured, an Income Statement, and a Balance Sheet

The total manufacturing cost of $86,720 represents the cost of direct materials, direct labor, and factory overhead incurred during the month of October. Note that the cost of the indirect materials is subtracted in calculating the cost of direct materials used in production because it is included as a separate item under factory overhead. To determine the cost of goods manufactured for October, which really means the cost of the goods completed for the month, you have to add the cost of the beginning work in process inventory, $4,000, and subtract the cost of the ending work in process inventory, $11,720, from the total manufacturing cost for October:

Jay Hawk Manufacturing Co.
Statement of Cost of Goods Manufactured
For the Month Ended October 31, 19—

Direct materials:			
Inventory, October 1	$ 8,000		
Purchases	58,000		
Total cost of available materials	$66,000		
Less inventory, October 31	19,500		
Cost of materials used	$46,500		
Less indirect materials used	5,500		
Cost of direct materials used in production		$41,000	
Direct labor		31,500	
Factory overhead:			
Indirect materials	$ 5,500		
Indirect labor	2,500		
Depreciation of building	520		
Depreciation of factory equipment	1,800		
Miscellaneous expenses	3,900		
Total factory overhead		14,220	
Total manufacturing cost		$86,720	
Add work in process inventory, October 1		4,000	
		$90,720	
Less work in process inventory, October 31		11,720	
Cost of goods manufactured		$79,000	

In preparing an income statement for a manufacturer, remember that the beginning finished goods inventory for the month must be added to the cost of goods manufactured to obtain the cost of goods available for sale. Then the ending finished goods inventory must be subtracted to obtain the cost of goods sold:

Jay Hawk Manufacturing Co.
Income Statement
For the Month Ended October 31, 19—

Net sales			$128,000
Cost of goods sold:			
Finished goods inventory, October 1	$ 25,000		
Add cost of goods manufactured	79,000		
Goods available for sale	$104,000		
Less finished goods inventory, October 31	17,000	87,000	
Gross profit on sales		$ 41,000	

Selling and administrative expenses:

Selling and administrative salaries	$ 5,000	
Depreciation of building	130	
Depreciation of office equipment	200	
Miscellaneous	1,300	6,630
Net income		$34,370

In preparing a balance sheet for a manufacturer, note that there are three separate inventory accounts rather than the single inventory account as for a merchandiser:

Jay Hawk Manufacturing Co.
Balance Sheet
October 31, 19—

Assets

Current assets:			
Cash			$ 26,000
Accounts receivable			41,000
Inventories:			
Finished goods		$ 17,000	
Work in process		11,720	
Materials		19,500	48,220
Total current assets			$115,220
Plant and equipment:			
Building	$156,000		
Less accumulated depreciation . .	24,050	$131,950	
Factory equipment	$108,000		
Less accumulated depreciation . .	55,800	52,200	
Office equipment	$ 12,000		
Less accumulated depreciation . .	2,200	9,800	
Total plant and equipment			193,950
Total assets			$309,170

Liabilities and Stockholders' Equity

Current liabilities:			
Accounts payable			$ 38,200
Stockholders' equity:			
Capital stock		$175,000	
Retained earnings*		95,970	
Total stockholders' equity			270,970
Total liabilities and			
stockholders' equity			$309,170

*$61,600 (bal. on 9/30) + $34,370 (Net income for Oct.) = $95,970

(Note that Problem 1-2 resembles this problem.)

QUESTIONS

1. How does the cost accounting function assist in the management of a business?

2. How do the activities of manufacturers, merchandisers, and service businesses differ?

3. In what ways does a typical manufacturing business differ from a merchandising concern? In what ways are they similar?

4. How are cost accounting data used by management?

5. Why is unit cost information important to management?

6. For a manufacturer, what does the planning process involve and how are cost accounting data used in planning?

7. How is effective control achieved in a manufacturing concern?

8. Define responsibility accounting.

9. What criteria must be met for a unit of activity within the factory to qualify as a cost center?

10. How is cost accounting related to financial accounting?

11. How does the computation of cost of goods sold for a manufacturer differ from that of a merchandiser?

12. How would you describe the following accounts? Finished Goods, Work in Process, and Materials

13. Compare the manufacturing, merchandising, and service sectors. How do they differ as to kinds of businesses in each category, the nature of their output, and type of inventory, if any?

14. What is the difference between a perpetual inventory system and a periodic inventory system.

15. What are the basic elements of production cost?

16. How would you define the following costs: direct materials, indirect materials, direct labor, indirect labor, and factory overhead?

17. How would you define prime cost and conversion cost? Does prime cost plus conversion cost equal the cost of manufacturing?

18. In what way does the accounting treatment of factory overhead differ from that of direct materials and direct labor costs?

19. How do cost of goods sold for a manufacturer and cost of goods manufactured differ?

20. How are nonfactory costs and costs that benefit both factory and nonfactory operations accounted for?

21. What is a mark-on percentage?

22. When is process costing appropriate and what types of businesses use it?

23. When is job order costing appropriate and what types of businesses use it?

24. What are the advantages of accumulating costs by departments or jobs rather than for the factory as a whole?

25. What is a job cost sheet and why is it useful?

26. What are standard costs, and what is the purpose of a standard cost system?

EXERCISES

E1-1
Cost of goods sold—merchandiser
Learning Objective 2

The following data were taken from the general ledger of Millicent Merchandisers on January 31, the end of the first month of operations in the current fiscal year:

Merchandise inventory, January 1,	22,000
Purchases	83,000
Merchandise inventory, January 31,	17,000

Compute the cost of goods sold for the month of January.

E1-2
Cost of goods sold—
manufacturer
Learning Objective 2

The data below were taken from the general ledger and other data of Mikko Manufacturing on July 31:

Finished goods, July 1   93,000
Cost of goods manufactured   343,000
Finished goods, July 31   85,000

Compute the cost of goods sold for the month of July.

E1-3
Cost classification
Learning Objective 3

Classify the following as direct materials, direct labor, factory overhead, or selling and administrative expense.
a. Steel used in an automobile plant.
b. Cloth used in a shirt factory.
c. Fiberglass used by a sailboat builder.
d. Lubricating oils used on machines in a tool factory.
e. Wages of a binder employed in a printing plant.
f. Insurance on factory machines.
g. Rent paid for factory buildings.
h. Wages of forklift operators employed in a factory.
i. Leather used in a shoe factory.
j. Wages of a factory janitor.
k. Electric power consumed in operating factory machines.
l. Depreciation on corporate offices.
m. Fuel used in heating a factory.
n. Paint used in the manufacture of automobiles.
o. Wages of an ironworker in the construction business.
p. Electricity used in lighting sales offices.

E1-4
Cost flow
Learning Objective 3

Explain in narrative form the flow of direct materials, direct labor, and factory overhead costs through the accounts.

E1-5
Journal entries
Learning Objective 3

The following is a list of manufacturing costs incurred by Pisgah Products Co. during the month of July:

Direct materials used $15,000
Indirect materials used   3,000
Direct labor employed   21,000
Indirect labor employed   5,000
Rent expense   4,000
Utilities expense   1,200
Insurance expense   500
Depreciation expense (machinery and equipment)   1,500

Prepare the journal entries necessary to record the preceding information and the entry transferring Factory Overhead to Work in Process.

E1-6
Statement of cost of
goods manufactured;
cost of goods sold
Learning Objective
3, 4

The following data are taken from the general ledger and other records of the Lyle Manufacturing Co. on January 31, the end of the first month of operations in the current fiscal year:

a. Prepare a statement of cost of goods manufactured.
b. Prepare the cost of goods sold section of the income statement.

Sales	$75,000
Materials inventory (January 1)	25,000
Work in process inventory (January 1)	24,000
Finished goods inventory (January 1)	30,000
Materials purchased	21,000
Direct labor cost	18,000
Factory overhead (including $1,000 of indirect materials used and $3,000 of indirect labor cost)	12,000
Selling and administrative expense	10,000
Inventories at January 31:	
Materials	22,000
Work in process	20,000
Finished goods	32,000

E1-7
Journal entries for job
order costing; total
and unit cost
computation
Learning Objectives 4

Magnus Manufacturing, Inc., uses the job-order cost system of accounting. The following information was taken from the company's books after all posting had been completed at the end of May:

Jobs Completed	Direct Materials Cost	Direct Labor Cost	Factory Overhead	Units Completed
1984	$3,600	$4,000	$1,600	400
2000	2,380	2,500	1,000	240
2525	1,800	1,700	680	200

a. Prepare the journal entries to charge the costs of materials, labor, and factory overhead to each job and to transfer the costs of jobs completed to Finished Goods.
b. Compute the total production cost of each job.
c. Compute the unit cost of each job.
d. Compute the selling price per unit for each job, assuming a mark-on percentage of 50%.

E1-8
Journal entries for
job-order costing
Learning Objective 4

Jet-Products Co. manufactures goods on a job-order basis. During the month of April, three jobs were started in process. (There was no work in process at the beginning of the month.) Jobs 707 and 727 were completed and sold during the month (Selling prices: Job 707, $22,000; Job 727, $27,000); Job 737 was still in process at the end of April.

The following data came from the job cost sheets for each job. These costs include a total of $1,200 of indirect materials and $900 of indirect labor. One work in process control account is used for all jobs.

	Job 707	Job 727	Job 737
Direct materials	$5,000	$6,000	$3,500
Direct labor	4,000	5,000	2,500
Factory overhead	2,000	2,500	1,250

Prepare journal entries to record the following:
a. Materials used.
b. Factory wages and salaries earned.
c. Factory Overhead transferred to Work in Process.
d. Jobs completed.
e. Jobs sold.

E1-9
Determining materials, labor, and cost of goods sold
Learning Objectives 3, 4

The following inventory data relate to Corinthian Corp.

	Inventories Ending	Beginning
Finished goods	$90,000	$110,000
Work in process	80,000	70,000
Direct materials	95,000	90,000

Revenues and Costs for the Period

Sales	$900,000
Cost of goods available for sale	775,000
Total manufacturing costs	675,000
Factory overhead	175,000
Direct materials used	205,000

Calculate the following for the year:
a. Direct materials purchased.
b. Direct labor costs incurred.
c. Cost of goods sold.
d. Gross profit.

(AICPA adapted)

PROBLEMS

P1-1
Cost of goods sold—merchandiser and manufacturer
Learning Objective 2

The following data were taken from the general ledgers and other data of Mountain Manufacturing and Mousetrap Merchandising on April 30 of the current year:

Merchandise inventory, April 1	$ 33,000
Finished goods, April 1	67,000
Purchases	121,000
Cost of goods manufactured	287,000
Merchandise inventory, April 30	38,000
Finished goods, April 30	61,000

Required:

1. Compute the cost of goods sold for Mousetrap Merchandising, selecting the appropriate items from the above list.
2. Compute the cost of goods sold for Mountain Manufacturing, selecting the appropriate items from the above list.

P1-2
Basic cost system;
journal entries;
financial statements.
Similar to self-study problem
Learning Objective 3

The post-closing trial balance of Buckler Manufacturing Co. on April 30 is reproduced as follows:

Buckler Manufacturing Co.
Post-Closing Trial Balance
April 30, 19—

Cash	25,000	
Accounts Receivable	65,000	
Finished Goods	120,000	
Work in Process	35,000	
Materials	18,000	
Building	480,000	
Accumulated Depr.—Building	456,000	72,000
Factory Equipment	220,000	
Accumulated Depr.—Factory Equipment		66,000
Office Equipment	60,000	
Accumulated Depr.—Office Equipment		36,000
Accounts Payable		95,000
Capital Stock		250,000
Retained Earnings		504,000
	1,023,000	1,023,000

During the month of May, the following transactions took place:

a. Purchased raw materials at a cost of $45,000 and general factory supplies at a cost of $13,000 on account (recorded materials and supplies in the materials account).
b. Issued raw materials to be used in production costing $47,000 and miscellaneous factory supplies costing $15,000.
c. Distributed wages and salaries earned for the month as follows: factory wages (including $12,000 indirect labor), $41,000, and selling and administrative salaries, $7,000. (Ignore payroll withholdings and deductions.)
d. Recognized depreciation for the month at an annual rate of 5% on the building, 10% on the factory equipment, and 20% on the office equipment. The

sales and administrative staff uses approximately one fifth of the building for its offices.
e. Incurred various other expenses totaling $11,000. One fourth of this amount is allocable to the office function.
f. Transferred total factory overhead costs to Work in Process.
g. Completed and transferred goods with a total cost of $91,000 to the finished goods storeroom.
h. Sold goods costing $188,000 for $345,000. (Assume all sales were made on account.)
i. Collected accounts receivable in the amount of $362,000.
j. Paid accounts payable totaling $206,000.

Required:

1. Prepare journal entries to record the transactions.
2. Set up T-accounts. Post the beginning trial balance and the journal entries prepared in Part 1 to the accounts and determine the balances in the accounts on May 31.
3. Prepare a statement of cost of goods manufactured, an income statement, and a balance sheet.

P1-3
Statement of cost of goods manufactured; income statement; balance sheet
Learning Objective 3

The adjusted trial balance for Western Furniture Company on September 30, the end of its first month of operation, is recorded as follows:

Western Furniture Company
Trial Balance
September 30, 19—

Cash	$ 24,500	
Accounts Receivable	16,200	
Finished Goods	13,900	
Work in Process	—	
Materials	7,400	
Building	300,000	
Accumulated Depr.—Building		$ 3,000
Machinery and Equipment	88,000	
Accumulated Depr.—Mach. and Equip.		2,200
Accounts Payable		7,900
Payroll	—	
Capital Stock		422,550
Sales		68,300
Cost of Goods Sold	41,450	
Factory Overhead	—	
Selling and Administrative Expenses	12,500	
	$503,950	$503,950

The general ledger reveals the following additional data:
a. There were no beginning inventories.
b. Materials purchases during the period were $33,000.
c. Direct labor cost was $18,500.

d. Factory overhead costs were as follows:

Indirect materials	$ 1,400
Indirect labor	4,300
Depr. of Building	3,000
Depr. of Machinery and Equipment	2,200
Utilities	1,750
	$12,650

Required:

1. Prepare a statement of cost of goods manufactured for the month of September.
2. Prepare an income statement for the month of September.
3. Prepare a balance sheet as of September 30.

P1-4
Job order cost;
journal entries; profit
analysis
Learning Objective 4

Dice Manufacturing Co. obtained the following information from its records for the month of July:

	Jobs Completed and Sold		
	Job 7	**Job 11**	**Job 12**
Direct materials cost	$ 15,000	$10,000	$ 25,000
Direct labor cost	50,000	50,000	50,000
Factory overhead	30,000	30,000	30,000
Units manufactured	5,000	4,000	10,000
Selling price	126,667	80,000	131,250

Required:

1. Prepare, in summary form, the journal entries that would have been made during the month to record the distribution of materials, labor, and overhead costs; the completion of the jobs; and the sale of the jobs. (Assume separate work in process accounts for each job.)
2. Prepare schedules showing the gross profit or loss for July for the following:
    a. The business as a whole.
    b. Each job completed and sold.
    c. For each unit manufactured and sold.(Round to the nearest cent.)

P1-5
Job cost; journal
entries; inventory
analysis;
manufacturing
statement
Learning Objective 4

Diesel Manufacturing Co. manufactures engines that are made only on customers' orders and to their specifications. During January, the company worked on Jobs 90AX, 90BZ, 90CK, and 90DQ. The following figures summarize the cost records for the month.

	Job 90AX (100 units)	Job 90BZ (60 units)	Job 90CK (25 units)	Job 90DQ (100 units)
Direct materials put into process:				
Jan. 2	$15,000	$ 5,000	—	—
18	20,000	16,000	$ 5,000	—
22	15,000	1,000	10,000	$ 6,000
28	—	—	3,500	2,000

Direct labor cost: week ending				
Jan. 2	$ 1,000	$ 1,000	—	—
9	27,000	9,000	—	—
16	32,000	27,000	—	—
23	20,000	3,000	$ 5,000	$ 500
30	—	—	18,000	11,500
Factory overhead	$60,000	$32,000	$17,500	$ 9,000
Engines completed	100	60	25	—

Jobs 90AX and 90BZ have been completed and delivered to the customer at a total selling price of $426,000, on account. Job 90CK is finished but has not yet been delivered. Job 90DQ is still in process. There was no work in process at the beginning of the month.

Required:

1. Prepare the summary journal entries for the month to record the distribution of materials, labor, and overhead costs; the completion of the jobs; and the sale of the jobs. (Assume a work in process account is kept for each job.)
2. Prepare a summary showing the total cost of each job completed during the month or in process at the end of the month. Also determine the cost of the inventories of completed engines and engines in process at the end of the month.
3. Prepare a statement of cost of goods manufactured.

P1-6
Job order cost; journal entries; ending work in process; inventory analysis
Learning Objective 4

Historic Company manufactures goods to special order and uses a job order cost system. During its first month of operations, the following selected transactions took place:

a.	Materials purchased on account	$37,000
b.	Materials issued to the factory:	
	Job 1066	$ 2,200
	Job 1215	5,700
	Job 1776	7,100
	Job 1865	1,700
	For general use in the factory	1,350
c.	Factory wages and salaries earned:	
	Job 1066	$ 2,700
	Job 1215	6,800
	Job 1776	9,200
	Job 1865	2,100
	For general work in the factory	2,250
d.	Miscellaneous factory overhead costs vouchered	$ 2,400
e.	Depreciation of $2,000 on the factory machinery recorded.	
f.	Factory overhead allocated as follows:	
	Job 1066	$ 1,200
	Job 1215	2,000
	Job 1776	3,800
	Job 1865	1,000
g.	Jobs 1066, 1215, and 1776 completed.	
h.	Jobs 1066 and 1215 shipped to the customer and billed at $30,900.	

Required:	1. Prepare a schedule reflecting the cost of each of the four jobs.
	2. Prepare journal entries to record the transactions. (One control account is used for Work in Process.)
	3. Compute the ending balance in Work in Process.
	4. Compute the ending balance in Finished Goods.

P1-7
Cash flow; journal entries; account analysis
Learning Objective 3

Selected account balances and transactions of The Kimbro Manufacturing Co. follow:

	Account Balances	
	May 1	May 31
Raw materials	$ 5,000	$ 6,500
Factory supplies	800	900
Work in process	6,000	5,300
Finished goods	12,000	13,200

May Transactions

a. Purchased raw materials and factory supplies on account at costs of $45,000 and $5,000, respectively. (One inventory account is maintained.)
b. Incurred wages during the month of $65,000 ($10,000 was for indirect labor).
c. Incurred factory overhead costs in the amount of $12,000.
d. Made adjusting entries to record $7,000 of factory overhead (credit Various Credits). Factory overhead was closed to Work in Process. Completed jobs were transferred to Finished Goods, and the cost of jobs sold was charged to Cost of Goods Sold.

Required:	Prepare journal entries for the following:
	1. The purchase of raw materials and factory supplies.
	2. The issuance of raw materials and supplies into production. (Hint: Be certain to consider the beginning and ending balances of raw materials and supplies as well as the amount of the purchases.)
	3. The recording of the payroll.
	4. The distribution of the payroll.
	5. The recording of factory overhead incurred.
	6. The adjusting entry for factory overhead.
	7. The entry to transfer factory overhead costs to Work in Process.
	8. The entry to transfer the cost of completed work to Finished Goods. (Hint: Be sure to consider the beginning and ending balances of Work in Process as well as the costs added to Work in Process this period.)
	9. The entry to record the cost of goods sold. (Hint: Be sure to consider the beginning and ending balances of Finished Goods as well as the cost of the goods finished during the month.)

P1-8
Data analysis; manufacturing statement
Learning Objective 4

Zuckerman Corporation manufactures one product and accounts for costs by a job-order cost system. You have obtained the following information for the year ended December 31 from the corporation's books and records:

a. Total manufacturing cost during the year was $1,000,000, including direct materials, direct labor, and factory overhead.

b. Cost of goods manufactured during the year was $970,000.
c. Factory overhead charged to work in process was 75% of direct labor cost and 27% of the total manufacturing cost.
d. Beginning work in process inventory, January 1, was 60% of ending work in process inventory, December 31.

Required:

Prepare a statement of cost of goods manufactured for the year ended December 31 for Zuckerman Corporation. (Hint: Set up a statement of cost of goods manufactured, putting the given information in the appropriate spaces and solving for the unknown information.)

(AICPA adapted)

P1-9
Data analysis, manufacturing statement, cost terminology
Learning Objectives 3, 4

Cecil Company's cost of goods sold for the month ended July 31 was $345,000. Ending work in process inventory was 90% of beginning work in process inventory. Factory overhead was 50% of direct labor cost. Other information pertaining to Cecil Company's inventories and production for the month of July is as follows:

Beginning inventories, July 1:	
Direct materials	$ 20,000
Work in process	40,000
Finished goods	102,000
Purchases of direct materials during July	110,000
Ending inventories, July 31:	
Direct materials	26,000
Work in process	?
Finished goods	105,000

Required:

1. Prepare a statement of cost of goods manufactured for the month of July. (Hint: Set up a statement of cost of goods manufactured, putting the given information in the appropriate spaces and solving for the unknown information.)
2. Prepare a schedule to compute the prime cost incurred during July.
3. Prepare a schedule to compute the conversion cost charged to Work in Process during July.

(AICPA adapted)

Accounting for Materials

The total cost of a finished product consists of the expenditures made for raw materials, direct labor, and the factory overhead generated by the manufacturing activities. The principles and procedures for controlling and accounting for these cost elements are the major subjects of Chapters 2, 3, and 4. Each chapter will examine the controls and accounting procedures that apply to each element. However, common controls and practices pertain to all cost control systems. The major function, in general, of any cost control system is to keep expenditures within the limits of a preconceived plan. The control system should also encourage cost reductions by eliminating waste and operational inefficiencies. An effective system of cost control is designed to control the people responsible for the expenditures because people control costs, costs do not control themselves.

An effective cost control system should include the following:

LEARNING OBJECTIVE
Identify the elements of an effective cost control system

1. A specific assignment of duties and responsibilities.
2. A list of individuals who are authorized to approve expenditures.

3. An established plan of objectives and goals.

4. Regular reports showing the differences between goals and actual performance. *Varian report*

5. A plan of corrective action designed to prevent unfavorable differences from recurring.

6. Follow-up procedures for corrective measures.⌉

Responsibility accounting is an integral part of a cost control system because it focuses attention on specific individuals who have been designated to achieve the established goals. Of the three major objectives of cost accounting—cost control, product costing, and inventory pricing—cost control is often the most difficult to achieve. A weakness in cost control can often be overcome by placing more emphasis on responsibility accounting. This makes the people who incur costs accountable for those costs.

MATERIALS CONTROL

LEARNING OBJECTIVE
Recognize the two basic aspects of materials control

The two basic aspects of ⌊**materials control** are (1) the physical control or safeguarding of materials and (2) control of the investment in materials.⌉ Physical control protects materials from misuse or misappropriation. Controlling the investment in materials maintains appropriate quantities of materials in inventory.

PHYSICAL CONTROL OF MATERIALS

Every business requires a system of internal control that includes procedures for the safeguarding of assets. Because highly liquid assets, such as cash and marketable securities, are particularly susceptible to misappropriation, the protection provided for such assets is usually more than adequate. However, other assets, including inventories, must also be protected from unauthorized use or theft.

Because inventories usually represent a significant portion of a manufacturer's current assets, a business must control its materials from the time they are ordered until the time they are shipped to customers in the form of finished goods. In general, to effectively control materials, a business must maintain

1. Limited access

2. Segregation of duties

3. Accuracy in recording

Limited Access. Only authorized personnel should have access to materials storage areas⌊ Materials should be issued for use in production only if requisitions for materials are properly documented and approved. Finished goods should also be safeguarded in limited access storage areas and not released for shipment in the absence of appropriate documentation and authorization. Procedures should be established within each production area or department for safeguarding work in process.

Segregation of Duties. A basic principle of internal control is the segregation of duties to minimize opportunities for misappropriation of assets. With respect to materials control, the following functions should be segregated: purchasing, receiving, storage, use, and recording. The independence of personnel assigned to these functions does not eliminate the danger of misappropriation or misuse because the possibility of collusion still exists. However, the appropriate segregation of duties limits an individual employee's opportunities for misappropriation and concealment. In smaller organizations, it is frequently not possible to achieve optimum segregation due to limited resources and personnel. Small businesses must therefore rely on specially designed control procedures to compensate for the lack of independence of assigned functions.

Accuracy in Recording. An effective materials control system requires accurate recording of purchases and issuances of materials. Inventory records should document the inventory quantities on hand and cost records should provide the data needed to assign a value to inventories for the preparation of financial statements. Periodically, recorded inventories should be compared with a physical inventory count, and any significant discrepancies should be investigated. Differences may be due to recording errors or may result from inventory losses through theft or spoilage. Once the cause has been determined, appropriate corrective action should be taken.

CONTROLLING THE INVESTMENT IN MATERIALS

Maintaining the proper balance of materials on hand is one of the most important objectives of materials control. An inventory of sufficient size and diversity for efficient operations must be maintained, but the size should not be excessive in relation to scheduled production needs.

Because funds invested in inventories are unavailable for other uses, management must consider other working capital needs in determining the amount of funds to be invested in inventories and whether alternative uses of these funds might yield a greater return. In addition to the usage of funds, management should consider the costs of materials handling, storage, and insurance against fire, theft, or other casualty. Also, higher than needed inventory levels could increase the possibility of loss from damage, deterioration, and obsolescence. The planning and control of the materials inventory investment requires that all of these factors be carefully studied to determine (1) when orders should be placed and (2) how many units should be ordered.

Order Point. A minimum level of inventory should be determined for each article of raw material, and inventory records should indicate how much of each article is on hand. This requires the establishment of a subsidiary ledger in which a separate account is maintained for each individual item of raw material used in the manufacturing process.

The point at which an item should be ordered, called the **order point** occurs when the predetermined minimum level of inventory on hand is reached. Calculating the order point is based on the following data:

1. **Usage**—the anticipated rate at which the material will be used.

2. **Lead time**—the estimated time interval between the placement of an order and receipt of the material.

3. **Safety stock**—the estimated minimum level of inventory needed to protect against **stockouts** (running out of stock). Stockouts may occur due to inaccurate estimates of usage or lead time or various other unforeseen events, such as the receipt of damaged or inferior materials from the supplier.

Assume that a company's expected daily usage of an item of material is 100 units, the anticipated lead time is 5 days, and the estimated safety stock is 1,000 units. The following calculation shows that the order point is reached when the inventory on hand reaches 1,500 units:

100 units (daily usage) × 5 days (lead time)	500 units
Safety stock required	1,000 units
Order point	1,500 units

If estimates of usage and lead time are accurate, when the new order is received the level of inventory would be equal to the safety stock of 1,000 units. If, however, the new order is delivered three days late, the company would need to issue 300 units of material from its safety stock to maintain the production level during the temporary delay.

Economic Order Quantity (EOQ). The order point establishes the time when an order should be placed, but it does not indicate the most economical number of units to be ordered. To determine the quantity to be ordered, the cost of placing an order and the cost of carrying inventory must be considered. **Order costs** generally include several factors:

1. Salaries and wages of employees engaged in purchasing, receiving, and inspecting materials.

2.   Communications costs associated with ordering, such as telephone (including fax) charges, postage, and forms or stationery.

3.   Materials accounting and record keeping.

A variety of factors must be considered in determining **carrying costs**:

1.   Materials storage and handling costs.

2.   Interest, insurance, and property taxes.

3.   Loss due to theft, deterioration, or obsolescence.

4.   Records and supplies associated with carrying inventories.

Order costs and carrying costs move in opposite directions—annual order costs decrease when order size increases, while annual carrying costs increase when order size increases. The optimal quantity to order at one time, called the **economic order quantity**, is the order size that minimizes total order and carrying costs over a period of time, for example, one year.

The factors to be considered in determining order and carrying costs for a particular company vary with the nature of operations and the organizational structure. Special analyses are usually required to identify relevant costs, because these data are not normally accumulated in an accounting system. Care must be exercised in determining which costs are relevant. For example, a company may have adequate warehouse space to carry a large additional quantity of inventory. If the space cannot be used for some other profitable purpose, the cost of the space is not a relevant factor in determining carrying costs. If, however, the space in the company warehouse could be used for a more profitable purpose or if additional warehouse space must be leased or rented to accommodate increased inventories, the costs associated with the additional space are relevant in determining carrying costs.

The interest cost associated with carrying an inventory in stock should be considered whether or not funds are borrowed to purchase the inventory. If these funds were not used for inventory, they could have been profitably applied to some alternate use. The rate of interest to be used in the calculations will vary depending on the cost of borrowing or the rate that could be earned by the funds if they were used for some other purpose.

Quantitative models or formulas have been developed for calculating the economic order quantity. One formula that can be used is the following:

$$\text{EOQ} = \sqrt{\frac{2CN}{K}}$$

where
EOQ = economic order quantity
C   = cost of placing an order
N   = number of units required annually
K   = carrying cost per unit of inventory

To illustrate this formula, assume that the following data have been determined by analyzing the factors relevant to materials inventory:

Number of units of material required annually 10,000
Cost of placing an order $10.00
Annual carrying cost per unit of intentory . . . . $.80

Using the EOQ formula:

$$EOQ = \sqrt{\frac{2(\text{cost of order}) (\text{number of units required annually})}{(\text{carrying cost per unit})}}$$

$$= \sqrt{\frac{2(\$10) (10,000)}{\$.80}}$$

$$= \sqrt{\frac{\$200,000}{\$.80}}$$

$$= \sqrt{250,000}$$

$$= 500 \text{ units}$$

The EOQ can also be determined by constructing a table using a range of order sizes. A tabular presentation of the data from the previous example, assuming no safety stock, follows:

1 Order Size	2 Number of Orders	3 Total Order Cost	4 Average Inventory	5 Total Carrying Cost	6 Total Order & Carrying Cost
100	100	$1,000	50	$ 40	$1,040
200	50	500	100	80	580
300	33	330	150	120	450
400	25	250	200	160	410
500	**20**	**200**	**250**	**200**	**400**
600	17	170	300	240	410
700	14	140	350	280	420
800	13	130	400	320	450
900	11	110	450	360	470
1,000	10	100	500	400	500

1. Number of units per order
2. 10,000 annual units ÷ order size
3. Number of orders × $10 per order
4. Order size ÷ 2 = average inventory on hand during the year
5. Average inventory × $.80 per unit carrying cost for one year
6. Total order cost + total carrying cost

The data presented in Figure 2-1 show the order cost decreasing as the order size increases. Meanwhile, the carrying costs increase as the order size increases because of the necessity to maintain a large quantity of inventory in stock. At the 500-unit level, the carrying and order costs are at their minimum point. This is the point at which the total carrying charges equal the total order costs, as demonstrated in the figure, when no safety stock is provided for. Assume in the preceding example that the company desires a safety stock of 400 units. The average number of units in inventory would be calculated as follows:

Average number
of units
in inventory $= (1/2 \times EOQ) + \text{Safety stock}$
$= (1/2 \times 500) + 400$
$= 650 \text{ units}$

The total carrying costs then would be

Carrying costs $= \text{Average inventory} \times \text{Carrying cost per unit}$
$= 650 \times \$.80$
$= 520$

FIGURE 2-1   Costs of Ordering and Carrying Inventory

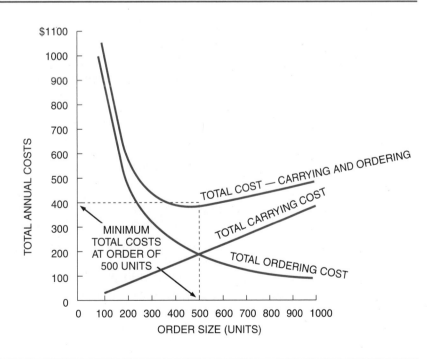

Note that the order cost of $200 is significantly less than the carrying costs of $520 when safety stock is present.

Limitations of Order Point and EOQ Calculations. The techniques illustrated for determining when to order (order point) and how much to order (EOQ) may give a false impression of exactness. However, because these calculations are based on estimates of factors such as production volume, lead time, and order and carrying costs, they are really approximations that serve as a guide to planning and controlling the investment in materials.

In addition, other factors may influence the time for ordering or the quantity ordered. Such factors include the availability of materials from suppliers, proximity of suppliers, fluctuations in the purchase price of materials, and trade (volume) discounts offered by suppliers.

MATERIALS CONTROL PROCEDURES

Specific internal control procedures should be tailored to a company's needs. However, materials control generally involves the following functions: (1) purchase and receipt of materials, (2) storage of materials, and (3) requisition and consumption of materials.

MATERIALS CONTROL PERSONNEL

Although actual job titles and duties may vary from one company to another, the personnel involved in materials control usually include the following:

1. Purchasing agent
2. Receiving clerk
3. Storeroom keeper
4. Production department supervisor

Purchasing Agent. The responsibility for buying the materials needed for the manufacturing enterprise should rest on the shoulders of one person. In a small plant the employee who does the buying may also perform other duties, while in a large plant the **purchasing agent** may head a department established to perform buying activities. Regardless of the size of an organization, it is important that one individual be responsible for the purchasing function. The duties of a purchasing agent may include the following:

1. Working with the production manager to prevent delays caused by the lack of materials.

2. Compiling and maintaining information that identifies where the desired materials can be obtained at the most economical price.

3. Placing purchase orders.

4. Supervising the order process until the materials are received.

5. Verifying purchase invoices and approving them for payments.

Receiving Clerk. The **receiving clerk** is responsible for supervising the receipt of incoming shipments. All incoming materials must be checked as to quantity and quality and sometimes as to price.

Storeroom Keeper. The **storeroom keeper**, who has charge of the materials after they have been received, must see that the materials are properly stored and maintained. The materials must be placed in stock and issued only on properly authorized requisitions. The purchasing agent should be informed of the quantities on hand as a guide to the purchasing of additional materials.

Production Department Supervisor. Each production department has a person who is responsible for supervising the operational functions within the department. This individual may be given the title of **production department supervisor** or another similar designation. One of the assigned duties of a department supervisor is to prepare or approve the requisitions designating the quantities and kinds of material needed for the work to be done in the department.

CONTROL DURING PROCUREMENT

Materials are ordered to maintain the adequate levels of inventory necessary to meet scheduled production needs. The storeroom keeper is responsible for monitoring quantities of materials on hand. When the order point is reached for a particular item of raw material, the procurement process is initiated. In many companies, computers store data pertaining to inventories on hand, predetermined order points, and economic order quantities. When properly programmed, computers can simplify the task of maintaining appropriate inventory levels.

Supporting documents are essential to maintaining control during the procurement process. In general, the documents should be prenumbered and protected from unauthorized use. The documents commonly used in procuring materials include (1) purchase requisitions, (2) purchase orders, (3) vendor's invoices, (4) receiving reports, and (5) debit-credit memoranda.

Purchase Requisitions. The form used to notify the purchasing agent that additional materials are needed is known as a **purchase requisition**. This requisition is an important part of the materials control process because it authorizes the agent to buy. Purchase requisitions should originate with the storeroom keeper or some other individual with similar authority and responsibility.

Purchase requisitions should be prenumbered serially to help detect the loss or misuse of any of these forms. They are generally prepared in duplicate. The first copy goes to the purchasing agent; the storeroom keeper retains the second copy. Figure 2-2 shows a purchase requisition.

Purchase Order. The purchase requisition gives the purchasing agent authority to order the materials described in the requisition. The purchasing agent should maintain or have access to an up-to-date list of vendors, which includes prices, available discounts, estimated delivery time, and any other relevant information. From this list, the purchasing agent selects a vendor from whom high-quality materials can be obtained when needed at a competitive cost. If this information is not available from the list for a particular item of material, the purchasing agent may communicate with several prospective vendors and request quotations on the materials needed.

The purchasing agent then completes a **purchase order**, as shown in Figure 2-3, and addresses it to the chosen vendor, describing the materials wanted, stating price and terms, and fixing the date and method of delivery. This purchase order should be prenumbered serially and prepared in quadruplicate. The first copy goes to the vendor, one copy goes to the accounting department, one copy goes to the receiving clerk, and the purchasing agent retains a copy.

The purchasing agent's copy of the order should be placed in an unfilled orders file. Before the order is filed, the purchase requisition on which it is based should be attached to it. This last important step begins the assembly of a complete set of all the forms pertaining to the purchase transaction. To identify each document relating to a transaction with all others of the same set, the purchase order number should be shown on each of the documents. The sets can then be compiled according to the respective purchase order numbers.

Vendor's Invoice. The company should receive a **vendor's invoice** before the materials arrive at the factory. As soon as it's received, the vendor's

FIGURE 2-2   Purchase Requisition. (Notifies purchasing agent that additional materials should
                          be ordered.)

WILDCAT MFG 🐾   PURCHASE REQUISITION   No. **3246**

Date ___January 3, 19--___

Date wanted ___February 1, 19--___

For { Job No.   300
      Account No.   1482

                                                    Authorization No.   3313

QUANTITY	DESCRIPTION
20,000 Gal.	Adhesive Compound -- Grade A102

Approved by ___*L. Merz*___   Signed by ___*G. Thomas*___

Purchase order No. ___1982___   Date ordered ___January 6, 19--___
Ordered from ___Hoosier Corporation___

---

invoice goes to the purchasing agent, who compares it with the purchase
order, noting particularly that the description of the materials is the
same, that the price and the terms agree, and that the method of shipment and the date of delivery conform to the instructions on the purchase order. When satisfied that the invoice is correct, the purchasing
agent initials or stamps the invoice indicating that it has been reviewed
and agrees with the purchase order. The invoice is then filed together
with the purchase order and the purchase requisition in the unfilled
orders file until the materials arrive.

FIGURE 2-3 Purchase Order. (Prepared by purchasing agent and sent to vendor to order materials.)

WILDCAT MFG

PURCHASE ORDER

Order No. **1982**

Mark Order No. on invoice
and on all packages

To: Hoosier Corporation
    Batesville, Indiana 47006

Date _January 6, 19--_

Terms _3/10 eom n/60_

Ship Via _Truck (to arrive_
January 25, 19--)

QUANTITY	DESCRIPTION	PRICE	
20,000 Gal.	Adhesive Compound -- Grade A102	$31,300	00

By _a. Lauren_

Purchasing Agent

Receiving Report. As noted previously, a copy of the purchase order goes to the receiving clerk to give advance notice of the arrival of the materials ordered. This is done to facilitate planning and to provide space for the incoming materials. The receiving clerk is in charge of the receiving department where all incoming materials are received, opened, counted or weighed, and tested for conformity with the order. If the materials received are of too technical a nature to be tested by the receiving clerk, an engineer from the production manager's office may perform the inspection, or the materials may be sent to the plant laboratory for testing.

The receiving clerk counts and identifies the materials received and prepares a **receiving report** similar to the one reproduced in Figure 2-4. Each report is numbered serially and shows the vendor, when the materials were received, what the shipment contained, and the number of the purchase order that identifies the shipment. The report should be prepared in quadruplicate. Two copies go to the purchasing agent, one copy goes with the materials or supplies to the storeroom keeper to ensure that all of the materials that come to the receiving department are put

FIGURE 2-4   Receiving Report. (Incoming materials opened, counted, weighed, or tested for conformity with purchase order.)

WILDCAT MFG

RECEIVING REPORT   No. **496**

Date ___January 21, 19--___

To the purchasing agent:

RECEIVED FROM ___Hoosier Corporation___

Via ___Ace Trucking___ Transportation Charges ___$210.85___

QUANTITY	DESCRIPTION
20,000 Gal.	Adhesive Compound -- Grade A102

Counted by ___R. S.___ Inspected by ___D. P.___

Purchase order No. ___1982___

into the storeroom, and the receiving clerk retains one copy. In some plants, the receiving clerk is given a copy of the purchase order with the quantity ordered omitted, thus ensuring that the items received will be counted.

The purchasing agent compares the receiving report with the vendor's invoice and the purchase order to determine that the materials received are those ordered and billed. If the documents agree, the purchasing agent initials or stamps the two copies of the receiving report. One copy is then attached to the other forms already in the file, and the entire set of forms is sent to the accounting department where a voucher is prepared and recorded in the voucher register. The other copy of the receiving report is sent to the person in the accounting department who maintains inventory records. The procedures for recording materials purchases are discussed later in this chapter.

Debit-Credit Memorandum. Occasionally, a shipment of materials does not match the order and the invoice. The purchasing agent will discover this discrepancy when comparing the receiving report with the purchase order and the invoice. Whatever the cause, the difference will lead to correspondence with the vendor, and copies of the letters should be added to the file of forms relating to the transaction. If a larger quantity has been received than has been ordered and the excess is to be kept for future use, a credit memorandum is prepared notifying the vendor of the amount of the increase in the invoice. Figure 2-5 shows one form of the debit-credit memorandum. This memo shows that the vendor has delivered materials that do not meet the buyer's specifications. The purchasing agent will prepare a return shipping order and return the materials to the vendor.

If, on the other hand, the shipment is short, one of two courses of action may be taken. If the materials received can be used, they may be retained and a debit memorandum prepared notifying the vendor of the amount of the shortage. If the materials received cannot be used, a return shipping order is prepared and the materials are returned.

CONTROL DURING STORAGE AND ISSUANCE

The preceding discussion outlined ways to maintain the control of materials during the procurement process. The procedures and forms described are necessary for control of the ordering and receiving functions and the transfer of incoming materials to the storeroom. The next problem to be considered is the storage and issuance of materials and supplies.

Materials Requisition. As discussed earlier, materials should be protected from unauthorized use. No materials should be issued from the store-

FIGURE 2-5   Debit-Credit Memorandum. (Discrepancy between order, shipment, and vendor invoice. Price adjustment request shown on debit-credit memo.)

WILDCAT MFG   (DEBIT) MEMORANDUM
CREDIT

Date __January 3, 19--__

To: Cardinal Machine Company
    Lousiville, Kentucky 40218

We have today (Debited) your account for the following:
             Credited

Explanation __wrong size__

QUANTITY	DESCRIPTION	UNIT PRICE	AMOUNT	
5 boxes	Brass machine screws, 8/32" x 1" flat head	$27.50	$137	50

Purchase order No. __1029__
Your invoice date __December 27, 19--__

By __a. Lauren__
                                    Purchasing Agent

room except on written authorization to lessen the chance of theft, carelessness, or misuse. The form used to provide this control is known as the **materials requisition** or **stores requisition** (see Figure 2-6) and is prepared by factory personnel authorized to withdraw materials from the storeroom. The personnel authorized to perform this function may differ from company to company, but such authority must be given to someone of responsibility. The most satisfactory arrangement would be to have the production manager prepare all materials requisitions, but this is usually not feasible. Another arrangement requires that the

FIGURE 2-6   Materials Requisition. (Authorization to withdraw materials from storeroom.)

WILDCAT MFG   MATERIALS REQUISITION

Date _January 19, 19--_   No. **632**

To: D. Graham

QUANTITY	DESCRIPTION	UNIT PRICE	AMOUNT	
100 Gal.	Adhesive Compound-- Grade A102	$1.565	$156	50

Approved by _E. B._   Issued by _B. W._

Received by _L. M._

Charged to Job/Dept. _300_   Factory Overhead Expense Account _____

department supervisors approve (sign) all materials requisitions for their respective departments. When the storeroom keeper receives a properly signed requisition, the requisitioned materials are released. Both the storeroom keeper and the employee to whom materials are issued should be required to sign the requisition.

The materials requisition is usually prepared in quadruplicate. Two copies go to the accounting department for recording; one copy goes to the storeroom keeper and serves as authorization for issuing the materials; and the production manager or department supervisor who prepared it retains one copy.

Identification is an important factor in the control of materials. For this reason, the materials requisition should indicate the job number (job order costing) or department (process costing) for which the materials are issued. When indirect materials are issued, such as cleaning materials, lubricants, and paint, the requisition will indicate the name or number of the factory overhead account to be charged.

Returned Materials Report. After materials are requisitioned, occasionally some or all of the materials must be returned to the storeroom. Perhaps more materials were requested than were needed or the wrong type of materials were issued. Whatever the reason, a written report, called a **returned materials report**, describing the materials and the reason for the return, must accompany the materials to the storeroom.

> **You should now be able to work the following: Questions 1–16; Exercise 1; Problems 1, 7, 8.**

ACCOUNTING FOR MATERIALS

A company's inventory records should show (1) the number of units of each kind of materials on hand and (2) their cost. The most desirable method of achieving this result is to integrate the materials accounting system with the general ledger accounts. All purchases of materials are recorded through the voucher register as a debit to Materials in the general ledger (the corresponding credit is to Accounts Payable). Materials is a control account supported by a subsidiary **stores** or **materials ledger** that contains an individual account for each item of material carried in stock. Periodically, the balance of the control account and the total of the individual accounts are compared, and any significant variation between the two is investigated.

Each of the individual materials accounts in the subsidiary stores ledger shows (1) the quantity on hand and (2) the cost of the materials. To keep this information current, it is necessary to record in each individual account the quantity and the cost of materials received, issued, and on hand. The stores ledger accounts are usually maintained on cards similar in design to the one shown in Figure 2-7.

Copies of the purchase order and receiving report are approved by the purchasing agent and sent to the accounting department. Upon receiving the purchase order, the stores ledger accountant enters the date, purchase order number, and quantity in the "On Order" columns of the appropriate stores ledger card. When materials arrive, the accounting

FIGURE 2-7 Stores Ledger Card

| Date | ON ORDER | | RECEIVED | | | | ISSUED | | | | BALANCE | | |
	Purchase Order No.	Quantity	Receiving Report No./ (Returned Shipping Order No.)	Quantity	Unit Price	Amount	Materials Requisition/ (Returned Materials Report No.)	Quantity	Unit Price	Amount	Quantity	Unit Price	Amount

Description White Lead

Maximum 15,000 lbs. **Minimum** 1,000 lbs.

Location in Storeroom Bin 8

Stores Ledger Acct. No. 1411

department's copy of the receiving report serves as the basis for posting the receipt of the materials to the stores ledger card. The posting shows the date of receipt, the number of the receiving report, and the number of units received and their cost. The cost may be expressed in both unit cost and total cost or in total only.

When materials are issued, two copies of the materials requisition go to the accounting department. One copy is used in posting the cost of requisitioned materials to the appropriate accounts in the job cost and factory overhead ledgers. Direct materials are charged to the job (or department), and indirect materials are charged to the appropriate factory overhead accounts. The other copy of the requisition goes to the stores ledger accountant and becomes the basis for posting to the ledger cards. The posting shows the date of issue, the number of the requisition, and the number of units issued and their cost.

When materials are returned to the storeroom, a copy of the returned materials report goes to the accounting department. The cost of the returned materials is entered on the report and posted to the appropriate stores ledger card. The cost assigned to the returned materials should be the same as that recorded when the materials were issued to the factory.

The copy of the returned materials report is then routed to the cost accountant in charge of the job cost and factory overhead ledgers. Direct materials returned are credited to the job or department, and indirect materials returned are credited to the appropriate factory overhead account.

After each receipt and issue of materials is posted to the stores ledger cards, the balance is extended. These extensions could be made at the end of the accounting period, when ending inventories are to be determined for financial reporting purposes. However, to wait until that time would defeat one of the advantages of this method of materials control because it would not be possible to determine from the stores ledger when stock is falling below the minimum requirements. Also, most companies have automated inventory systems that enable current balances to be available in a timely and cost-efficient manner.

DETERMINING THE COST OF MATERIALS ISSUED

An important area of materials accounting is the cost of materials requisitioned from the storeroom for factory use. The unit cost of incoming materials is known at the time of purchase. The date of each purchase is also known, but the materials on hand typically include items purchased on different dates and at different prices. Items that look alike usually are commingled in the storeroom. As a result, it may be difficult or impossible to identify an issue of materials with a specific purchase when determining what unit cost should be assigned to the materials being issued.

Several practical methods of solving this problem are available. In selecting the method to be employed, the accounting policies of the firm and the federal and state income tax regulations must be considered. As the methods are discussed, it is important to remember that the flow of materials does not dictate the flow of costs. The **flow of materials** is the order in which materials are actually issued for use in the factory. The **flow of costs** is the order in which unit costs are assigned to materials issued. The following examples assume the use of a perpetual inventory system where the materials ledger card is updated each time materials are received or issued. FIFO and LIFO may also be used with a periodic inventory system where the inventory is counted and costed at the end of the period. In a periodic inventory system, the moving average method is replaced by the weighted or month-end average method.

First-In, First-Out Method. The **first-in, first-out (FIFO)** method of costing has the advantages of simplicity and wide adoption. The FIFO method assumes that materials issued are taken from the oldest materials in stock. Therefore, the materials are costed at the prices paid for the oldest materials. In many companies, the flow of costs using FIFO closely parallels the physical flow of materials. For example, if materials have a tendency to deteriorate in storage, the oldest materials would be issued first. However, as noted previously, the flow of costs does not have to be determined on the basis of the flow of materials. As a result, any organization may use FIFO.

The FIFO method can be illustrated using the following data:

Dec.	1	Balance, 1,000 units @ $20.
	10	Issued 500 units.
	15	Purchased 1,000 units @ $24.
	20	Issued 250 units.
	26	Issued 500 units.
	28	Purchased 500 units @ $26.
	30	Issued 500 units.
	31	Balance, 750 units.

Using FIFO, costs would be assigned to materials issued during the month and to materials on hand at the end of the month as follows:

Dec.	10	Issued from the December 1 balance: 500 units @ $20 total cost, $10,000.
	20	Issued from the December 1 balance: 250 units @ $20, total cost, $5,000.
	26	Issued from the December 1 balance: 250 units @ $20, total cost, $5,000.

Dec. 26   Issued from the December 15 purchase: 250 units @ $24, total
           cost, $6,000.
     26   Total cost of materials issued: $5,000 + $6,000 = $11,000.
     30   Issued from the December 15 purchase: 500 units @ $24, total
           cost, $12,000.
     31   The ending inventory of materials, 750 units, consists of the fol-
           lowing:

Date of Purchase	Units	Unit Cost	Total Cost
December 15	250	$24	$ 6,000
December 28	500	26	13,000
	750		$19,000

As illustrated in the example, ending inventories using FIFO are costed at the prices paid for the most recent purchases. Thus, 500 of the units on hand are assigned a unit cost of $26, the unit cost of the December 28 purchase. The remaining 250 units on hand are costed at $24 per unit, reflecting the unit cost of the next most recent purchase on December 15.

Last-In, First-Out Method. The **last-in, first-out (LIFO)** method of costing materials, as the name implies, assumes that materials issued for manufacturing are the most recently purchased materials. Thus, materials issued are costed at the most recent purchase prices, and inventories on hand at the end of the period are costed at prices paid for the earliest purchases. The LIFO method of costing closely approximates the physical flow of materials in some industries. For example, in the smelting of iron ore, the raw material is stored in mountainous piles. As ore is needed for production, it is drawn from the pile in such a way that the material being used is the last ore to have been received. As emphasized previously, however, physical flow does not determine the costing method used.

Using the same data given to illustrate the FIFO method, costs under the LIFO method would be determined as follows:

Dec. 10   Issued from the December 1 balance: 500 units @ $20, total cost,
           $10,000.
     20   Issued from the December 15 purchase: 250 units @ $24, total
           cost, $6,000.
     26   Issued from the December 15 purchase: 500 units @ $24, total
           cost, $12,000.
     30   Issued from the December 28 purchase: 500 units @ $26, total
           cost, $13,000.
     31   The ending inventory of materials, 750 units, consists of the fol-
           lowing:

Date of Purchase	Unit	Unit Cost	Total Cost
Balance, December 1	500	$20	$10,000
December 15	250	24	6,000
	750		$16,000

Moving Average Method. The **moving average** method assumes that the materials issued at any time are simply withdrawn from a mixed group of like materials in the storeroom and that no attempt is made to identify the materials as being from the earliest or the latest purchases. This method has the disadvantage of requiring more frequent computations than the other methods. However, the use of computers has overcome this disadvantage, and many firms are adopting this method. A basic requirement of the moving average method is that an average unit price must be computed every time a new lot of materials is received and this average unit price must be used to cost all issues of materials until another lot is purchased. Thus, the issues in the illustration would be computed as follows:

Dec. 10   Issued from the December 1 balance: 500 units @ $20 total cost, $10,000.

15   The balance of materials on hand on December 15 consists of 500 units from December 1 and 1,000 units acquired on December 15, for a total of 1,500 units that cost $34,000. The average cost is $22.66 2/3 per unit ($34,000 ÷ 1,500).

20   Issued 250 units @ $22.66 2/3, total cost, $5,666.67.

26   Issued 500 units @ $22.66 2/3, total cost, $11,333.33.

28   The balance of materials on hand on December 28 consists of 750 units costing $17,000 (purchased prior to December 28) and 500 units @ $26 (purchased on December 28) costing $13,000. The total cost is $30,000 for 1,250 units, representing an average cost of $24 per unit ($30,000/1,250).

30   Issued 500 units @ $24, total cost, $12,000.

31   The ending inventory of materials consists of the following:

Units	Unit Cost	Total Cost
750	$24	$18,000

Analysis of FIFO, LIFO, and Moving Average. FIFO, LIFO, and moving average are the most commonly used methods of inventory costing. Any of these methods may be adopted to maintain the stores ledger as shown in Figure 2-8.

Because no one method best suits all manufacturing situations, the method chosen should be the one that most accurately reflects the income for the period in terms of the current economic conditions. One factor to consider is the effect the costing method has on reported net

FIGURE 2-8   Comparison of Inventory Valuation Methods

First-In, First-Out Method

Date	Received Quantity	Unit Price	Amount	Issued Quantity	Unit Price	Amount	Balance Quantity	Unit Price	Amount
Dec. 1							1,000	20 00	20,000 00
10				500	20 00	10,000 00	500	20 00 }	10,000 00
15	1,000	24 00	24,000 00				500	20 00 }	
							1,000	24 00 }	34,000 00
20				250	20 00	5,000 00	250	20 00 }	
							1,000	24 00	29,000 00
26				250	20 00 }				
				250	24 00 }	11,000 00	750	24 00 }	18,000 00
28	500	26 00	13,000 00				750	24 00 }	
							500	26 00 }	31,000 00
30				500	240 00	12,000 00	250	24 00 }	
							500	26 00	19,000 00

First-In, First-Out Method

Date	Received Quantity	Unit Price	Amount	Issued Quantity	Unit Price	Amount	Balance Quantity	Unit Price	Amount
Dec. 1							1,000	20 00	20,000 00
10				500	20 00	10,000 00	500	20 00	10,000 00
15	1,000	24 00	24,000 00				500	20 00 }	
							1,000	24 00 }	34,000 00
20				250	24 00	6,000 00	500	20 00 }	
							750	24 00 }	28,000 00
26				500	24 00	12,000 00	500	20 00 }	
							250	24 00 }	16,000 00
28	500	26 00	13,000 00				500	20 00 }	
							500	24 00	
							500	26 00 }	29,000 00
30				500	26 00	13,000 00	500	20 00 }	
							250	24 00 }	16,000 00

income. Overstating net income will subject a firm to higher taxes than those of a competitor who is using a different costing method.

FIGURE 2-8   Continued

Moving Average Method

Date	Received Quantity	Received Unit Price	Received Amount	Issued Quantity	Issued Unit Price	Issued Amount	Balance Quantity	Balance Unit Price	Balance Amount
Dec. 1							1,000	20 00	20,000 00
10				500	20 00	10,000 00	500	20 00	10,000 00
15	1,000	24 00	24,000 00				1,500	22 66⅔	34,000 00
20				250	22 66⅔	5,666 67	1,250	22 66⅔	28,333 33
26				500	22 66⅔	11,333 33	750	22 66⅔	17,000 00
28	500	26 00	13,000 00				1,250	24 00	30,000 00
30				500	24 00	12,000 00	750	24 00	18,000 00

In an inflationary environment, LIFO is sometimes adopted so that the higher prices of the most recently purchased materials may be charged against the increasingly higher sales revenue. The resulting lower gross margin is assumed to reflect a more accurate picture of earnings because the firm will have to replace its inventory at the new higher costs. Also, the lower gross margin, brought about by the use of the LIFO method, results in a smaller tax liability for the firm. This LIFO benefit, however, does not mean that all companies should adopt LIFO.

To illustrate the effects that the different costing methods have on profit determination, assume that A, B, and C are competing companies that use FIFO, moving average, and LIFO, respectively. The companies have no beginning inventories, and they purchase identical materials at the same time as follows (assume also that each purchase is for one unit):

Purchase No. 1 @ $.10
Purchase No. 2 @ $.50
Purchase No. 3 @ $.90

Assume that one unit of materials is used and sold at a price of $1.00 after the last purchase has been made. The net income is calculated as follows:

	Co. A FIFO (Per Unit)	Co. B Moving Avg. (Per Unit)	Co. C LIFO (Per Unit)
Net sales	$1.00	$1.00	$1.00
Less cost of goods sold	.10	.50*	.90
Gross margin on sales	$ .90	$ .50	$ .10
Operating expenses	.08	.08	.08
Income before income taxes	$ .82	$ .42	$ .02
Less income taxes (50%)	.41	.21	.01
Net income	$ .41	$ .21	$ .01

*$.10 + $.50 + $.90 = $1.50/3 units = $.50 per unit.

As shown in the example, LIFO costing has a definite tax advantage when prices are rapidly rising. Notice that Company C pays $.01 per unit for taxes, while Companies A and B pay taxes per unit of $.41 and $.21, respectively. Thus, Company C has $.99 of each sales dollar to pay for merchandise, operating expenses, and dividends, while Company A has only $.59 and Company B has only $.79 available.

As previously mentioned, each unit of material currently costs $.90 (Purchase No. 3). Therefore, Company A requires additional funding of $.31 ($.90 – $.59) and Company B requires additional funding of $.11 ($.90 – $.79) to replace a unit of material. Only Company C can replace materials, pay operating expenses and taxes, and retain its profit per unit.

The companies, using their respective costing methods, have the following ending materials inventory balances:

Company A (FIFO)	$1.40 ($.50 + $.90)
Company B (moving average)	$1.00 ($.50 + $.50)
Company C (LIFO)	$ .60 ($.10 + $.50)

Company C has the most conservatively valued inventory at $.60, and Company A shows the highest inventory value at $1.40. The Company A inventory value also may be detrimental because inventory often is subject to state and local property taxes that are based on the inventory valuation chosen by the company. It is important to realize that differences between the three methods usually will not be as extreme as they were in this example. Companies that turn their inventory over very rapidly will not be as concerned with the choice of methods as will companies who hold their inventory for a longer time.

Many companies have adopted the LIFO method to match current materials costs with current revenue as well as to minimize the effect of income taxes in periods of rising prices. Companies considering the adoption of the LIFO method, however, should carefully analyze economic conditions and examine the tax regulations that pertain to LIFO. If there should be a downward trend of prices, these companies would probably desire to change to the FIFO method to have the same competitive advantages that were gained by using LIFO when prices were rising. However, the LIFO election cannot be rescinded unless authorized or required by the Internal Revenue Service.

ACCOUNTING PROCEDURES

LEARNING OBJECTIVE
Account for materials and relate materials accounting to the general ledger

The purpose of materials accounting is to provide a summary from the general ledger of the total cost of materials purchased and used in manufacturing. The forms commonly used in assembling the required data have already been discussed. The purchase invoices provide the information needed to prepare the vouchers. The vouchers are then recorded in a voucher register where a special column is provided for recording materials purchased. At the end of the month, the total materials purchased during the month is posted by debiting Materials and crediting Accounts Payable. The materials account in the general ledger serves as a control account for the stores ledger.

All materials issued during the month and materials returned to stock are recorded on a **summary of materials issued and returned** form (see Figure 2-9). When the summary is completed at the end of the month, the total cost of direct materials requisitioned is recorded by debiting Work in Process and crediting Materials. The total of indirect materials requisitioned is recorded by debiting the appropriate factory overhead account and crediting Materials. The work in process account in the general ledger serves as a control account for the job cost ledger.

Any undamaged materials returned to the storeroom should also be recorded on the summary of materials issued and returned so that the totals may be recorded at the end of the month. The entries required to record undamaged materials returned are the reverse of the entries required to record materials requisitioned. Thus, the total cost of direct materials returned to the storeroom should be debited to Materials and credited to Work in Process, while the total cost of indirect materials returned should be debited to Materials and credited to the proper factory overhead account.

Any materials returned to the original vendors should be debited to Accounts Payable and credited to Materials. Unless a special journal is provided for recording such returns, the entries may be made in the general journal. All transactions relating to materials should be recorded so that the balance of the materials account in the general ledger will represent the cost of materials on hand at the end of a period. The balance of the materials account in the general ledger may be proved by listing the stores ledger account balances.

A summary of the procedures involved in accounting for materials is shown in Figure 2-10, which presents the recordings required for the

FIGURE 2-9　　Summary of Materials Issued and Returned

SUMMARY OF MATERIALS ISSUED AND RETURNED　　Month Ending _____ 19 ___

| | | Materials Issued | | | | | Materials Returned to Storeroom | | | | |
| | | Direct Materials | | Indirect Materials | | | Direct Materials | | Indirect Materials | |
Date	Req. No.	Job	Amount	Overhead Acct. No.	Amount	Report No.	Job	Amount	Overhead Acct. No.	Amount
Mar. 5	825	315	$2,150 00							
8	826	316	3,210 00							
11	827	317	280 00	3121	$ 440 00				3121	$ 12 50
14	828	317	415 00	3121	132 50					
17	829	316	340 00							
17	830	317	820 00							
18	831	318	290 00	3121	135 00				3121	15 00
19	832	319	224 20			232	319	$ 12 10		
20	833	319	975 90							
24	834	320	4,350 00	3121	432 00	233	320	448 90		
27	835	321	6,500 00			234	321	318 20		
29	836	322	550 00							
30	837	321	785 40							
31	838	320	870 00							
			$21,760 50		$1,139 50			$ 779 20		$ 27 50

FIGURE 2-10   Summary of Materials Transactions

Transaction	Entry at Time of Transaction			Entry at End of Accounting Period		
	Source of Data	Book of Original Entry	Subsidiary Ledger Posting	Source of Data	Book of Original Entry	General Ledger Posting
Purchase of materials	Vendor's Invoice Receiving Report	Voucher Register	Stores Ledger	Voucher Register	None	Materials Accounts Payable
Materials returned to vendor	Return Shipping Order	General Journal	Stores Ledger	General Journal	None	Accounts Payable Materials
Payment of invoices	Approved Voucher	Check Register	None	Check Register	None	Accounts Payable Cash
Direct materials issued	Materials Requisitions	None	Stores Ledger Job Cost Ledger	Materials Summary	General Journal	Work in Process Materials
Indirect materials issued	Materials Requisitions	None	Stores Ledger Factory Overhead Ledger	Materials Summary	General Journal	Factory Overhead Materials
Direct materials returned from factory to storeroom	Returned Materials Report	None	Stores Ledger Job Cost Ledger	Materials Summary	General Journal	Materials Work in Process
Indirect materials returned from factory to storeroom	Returned Materials Report	None	Stores Ledger Factory Overhead Ledger	Materials Summary	General Journal	Materials Factory Overhead
Inventory adjustment: (a) Materials on hand less than stores ledger balance	Inventory Report	General Journal	Factory Overhead Ledger Stores Ledger	General Journal	None	Factory Overhead Materials
(b) Materials on hand more than stores ledger balance	Inventory Report	General Journal	Factory Overhead Ledger Stores Ledger	General Journal	None	Materials Factory Overhead

more typical materials transactions, both at the time of the transaction and at the end of the period. At the time of the transaction, the recordings to be made affect the subsidiary ledgers, such as the stores ledger and the job cost ledger. At the end of the period, the recordings to be made affect the control accounts for materials, work in process, and factory overhead in the general ledger.

The Voucher System. Throughout this discussion, the **voucher system** of accounting has been in use. The voucher system, due to its many advantages, is more widely used than the simpler but less efficient purchases journal system, particularly in large manufacturing enterprises.

The two systems differ only in their effect on general accounting procedures, as Figure 2-11 illustrates.

FIGURE 2-11   Voucher System vs. Purchases Journal System

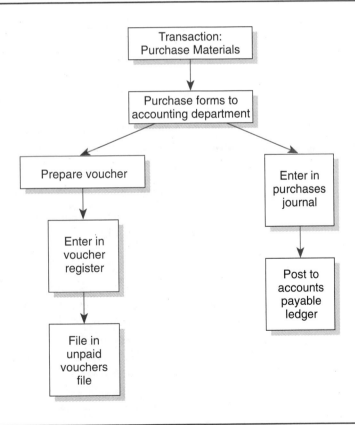

Inventory Verification. The stores ledger contains an account for each material used in the manufacturing process. Each account shows the number of units on hand and their cost. In other words, the stores ledger provides a perpetual inventory of the individual items of material in the storeroom. From the information in the stores ledger, the necessary materials inventory data can be obtained for preparation of a balance sheet, an income statement, and a manufacturing statement.

However, errors in recording receipts or issues of materials in the stores ledger may affect the reliability of the inventory totals. To guard against error, the materials on hand should be checked periodically against the individual stores ledger accounts. The usual practice is to count one lot of materials at a time, spacing the time of the counts so that a complete check of all inventories in the storeroom can be made within a fixed period of time, such as three months. These periodic checks have the advantage of eliminating the costly and time-consuming task of counting all the materials at one time. To guard against carelessness or dishonesty, the count should be made by someone other than the storeroom keeper or the stores ledger clerk.

The person making the count should prepare an **inventory report** similar to the one shown in Figure 2-12. If the total indicated in the report differs from the balance in the stores ledger account, an immediate correcting entry should be made in the proper stores ledger account. The entries in the general ledger accounts may be made in total at the end of the month. If the materials on hand exceed the balance in the control account, the control account balance should be increased by the following entry:

Materials   xxx
    Factory Overhead (Inventory Short and Over)   xxx

If the amount of materials on hand is less than the control account balance, the balance should be decreased by the following entry:

Factory Overhead (Inventory Short and Over)   xxx
    Materials   xxx

Such inventory differences are almost always a shortage and may arise from carelessness in handling materials, shrinkage in goods as a result of handling, or issuing excess quantities of materials to production. Such shortages are considered unavoidable and constitute part of the cost of operating a manufacturing plant. Shortages (or overages) are recorded in a factory overhead account, usually entitled Inventory Short and Over, as indicated in the preceding entries.

FIGURE 2-12   Inventory Report. (Compares book inventory and physical inventory quantities.)

WILDCAT MFG   INVENTORY REPORT

Material _____ 3/4" valves

Location in storeroom _____ Bin L123

Stores ledger acct. No. _____ 12345

Date of Verification _____ January 27, 19--

Units in storeroom _____ 590

Units in receiving
    department _____ 300

Total number units on hand _____ 890

Balance per stores ledger _____ 910

Difference _____ 20

Counted by _____ P. Valence

Supervised by _____ W. Cox

Visual Aid. For a cost accounting system to function properly, each employee must understand the assigned duties and the purpose of the various forms and records. Figure 2-13 shows the interrelationship of the accounts and how internal control procedures can be established.

You should now be able to work the following: Questions 17–21; Exercises 2–10; Problems 2–9, 12.

FIGURE 2-13   Interrelationship of Materials Documents and Accounts

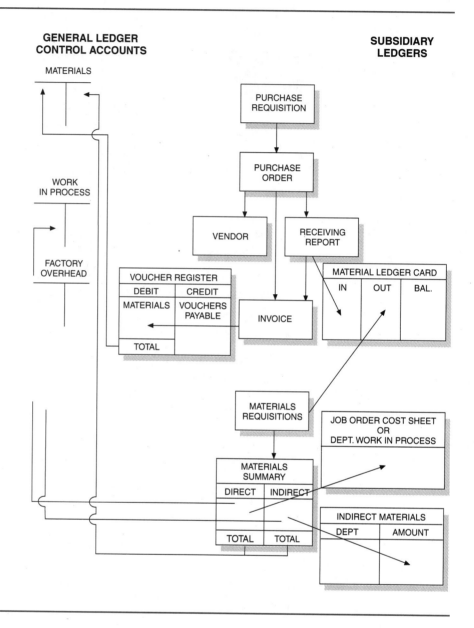

CONTROLLING INVENTORY ERRORS

An article in *Management Accounting* reported that of the 68.5% of manufacturing companies surveyed that reported an inventory loss, the average loss was $521,952. The authors made this observation:

[T]he inventory record has far more important implications for manufacturing companies than for retail companies because many management decisions—purchasing raw materials, pricing products, hiring workers, and scheduling production—are based on current inventory levels.

They describe a number of steps that manufacturers can take to control inventory errors, including the following:

Once problem areas are identified, an internal control system must be developed to correct the problems and to prevent the same errors from recurring. Tight controls on the following areas in particular are essential: accounts receivable, accounts payable, credit refunds, debit memos, price changes, and vendor returns. For inventories vulnerable to errors, it is recommended that a physical inventory be taken more often. Even companies with well-developed inventory control systems have some unavoidable inventory errors—it is practically impossible to eliminate all of them. Hence, it is sometimes beneficial to count inventories more often than once a period.

If the plant manager is usually busy with other daily operations and is not an expert in reducing inventory discrepancies, it is recommended that an inventory discrepancy committee be formed. This committee would be in charge of reviewing and evaluating inventory error reduction efforts of individual line managers and would recommend changes to the line managers and top management.

In connection with internal control and performance evaluation systems, it is important to develop a good accounting system to trace the inventory record. Under a periodic inventory system, it is difficult to measure inventory loss because the inventory account is not updated daily. The actual ending inventory is determined by count and is subtracted from the goods available for sale to get the cost of goods sold. Hence, the cost of goods sold will include any inventory shrinkage occurring during the period.

The inventory records are updated continuously under perpetual inventory systems. Here the records should show the proper balances on hand at all times. At any time during the accounting period, a physical count will reveal inventory gains or losses accumulated from the beginning of the period to date.

A seemingly passive but very effective approach for reducing inventory errors is to reduce inventories. Inventory errors occur because of the existence of inventories. Hence, the number of inventory errors will depend on the amount of existing inventories. As inventories decrease, inventory errors probably will decrease in the same proportion. The just-in-time (JIT) inventory control technique is used widely by many manufacturing companies in the United States in an attempt to reduce inventories.

Retail businesses have been using bar codes for many years to improve accuracy and timeliness in inventory control. Bar codes are electronic symbols that can be read and processed in an integrated computerized system. Manufacturers also can use bar codes to establish an up-to-date inventory database from the shop floor.

Il-woon Kim and Arjan T. Sadhwani, "Is Your Inventory Really All There," *Management Accounting,* July 1991, pp. 37–40.

SCRAP, SPOILED GOODS, AND DEFECTIVE WORK

LEARNING OBJECTIVE
Account for scrap materials, spoiled goods, and defective work

Manufacturing operations usually produce some imperfect units that cannot be sold as regular items. The controls over imperfect items and operations that waste materials are important elements of inventory control. **Scrap** or **waste materials** may result naturally from the production process, or they may be spoiled or defective units that result from avoidable or unavoidable mistakes during production. A company usually introduces quality control techniques that prevent imperfect items from being sold, thereby damaging the reputation of the company. Since scrap, spoiled goods, and defective work usually have some value, each of their costs is accounted for separately.

SCRAP MATERIALS

The expected sales value of the scrap produced by the manufacturing process determines which accounting procedures are used. When the scrap value is small, no entry is made for it until the scrap is sold. Then Cash (or Accounts Receivable) is debited, and an account such as Scrap Revenue is credited. The income from scrap sales is usually reported as "Other income" in the income statement.

When the value of the scrap is relatively high, an inventory card should be prepared, and the scrap is transferred to a controlled materials storage area. If both the quantity and the market value of the scrap are known, the following journal entries are recorded:

Scrap Materials	xxx	
Scrap Revenue (or Work in Process or Factory Overhead)		xxx
Transferred scrap to inventory.		
Cash (or Accounts Receivable)	xxx	
Scrap Materials		xxx
Sold scrap.		

If the market value of the scrap is not known, no journal entry is made until the scrap is sold. At the time of sale, the following entry is then recorded:

Cash (or Accounts Receivable)	xxx	
Scrap Revenue (or Work in Process or Factory Overhead)		xxx
Sold scrap.		

If income from scrap is to be treated as a reduction in manufacturing costs rather than as other income, Work in Process may be credited if the scrap can be readily identified with a specific job. If the scrap cannot be identified with a specific job, Factory Overhead may be credited.

SPOILED AND DEFECTIVE WORK

Scrap is an unexpected by-product of the production of the primary product. Spoiled or defective goods are not by-products but imperfect units of the primary product. **Spoiled units** have imperfections that cannot be economically corrected. They are sold as items of inferior quality or "seconds." **Defective units** have imperfections considered correctable because the market value of the corrected unit will be greater than the total cost incurred for the unit.

Spoiled Work. The loss associated with spoiled goods may be treated as part of the cost of the job or department that produced the spoiled units, or the loss may be charged to Factory Overhead and allocated among all jobs or departments. Generally, Factory Overhead is charged unless the loss results from a special order and the spoilage is due to the type of work required on that particular order. In both cases, the spoiled goods are recorded in Spoiled Goods Inventory at the expected sales price.

To illustrate, assume a garment manufacturer using job order costing completes an order for 1,000 denim jackets (Job 350) at the following unit costs:

Materials	$20
Labor	20
Factory overhead	10
Total cost per unit	$50

The journal entry to record the costs of production is as follows:

Work in process—Job 350	50,000	
Materials		20,000
Payroll		20,000
Factory Overhead		10,000
Recognized production costs for Job 350.		

During the final inspection, 50 jackets are found to be inferior and are classified as irregulars or seconds. They are expected to sell for $10 each. If the unrecovered costs of spoilage are to be charged to Factory Overhead, the following entry is recorded:

Spoiled Goods Inventory	500	
Factory Overhead	2,000	
Work in Process—Job 350		2,500

    Recognized spoiled goods at market value (50 jackets @ $10, charged Factory Overhead for loss of $40 per unit, and reduced cost of Job 350 (50 jackets @ $50).

If the loss from spoilage is considered a cost of the specific job, the entry to record the market value is as follows:

Spoiled Goods Inventory	500	
Work in Process—Job 350		500

    Recognized spoiled goods at market value and reduced the cost of Job 350 by $500 sales price of spoiled goods.

Spoilage costs charged to Factory Overhead are allocated among all jobs in production. When spoilage is attributed to a specific job, however, the entire cost of spoilage is reflected in the cost of that job. In the example, Job 350 will be charged with only a portion of the $2,000 loss from spoilage when Factory Overhead is allocated to the various jobs. When Factory Overhead is not charged for the spoilage costs, however, the entire $2,000 loss is included in the total cost of Job 350.

Defective Work. The procedures for recording the cost associated with defective work are similar to those employed in accounting for spoiled work. There are, however, additional costs for correcting the imperfections on defective units. If these costs are incurred on orders that the company regularly produces, they are charged to Factory Overhead. For special orders, the additional costs are charged to the specific job on which the defective work occurs. An inventory account is not established for goods classified as defective because the defects are corrected and the units become first-quality merchandise.

As in the previous illustration, assume it costs $50 to manufacture each jacket. Upon final inspection of the 1,000 jackets completed, 50 jackets are considered defective because one sleeve on each jacket is a slightly different shade of blue than the other parts of the jacket. Management decides to recut the sleeves from a bolt of material identical in color to the rest of the jacket. The costs of correcting the defects are $500 for materials, $400 for labor, and $300 for factory overhead, representing a total cost of $1,200.

If the additional costs are charged to Factory Overhead, the cost of correcting defective work is spread over all jobs that go through the production cycle. The journal entry is as follows:

Factory Overhead (Costs to Correct Defective Work) .	1,200	
Materials		500
Payroll		400
Factory Overhead		300

Recognized costs of correcting defective units.

If the order for 1,000 jackets was a special order and the defects resulted from the exacting specifications of the order, the additional costs would be charged to the job as follows:

Work in Process—Job 350	1,200	
Materials		500
Payroll		400
Factory Overhead		300

Charged Job 350 with cost of correcting defective work.

The total cost of Job 350 will be higher because the additional costs to correct the defects were charged to the order rather than to the factory overhead account. The unit cost of each completed jacket is increased from $50 ($50,000/1,000) to $51.20 ($51,200/1,000) because of the additional costs charged to the work in process account.

You should now be able to work the following: Questions 22–23; Exercises 11–13; Problems 9–11.

APPENDIX 2A: JUST-IN-TIME MATERIALS CONTROL

In a **just-in-time (JIT) inventory system**, materials are delivered to the factory immediately prior to their use in production. A JIT system significantly reduces inventory carrying costs by requiring that the raw materials be delivered just in time to be placed into production. Additionally, work in process inventory is minimized by eliminating inventory buffers between work centers. For example, the work is performed on a unit in Department A only after the department receives the request from Department B for a certain number of the units. This contrasts with traditional manufacturing systems that produce goods for inventory with the hope that the demand for these goods then will be created. For JIT to work successfully, a high degree of coordination and cooperation must exist between the supplier and the manufacturer and among manufacturing work centers.

Just-in-time production techniques first were utilized by Japanese industry, and they have become popular with U.S. manufacturers only in recent years. U.S. companies that have adopted the principles of JIT include Harley-Davidson, Hewlett-Packard, IBM, and Motorola. It is not unusual in JIT manufacturing for a finished product to be shipped to the customer during the same eight-hour shift that the raw materials used in the product were received from the supplier.

JIT and Cost Control. Reducing inventory levels may increase processing speed, thereby reducing the time it takes for a unit to make it through production. For example, if 10,000 units are produced each day and the average number of units in work in process is 40,000, then the **through-put time**, or time that it takes a unit to make it through the system, is 40,000/10,000, or four days. If the same daily output can be achieved while reducing the work in process by 50%, the throughput time will be reduced to two days, 20,000/10,000, and the **velocity**, or speed with which units are produced in the system, will have doubled. If production speed can be increased dramatically, all products may be made to order, thus eliminating the need for finished goods inventory. Additionally, reducing throughput time can lower costs because there will be fewer **nonvalue added activities**, operations that include costs but do not add value to the product, such as moving, storing, and inspecting.

If the velocity of production is doubled as in the preceding example, the inventory carrying costs can be reduced. For example, assume an annual inventory carrying cost percentage of 20% and an average work in process of $400,000 resulting in annual carrying costs of $80,000 (20% × $400,000). Further assume that through the use of JIT production techniques, the velocity of production is doubled without changing the total annual output, thus necessitating only one-half as much work in process (WIP). The new annual carrying costs would be calculated as follows:

Carrying cost percentage × Average WIP
20% × (1/2 × $400,000) = $40,000

or a $40,000 reduction from the previous level of $80,000.

Further advantages of reduced throughput time include increased customer satisfaction due to quicker delivery and reduced production losses due to not having great quantities of partially completed units piling up at the next work station before an error in their production is detected.

JIT and Cost Flows. Figure 2-14 contrasts the journal entries made in a traditional manufacturing cost accounting system with the entries made in a JIT system. **Backflush costing** is the name for the accounting system

FIGURE 2-14   Journal Entries for Traditional and Backflush Accounting Systems

Transaction	Journal Entries: Traditional System	Journal Entries: Backflush System
A Purchase of raw materials	Materials . . . . 50,000 　Accounts Payable 50,000	Raw and In-Process . 50,000 　Accounts Payable 50,000
B Raw materials requisitioned to production	Work in Process . . . . 50,000 　Materials 50,000	No Entry
C Direct labor cost distributed	Work in Process . . . . 25,000 　Payroll 25,000	Conversion Costs . . 25,000 　Payroll 25,000
D Manufacturing overhead costs incurred	Factory Overhead . . . 75,000 　Various Credits 75,000	Conversion Costs . . 75,000 　Various Credits 75,000
E Transfer of factory overhead costs to work in process	Work in Process . . . . 75,000 　Factory Overhead 75,000	No Entry
F Completion of products	Finished Goods . . . . . 150,000 　Work in Process 150,000	No Entry
G Sale of products	Cost of Goods Sold . . . 150,000 　Finished Goods 150,000	Cost of Goods Sold . 150,000 　Raw and In-Process . . . . 50,000 　Conversion Costs 100,000

used with JIT manufacturing. It derives its name from the fact that costs are not "flushed out" of the accounting system and charged to the products until the goods are completed and sold.

Entries A and B in Figure 2-14 indicate that a single account, Raw and In-Process, is used in backflush costing for both raw materials and work in process inventories. This is done because raw materials are issued to production as soon as received in a JIT system, thus negating the need for a separate raw materials inventory account. Entries C, D, and E illustrate that a single account, Conversion Costs, contains both direct labor and factory overhead costs in a backflush system. Direct labor usually is so insignificant in a highly automated JIT setting that it is not cost-effective to account for it separately.

Entries F and G illustrate that in a true JIT setting, there is no need for a finished goods account because goods are shipped to customers immediately upon completion. Entry G also illustrates that materials, labor, and overhead costs are not attached to products in a backflush system until they are completed and sold. The rationale for this approach is that products move through the system so rapidly in a JIT environment it would not be cost-effective to track production costs to them while in process.

You should now be able to work the following: Questions 24–25; Exercises 13–14; Problems 11–12.

K E Y   T E R M S

Backflush costing, p. 88
Carrying costs, p. 55
Credit memorandum, p. 64
Debit memorandum, p. 64
Defective units, p. 85
Economic order quantity, p. 55
First-in, first-out (FIFO), p. 70
Flow of costs, p. 70
Flow of materials, p. 70
Inventory report, p. 80
Just-in-time (JIT) inventory system, p. 87
Last-in, first-out (LIFO), p. 71
Lead time, p. 54
Materials control, p. 52
Materials ledger, p. 67
Materials requisition, p. 65
Moving average, p. 72
Nonvalue added activities, p. 88
Order costs, p. 54
Order point, p. 54
Production department supervisor, p. 59

Purchasing agent, p. 58
Purchase order, p. 60
Purchase requisition, p. 60
Receiving clerk, p. 59
Receiving report, p. 63
Returned materials report, p. 67
Return shipping order, p. 64
Safety stock, p. 54
Scrap materials, p. 84
Spoiled units, p. 85
Stockout, p. 54
Storeroom keeper, p.59
Stores ledger, p. 67
Stores requisition, p. 65
Summary of materials issued and returned, p. 76
Throughput time, p. 88
Usage, p. 54
Velocity, p. 88
Vendor's invoice, p. 60
Voucher system, p. 79
Waste materials, p. 84

S E L F - S T U D Y   P R O B L E M

ORDER POINT; ECONOMIC ORDER QUANTITY; ORDERING AND CARRYING COSTS

The Wonderboy Company, manufacturer of top of the line baseball bats from Northern White Ash, predicts that 8,000 billets of lumber will be used during the year. (A billet is the quantity of rough lumber needed to make one bat.) The expected daily usage is 32 billets. There is an expected lead time of 10 days and a safety stock of 500 billets. The Wonderboy Company expects the lumber to cost $4 per billet. It anticipates that it will cost $40 to place each order. The annual carrying cost is $.25 per billet.

Required:

1. Calculate the order point.
2. Calculate the most economical order quantity (EOQ).
3. Calculate the total cost of ordering and carrying at the EOQ point.

SOLUTION TO SELF-STUDY PROBLEM

Suggestions:

Read the entire problem thoroughly, keeping in mind that you are required to calculate the following:

1. Order point.
2. EOQ.
3. Total ordering and carrying costs.

The specifics in the problem highlight the following facts relevant to computing the order point:

> Expected daily usage is 32 billets.
> Expected lead time is 10 days.
> Required safety stock is 500 billets.

The order point is the inventory level at which an order should be placed. It is determined by adding the estimated number of billets to be used between placement and receipt of the order:

> Estimated usage during lead time
> = 32 units (daily usage) × 10 days (lead time)
> = 320

The number of units of safety stock (500 in this problem) needed to protect against abnormally high usage and unforeseen delays in receipt of good materials from the supplier:

> Order Point = Expected usage during lead time + safety stock
> = 320   + 500
> = 820 units

The specifics in the problem highlight the following facts relevant to computing the EOQ:

Estimated annual usage of materials	8,000 billets
Cost of placing an order	$40
Annual carrying cost per billet	$.25

The EOQ is the order size that minimizes total order and carrying costs. It can be calculated by using the EOQ formula:

$$EOQ = \sqrt{\frac{2 \times \text{order cost} \times \text{annual demand}}{\text{annual carrying cost per unit}}}$$

$$= \sqrt{\frac{2 \times \$40 \times 8{,}000}{\$.25}}$$

$$= \sqrt{\frac{\$640{,}000}{\$.25}}$$

$$= \sqrt{2{,}560{,}000}$$

$$= \underline{\underline{1{,}600}} \text{ billets}$$

The specifics in the problem highlight the following facts that are relevant to computing the total ordering and carrying costs at the EOQ point:

Annual usage	8,000 billets
EOQ	1,600 billets
Ordering costs	$40 per order
Carrying cost	$.25 per billet
Safety Stock	500 billets

To determine the annual ordering cost, you must first determine the number of orders by dividing the annual usage by the EOQ:

$$\text{Number of orders} = \text{annual usage} / \text{EOQ}$$
$$= 8{,}000 \text{ billets} / 1{,}600 \text{ units}$$
$$= 5$$

The annual order cost is determined by multiplying the number of orders by the cost per order:

$$5 \text{ orders} \times \$40 \text{ per order} = \$200$$

To determine the annual carrying cost, you must first determine the average number of units in inventory:

$$(1/2 \times \text{EOQ}) + \text{Safety stock}$$
$$(1/2 \times 1{,}600) + 500 \qquad = 1{,}300 \text{ units}$$

The average number of billets in inventory would consist of one-half of the amount ordered plus the 500 billets that are kept as a cushion against unforeseen events. The total carrying cost would then be as follows:

$$\text{Average inventory} \times \text{carrying cost per billet}$$
$$1{,}300 \qquad \times \; \$.25 \qquad\qquad = \$325$$

Total cost of ordering and carrying:

$$\text{Order costs} + \text{carrying costs}$$
$$\$200 + \$325 \qquad = \$525$$

(Note: Problem 2-1 is similar to this problem.)

QUESTIONS

1. What are the two major objectives of materials control?

2. Materials often represent a substantial portion of a company's assets; therefore, they should be controlled from the time orders are placed to the time finished goods are shipped to the customer. What are the control procedures used for safeguarding materials?

3. What factors should management consider when determining the amount of investment in materials?

4. Maintaining and replenishing the stock of materials used in manufacturing operations is an important aspect of the procurement process. What is the meaning of the term "order point"?

5. What kind of information and data are needed to calculate an order point?

6. How would you define the term "economic order quantity"?

7. What factors should be considered when determining the cost of an order?

8. What are the costs of carrying materials in stock?

9. Briefly what are the duties of the following employees?

    a. Purchasing agent

    b. Receiving clerk

    c. Storeroom keeper

    d. Production supervisor

10. Proper authorization is required before orders for new materials can be placed. What is the difference between a purchase requisition and a purchase order?

11. Purchasing agents are responsible for contacting vendors from which to purchase materials required by production. Why is the purchasing agent also responsible for reviewing and approving incoming vendors' invoices?

12. Illustrations of forms for requisitioning, ordering, and accounting for materials are presented in the chapter. Would you expect these forms, as shown, to be used by all manufacturers? Discuss.

13. What internal control procedures should be established for incoming shipments of materials purchased?

14. What is the purpose of a debit-credit memorandum?

15. Who originates each of the following forms?

    a. Purchase requisition

    b. Purchase order

    c. Receiving report

    d. Materials requisition

16. Normally a manufacturer maintains an accounting system that includes a stores ledger and a general ledger account for Materials. What is the relationship between the stores ledger and the materials account?

17. A company may select an inventory costing method from a number of commonly used procedures. Briefly how would you describe each of the following methods?

    a. First-in, first-out

    b. Last-in, first-out

    c. Moving average

18. Why do companies adopt the LIFO method of inventory costing? Your discussion should include the effects on both the income statement and balance sheet.

19. Which of the forms shown in the chapter is the source for the following entries to subsidiary ledger accounts?

    a. Debits to record materials purchased in stores ledger.

    b. Credits to record materials requisitioned in stores ledger.

    c. Debits to record materials placed in process in job cost ledger.

20. Which book of original entry is the source for each of the following entries in the general ledger, assuming that a general journal, voucher register, and check register are used?

    a. Debits to materials account to record materials purchased.

    b. Credits to materials account to record materials placed in production.

    c. Debits to vouchers payable account to record vouchers paid.

    d. Debits to work in process account to record materials placed in production.

    e. Credits to work in process account to record materials returned to storeroom.

21. What are some of the steps manufacturers can take to control inventory costs.

22. A manufacturing process may produce a considerable quantity of scrap material because of the nature of the product. What methods can be used to account for the sales value of scrap material?

23. After a product is inspected, some units are classified as spoiled and others as defective. What distinguishes a product as being spoiled or defective?

24. How does the just-in-time approach to production differ from the traditional approach? (Appendix)

25. What is the difference between throughput time and velocity? (Appendix)

E X E R C I S E S

E2-1
Economic order
quantity; order cost;
carrying cost
Learning Objective 2

Gordon Company predicts that it will use 100,000 units of material during the year. The material is expected to cost $5 per unit. Gordon anticipates that it will cost $18 to place each order. The annual carrying cost is $.10 per unit.

a. Determine the most economical order quantity by using the EOQ formula.
b. Determine the total cost of ordering and carrying at the EOQ point.

E2-2
Journalizing materials
requisitions
Learning Objective 4

Everett Corporation records the following use of materials during the month of June:

| | | | Materials Requisitions | |
| | | | Direct | Indirect |
Date	Req. No.	Use	Materials	Materials
1	110	Material A, Job 10	$20,000	
5	111	Material B, Job 11	18,000	
9	112	Material B, Job 12	16,000	
12	113	Factory supplies		$ 800
18	114	Material C, Job 10	3,000	
21	115	Material D, Job 10	9,000	
23	116	Material E, Job 13	2,000	
28	117	Factory supplies		1,300
30	118	Factory supplies		1,700

Prepare a summary journal entry for the materials requisitions.

E2-3
Recording materials
transactions
Learning Objective 4

Prepare a journal entry to record each of the following materials transactions:

a. The voucher register shows that the total materials purchased during the month amounted to $200,000.
b. Direct materials requisitioned for the month totaled $175,000.
c. Indirect materials requisitioned during the month totaled $12,000.
d. Direct materials returned to the storeroom from the factory amounted to $2,500.
e. Total materials returned to vendor during the month amounted to $800.
f. Vouchers paid during the month for materials purchases totaled $160,000 less 2% discount.

E2-4
FIFO costing
Learning Objective 3

Using first-in, first-out, and perpetual inventory costing, determine the cost of materials used and the cost of the May 31 inventory from the following information:

May 1　Balance on hand, 1,000 units (bearings, $4 each).
　　 3　Issued 250 units.
　　 5　Received 500 units at $4.50 each.
　　 6　Issued 150 units.
　 10　Issued 110 units.
　 11　Factory returned 10 units to the storeroom that were issued on the 10th.

15   Received 500 units at $5.00 each.
20   Returned 300 units to vendor from May 15 purchase.
26   Issued 600 units.

E2-5
LIFO costing
Learning Objective 3

Using last-in, first-out, and perpetual inventory costing, compute the cost of materials used and cost of the May 31 inventory, based on the information presented in E2-4.

E2-6
Moving average costing
Learning Objective 3

Using the moving average method and perpetual inventory costing, compute the cost of materials used and the cost of the May 31 inventory based on the information presented in E2-4. (Round unit prices to five decimal places and amounts to the nearest whole dollar.)

E2-7
Comparison of FIFO, LIFO, and moving average methods
Learning Objective 3

In tabular form, compare the total cost transferred to Work in Process and the cost of the ending inventory for each method used in E2-4, E2-5, and E2-6. Discuss the effect that each method will have on profits,depending on whether it is a period of rising prices or a period of falling prices.

E2-8
Impact of costing methods on net income
Learning Objective 3

Bracer Company was franchised on January 1, 19AI. At the end of its third year of operations, December 31, 19A3, management requested a study to determine what effect different materials inventory costing methods would have had on its reported net income over the three-year period.

The materials inventory account, using LIFO, FIFO, and moving average, would have had the following ending balances:

| | | Materials Inventory Balances | |
December 31	LIFO	FIFO	Average
19AI	$20,000	$22,000	$21,000
19A2	22,000	24,000	23,000
19A3	26,000	30,000	28,000

a. Assuming a constant physical count in ending inventory at the end of each year, were material costs rising or falling from 19A1 to 19A3?
b. Which costing method would show the highest net income for 19A1?
c. Which method would show the highest net income for 19A3?
d. Which method would show the lowest net income for the three years combined?
e. For the year 19A2, how would the profit using LIFO compare to the profit if average cost was used?

E2-9
Recording materials transactions
Learning Objective 4

Motown Manufacturing Company maintains the following accounts in the general ledger: Materials, Work in Process, Factory Overhead, and Accounts Payable. On June 1, the materials account had a debit balance of 8,000. Following is a summary of material transactions for the month of June:

1. Materials purchased, per voucher register, $18,750.
2. Direct materials requisitioned, $21,250.
3. Direct materials returned to storeroom, $1,400.

4. Indirect materials requisitioned, $1,975.
5. Indirect materials returned to storeroom, $185.

a. Prepare journal entries to record the materials transactions.
b. Post the journal entries to ledger accounts (in T-account form).
c. What is the balance of the materials inventory account at the end of the month?

E2-10
Scrap materials
Learning Objective 5

A machine shop manufactures a stainless steel part that is used in an assembled product. Materials charged to a particular job amounted to $600. At the point of final inspection, it was discovered that the material used was inferior to the specifications required by the engineering department; therefore, all units had to be scrapped.

Record the entries required for scrap under each of the following conditions:

a. The revenue received for scrap is to be treated as a reduction in manufacturing cost but cannot be identified with a specific job. The value of stainless steel scrap is stable. The scrap is sold two months later for $125.
b. Revenue received for scrap is to be treated as a reduction in manufacturing cost but cannot be identified with a specific job. A firm price is not determinable for the scrap until it is sold. It is sold eventually for $75.
c. The production job is a special job and the $85 received for the scrap is to be treated as a reduction in manufacturing cost. (A firm price is not determinable for the scrap until it is sold.)
d. Only $40 was received for the scrap when it was sold in the following fiscal period. (A firm price is not determinable for the scrap until it is sold and the amount to be received for the scrap is to be treated as other income.)

E2-11
Spoiled work
Learning Objective 5

Advantage Company manufacturers tennis clothing. During the month, the company cut and assembled 8,000 sweaters. One hundred of the sweaters did not meet specifications and were considered "seconds." Seconds are sold for $9.95 per sweater, whereas first-quality sweaters sell for $39.95. During the month, Work in Process was charged $108,000: $36,000 for materials, $48,000 for labor, and $24,000 for factory overhead.

Record the entries required to charge production costs for the period and to record the loss due to spoiled work, under each of the following conditions:

a. The loss due to spoiled work is spread over all jobs in the department.
b. The loss due to spoiled work is charged to this job because it is a special order.

E2-12
Defective work
Learning Objective 5

Micro Mfg. Company manufactures an integrated transistor circuit board for repeat customers but also accepts special orders for the same product. Job No. 1OA1 incurred the following unit costs for 1,000 circuit boards manufactured:

Materials	$5.00
Labor	2.00
Factory overhead	2.00
Total cost per unit	$9.00

When the completed products were tested, 50 circuit boards were found to be defective. The costs per unit of correcting the defects follow:

Materials	$3.00
Labor	1.00
Factory overhead	1.00

Record the journal entry required for the following:

a. If the cost of the defective work is charged to factory overhead.
b. If the cost of the defective work is charged to the job.

E2-13
JIT and Cost Control.
Appendix

Ajax Industries produces 5,000 units each day and the average number of units in work in process is 25,000.

1. Determine the throughput time.
2. If the same daily output can be achieved while reducing the work in process by 40%, determine the new throughput time.

E2-14
Backflush costing
Appendix

Hervis Company uses backflush costing to account for its manufacturing costs. Prepare journal entries to account for the following:

a. Purchased raw materials, on account, $80,000.
b. Requisitioned raw materials to production, $40,000.
c. Distributed direct labor costs, $10,000.
d. Manufacturing overhead costs incurred, $60,000. (Use Various Credits for the account in the credit part of the entry.)

P R O B L E M S

P2-1
Economic order quantity; ordering and carrying costs
Learning Objective 2

 SS

Required:

Brittany Company predicts that it will use 25,000 units of material during the year. The expected daily usage is 200 units, there is an expected lead time of five days and a safety stock of 500 units. The material is expected to cost $5 per unit. Brittany anticipates that it will cost $50 to place each order. The annual carrying cost is $.10 per unit.

1. Compute the order point.
2. Determine the most economical order quantity by use of the formula.
3. Calculate the total cost of ordering and carrying at the EOQ point.

P2-2
Inventory costing methods
Learning Objective 3

The purchases and issues of copper flanges (Stores Ledger #11216) as shown in the records of Jurgen Corporation for the month of November follow:

		Units	Unit Price
Nov. 1	Beginning balance	30,000	$3.00
4	Received, Rec. Report No. 112	10,000	3.10
5	Issued, Mat. Req. No. 49	30,000	
8	Received, Rec. Report No. 113	50,000	3.30
15	Issued, Mat. Req. No. 50	20,000	
22	Received, Rec. Report No. 114	25,000	3.50
28	Issued, Mat. Req. No. 51	30,000	

Required:

1. Complete a stores ledger card similar to Figure 2-7 (the "on order" columns may be omitted) for each of the following inventory costing methods using a perpetual inventory system:
   a. FIFO
   b. LIFO
   c. Moving average (Carry unit prices to five decimal places.)
2. For each method, prepare a schedule that shows the total cost of materials transferred to Work in Process and cost of the ending inventory.
3. If prices continue to increase, would you favor adopting the FIFO or LIFO method? Explain.
4. When prices continue to rise, what is the effect of FIFO versus LIFO on the inventory balance reported in the balance sheet? Discuss.

P2-3
Inventory costing methods
Learning Objective 3

The following transactions affecting materials occurred in February:

Dec. 1	Balance on hand, 1,200 units @ $2.76, $3,312.00 (plastic tubing, 100 feet per unit, stores ledger account # 906).
5	Issued 60 units on Materials Requisition No. 108.
11	Issued 200 units on Materials Requisition No. 210.
14	Received 800 units, Receiving Report No. 634, price $2.8035 per unit.
15	Issued 400 units, Materials Requisition No. 274.
16	Returned for credit 90 units purchased on February 14, which were found to be defective.
18	Received 1,000 units, Receiving Report No. 712, price $2.82712 per unit.
21	Issued 640 units, Materials Requisition No. 318.

Required:

Record the transactions on stores ledger cards similar to Figure 2-7. (The "on order" column may be omitted.) Use the following inventory methods, assuming the use of a perpetual inventory system. Carry units prices to five decimal places.

1. FIFO
2. LIFO
3. Moving average

P2-4
Journalizing materials transactions
Learning Objective 4

Jersey Cloth Company uses a job-order cost system. A partial list of the accounts being maintained by the company, with their balances as of November 1, is shown below:

Cash	$32,250
Materials	29,500
Work in process	27,000
Accounts payable (credit)	21,000
Factory overhead	none

The following transactions were completed during the month of November:

a. Materials purchases during the month, per voucher register, $24,000
b. Materials requisitioned during the month:

1. Direct materials, $31,000.
2. Indirect materials, $6,000.

c. Direct materials returned by factory to storeroom during the month, $1,100.
d. Materials returned to vendors during the month prior to payment,$500.
e. Vouchers paid during the month, $23,000.

Required:

1. Prepare general journal entries for each of the transactions.
2. Post the general journal entries to T-accounts.
3. Balance the accounts and report the balances of November 30 for the following:
   a. Cash.
   b. Materials.
   c. Accounts Payable.

P2-5
Analyzing materials and other transactions
Learning Objective 4

Arthur Manufacturing Company uses a job-order cost system. The following accounts have been taken from the books of the company:

Materials			
Bal. Inventory	7,000	b. Requisitions for month	23,000
a. Purchases for month	20,000		

Work in Process			
Bal. Inventory	3,600	e. To finished goods	50,000
b. Material Requisitions	23,000		
c. Direct Labor	17,000		
d. Factory Overhead	12,000		

Finished Goods			
Bal. Inventory	11,650	f. Cost of Goods Sold	55,000
e. Goods Finished	50,000		

Required:

1. Analyze the accounts and describe in narrative form what transactions took place. (Use the reference letters a through f in your explanations.)
2. List the supporting documents or forms required to record each transaction involving the receipt or issuance of materials.
3. Determine the ending balances for Materials, Work in Process, and Finished Goods.

P2-6
Comprehensive analysis of materials accounting procedures
Learning Objectives 3, 4

The following decisions and transactions were made by Maui Sheet Metal Company in accounting for materials costs for April.

Mar. 31 The factory manager informs the storeroom keeper that for the month of April, 2,000 sheets of aluminum are the forecasted usage. A check of the stock shows 500 aluminum sheets, costing $23 each, on hand. A minimum stock of 300 sheets must be maintained, and the purchasing agent is notified of the need for

1,800 sheets. This quantity will cover the April production requirements and, at the same time, maintain the minimum inventory level.

Apr.   1   After checking with a number of different vendors, the purchasing agent orders the requested number of sheets at $25 each.

6   The shipment of aluminum sheets is received, inspected, and found to be in good condition. However, the order is short 200 sheets, which are back ordered and expected to be shipped in five days.

6   The invoice from the vendor covering the aluminum sheets is received and is approved for payment.

11   The aluminum sheets that were back ordered are received and approved.

11   The vendor's invoice for the back-ordered shipment is received and approved for payment.

16   The April 6 invoice is paid, less a cash discount of 2%.

30   During the month, 1,900 sheets are issued to the factory. The company uses FIFO costing and a job order cost system.

30   The factory returns 20 unused sheets to stores. The returned sheets have a cost of $25 each.

30   At the end of the day, 398 sheets are on hand.

Required:

1. In tabular form, answer the following questions pertaining to each of the preceding decisions and transactions:
    a. What forms, if any, were used?
    b. What journal entries, if any, were made?
    c. What books of original entry, if any, were used to record the data?
    d. What subsidiary records were affected?
2. Calculate and show your computations for the following:
    a. The materials inventory balance as of April 30.
    b. The cost of materials used in production during April.

P2-7
Materials inventory shortage; returns; scrap; spoiled goods
Learning Objectives 4, 5

An examination of Sherwood Forest Corporation's records reveals the following transactions:

a. On December 31, the physical inventory of raw material was 9,970 units. The book quantity, using the moving average method, was 11,000 units @ $.525 per unit.

b. Production returned to stores materials costing $775.

c. Materials valued at $770 were charged to Factory Overhead (Repairs and Maintenance) but should have been charged to Work in Process.

d. Defective material, purchased on account, was returned to the vendor. The material returned cost $234, and the shipping charges (our cost) of $35 were paid in cash.

e. Goods sold to a customer, on account, for $5,000 (cost $2,500) were returned because of a misunderstanding of the quantity ordered. The customer stated that the goods returned were in excess of the quantity needed.

f. Materials requisitioned totaled $22,300, of which $2,100 represented supplies used.

g. Materials purchased on account totaled $25,500. Freight on the materials purchased was $185.

h. Direct materials returned to stores amounted to $950.

i. Scrap materials sent to the storeroom were valued at an estimated selling price of $685 and treated as a reduction in the cost of all jobs worked on during the period.

j. Spoiled work sent to the storeroom valued at a sales price of $60 had production costs of $200 already charged to it. The cost of the spoilage is to be charged to the specific job worked on during the period.

k. The scrap materials in (i) were sold for $685 cash.

Required:

Record the entries, in general journal form, for each transaction.(Round amounts to the nearest whole dollar.)

P2-8
Spoiled goods; loss charged to factory overhead; loss charged to job
Learning Objective 5

Big Company manufactures Brobdingnagians, which sell for $.99 each. The cost of each Brobdingnagian consists of:

Materials	$.35
Labor	.15
Factory overhead	.20
Total	$.70

Job 100 produced 10,000 Brobdingnagians, of which 600 units were spoiled and classified as seconds. Seconds are sold to department stores for $.50 each.

Required:

1. Under the assumption that the loss from spoilage will be distributed to all jobs produced during the current period, use general journal entries to (a) record the costs of production, (b) put spoiled goods into inventory, and (c) record the cash sale of spoiled units.

2. Under the assumption that the loss due to spoilage will be charged to Job 100, use general journal entries to (a) record the costs of production, (b) put spoiled goods into inventory, and (c) record the cash sale of spoiled units.

P2-9
Spoiled goods and defective work
Learning Objective 5

Wrigley Company manufactures electrical equipment from specifications received from customers. Job X10 was for 1,000 motors to be used in a specially designed electrical complex. The following costs were determined for each motor:

Materials	$117
Labor	100
Factory overhead	83
Total	$300

At final inspection, Wrigley discovered that 33 motors did not meet the exacting specifications established by the customer. An examination indicated that 15 motors were beyond repair and should be sold as spoiled goods for $75 each. The remaining 18 motors, although defective, could be reconditioned as first-quality units by the addition of $1,650 for materials, $1,500 for labor, and $1,200 for factory overhead.

Required:

Prepare the journal entries to record the following:

1. The scrapping of the 15 units with the income from spoiled goods treated as a reduction in the manufacturing cost of the specific job.

2. The correction of the 18 defective units with the additional cost charged to the specific job.
3. The additional cost of replacing the 15 spoiled motors with new motors.
4. The sale of the spoiled motors.

P2-10
Review problem;
transactions and
statements
Learning Objective 4

Vertigo Company manufactures chain hoists. The raw material inventories on hand October 1 were as follows:

Chain	12,000 pounds, $24,000
Pulleys	4,000 sets, $20,000
Bolts and taps	10,000 sets, $5,000
Steel plates	4,000 units, $2,000

The balances in the ledger accounts on October 1 were as follows:

Cash	$ 12,000	
Work in process	15,000	
Materials	51,000	
Prepaid insurance	3,000	
Machinery	125,000	
Office equipment	30,000	
Office furniture	20,000	
Accounts payable		$ 30,000
Capital stock		200,000
Retained earnings		26,000
	$256,000	$256,000

Transactions during October were as follows:
a. Payroll recorded during the month: direct labor, $28,000; indirect labor, $3,000.
b. Factory supplies purchased for cash, $1,000. (Use a separate inventory account, Factory Supplies.)
c. Materials purchased on account: chain—4,000 pounds, $8,800; pulleys—2,000 units, $10,200; steel plates—5,000 units, $3,000.
d. Sales on account for the month, $126,375.
e. Accounts receivable collected, $72,500.
f. Materials used during October (FIFO costing): chain, 14,000 pounds; pulleys, 4,400 units; bolts and taps, 4,000 sets; steel plates, 3,800 units.
g. Payroll paid, $31,000.
h. Factory supplies on hand, October 31, $350.
i. Factory heat, light, and power costs for October $3,000 (not yet paid).
j. Office salaries paid, $6,000.
k. Advertising paid, $2,000.
l. Factory superintendence paid, $1,800.
m. Expired insurance—on office equipment, $100; on factory machinery, $300.
n. Factory rent paid, $2,000.
o. Depreciation on office equipment, $400; on office furniture, $180; on machinery, $1,200.
p. Factory overhead charged to jobs, $11,950.

q. Work in Process, October 31, $11,000. (Hint: The difference between the total charges to Work in Process during the period and the ending balance in Work in Process represents the cost of the goods completed.)
r. Cost of goods sold during the month, $84,250.
s. Accounts payable paid, $33,750.

Required:

1. Set up T-accounts and enter the balances as of October 1.
2. Prepare journal entries to record each of the above transactions.
3. Post the journal entries to the accounts, setting up any new ledger accounts necessary. Only controlling accounts are to be maintained; however, show the calculation for the cost of materials used.
4. Prepare a statement of cost of goods manufactured for October.
5. Prepare an income statement.
6. Prepare a balance sheet showing the classifications of current assets, plant and equipment, current liabilities, and stockholders' equity.

P2-11
JIT and Cost Control
Appendix

Felton Fixtures produces 50,000 units each day and the average number of units in work in process is 200,000. The average annual inventory carrying cost percentage is 20% and the average work in process is $1,000,000.

Required:

1. Determine the throughput time.
2. Compute the annual carrying costs.
3. If the same daily output can be achieved while reducing the work in process by 50%, determine the new throughput time.
4. What has happened to the velocity of production in part 3 above.
5. Compute the annual carrying costs for part 3.

P2-12
Backflush Costing
Appendix

Ellison Company uses backflush costing to account for its manufacturing costs.

Required:

Prepare journal entries, if needed, to account for the following transactions.
a. Purchased raw materials on account, $150,000.
b. Requisitioned raw materials to production, $150,000.
c. Distributed direct labor costs, $25,000.
d. Manufacturing overhead costs incurred, $100,000. (Use Various Credits for the credit part of the entry.)
e. Cost of products completed, $275,000.
f. Completed products sold for $400,000, on account.

Accounting for Labor

LEARNING OBJECTIVES

After studying this chapter, you should be able to:

1. Differentiate between direct and indirect labor costs
2. Distinguish between features of hourly rate and piece-rate plans
3. Enumerate procedures for controlling labor costs
4. List functions of timekeeping and payroll departments
5. Enumerate procedures involved in accounting for labor costs
6. Compute and report payroll taxes
7. Account for special problems encountered in labor costing

LEARNING OBJECTIVE
Differentiate between direct and indirect labor costs

Factory payroll costs are divided into two categories: direct labor and indirect labor. **Direct labor** represents payroll costs traced directly to the product. The cost of direct labor is debited to Work in Process. **Indirect labor** consists of labor costs incurred for a variety of jobs related to the production process but not readily identifiable with the individual jobs worked on during the period. Indirect labor costs include the salaries and wages of the factory superintendent, supervisors, janitors, clerks, factory accountants, and timekeepers. Indirect labor costs are charged to Factory Overhead.

The accounting system of a manufacturer must include the following procedures for recording payroll costs:

1. Recording the hours worked or quantity of output by employees in total and by job, process, or department.

2. Analyzing the hours worked by employees to determine how time is to be charged.

3. Charging payroll costs to jobs, processes, departments, and factory overhead accounts.

4. Preparing the payroll, which involves computing and recording employee gross earnings, withholdings and deductions, and net earnings.

WAGE PLANS

LEARNING OBJECTIVE
Distinguish between features of hourly rate and piece-rate plans

Employees' wages are based on plans that have been established by management, approved by the unions, if present, and that comply with the regulations of governmental agencies. A manufacturer may use many variations of wage plans. This chapter covers the wage plans most frequently encountered including hourly rate, piece-rate, and modified wage plans.

HOURLY RATE PLAN

An **hourly rate plan** establishes a definite rate per hour for each employee. An employee's wages are computed by multiplying the established rate per hour times the number of hours worked by the employee in the payroll period. The hourly rate plan is widely used and is simple to apply. Critics argue that it provides no incentive for the employee to maintain or achieve a high level of productivity. An employee is paid for merely "being on the job" for an established period of time. The plan gives no extra recognition or reward for doing more than the minimum required of the position. Proponents of the plan argue that because productivity is not an important factor of such a plan, employees will not be tempted to sacrifice the quality of the product by speeding up production to earn a higher wage.

To illustrate the hourly rate plan, assume an employee earns $10 per hour and works 40 hours per week. The employee's gross earnings would be $400 (40 × $10 per hour).

PIECE-RATE PLAN

A company that gives a high priority to the quantity produced by each worker should consider using an **incentive wage plan** such as a **piece-rate plan,** which bases earnings on the employee's quantity of production. To illustrate, assume a machine operator will earn $.20 for each part (or "piece") finished. If the operator finishes 2,200 in a week, he or she will earn $440 ($.20 × 2,200 parts). The plan provides an incentive for employees to produce a high level of output, thereby maximizing their earnings and also increasing the company's revenue. However, a serious shortcoming of such plans is that they may encourage employees to sacrifice quality in order to maximize their earnings unless the plan is based on good units only. Also, piece rates are not appropriate if machines control production speed.

MODIFIED WAGE PLANS

Modified wage plans combine some features of the hourly rate and piece-rate plans. An example of a modified wage plan would be to set a minimum hourly wage that will be paid by the company even if an employee does not attain an established quota of production. If the established quota is exceeded, an additional payment per piece would be added to the minimum wage level. This type of plan directs management's attention to the employee unable to meet the established quotas.

Labor-management negotiations create many variations of the hourly rate and piece-rate plans. These variations occur because management wishes to minimize costs and maximize profits, while labor attempts to maximize employee earnings.

To illustrate a modified wage plan, assume an employee earns an hourly rate of $10 per hour for up to 100 units of production per day. The employee who produces more than 100 units per day will receive an additional piece rate of $0.80 per unit [($10 × 8 hours) / 100 units]. When the employee produces fewer than 100 units, the difference, often referred to as a **make-up guarantee**, will be charged to Factory Overhead rather than to Work in Process because it represents the cost of inefficient production.

Assume an employee's production and earnings for one week are as follows:

	Hours Worked	Pieces Finished (Quota 100)	Earnings @ $10 per Hour	Earnings @ $.80 per Unit	Make-Up Guarantee	Payroll Earnings
Mon.	8	120	$ 80	$ 96		$ 96
Tues.	8	90	80	72	$ 8	80
Wed.	8	80	80	64	16	80
Thurs.	8	110	80	88		88
Fri.	8	80	80	64	16	80
	40		$400	$384	$40	$424

The employee earned $384 on the piece-rate basis, but the daily guarantee of $80 per day compensated for the days when the employee did not reach the quota. A make-up guarantee of $40 is charged to Factory Overhead because the employee did not meet the quota on Tuesday ($8), Wednesday ($16), and Friday ($16). The payroll distribution for the week would be as follows:

AT MOTOROLA, IMPROVING QUALITY IS A TEAM SPORT

Anyone looking for the thrill of victory and the agony of defeat would have been disappointed. But there was no absence of enthusiasm at an all-day Olympics of sorts held by Motorola Inc.

Today's championship round of a yearlong contest highlighted the successes of employee teams from around the world in improving the quality of things the company does and makes for itself and others.

The telecommunications and electronics manufacturer, based just west of here in Schaumburg, Ill., estimates that it is now saving about $2.2 billion annually from quality programs that in recent years have increasingly emphasized teamwork. . . .

Today's finale to what is formally called the Total Customer Satisfaction Team Competition provided a window on how Motorola has progressed since being selected in 1988 as one of the first companies to win the federal government's top quality prize, the Malcolm Baldridge National Quality Award. The winners were judged not only by the benefits they passed on to Motorola's bottom line, but also on how they achieved them. And the stories that unfolded today help explain why no other company is so frequently rated by consultants and other companies as among the deftest when it comes to making nitty-gritty measurements and adjustments that further its strategic goals.

Company prizes for quality teams are common in industry. So are meetings where teams come together to share experiences and present them to management. But, experts say, only Motorola has gone so far as to organize a worldwide event that ends up with the company's top managers acting as judges of the finalists. . . .

The contest has grown each year. This year, the 24 finalists from Europe, North America and Asia are the survivors of a weeding-out process that began with almost 4,000 teams involving nearly 40,000 of Motorola's 107,000 employees, up from 20,000 two years ago.

Many of the contestants also said they were excited by the opportunity the competition provided for sharing the experience with other parts of the far-flung multinational and gathering ideas to take back to their own plants. That kind of talk does not surprise Mr. Simpson (Motorola executive who oversees competition).

"We don't even bother to track the costs because the benefits are so overwhelming," he said.

It was not exactly white-knuckled competition, what with 12 teams winning gold medals at a banquet tonight. Everyone else got silver medals and liberal praise. . . .

The contest is one of only several ways that Motorola acknowledges quality achievement. Each year, 15 or so trophies get presented by Mr. Fisher (Motorola's chairman and CEO), Gary Tooker, president and chief operating officer, or Chris Galvin, senior executive vice president, to individuals or groups whose work has been brought to their attention. Suppliers also get awards. Mr. Simpson said that the idea for the contest came from seeing the enthusiasm with which employees from some of Motorola's Asian plants participated in national competition. . . .

Mr. Simpson said Motorola was continuing to tinker with the contest format. This year, it set aside the day after the finals to allow the contestants to tour Chicago, shop and visit local museums, and enjoy an evening at a local nightclub. But the kind of employees who make it this far sometimes have other ideas about how to unwind.

"I think I'll go to our sister plant in Northbrook instead," said Fred Clark, a member of the Wippersnappers from Elma. "There's some things that they are doing there that have been called to our attention that might be of interest."

Barnaby Feder, "At Motorola, Improving Quality is a Team Sport," *The New York Times* (January 21, 1993), pp. D1.

Work in Process	384
Factory Overhead	40
Payroll	424

Distributed payroll.

If the number of pieces finished depends on a group effort, then a single incentive plan for the group would be appropriate. In recent years, U.S. manufacturers have adopted the concept of **production work teams** where output is dependent upon contributions made by all members of the work crew or department. The wages may be computed in a manner similar to the previous illustration except that the piece-rate bonus would be shared by all members of the group. Work teams may also participate in company-wide competition for awards and prizes.

CONTROLLING LABOR COST

LEARNING OBJECTIVE
Enumerate procedures for controlling labor costs

The timekeeping and payroll departments have the responsibility of maintaining labor records. The timekeeping and payroll functions may be established as separate departments or organized as subdivisions of a single department. In either case, they should function as independent units to provide an internal check on the accuracy of computing and recording labor costs.

The **timekeeping department** accounts for the time spent by the hourly employees in the factory. The overall objective of the department is to determine the number of hours that should be paid for and the type of work performed by the employees during the working day.

The **payroll department** computes each employee's gross earnings, the amount of withholdings and deductions, and the net earnings to be paid to the employee.

The departmental responsibilities of timekeeping and payroll include completing and maintaining the following forms and records:

Timekeeping	Payroll
Clock cards	Payroll records
Time tickets	Employees earnings records
Production reports	Payroll summaries

CLOCK CARDS AND TIME TICKETS

A **clock card** is provided for each company employee required to use a time clock (time recorder). The card provides a record of the total amount of time the employee spends in the plant. The preprinted card contains such information as the employee's name, social security number, department number, clock number, and the week or pay period. The completed card shows the time a worker started and stopped work each day and the total regular and overtime hours and wages for the period. The clock number also identifies the employee in the payroll records. Figure 3-1 shows an example of a clock card.

Each entrance to the factory may be a clock card station with time clocks and a rack of clock cards for the employees assigned to that entrance. The clock card should show the time of each employee's entrance and exit. Currently, mechanical time recorders and clock cards are being replaced by bar-coding technology. **Bar codes** are symbols that can be processed electronically to identify numbers, letters, or special characters. Each employee receives a bar-coded identification card that is read by **optical scanners** positioned at the factory entrances, thus recording arrival and departure times in the computer database.

Upon reporting to a work station, the employee receives a **time ticket** (Figure 3-2) for recording the hours worked on specific assignments. The time spent on each assignment may be entered by the employee manually on the time ticket, a production supervisor, or by an individual from the timekeeping department. Many companies have computer terminals located throughout the factory that when used in conjunction with bar coding technology can enter employee time distributions directly into the computer without the need for the hard copy.

NAME	Denise R. Sweeney					
SOCIAL SEC. NO.	410-80-7865					

	DEPT. NO.	CLOCK NO.
	04	2316

WEEK ENDING   2/16

AUTHORIZED   Henry Johnson

DAY	IN	OUT	IN	OUT	TOTAL	FOR PAYROLL USE ONLY
M	7:56	12:01	12:59	5:03	8	60.00
T	8:28	12:03	12:58	5:07	7 1/2	56.25
W	7:54	12:01	12:57	5:00	8	60.00
TH	7:58	12:05	1:00	5:05	8	60.00
F	7:55	12:00	12:55	5:02	8	60.00
S						
S						

	RATE		HOURS	AMOUNT
REGULAR	7.50/hr.	REGULAR	39 1/2	296.25
OVERTIME		OVERTIME		

The time ticket shows the employee's starting and stopping time on each job, the rate of pay, and the amount of earnings. When job transfers occur during a working day, the times of the transfers to and from different jobs are recorded on the ticket. The labor hours recorded on the time ticket should be approved by a supervisor because the ticket is the source document for allocating the cost of labor to jobs or departments in the cost ledger and factory overhead ledger. The preparation of separate or unit time tickets for each job or operation on which an employee works may be a requirement of the accounting system (Figure 3-3). Different colors may be selected for these time tickets to facilitate the sorting of the tickets into direct labor and indirect labor categories.

After employees clock in, the timekeeper collects the preceding day's time tickets from supervisors and compares the time tickets and clock

FIGURE 3-2   Time Ticket (Daily)

Name Denise R. Sweeney					Clock No. 2316		

Dept. Grinding (04)

Job or Type of Work	Time Started	Time Stopped	Hours Worked Reg.	O.T.	Rate Reg.	O.T.	Amount Earned
402	8:00	12:00	4		7.50		30 00
437	1:00	4:00	3		7.50		22 50
Machine repair	4:00	5:00	1		7.50		7 50

Date 2/14   Signed Denise R. Sweeney

                                            Employee

               Approved Shawna Campo

                                            Supervisor

cards. The purpose of the comparison is to determine that all time spent by the employee in the factory is accounted for. Total time worked, as shown on the employee's clock card, should correspond to the time reported on the time ticket. Discrepancies should be investigated immediately. If the clock card shows more hours than the time ticket, the difference is reported as idle time. Some companies compare time tickets with clock cards at the end of each shift rather than waiting until the next day. That way, accurate efficiency reports can be prepared overnight and made available to the supervisor at the beginning of the next day.

The employer must compensate the employee for the time spent on assigned jobs. When time is not fully utilized, the employer suffers a loss just as if a theft of some tangible good had occurred. Therefore, if time spent in the factory has been unproductive, the idle time, along with the reason for it, should be recorded.

After the clock cards and time tickets have been compared, the cards are returned to the racks and the time tickets are forwarded to payroll. The pay rates are entered, and the employee's gross earnings are com-

FIGURE 3-3   Time Ticket (Unit)

DEPT.	CLOCK NO.	NAME			
04	2316	Denise R. Sweeney			
JOB	DESCRIPTION OF WORK 3 HP gear				
402	Semi-finishing housings				

				PAYROLL USE ONLY	
			HOURS	AMOUNT	TOTAL
STOP	12:00	OVERTIME			
START	8:00	REGULAR	4	7.50	30.00

Date 2/14

Signed _Denise R. Sweeney_
                                                                Employee

Approved _Shawna Campo_
                                                                Supervisor

puted and recorded on the time tickets. At the end of the week, the clock cards are removed from the rack, and the total hours worked by the employee are computed and recorded. The cards are then forwarded to payroll where the pay rate and gross earnings are entered on the clock cards and recorded in the payroll records. The cards are then filed by employee name or number.

Individual production reports are used instead of time tickets when labor costs are computed using piece rates. A daily report is prepared for each employee that shows work assignments by job number or type of work performed and the total number of units completed. After approval by the supervisor, the report is forwarded to payroll for earnings computation.

PAYROLL DEPARTMENT

The payroll department's primary responsibility is to compute the employees' wages and salaries. It involves combining the daily wages, determining the total earnings, and computing deductions and with-holdings for each employee.

The department must maintain current information concerning regulatory requirements regarding wages and salaries because a specified amount of the employee's wages are subject to social security and income tax deductions. Additional deductions, approved by the employee, can be taken for group insurance premiums, union dues, contribution to a tax-sheltered annuity, and so on.

Payroll Records. Forms used to record earnings information may vary considerably from company to company; however, all forms possess some common characteristics. The **payroll record**, shown in Figure 3-4 provides typical information. It assembles and summarizes each period's payroll data and serves as a subsidiary record for the preparation of a general journal entry. For example, the entry to record the payroll data in Figure 3-4 would be as follows:

Payroll		920.25
FICA Tax Payable		73.62
Employee Income Tax Payable		142.40
Health Insurance Payable		45.00
Employee Receivables		25.00
Wages Payable		634.23
Recognized incurred payroll.		

Employee Earnings Records. In addition to the payroll record, the payroll department keeps a record of the earnings for each employee. Figure 3-5 shows an **employee earnings record**. This cumulative record of employee earnings is needed to compute the amount of employee earnings subject to FICA and other payroll taxes.

Payment of Net Earnings. The payroll department sends the payroll record (Figure 3-4) to the treasurer's office, which is responsible for making the payments to the employees. The earnings usually are paid by check. A check for the total amount to be paid is drawn to create a special payroll fund from which the employees will be paid. The special account is used only for payroll, and the individual payroll checks, when cashed, are charged to the special account. A new payroll account may be established for each payroll period, numbering the accounts sequentially. The checks drawn for each payroll period can then be identified as belonging to a special payroll period. This system facilitates the reconciliation of bank statements. The entry in general journal form to record the payment of net pay to employees would be as follows:

FIGURE 3-4　　　　**Payroll Record**

FOR PERIOD ENDING 2/16/19—

					EARNINGS				
	CLOCK		NO. OF		REGULAR		OVERTIME		TOTAL
NAME	NO.	M/S	ALLOW.	RATE	HOURS	AMOUNT	HOURS	AMOUNT	EARNINGS
DONOVAN, P.	1987	M	0	7.00	40.0	280.00	0	00.00	280.00
FRY, R.	2403	M	2	8.00	40.0	320.00	2	24.00	344.00
SWEENEY, D.	2316	S	1	7.50	39.5	296.25	0	00.00	296.25

WITHHOLDINGS					DEDUCTIONS		NET PAY	
FICA TAXABLE	FICA	INCOME TAXES			HEALTH		OTHER	CHECK
EARNINGS	TAX	FEDERAL	STATE	LOCAL	INSURANCE	OTHER	NO.	AMOUNT
280.00	22.40	28.00	11.30	5.60	15.00		8441	197.70
344.00	27.52	25.00	12.40	7.10	15.00	25.00 ADVANCE	8442	231.98
296.25	23.70	35.00	12.00	6.00	15.00		8443	204.55

FIGURE 3-5   Employee Earnings Record

02/16/19—

CLOCK NUMBER: 2316   EMPLOYEE NAME: DENISE R. SWEENEY   SOCIAL SECURITY NO.: 410-80-7865

MAR. ST.: S   NO. ALLOW.: 1   SEX: F   DEPARTMENT: GRINDING   OCCUPATION: MACHINIST   DATE OF BIRTH: 4/4/47

PERIOD NO.	DATE 19—	RATE	REGULAR HOURS	REGULAR AMOUNT	OVERTIME HOURS	OVERTIME AMOUNT	TOTAL EARNINGS	FICA TAX	FEDERAL	STATE	LOCAL	HEALTH INS.	OTHER	CHECK NO.	AMOUNT
1	1/05	7.20	40	288.00			288.00	23.04	33.70	7.20	4.32	15.00		7971	204.74
2	1/12	7.20	40	288.00	4	43.20	331.20	26.50	41.00	8.28	4.97			8046	250.45
3	1/19	7.20	40	288.00	4	43.20	331.20	26.50	41.00	8.28	4.97	15.00		8129	235.45
4	1/16	7.20	40	288.00			288.00	23.04	33.70	7.20	4.32		18.75	8203	200.99
5	2/02	7.50	40	300.00	6	67.50	367.50	29.40	47.50	9.19	5.51	15.00		8298	260.90
6	2.09	7.50	40	300.00			300.00	24.00	35.60	7.50	4.50			8371	228.40
7	2/16	7.50	39.5	296.25			296.25	23.70	35.00	12.00	6.00	15.00		8443	204.55
8															
9															
10															
11															
12															
13															
QTR TTL				2048.25		153.90	2202.15	176.18	267.50	59.65	34.59	60.00	18.75		1585.48
YRL TTL				2048.25		153.90	2202.15	176.18	267.50	59.65	34.59	60.00	18.75		1585.48

Wages Payable	. . . .	.634.23
Cash	. . . .	.634.23

    Paid employees.

Note that in a voucher system, a voucher first must be prepared for the amount due to the workers. The entry in the voucher register is a debit to Wages Payable and a credit to Accounts Payable. The payment of the voucher then would be recorded in the check register as a debit to Accounts Payable and a credit to Cash.

In the rare instance where employees are paid cash, a check is cashed for the total amount of net earnings. The cash is then divided into amounts earned by individual employees. These cash amounts are placed in envelopes and distributed to the employees. The employee's receipt or signature acknowledges the payment. Many employers now allow employees to authorize the direct electronic deposit of their net pay to their checking accounts.

> **You should now be able to work the following: Questions 1–10, Exercises 2, 3, and Problem 4.**

ACCOUNTING FOR LABOR COSTS

LEARNING OBJECTIVE
Enumerate procedures involved in accounting for labor costs

For all regular hourly employees, the hours worked should be recorded on a time ticket or individual production report. The time tickets and production reports are sent to payroll on a daily basis. The payroll department enters pay rates and gross earnings and forwards the reports to accounting. Cost accountants sort the time tickets and production reports and charge the labor costs to the appropriate jobs or department and to factory overhead. This analysis of labor costs is recorded on a **labor cost summary** (Figure 3-6) in the job cost ledger and in the factory overhead ledger.

Salaried employees, such as department supervisors, are not required to punch time clocks or prepare daily time tickets. Payroll sends a list of salaried employees to accounting showing the names of employees, the nature of work performed, and the salaries. The accounting department records the earnings in factory overhead ledger accounts, because the salaried factory employees are indirect labor, and on the labor cost summary.

The labor cost summary becomes the source for making a general journal entry to distribute payroll to the appropriate accounts:

FIGURE 3-6   Labor Cost Summary

LABOR COST SUMMARY						
Dept. _Grinding_			Month Ending _May 31, 19--_			
Date	Dr. Work in Progress (Direct labor-regular time)		Dr. Factory Overhead (Indirect labor and overtime premium)		Cr. Payroll (Total)	
5/14	11,050	00	1,950	00	13,000	00
5/28	13,000	00	2,600	00	15,600	00
5/31	3,900	00	780	00	4,680	00

Work in Process	27950	
Factory Overhead	5330	
Payroll		33,280
Distributed payroll.		

The entry is then posted to the control accounts, Work in Process and Factory Overhead, in the general ledger. The time tickets and individual production reports have been used to record the labor costs in the subsidiary job cost and factory overhead ledgers and in the labor cost summary. Therefore, the debit to the work in process control account must equal the direct labor cost charged to the jobs, and the charge to the factory overhead control account must equal the labor costs recorded in the factory overhead ledger.

In preparing the labor cost summary from the time tickets, any overtime must be separated from an employee's regular time because the accounting treatment may be different for each type of pay. Regular time worked is charged to Work in Process. Overtime pay may be charged to Work in Process, to Factory Overhead, or allocated partly to Work in Process and partly to Factory Overhead. Overtime distribution depends upon the conditions creating the need for overtime hours.

If an employee works beyond the regularly scheduled time but is paid at the regular hourly rate, the extra pay is called **overtime pay**. If an additional rate is allowed for the extra hours worked, the additional rate earned is referred to as an **overtime premium**. The premium pay rate is added to the employee's regular rate for the additional hours worked. The premium rate is frequently one-half the regular rate, resulting in a total hourly rate for overtime that is 150% of the regular rate. Under these circumstances, overtime pay is often referred to as "time-and-a-half" pay. In some cases, the overtime premium may be equal to or even twice the regular rate, resulting in "double-time" or "triple-time" pay. The double- or triple-time pay rates are not as common as the time-and-a-half pay rate.

To illustrate how a payroll is computed where overtime premium is a factor, assume an employee regularly earns $10 per hour for an 8-hour day. If called upon to work more than 8 hours in a working day, the company pays time-and-a-half for overtime hours. Assuming the employee works 12 hours on Monday, the earnings would be computed as follows:

Direct labor—8 hours @ $10		$ 80
Direct labor—4 hours @ $10	$40	
Factory overhead (overtime premium)—4 hours @ $5 . . .	20	60
Total earnings		$140

The preceding analysis shows that the regular rate of pay was used to charge Work in Process for the direct labor. The additional rate was used to compute the cost of the overtime hours, which was charged to Factory Overhead. By charging the overtime premium to the factory overhead account, all jobs worked on during the period share the cost of overtime premiums paid. If the job contract stipulated that it was a rush order and the overtime premium resulted from the time limitation in the contract, it would be appropriate to charge the premium pay to the specific job worked on during the overtime period instead of to a factory overhead account.

EMPLOYERS' PAYROLL TAXES

LEARNING OBJECTIVE
Compute and report payroll taxes

Payroll taxes imposed on employers include social security tax and federal and state unemployment taxes. Employers must periodically report and pay the taxes to the appropriate government agencies. Employers who fail to file required reports or pay taxes due are subject to civil and, in some cases, criminal penalties.

The **Federal Insurance Contributions Act (FICA)** requires employers to pay social security taxes on wages and salaries equal to the amount withheld from employees' earnings. The employers and employees, therefore, share equally in the cost of the social security program. FICA includes a tax to finance the federal old age, survivors, and disability insurance program (OASDI) and the hospital insurance (HI) or Medicare program. The legislation that governs FICA is frequently amended. These amendments change the wage base subject to FICA and the percentage rate of tax to be charged. For example, in 1980 the tax rate for the employer was 6.13% and the wage base was $25,900. For 1994, the FICA tax rate was 7.65% on the first $60,600 in annual earnings; earnings beyond $60,600 were taxed 1.45% for Hospital Insurance. (Due to the uncertainty that surrounds both the rate and the base wage, an arbitrary FICA tax rate of 8% will be applied to the first $60,000 of earnings in all discussions, examples, and problems in this text.) The selected arbitrary rate and wage base will simplify the tax calculations related to FICA, but they are not predictive of future legislation that may alter the social security system.

The **Federal Unemployment Tax Act (FUTA)** requires employers to pay an established rate of tax on wages and salaries to provide for compensation to employees if they are laid off from their regular employment. For 1994, employers were subject to a tax of 6.2% on the first $7,000 of wages or salaries paid to each employee during the calendar year.

Unemployment benefits, however, are actually paid by individual states and not the federal government. The employer's contributions are apportioned between the federal and state governments as follows: (1) 0.8% goes to the federal government for administration costs relating to the program and (2) 5.4% goes to the state government to accumulate funds for paying unemployment compensation. Each state has its own unemployment tax laws, although such laws must conform to certain requirements established under FUTA. Both tax rates and wage bases vary among states, and the actual amount of combined federal and state unemployment taxes paid depends on a number of factors, including an experience rating for an employer who provides steady employment that may result in a state rate substantially below the 5.4% maximum. (Because of the variation among states and because FUTA taxes are subject to amendments, the examples, exercises, and problems in the text will assume a 4% rate for state taxes and a 1% rate for federal taxes.) These tax rates will be applied to the first $8,000 of an employee's annual earnings.

The employer's payroll taxes are directly related to the costs of direct labor and indirect labor, and theoretically should be charged to these categories of labor cost. However, due to the additional expense and time such allocations would require, it is usually more practical to record all factory-related payroll taxes as factory overhead. The entry, in general journal form, to record the payroll taxes for the payroll in Figure 3-4, assuming that no employee had exceeded the maximum for unemployment taxes, would be as follows:

Factory Overhead	119.63	
FICA Tax Payable		73.62
Federal Unemployment Tax Payable		9.20
State Unemployment Tax Payable		36.81
Recognized payroll taxes.		

ILLUSTRATION OF ACCOUNTING FOR LABOR COSTS

Bowen Manufacturing Company pays employees every two weeks. Monday, May 1, is the beginning of a new payroll period. The company maintains the following records:

Payroll record

Employee earnings records

General journal

General ledger

Job cost ledger

Factory overhead ledger

Bowen uses the following general ledger accounts in accounting for labor costs:

Cash

Work in Process

Wages Payable

FICA Tax Payable

Employees Income Tax Payable

Federal Unemployment Tax Payable

State Unemployment Tax Payable

Health Insurance Premiums Payable

Payroll

Factory Overhead

Administrative Salaries

Sales Salaries

Payroll Tax Expense—Administrative Salaries

Payroll Tax Expense—Sales Salaries

Applicable withholding and payroll tax rates and wage bases follow:

	Rates		Annual
	Employee Withholdings	Employer Payroll Taxes	Wages/Salaries Subject to Tax
Federal income tax	Graduated*		100%
FICA	8%	8%	$60,000
Federal unemployment . .		1%	$ 8,000
State unemployment . . .		4%	$ 8,000

*Federal income tax withholdings are determined from tables. State and local income taxes are not shown in this example.

The following payroll summary is prepared by the payroll department and forwarded to accounting for recording:

Payroll Summary For the Period May 1–14			
	Factory Employees	Sales and Administrative Employees	Total
Gross earnings	$100,000	$30,000	$130,000
Withholdings and deductions:			
FICA tax	$ 8,000	$ 2,400	$ 10,400
Income tax	11,250	3,500	14,750
Health insurance premiums .	2,100	700	2,800
Total	$ 21,350	$ 6,600	$ 27,950
Net earnings	$ 78,650	$23,400	$102,050

After the data are verified, a general journal entry records the payroll:

(A)	Payroll	130,000	
	FICA Tax Payable		10,400
	Employees Income Tax Payable		14,750
	Health Insurance Premiums Payable		2,800
	Wages Payable		102,050
	Incurred payroll for period ended May 14.		

To record the payment of the net earnings to employees, the following entry must be made:

(B)	Wages Payable	102,050	
	Cash		102,050
	Paid payroll for period ended May 14.		

The following labor cost summary and summary of payroll taxes provides the information necessary to distribute the total payroll of $130,000 to the appropriate accounts and to record the employer's payroll taxes for the period.

Schedule of Earnings and Payroll Taxes
For Payroll Period, May 1–14

Nonfactory Employees	Gross Earnings	FICA 8%	Federal 1%	State 4%	Total Payroll Taxes
			Unemployment Taxes		
Sales	$ 20,000	$ 1,600	$ 200	$ 800	$ 2,600
Administrative	10,000	800	100	400	1,300
	$ 30,000	$ 2,400	$ 300	$1,200	$ 3,900
Factory Employees					
Direct labor:					
Regular	$ 85,000	$ 6,800	$ 850	$3,400	$11,050
Overtime premium .	10,000	800	100	400	1,300
Indirect labor	5,000	400	50	200	650
	$100,000	$ 8,000	$1,000	$4,000	$13,000
Total	$130,000	$10,400	$1,300	$5,200	$16,900

The distribution of the payroll and the employer's payroll taxes are recorded as follows:

(C)	Work in Process	85,000	
	Factory Overhead	15,000*	
	Sales Salaries	20,000	
	Administrative Salaries	10,000	
	Payroll		130,000
	Distributed payroll for period ended May 14.		

*Overtime premium ($10,000) + indirect factory labor ($5,000)

(D)	Factory Overhead	13,000**	
	Payroll Tax Expense—Sales Salaries	2,600***	
	Payroll Tax Expense—Administrative Salaries . .	1,300****	
	FICA Tax Payable		10,400
	Federal Unemployment Tax Payable		1,300
	State Unemployment Tax Payable		5,200
	Recognized employer's payroll taxes for period ended May 14.		

**FICA ($8,000) + FUTA ($1,000) + SUTA ($4,000)
***FICA ($1,000) + FUTA ($200) + SUTA ($800)
****FICA ($850) + FUTA ($100) + SUTA ($400)

The general ledger accounts that reflect the entries related to the May 1–14 payroll period follow:

Payroll			
(A)	130,000	(C)	130,000

FICA Tax Payable		
	(A)	10,400
	(D)	10,400

Employees Income Tax Payable		
	(A)	14,750

Health Insurance Premiums Payable		
	(A)	2,800

Wages Payable			
(B)	102,050	(A)	102,050

Cash		
	(B)	102,050

Work in Process	
(C)	85,000

Factory Overhead		
(C)	15,000	
(D)	13,000	

Sales Salaries	
(C)	20,000

Administrative Salaries	
(C)	10,000

Payroll Tax Expense—Sales Salaries	
(D)	2,600

Payroll Tax Expense—Admin. Salaries	
(D)	1,300

Federal Unemployment Tax Payable		
	(D)	1,300

State Unemployment Tax Payable		
	(D)	5,200

The next payroll period is May 15 to May 28. At the end of the two-week period, the following schedule for payroll is prepared:

Payroll Summary
For the Period May 15–28

	Factory Employees	Sales and Administrative Employees	Total
Gross earnings	$120,000	$30,000	$150,000
Withholdings and deductions:			
FICA tax	$ 9,600	$ 2,400	$ 12,000
Income tax	13,000	3,500	16,500
Health insurance premiums . .	2,300	700	3,000
Total	$ 24,900	$ 6,600	$ 31,500
Net earnings	$ 95,100	$23,400	$118,500

The payroll data are verified, and a general journal entry is prepared as follows:

(E)	Payroll	150,000	
	FICA Tax Payable		12,000
	Employees Income Tax Payable		16,500
	Health Insurance Premiums Payable		3,000
	Wages Payable		118,500
	Incurred payroll for period ending May 28.		

The payment of the net earnings to employees requires the following entry:

(F)	Wages Payable	118,500	
	Cash		118,500
	Paid payroll for period ended May 28.		

The following labor cost summary and summary of payroll taxes provides the information necessary to distribute the total payroll of $150,000 to the appropriate accounts and to record the employer's payroll taxes for the period.

Schedule of Earnings and Payroll Taxes
For Payroll Period May 15–28

			Unemployment Taxes		
Nonfactory Employees	Gross Earnings	FICA 8%	Federal 1%	State 4%	Total Payroll Taxes
Sales	$ 20,000	$ 1,600	$ 200	$ 800	$ 2,600
Administrative	10,000	800	100	400	1,300
	$ 30,000	$ 2,400	$ 300	$1,200	$ 3,900
Factory Employees					
Direct labor:					
Regular	$100,000	$ 8,000	$1,000	$4,000	$13,000
Overtime premium .	12,000	960	120	480	1,560
Indirect labor	8,000	640	80	320	1,040
	$120,000	$ 9,600	$1,200	$4,800	$15,600
Total	$150,000	$12,000	$1,500	$6,000	$19,500

The distribution of the payroll and the employer's payroll taxes are recorded as follows:

(G)	Work in Process	100,000	
	Factory Overhead	20,000*	
	Sales Salaries	20,000	
	Administrative Salaries	10,000	
	Payroll		150,000

Distributed payroll for period ended May 28.

*Overtime premium ($12,000) + indirect factory labor ($8,000)

(H)	Factory Overhead	15,600	
	Payroll Tax Expense—Sales Salaries	2,600	
	Payroll Tax Expense—Administrative Salaries	1,300	
	FICA Tax Payable		12,000
	Federal Unemployment Tax Payable		1,500
	State Unemployment Tax Payable		6,000

Recognized employer's payroll taxes for period ended May 28.

PAYROLL ACCRUAL

When the financial statement date does not coincide with the ending date for a payroll period, an accrual for payroll earnings and payroll tax expense should be made. The accrual computations will not include the employees' withholdings because they do not affect the employer's income or total liabilities to be reported. However, the employer's payroll taxes are accrued to avoid understating the expenses and liabilities for the period.

The next payroll period for the Bowen Manufacturing Company begins on May 29 and ends June 11. However, the financial statements to be prepared for May will require an accrual of payroll earnings and taxes for the period May 29–31. The employee earnings and the payroll taxes for the accrual period are shown here, followed by the journal entries required to record and distribute the accrued payroll and to record the employer's payroll taxes.

Schedule of Earnings and Payroll Taxes
For Payroll Period May 29–31

Nonfactory Employees	Gross Earnings	FICA 8%	Unemployment Taxes Federal 1%	State 4%	Total Payroll Taxes
Sales	$ 6,000	$ 480	$ 60	$ 240	$ 780
Administrative	3,000	240	30	120	390
	$ 9,000	$ 720	$ 90	$ 360	$1,170

Factory Employees

	Gross Earnings	FICA 8%	Federal 1%	State 4%	Total Payroll Taxes
Direct labor:					
Regular	$30,000	$2,400	$300	$1,200	$3,900
Overtime premium .	4,000	320	40	160	520
Indirect labor	2,000	160	20	80	260
	$36,000	$2,880	$360	$1,440	$4,680
Total	$45,000	$3,600	$450	$1,800	$5,850

(I)	Payroll	45,000	
	Wages Payable		45,000
	Incurred payroll for May 29–31.		
(J)	Work in Process	30,000	
	Factory Overhead	6,000*	
	Sales Salaries	6,000	
	Administrative Salaries	3,000	
	Payroll		45,000
	Distributed payroll for period May 29–31.		
	*Overtime premium ($4,000) + indirect labor ($2,000)		
(K)	Factory Overhead	4,680	
	Payroll Tax Expense—Sales Salaries	780	
	Payroll Tax Expense—Administrative Salaries . .	390	
	FICA Tax Payable		3,600
	Federal Unemployment Tax Payable		450
	State Unemployment Tax Payable		1,800
	Recognized employer's payroll taxes for period May 29–31.		

Before June transactions are recorded, the entry for accruing payroll should be reversed:

| (L) | Wages Payable | . . . . | 45,000 | |
| | Payroll | . . . . | | 45,000 |

Reversed May 31 adjusting entry for accrued payroll.

The amount earned by the employees during the May 29–31 period is a portion of the total costs and expenses for production, sales, and administration for the month of May. However, the employees will not be paid until June 11 for the payroll period from May 29 to June 11. The credit balance in the payroll account, created by the reversing entry, will assure that only the payroll costs accumulated during the June 1 to June 11 period will be included in the June production, sales, and administrative costs. The ledger accounts would appear as follows after posting all of the preceding entries:

Payroll					FICA Tax Payable		
(A)	130,000	(C)	130,000			(A)	10,400
(E)	150,000	(G)	150,000			(D)	10,400
(I)	45,000	(J)	45,000			(E)	12,000
	325,000	(L)	45,000			(H)	12,000
			370,000			(K)	3,600
			45,000				48,400

Employees' Income Tax Payable			Health Insurance Premiums Payable		
	(A)	14,750		(A)	2,800
	(E)	16,500		(E)	3,000
		31,250			5,800

Wages Payable				Cash		
(B)	102,050	(A)	102,050		(B)	102,050
(F)	118,500	(E)	118,500		(F)	118,500
(L)	45,000	(I)	45,000			

Work in Process			Factory Overhead	
(C)	85,000		(C)	15,000
(G)	100,000		(D)	13,000
(J)	30,000		(G)	20,000
	215,000		(H)	15,600
			(J)	6,000
			(K)	4,680
				74,280

Administrative Salaries

(C)	10,000	
(G)	10,000	
(J)	3,000	
	23,000	

Payroll Tax Expense—
Administrative Salaries

(D)	1,300	
(H)	1,300	
(K)	390	
	2,990	

Sales Salaries

(C)	20,000	
(G)	20,000	
(J)	6,000	
	46,000	

Payroll Tax Expense—Sales Salaries

(D)	2,600	
(H)	2,600	
(K)	780	
	5,980	

State Unemployment Tax
Payable

	(D)	5,200
	(H)	6,000
	(K)	1,800
		13,000

Federal Unemployment Tax Payable

	(D)	1,300
	(H)	1,500
	(K)	450
		3,250

You should now be able to work the following: Questions 11–17, Exercises 1, 4, 5, 7–11, and Problems 1–3, 5, 6, 9, 10.

SPECIAL LABOR COST PROBLEMS

LEARNING OBJECTIVE
Account for special problems encountered in labor costing

An employer may be required to account for a variety of labor-related costs that do not fall into the normal routine of accounting for payroll costs. These special labor-related cost problems may include shift premiums, pensions, bonuses, and vacation and holiday pay. If encountered, the employer should systematically record and recognize each of these costs as a cost of the production process.

SHIFT PREMIUM

A **work shift** is defined as a regularly scheduled work period for a designated number of hours. If a company divides each work day into two or three 8-hour shifts, the employees working on shifts other than the regular daytime shift may receive additional pay, called a **shift premium**. For example, assume the company operates three shifts: day shift, 8 a.m. to 4 p.m.; evening shift, 4 p.m. to 12 p.m.; night shift, 12 p.m. to 8 a.m. The company pays an additional $1.00 per hour to employees who work the evening shift and an additional $1.50 per hour to workers on the night shift. The additional payroll costs for the shift premiums do not increase the productivity of the shifts but are paid because of the social and other life-style adjustments required of the late shift workers. The "other-than-normal" sleep and work schedules deprive the workers from participating in the normal, established social activities and routines. The shift premiums are designed to attract workers to the later shifts scheduled by a company. In reality, even though later shift workers are paid at higher rates, the productivity level of the day workers usually exceeds the productivity of the higher paid, late-shift employees. In order to avoid a distortion in costing products depending upon the time of day that they are worked on, shift premiums are usually charged to Factory Overhead and allocated to all jobs worked on during the period, regardless of shift.

EMPLOYEE PENSION COSTS

Pension costs originate from an agreement between a company and its employee group whereby the company promises to provide income to employees after they retire. The amount of pension benefits paid to a retired employee is commonly based on the employee's past level of earnings and length of service with the company. Some plans are completely funded (paid for) by the company. Others require a partial contribution from the employee. When a pension plan is initiated by a company, the plan is usually retroactive and recognizes the previous years of each employee's service with the company.

A basic provision of all plans is to systematically accrue, over the period of active service, the total estimated pension cost from the beginning date of the pension plan to the employee's retirement date. If, for example, an employee works a 40 hour week and the company incurs a pension cost of $2 per hour, the amount of pension cost chargeable to the payroll period for this employee is $80. The pension costs related to the factory employees could be charged to general or administrative expenses under the premise that the costs of pensions is beneficial to the company as a whole. However, it is also considered appropriate to charge pension costs directly to the individual employee's department or to apportion the cost of pensions, using a percentage of total payroll, to all departments within the company. A percentage allocation plan would seem to be the most desirable to avoid charging the highest pension costs to those departments that employ the most senior workers.

BONUSES

Employees may receive **bonus pay** for a variety of reasons, such as higher-than-usual company profits, exceeding departmental quotas for selling or production, or for any other achievement that the company feels merits additional pay. Bonus plans may include some or all employees. The cost of bonuses is generally charged to the department in which the employee works. Therefore, factory workers' bonuses are charged to Factory Overhead, and sales employees' bonuses are charged to Selling Expense.

VACATION AND HOLIDAY PAY

All permanent employees of a company expect a vacation period each year that will be paid by their employer. Usually the **vacation pay** is earned gradually by the employee for daily service on the job.

Vacation plans generally stipulate that an employee will be granted a specified period of paid vacation time each year for services rendered during the year. The vacation cost is accrued throughout the year and assigned to the employee's department. For example, assume an employee earns $600 per week and is entitled to a four-week vacation. The total cost of the vacation to the company would be $2,400. Each week that the employee works, the employee's department would be charged $50 ($2,400/48 weeks) for vacation pay expense.

Holiday pay is based on an agreement between management and company employees that stipulates that certain holidays during the year will be paid for by the company but are nonworking days for the employees.

ACCOUNTING FOR BONUSES, VACATIONS, AND HOLIDAY PAY

To illustrate accounting for bonuses, vacations, and holiday pay, assume a factory worker earns $700 each week. In addition, the worker will receive a $1,000 bonus at year end, a two-week paid vacation, and five paid holidays. The entry to record the weekly payroll and the costs and liabilities related to the bonus, vacation, and holiday pay as an expense of the 50 weeks that the employee actually worked follows:

Work in Process	700	
Factory Overhead (Bonus)*	20	
Factory Overhead (Vacation)**	28	
Factory Overhead (Holiday)***	14	
Payroll		700
Bonus Liability		20
Vacation Pay Liability		28
Holiday Pay Liability		14

Incurred payroll and bonus, vacation, and holiday pay.

*Bonus: $1,000 / 50 weeks = $20 per week.
**Vacation Pay: $700 × 2 weeks = $1,400 / 50 = $28 per week.
***Holiday Pay: $700 / 5 = $140 per day × 5 = $700
                 $700 / 50 weeks = $14 per week.

Note in the previous example that Factory Overhead was debited for the cost of the bonus, vacation, and holiday pay. If these fringe benefits had related to sales workers or general office workers, Sales Salaries and Administrative Salaries would have been debited respectively.

You should now be able to work the following: Questions 18–21, Exercise 12, and Problems 7, 11.

REAL-WORLD EXAMPLE

DIRECT LABOR COST NOT ALWAYS RELEVANT AT HEWLETT-PACKARD

In certain environments, traditional ways of measuring labor costs may not provide the best information. Hewlett-Packard Company's printed circuit fabrication facility is highly automated. The printed circuit boards are manufactured using "repetitive manufacturing," in which a high volume of standardized units are produced. Hewlett-Packard Company had used job order costing in this facility, but found that it was not suited for controlling a very high volume of standardized products. An article in *Management Accounting* explains how Hewlett-Packard Company simplified its accounting system so that it could provide better information more efficiently.

Attempted use of a job order costing system at Hewlett-Packard frustrated line managers and production workers because they could not physically differentiate between the products in different orders that were being worked on. In order to keep the process flowing efficiently, workers and materials were frequently traded between orders which confounded the cost accounting system's attempt to track the costs of each order.

Repetitive manufacturing also differs from the environment suited to process costing. Process costing works best for the continuous processing of products consisting of fluids or powders. Repetitive manufacturing deals with discrete physical units rather than fluids or powders and is not an inherently continuous process.

Hewlett-Packard changed several cost accounting procedures in order to adapt to its manufacturing environment. A major change was to eliminate the direct labor cost category.

Prior to this change, great amounts of worker, manager, and accountant time were consumed in tracking direct labor costs to specific work orders. Because direct labor comprises such a small percent of total product cost—only 3% to 5%—the continual effort to prepare standard labor costs and then variances from these standards had little potential impact upon overall cost control. In addition, if labor variances occurred, these variances resulted more from how efficiently the process was working on a particular day rather than worker efficiency. The cost accounting staff had tremendous difficulty correcting labor vouchers because the workers and managers could not always distinguish between work orders. For all of these reasons, both the accounting and production managers agreed to include direct labor within manufacturing overhead.

The accounting system became much simpler when direct labor was eliminated as a separate product cost. All manufacturing labor became part of overhead, thus simplifying the accounting for work-in-process inventories and eliminating an estimated 100,000 journal entries per month. Labor variances are now reported weekly or monthly, but the variances are not traced to a particular product lot. Simplifying the cost system allowed the cost accountants to spend more time working with management to provide better reports to improve productivity.

[1]Rick Hunt, Linda Garrett, and C. Mike Merz, "Direct Labor Cost Not Always Relevant at H-P," *Management Accounting* (February 1985), pp. 58–62.

KEY TERMS

Bar codes, p. 109
Bonus pay, p. 130
Clock card, p. 109
Direct labor, p. 104
Employee earnings record, p. 113
Federal Insurance Contributions Act (FICA), p. 118
Federal Unemployment Tax Act (FUTA), p. 119
Holiday pay, p. 130
Hourly rate plan, p. 105
Incentive wage plan, p. 105

Indirect labor, p. 104
Individual production report, p. 112
Labor cost summary, p. 116
Make-up guarantee, p. 106
Modified wage plan, p. 106
Optical scanners, p. 109
Overtime pay, p. 118
Overtime premium, p. 118
Payroll department, p. 109
Payroll record, p. 113

SELF-STUDY PROBLEM

PAYMENT AND DISTRIBUTION OF PAYROLL

The general ledger of the La Luna Company showed the following credit balances on March 15:

FICA Tax Payable	$1,550
Employees Income Tax Payable	975
FUTA Tax Payable	95
State Unemployment Tax Payable	380

Direct labor earnings amounted to $5,100 and indirect labor was $3,400 for the period from March 16 to March 31. The sales and administrative salaries for the same period amounted to $1,500.

Use the following tax rates and bases for this problem:

FICA: 8% on the first $60,000.
State unemployment: 4% on the first $8,000.
FUTA: 1% on the first $8,000.
Federal income tax: 10% of each employee's gross earnings unless otherwise stated.

Required:

1. Prepare the journal entries for the following:
   a. Recording the payroll.
   b. Paying the payroll.
   c. Recording the employer's payroll tax liability.
   d. Distributing the payroll for March 16 to 31.
2. Prepare the journal entries to record the payment of the amounts due for the month for FICA and income tax withholdings.

Suggestions:

Read the entire problem thoroughly, keeping in mind what you are required to do:

1. Journal entries to record the payroll, pay the payroll, record the employer's payroll taxes, and distribute the payroll.
2. Journal entries for the payment of FICA taxes and federal income tax withholdings.

The specifics of the problem highlight the following facts:

1. There are three separate categories of labor: direct labor, indirect factory labor, salespersons and administrators.
2. The company uses a voucher system.

SOLUTION TO SELF-STUDY PROBLEM

1. a. Journal entry to record the payroll for the period March 16–31. To determine the amount of the debit to Payroll, the earnings of direct labor, indirect labor, sales and administrative must be added together to obtain $10,000. The amount of FICA to be withheld from $800 can be obtained by multiplying the 8% rate by the $10,000 payroll (assuming that no employee's salary has already exceeded the $60,000 base for the year). The $1,000 withholding for income taxes is determined by multiplying the $10,000 payroll by the assumed withholding percentage of 10%. Lastly, the credit to Wages Payable for $8,200 represents the amount of net pay that is to appear on employees' paychecks.

A. Payroll 10,000
        FICA Tax Payable   800
        Employees Income Tax Payable   1,000
        Wages Payable   8,200

b. Journal entry to pay the payroll. A check drawn by the company for the total payroll net earnings is deposited in a separate payroll account at the bank and individual checks are issued to the employees. Because the voucher system is used, it is necessary to first prepare a voucher for the net amount to be paid the employees. The voucher is then recorded in the voucher register.

B. Wages Payable   8,200
        Accounts Payable   8,200

The payment of the voucher is recorded in the check register as follows:

C. Accounts Payable   8,200
        Cash   8,200

c. Journal entry to record the payroll tax liability. Payroll taxes consist of the employer's share of the FICA taxes and the federal and state unemployment insurance premiums. The employer pays an amount of FICA taxes that matches the employees' contributions and unemployment insurance premiums that are based on an experience rating related to the business' employment history. (In this example, $800 represents the employees' contributions, $400 is the state unemployment insurance premium, and $100 is the federal unemployment insurance premium.) An important fact to note in the following journal entry is that the payroll taxes on factory labor, whether direct or indirect, are all charged to Factory Overhead, whereas the payroll taxes on the sales and administrative salaries are charged to Payroll Tax Expense (Sales and Administrative Salaries).

D. Factory Overhead 1,105*
      Payroll Tax Expense (Sales and
      Administrative Salaries) 195**
        FICA Tax Payable   800
        Federal Unemployment Tax Payable   100
        State Unemployment Tax Payable   400
      *[.08 ($5,100 + $3,400) + .01 ($8,500) + .04 ($8,500)]
      **[.08 ($1,500) + .01 (1,500) + .04 ($1,500)]

d. Journal entry to distribute the payroll. In distributing the payroll to the appropriate accounts, it is important to distinguish direct labor, which is charged to Work in Process, from indirect labor, which is debited to Factory Overhead.

E. Work in Process	5,100	
Factory Overhead	3,400	
Sales and Administrative Salaries	1,500	
Payroll		10,000

2. At appropriate times as designated by law, the employer payroll taxes and employee withholdings must be remitted to the proper authorities. In this example, FICA taxes and employee income taxes are remitted monthly. The entries in the voucher register and check register, respectively, would be as follows:

FICA Tax Payable	3,150	
Employees Income Tax Payable	1,975	
Accounts Payable		5,125
Accounts Payable	5,125	
Cash		5,125

(Note that Problem 3-3 is similar to this problem.)

QUESTIONS

1. What is the difference between direct and indirect labor?

2. Briefly stated, what are the advantages and disadvantages of (a) the hourly rate wage plan and (b) the piece-rate wage plan?

3. What is a modified-wage plan?

4. What is the concept of production work teams as it relates to incentive-wage plans?

5. What are the functions of the timekeeping and payroll departments?

6. The timekeeping and payroll departments are expected to operate, to a degree, independently of each other. Why is this independence important?

7. a. In a payroll system, what purpose is served by the clock card and time ticket? b. How is the information recorded on clock cards and time tickets used?

8. What technology is replacing mechanical time recorders and clock cards in the modern factory? Explain.

9. How do the clock cards and time tickets complement each other?

10. Although payroll records may vary in design, what types of employee data would be found in the payroll records of most manufacturing companies?

11. What is the source for posting direct labor cost to (a) individual jobs in the job cost ledger and (b) the work in process account in the general ledger?

12. What is the source for posting indirect labor cost to the indirect labor account in the factory overhead ledger?

13. In accounting for labor costs, what is the distinction between regular pay and overtime premium pay?

14. Maintaining internal control over labor cost is necessary for a cost accounting system to function effectively. What are the internal control procedures regarding the charge to the work in process account and the credit to the payroll account in the general ledger?

15. What accounts are used to record employees' withholding taxes and the employer's payroll taxes?

16. What are the procedures involved in accounting for labor cost, and what supporting forms are used for each procedure.

17. What are the sources of data and the books of original entry for each of the following?

    a. Recording the wages and salaries earned during the payroll period.

    b. Paying the wages and salaries earned if a voucher system is being used.

    c. Recording the payroll taxes imposed on the employer.

18. What is a shift premium?

19. What is a basic requirement in all pension plans?

20. What accounting treatments do factory bonuses, vacation pay, and holiday pay for employees have in common?

21. Under what set of circumstances might direct labor be an insignificant amount that would not be accounted for as a separate cost category?

EXERCISES

NOTE: For the exercises and problems in this chapter, use the following tax rates:

FICA—Employer and employee, 8% of the first $60,000 of earnings per employee per calendar year.

State unemployment—4% of the first $8,000 of earnings per employee per calendar year.

FUTA—1% of the first $8,000 of earnings per employee per calendar year.

Federal income tax withholding—10% of each employee's gross earnings, unless otherwise stated.

E3-1
Payroll taxes
Learning Objective 5

The Fucia Company paid wages to its employees during the year as follows:

Brooks	$11,400
Coombs	12,700
Durkins	9,000
Evans	19,300
Hull	29,200
Massey	32,100
Oliver	62,700
Sanders	75,000

a. How much of the total payroll is exempt from FICA tax?

b. How much of the total payroll is exempt from federal and state unemployment taxes?

c. How much of the total payroll is exempt from federal income tax withholding?

E3-2
Computing payroll earnings and taxes
Learning Objectives 2, 3

H. Prince of the Royalty Manufacturing Company is paid at the rate of $12 an hour for an 8-hour day, with time and a half for overtime and double time for Sundays and holidays. Regular employment is on the basis of 40 hours a week, five days a week. The regular workday is from 7:00 a.m. to 12:00 noon and from 12:30 p.m. to 3:30 p.m. At the end of a week the clock card shows the following:

	A.M.		P.M.		Overtime	
	In	Out	In	Out	In	Out
Sunday	8:00	12:00				
Monday	6:58	12:01	12:25	3:35		
Tuesday	7:00	12:03	12:28	3:32		
Wednesday	6:56	12:02	12:30	3:33		
Thursday	6:55	12:05	12:28	3:35	6:00	9:30
Friday	6:55	12:01	12:29			6:32
Saturday	6:55			1:30		

On Monday through Friday night, Prince worked on the production line. The hours worked on Saturday and Sunday were used to repair machinery.
a.   Compute Prince's total earnings for the week. (Ignore odd minutes.)
b.   Present the journal entry to distribute Prince's total earnings.

E3-3
Recording payroll
Learning Objectives
2, 3

Using the earnings data developed in E3-2, and assuming that this was the first week of employment for H. Prince with the Royalty Manufacturing Company, prepare the journal entries for the following:

a.   Recording the week's payroll.
b.   Recording payment of the payroll.

Note: *These single journal entries here and in E3-4 and E3-5 are for the purpose of illustrating the principle involved. Normally the entries would be made for the total factory payroll plus the administrative and sales payroll.*

E3-4
Recording the payroll
and payroll taxes
Learning Objective 5

Using the earnings data developed in E3-2, and assuming that this was the tenth week of employment for Prince and the previous earnings to date were $7,900, prepare the journal entries for the following:

a.   Recording the week's payroll.
b.   Recording payment of the payroll.
c.   Recording the employer's payroll taxes.

E3-5
Recording the payroll
and payroll taxes
Learning Objective 6

Using the earnings data developed in E3-2, and assuming that this was the fiftieth week of employment for Prince and the previous earnings to date were $59,800, prepare the journal entries for the following:

a.   Recording the week's payroll.
b.   Recording payment of the payroll.
c.   Recording the employer's payroll taxes.

E3-6
Determining payroll
earnings
Learning Objective 3

The J.P. Julian Company requires all factory workers to record the time of arrival and departure by means of a time clock. The company operates on a 40-hour basis, time and a half allowed for overtime. The regular work day is from 8:30 a.m. to 12:00 noon and from 1:00 p.m. to 5:00 p.m., Monday through Friday, and from 8:30 a.m. to 11:00 a.m. on Saturday.

The clock card record of a group of employees for Monday is as follows:

Employee No.	Morning In	Noon Out	Noon In	Night Out	Extra In	Extra Out
51	8:29	12:10	12:51	4:57		
52	8:30	12:01	12:56	4:58		
53	8:21	12:05				
54	8:20	12:02	12:57	4:53		
55	8:24	12:04	12:57	4:50		
56	8:29	12:04	12:53	4:57		
57	8:25	12:04				
58	8:27	12:00	12:48	4:56		
59	8:28	12:01	12:57			6:50
60	8:26	12:03	12:56			5:20
61	8:26	12:05	12:59	4:58		
62	8:23	12:00	12:52	4:59	5:30	9:30

a. Compute the regular and overtime hours for each employee for the day. (Ignore odd minutes.)

b. Assuming that all of the employees are paid at the rate of $9.20 an hour, compute the amount of each employee's earnings for the day.

E3-7
Payroll distribution
Learning Objective 5

The total wages and salaries earned by all employees of The Carrasco Manufacturing Company during the month of March as shown in the labor cost summary and the schedule of fixed administrative and sales salaries are classified as follows:

Direct labor	$ 625,125
Indirect labor	162,120
Administrative salaries	140,200
Sales salaries	172,500
Total wages earned	$1,099,945

a. Prepare a journal entry to distribute the wages earned during March.

b. What is the total amount of payroll taxes that will be imposed on the employer for the payroll, assuming that two administrative employees with combined earnings this period of $1,500 have exceeded $8,000 in earnings prior to the period?

E3-8
Overtime allocation
Learning Objective 3

The Boris Machine Tool Company produces tools on a job order basis. During May, two jobs were completed, and the following costs were incurred:

	Job 401	Job 402
Direct materials	$28,000	$37,000
Direct labor: regular	18,000	23,000
overtime premium	—	6,000

Other factory costs for the month totaled $16,800. Factory overhead costs are allocated one-third to Job 401 and two-thirds to Job 402.

a. Describe two alternative methods for assigning the overtime premium cost to Jobs 401 and 402 and explain how the appropriate method would be determined.

b. Compute the cost of Job 401 and Job 402 under each of the two methods described in part a.

E3-9
Employees' earnings and taxes
Learning Objectives 3, 4

A weekly payroll summary made from time tickets shows the following data:

Employee	Classification	Hourly Rate	Hours Regular	Hours Overtime
Ewing, P.	Direct	$12	40	2
Hardaway, A.	Direct	12	40	3
Majerle, D.	Direct	15	40	4
Robinson, D.	Indirect	9	40	
Webber, C.	Indirect	18	40	

Overtime is payable at one-and-a-half times the regular rate of pay for an employee and is distributed to all jobs worked on during the period.

a. Determine the net pay of each employee. The income taxes withheld for each employee amount to 15% of the gross wages.
b. Prepare journal entries for the following:
    1. Recording the payroll.
    2. Payment of the payroll.
    3. Distribution of the payroll. (Assume that overtime premium will be charged to all jobs worked on during the period.)
    4. The employer's payroll taxes. (Assume that none of the employees has achieved the maximum wage bases for FICA and unemployment taxes.)

E3-10
Employees' earnings using hourly and piece-rate methods
Learning Objectives 2, 4

The payroll records of Eastern-Northern Manufacturing Company show the following information for the week ended April 17:

Employee	Classification	Hours Worked	Production (Units)	Hourly Rate	Piece Rate	Weekly Rate	Income Tax W/held
Charles, A.	Direct	42		$9.00			$40
Donn, B.	Direct	48		8.80			42
Johns, C.	Direct	39	2,000		$.22		55
Peter, D.	Direct	40	1,800		.22		50
Raymond, E.	Indirect	40				$200	25
Stephens, F.	Indirect	40				400	60
Williams, G.	Indirect	40				350	30

Hourly workers are paid time-and-a-half for overtime.

a. Determine the net earnings of each employee.
b. Prepare the journal entries for the following:
    1. Recording the payroll.
    2. Paying the payroll.
    3. Distributing the payroll.
    4. Recording the employer's payroll taxes. Assume that none of the employees has achieved the maximum wage bases for FICA and unemployment taxes.

E3-11
Journal entries for payroll
Learning Objectives 3, 4

A partial summary of the payroll data for The Luxor Manufacturing Company for each week of June is as follows:

	June 7	June 14	June 21	June 28
Total earnings	$36,500	$34,200	$37,300	$38,400
Deductions:				
FICA tax, 8%	$?	$?	$?	$?
Tax-sheltered annuity . . .	1,825	1,780	1,855	1,870
Income tax	4,215	4,120	4,320	4,410
Health insurance	600	600	600	600
Total deductions	$?	$?	$?	$?
Net earnings	$?	$?	$?	$?

a. Compute the missing amounts in the summary assuming that no employees have reached the $60,000 FICA maximum.
b. For each payroll period, prepare journal entries to (1) record the payroll and (2) record the payments to employees.

E3-12
Accounting for Bonus and Vacation Pay
Learning Objective 6

Jane Johnson, a factory worker, earns $800 each week. In addition, she will receive a $2,000 bonus at year end and a four-week paid vacation.

    Prepare the entry to record the weekly payroll and the costs and liabilities related to the bonus and the vacation pay, assuming that Johnson is the only employee.

P R O B L E M S

P3-1
Computing and journalizing employer's payroll taxes
Learning Objective 5

The following form is used by The Paris Manufacturing Company to compute payroll taxes incurred during the month of April.

Classification of Wages and Salaries	Earnings for Month	FICA Tax 8%	Federal Tax 1%	State Tax 4%	Total Payroll Taxes Imposed on Employer
			Unemployment Taxes		
Direct labor	88,180				
Indirect labor	16,220				
Payroll taxes on factory					
wages					
Administrative					
salaries	12,000				
Sales salaries	11,500				
Total payroll taxes . .					

Required:

1. Using the above form, calculate the employer's payroll taxes for April. Assume that none of the employees has achieved the maximums for FICA and unemployment taxes.

2. Assuming that the employer payroll taxes on factory wages are treated as factory overhead, the taxes covering administrative salaries are an administrative expense, and the taxes covering sales salaries are a selling expense, prepare a general journal entry to record the employer's liability for the April payroll taxes.

P3-2
Payroll for piece-rate wage system
Learning Objectives 2, 4

The Ringside Manufacturing Company operates on a modified wage plan. During one week's operation, the following direct labor costs were incurred.

Employee	Piece Rate per 100 Units	M	T	W	T	F
			Units Completed			
R. Bowe	$ .90	6,800	7,100	6,500	8,000	4,800
L. Lewis	1.10	6,300	6,400	2,900	2,800	7,000
M. Moorer	1.30	6,200	6,100	7,100	6,000	2,800

The employees are machine operators. Piece rates vary with the kind of product being produced. A minimum of $45 per day is guaranteed each employee by union contract.

Required:

1. Compute Bowe's, Lewis', and Moorer's earnings for the week.
2. Prepare journal entries to:
   a. Record the week's payroll assuming that none of the employees have achieved the maximum base wage for FICA Taxes and Federal Income Tax Withholding is 10%.
   b. Record payment of the payroll.
   c. Record the employer's share of payroll taxes, assuming none of the employees have achieved the maximum base wage for FICA or unemployment taxes.

P3-3
Payment and distribution of payroll
Learning Objective 4
(Similar to Self-Study Problem)

The general ledger of the Throop Company showed the following credit balances on May 15.

FICA Tax Payable 3,100.00
Employees Income Tax Payable 1,938.00
FUTA Tax Payable 193.75
State Unemployment Tax Payable 775.00

Direct labor earnings amounted to $10,500 from May 16 to May 31. Indirect labor was $5,700 and sales and administrative salaries for the same period amounted to $3,800. All wages are subject to FICA, FUTA, state unemployment taxes, and 10% income tax withholding.

Required:

1. Prepare the journal entries for the following:
   a. Recording the payroll.
   b. Paying the payroll assuming the use of a voucher system.
   c. Recording the employer's payroll tax liability.
   d. Distributing the payroll costs for May 16 to 31.
2. Prepare the journal entry to record the payment of the amounts due for the month for FICA and income tax withholdings.
3. Calculate the amount of total earnings for the period from May 1 to May 15.

P3-4
Payroll computation
with incentive bonus
Learning Objective 2

Fifteen workers are assigned to a group project. The production standard calls for 500 units to be completed each hour to meet a customer's set deadline for the products. If the required units can be delivered before the target date on the order, a substantial premium for early delivery will be paid by the customer. The company, wishing to encourage the workers to produce beyond the established standard, has offered a bonus that will be added to each project employee's pay for excess production. The bonus is to be computed as follows:

a. $\dfrac{\text{Group's excess production over standard}}{\text{Standard units for week}} \times 50\% = \text{bonus percentage}$

b. Individual's hourly wage rate × bonus percentage = hourly bonus rate
c. Hourly wage rate + hourly bonus rate = new hourly rate for week
d. Total hours worked × new hourly rate = earnings for week

The average wage rate for the project workers is $8 per hour. The production record for the week shows the following:

	Hours Worked	Production (Units)
Monday	112	61,040
Tuesday	112	60,032
Wednesday	112	60,480
Thursday	112	65,632
Friday	108	57,344
Saturday	60	26,000
	616	330,528

Required:

1. Determine the hourly bonus rate and the total amount of the bonus for the week.
2. What are the total wages of N. Brown, who worked 40 hours at a base rate of $8 per hour?
3. What are the total wages of C. Long, who worked 35 hours at a base rate of $9 per hour?

P3-5
Payroll work sheet
and journal entries
Learning Objectives
3, 4

The payroll records of the Delancey Corporation for the week ending October 7, the fortieth week in the year, show the following:

Employee	Classification	Pay Rate per 40-Hour Week	Hours Worked	Income Tax Withheld	Gross Earnings through Thirty-Ninth week
Coster	President	$1,540	40	$300	$60,060
Davis	Vice-President—Administration	1,275	40	240	49,725
Evans	Supervisor—Production	700	40	180	27,300
Frank	Factory—Direct	500	48	150	19,820
Gregg	Factory—Direct	400	46	160	17,200
Haynes	Factory—Direct	400	44	110	16,600
Porter	Factory—Direct	380	42	120	15,200
Revoz	Factory—Indirect	300	42	80	7,800
Stover	Factory—Indirect	300	42	60	6,600

Required:

1. Complete a work sheet with the following column headings:
   Employee
   3 columns for Earnings for Week:
     Use one for Regular Pay
     Use one for Overtime Premium Pay (The company pays time-and-one-half-for overtime for all employees below the supervisory level.)
     Use one for Total for Week
   Total Earnings through Fortieth Week
   FICA Taxable Earnings
   FICA
   Income Tax Withheld
   Net Earnings
2. Prepare journal entries for the following:
   a. Payroll for fortieth week.
   b. Payment of payroll for week.
   c. Distribution of the payroll costs assuming that overtime premium is charged to all jobs worked on during the period.
   d. Employer's payroll tax liability.
3. The company carries a disability insurance policy for the employees at a cost of $7.80 per week for each employee. Journalize the employer's cost of insurance premiums for the week.

P3-6
Payroll calculation and distribution; overtime and idle time
Learning Objectives 3, 4

A rush order was accepted by the Victory Van Trailer Company for five van conversions. The time tickets and clock cards for the week ended March 27 show the following:

		Time Tickets—Hour Distribution				
Employees	Clock Hours	Van #1	Van #2	Van #3	Van #4	Van #5
Johnson (Supervisor)	42					
Dorsett	45	10	10	10	10	5
Fernandez	48	24	24			
Larkin	48			24	24	
Mitchell	45	15	15	15		
Rijo	42	24	8			
Sanders	40	20	10			

All employees are paid $10.00 per hour, except Johnson, who receives $15 per hour. All overtime premium pay except Johnson's is chargeable to the job and all employees, including Johnson, receive time and a half for overtime hours.

Required:

1. Calculate the total payroll and total net earnings for the week. Assume that an 18% deduction for federal income tax is required in addition to FICA deductions. Assume that none of the employees has achieved the maximums for FICA and unemployment taxes. Hours not worked on vans are idle time and are not charged to the job.
2. Prepare the journal entries to record and pay the payroll.
3. Prepare the journal entry to distribute the payroll to the appropriate accounts.
4. Determine the dollar amount of labor that is chargeable to each van, assuming the overtime costs are proportionate to the regular hours used on the

vans. (First compute an average labor rate for each worker, including overtime premium.)

P3-7
Allocating overtime
premium and bonus
costs
Learning Objectives
4, 6

The Inmont Manufacturing Company uses a job order cost system to cost its
products. It recently signed a new contract with the union that calls for time and
a half for all work over 40 hours a week and double time for Saturday and
Sunday. Also, a bonus of 1% of the employees' earnings for the year is to be
paid to the employees at the end of the fiscal year. The controller, the plant manager, and the sales manager disagree as to how the overtime pay and the bonus
should be allocated.

An examination of the first month's payroll under the new union contract
provisions shows the following:

Direct labor:
Regular—40,200 hours @ $10 . . . . $402,000
Overtime:
  Weekdays—1,700 hours @ $15 . . . . . . $25,500
  Saturdays—400 hours @ $20   8,000
  Sundays—300 hours @ $20   6,000   39,500
Indirect labor   14,800
                                             $456,300

Analysis of the payroll supporting documents revealed the following:

a. More production was scheduled each day than could be handled in a regular
work day, resulting in the need for overtime.
b. The Saturday and Sunday hours resulted from rush orders with special contract arrangements with the customers.

The controller believes that the overtime premiums and the bonus should
be charged to factory overhead and spread over all production of the accounting
period, regardless of when the jobs were completed.

The plant manager favors charging the overtime premiums directly to the
jobs worked on during overtime hours and the bonus to administrative expense.

The sales manager states that the overtime premiums and bonus are not
factory costs chargeable to regular production but are costs created from administrative policies and, therefore, should be charged only to administrative
expense.

Required:

1. Evaluate each position—the controller's, the plant manager's, and the sales
manager's. If you disagree with all of the positions taken, present your view
of the appropriate allocation.
2. Prepare the journal entries to illustrate the position you support, including the
accrual for the bonus.

P3-8
Estimating labor costs
for bids
Learning Objective 2

The Mugabe Manufacturing Company prepares cost estimates for projects on
which it will bid. In order to anticipate the labor cost to be included in a request
to bid on a contract for 1,200,000 units that will be delivered to the customer at
the rate of 100,000 units per month, the company has compiled the following
data related to labor:

a. The first 100,000 units will require 5 hours per unit.
b. The second 100,000 units will require less labor due to the skills learned on the first 100,000 units finished. It is expected that labor time will be reduced by 15% if an incentive bonus of one-half of the labor savings is paid to the employees.
c. For the remaining 1,000,000, it is expected that the labor time will be reduced 25% from the original estimate (the first 100,000 units) if the same incentive bonus (1/2 of the savings) is paid to the employees.
d. Overtime premiums are to be excluded when savings are computed.

The contract will require 2,250 employees at a base rate of $10.00 per hour with time and a half for overtime. The plant operates on a 5-day, 40-hour-per-week basis. Employees are paid for a 2-week vacation in August and for eight holidays.

The scheduled production for the 50-week work-year shows:

January—June: 26 weeks with 4 holidays
July—December: 24 weeks with 4 holidays

Required:

Prepare cost estimates for direct labor and labor related costs for the contract showing the following:

1. Wages paid at the regular rate.
2. Overtime premium payments. (Don't forget holidays in computing regular hours available.)
3. Incentive bonus payments.
4. Vacation and holiday pay.
5. Employer's payroll taxes (13% of total wages assuming that no employee has exceeded the wage bases for FICA and the Unemployment Insurance Taxes).

P3-9
Summary of payroll procedures
Learning Objectives 3, 4

An analysis of the time tickets for the month of November of the Howard Manufacturing Company reveals the information shown:

	Gross Earnings*—Week Ending			
Employee Name	11/8	11/15	11/22	11/29
A. Arthur	$ 300	$ 280	$ 290	$ 320
B. Bennett	280	270	260	280
C. Carletto	320	300	340	280
D. Davenport	1,350	1,350	1,350	1,350
E. Evans	800	760	850	870

*All regular time

Arthur, Bennett, and Carletto are production workers, and Davenport is the supervisor of the group. Evans is in charge of the office.

Cumulative earnings paid (before deductions) in this calendar year prior to the payroll period ending November 8 were as follows: Arthur, $12,000; Bennett, $7,800; Carletto, $11,500; Davenport, $59,400; and Evans, $32,800.

Required:

The solution to this problem requires the following forms, using the indicated column headings:

| Employee | | |
| Earnings Record | Payroll Record | Labor Cost Summary |

Employee Earnings Record
Week Ending
Weekly Gross Earnings
Accumulated Gross
    Earnings
Weekly Earnings Subject
    to FICA
Withholdings
    (2 columns):
    FICA Tax
    Income Tax (10%)
Net Amount Paid

Payroll Record
Employee's Name
Gross Earnings
Withholdings
    (2 columns):
    FICA Tax
    Income Tax (10%)
Net Amount Paid

Labor Cost Summary
Week Ending
Dr. Work in Process
    (Direct Labor)
Dr. Factory Overhead
    (Indirect Labor)
Dr. Administrative
    Salaries (Office)
Cr. Payroll (Total)

1. Prepare an employee earnings record for each of the five employees.
2. Prepare a payroll record for each of the four weeks.
3. Prepare a labor cost summary for the month.
4. Prepare journal entries to record the following:
    a. The payroll for each of the four weeks.
    b. The payment of wages for each of the four payrolls.
    c. The distribution of the monthly labor costs per the labor cost summary.
    d. The company's payroll taxes covering the four payroll periods.

P3-10
Summary of payroll procedures
Learning Objective 4

The Elle Construction Company uses the job order cost system. In recording payroll transactions, the following accounts are used:

Cash
Wages Payable
FICA Tax Payable
Federal Unemployment Tax Payable
State Unemployment Tax Payable
Employees Income Tax Payable
Payroll

Administrative Salaries
Miscellaneous Administrative Expense
Sales Salaries
Miscellaneous Selling Expense
Factory Overhead
Work in Process

Factory employees are paid weekly, while all other employees are paid semimonthly on the fifteenth and the last day of each month. All salaries and wages are subject to all taxes.

Following is a narrative of transactions completed during the month of March:

Mar. 7   Recorded total earnings of factory employees amounting to $68,200 less deductions for employees' income taxes at a withholding rate of 10% and FICA taxes.

7   Issued check for payment of the payroll.

14   Recorded total earnings of factory employees amounting to $66,300 less deductions for employees' income taxes and FICA taxes.

14   Issued check for payment of the payroll.

15   Recorded administrative salaries, $9,000, and sales salaries,
      $17,000, less deductions for employees' income taxes and FICA
      taxes.
15   Issued check for payment of the salaries.
21   Recorded total earnings of factory employees amounting to
      $72,500 less deductions for employees' income taxes and FICA
      taxes.
21   Issued check for payment of the payroll.
28   Recorded total earnings of factory employees amounting to
      $74,200 less deductions for employees' income taxes and FICA
      taxes.
28   Issued check for payment of the payroll.
31   Recorded administrative salaries, $9,000, and sales salaries,
      $17,000 less deductions for employees' income taxes and FICA
      taxes.
31   Issued check for payment of the salaries.
31   The following wages and salaries were earned or accrued during
      March:

Direct labor	$302,500
Indirect labor	22,500
Administrative salaries	18,000
Sales salaries	34,000
Total	$377,000

The Elle Construction Company used the following form to compute the amount
of payroll taxes incurred:

	Taxable Earnings				State Unemployment Tax	Total Taxes Imposed on Employer
Items	FICA	FUTA	FICA	FUTA		
Factory wages	325,000	325,000				
Administrative salaries						
Sales salaries	_____	_____				
Total	377,000	377,000				

Required:

1. Complete the above form to show the payroll taxes imposed on the
   employer for the month of March.
2. Prepare the journal entries to record the foregoing transactions including the
   distribution of payroll costs and payroll taxes, assuming that the payroll
   taxes imposed on the employer for factory wages are to be charged to
   Factory Overhead, the taxes for administrative salaries are to be charged to
   Miscellaneous Administrative Expense, and the taxes for sales salaries are
   to be charged to Miscellaneous Selling Expense.
3. Assume the factory employees worked on March 29, 30, and 31. What was
   the amount of accrued wages on March 31?

P3-11
Accounting for bonus,
vacation pay, and
holiday pay
Learning Objective 6

The factory payroll for the week is $100,000, consisting of $70,000 earned by 100 direct laborers and $30,000 earned by 30 indirect laborers. The total of factory bonuses to be received at year end is estimated at $200,000. All factory workers receive a two-week paid vacation and five paid holidays.

Prepare the entry to record the weekly payroll and the costs and liabilities related to the bonus, vacation, and holiday pay.

Accounting for Factory Overhead

LEARNING OBJECTIVES

After studying this chapter, you should be able to:

1. Identify cost behavior patterns
2. Separate semivariable costs into variable and fixed components
3. Prepare a budget for factory overhead costs
4. Account for actual factory overhead costs
5. Distribute service department factory overhead costs to production departments
6. Apply factory overhead using predetermined rates

All costs incurred in the factory not chargeable directly to the finished product are called **factory overhead**. These operating costs of the factory cannot be traced specifically to a unit of production. A variety of other terms have been used to describe this type of cost, such as indirect expenses, indirect manufacturing costs, or factory burden. These costs are also referred to simply as "overhead" or "burden."

One method to determine whether a factory expenditure is a factory overhead item is to compare it to the classification standards established for direct materials and direct labor costs. If the expenditure cannot be charged to either of these two "direct" factory accounts, it is classified as factory overhead. Thus, all indirect factory expenditures are factory overhead items. Generally, factory overhead accounts include (1) indirect materials consumed in the factory, such as cleaning materials and lubricants required for production; (2) indirect factory labor, such as wages of janitors, forklift operators, and supervisors; and overtime premiums paid to all factory workers; and (3) other indirect manufacturing expenses, such as rent, insurance, property taxes, depreciation, heat, light, and power.

Accounting for factory overhead involves the following procedures:

1. Identifying cost behavior patterns
2. Budgeting factory overhead costs
3. Accumulating actual overhead costs
4. Applying factory overhead estimates to production
5. Calculating and analyzing differences between actual and applied factory overhead

IDENTIFYING COST BEHAVIOR PATTERNS

LEARNING OBJECTIVE
Identify cost behavior patterns

Direct materials and direct labor are classified as variable costs. **Variable costs** are costs that vary in direct proportion to volume changes. In contrast are those costs that remain the same, in total, when production levels increase or decrease. These unchanging costs are referred to as **fixed costs**. A third type of cost is erratic or irregular and does not respond in a predictable way to a change in volume. These costs, which are difficult to predict, are called **semivariable costs**.

Factory overhead expenses include costs that may be classified as variable, fixed, or semivariable. Therefore, factory overhead creates a difficult problem for most companies because they must predict costs that will be incurred at various levels of production. The factory overhead costs that behave in the same pattern as direct materials cost and direct labor costs are considered variable costs and are readily forecasted because they move up or down proportionately with production volume changes. The factory overhead charges deemed to be fixed costs remain unchanged when production varies; therefore, they are also considered predictable. The factory overhead costs that are semivariable require additional analysis and attention because they are not readily predictable. In many companies, semivariable costs constitute a substantial portion of the factory overhead charges, and the method used to forecast these costs must be carefully selected.

Figure 4-1 shows the basic patterns of factory overhead costs as volume changes are encountered.

Examples of variable, fixed, and semivariable factory overhead costs include the following:

Variable: Power costs directly associated with production, depreciation expense computed on the basis of hours equipment is used, repairs directly related to usage, supplies, spoilage, small tools expense.

FIGURE 4-1 Cost Behavior Patterns

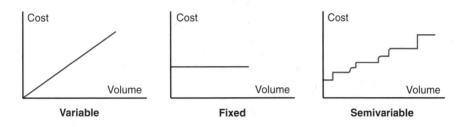

Fixed: Factory property taxes, depreciation of equipment computed on a straight-line basis, periodic rent payments, production executives' salaries, insurance on factory building and equipment.

Semivariable:

Type A: Changes as various levels of production are reached. This type of cost, also known as a **step variable cost,** will remain constant over a range of production, then abruptly change. The increases are not continuous, and costs will plateau before another cost change occurs. Examples are inspection and handling costs, factory supervision and other indirect labor costs, and some indirect materials.

Type B: Varies continuously, but not in direct proportion (ratio) to volume changes. Examples include fuel costs, some utilities costs, and maintenance of factory equipment.

The composition of the different semivariable factory overhead costs make the prediction of a specific amount of overhead cost for a given level of production very difficult. Mathematical techniques can be used to establish fixed and variable components that comprise semivariable costs and, to a degree, remove some of the uncertainty.

ANALYZING SEMIVARIABLE FACTORY OVERHEAD COSTS

LEARNING OBJECTIVE
Separate semivariable costs into variable and fixed components

Many different techniques and theories exist regarding the prediction of future events. Most mathematical techniques attempt to establish a pattern from the historic evidence available, then use the pattern as a model for predicting future outcomes. If history repeats itself, the model will satisfactorily simulate the future events, and the predictions will be beneficial to the decision-making process.

The mathematical (statistical) techniques to be discussed use the relationships of historic costs to isolate variable and fixed elements that can be used to determine future costs. The nonmathematical (observation) method relies on personal experience and managerial judgement.

OBSERVATION METHOD

The **observation method** relies heavily on the ability of an observer to detect a pattern of cost behavior by reviewing past cost and volume data. The reaction of an expense to past changes in production is observed, and a decision is made to treat the expense as either a variable item or a fixed item, depending on which type of cost behavior it more closely resembles. The analyzed overhead item will thereafter be treated as either a variable or fixed cost, ignoring the fact that many costs are semivariable. Companies that use this method believe that the discrepancy between the actual costs and the forecast costs will be insignificant and will not affect management strategies or operations.

The observation method still is used by some companies. However, due to an increasing emphasis on quantifying business data and the need to separate semivariable costs into their fixed and variable components, mathematical methods have increased in popularity. Two of these methods are discussed in the following sections: (1) the high-low method and (2) the statistical scattergraph method. Both of these methods isolate an element of a semivariable cost, then suggest the remainder of the cost is the other element.

HIGH-LOW METHOD

The **high-low method** compares a high production volume and its related cost to a low production volume with its related cost. The difference in volume between the two points being compared is linear and will fall along a straight line.

To illustrate, assume the following overhead costs were incurred at two different levels of production:

	1,000 Units	2,000 Units
Depreciation (fixed)	$2,000	$2,000
Inspection costs (semivariable)	3,000	5,000
Factory supplies (variable)	1,000	2,000

Depreciation is a fixed cost and remained unchanged. Factory supplies varied proportionately with the change in volume, but the unit cost remained constant at $1 per unit. Inspection costs, however, were neither fixed nor did they change proportionately with volume. By using the high-low technique, part of the inspection cost will be considered variable and the remaining part fixed:

Variable element:

	Units	Costs
High volume	2,000	$5,000
Low volume	1,000	3,000
Difference	1,000	$2,000

Variable cost per unit ($2,000 / 1,000 units) = $2

Fixed element:

	1,000 Units	2,000 Units
Cost	$3,000	$5,000
Variable @ $2 per unit	2,000	4,000
Fixed cost (remainder)	$1,000	$1,000

Inspection costs at various levels of production can be estimated using the following formula:

$$\text{Inspection costs} = \$1,000 + \$2 \text{ (number of units produced)}$$

Assume that management wishes to estimate total factory overhead costs for one month at a production level of 4,000 units. Using the above data and the formula for the semivariable cost, projected factory overhead costs for the month would be $15,000, computed as follows:

Depreciation (fixed)	$ 2,000
Inspection costs [semivariable, $1,000 + $2 (4,000)]	9,000
Factory supplies (variable, $1 × 4,000)	4,000
Total estimated factory overhead at 4,000 units	$15,000

SCATTERGRAPH METHOD

The **scattergraph method** estimates a straight line along which the semivariable costs will fall. The cost being analyzed is plotted on the y-axis of the graph and the activity level, such as direct labor hours or machine hours, is plotted on the x-axis. After the observations of cost and production data are plotted on graph paper, a line is drawn by visual inspection representing the trend shown by most of the data points. Usually an equal number of data points fall above and below the line. The point where the straight line intersects the y-axis represents the total fixed costs. The variable cost per unit is computed by subtracting fixed costs from total costs at any point on the graph and then dividing by the volume level for that point read from the x-axis.

Principles of Cost Accounting

The following data will be used to illustrate the determination of the fixed and variable components of inspection cost, using cost and production data for the past six months:

Month	Inspection Cost for Month	Units Produced
July	$4,500	1,600
August	3,000	1,000
September	4,600	1,800
October	5,000	2,000
November	4,050	1,500
December	3,350	1,200

Figure 4-2 shows the scattergraph of these data. A line is visually fit to these data by laying a ruler on the data points. Note that an equal num-

FIGURE 4-2   Scattergraph Method

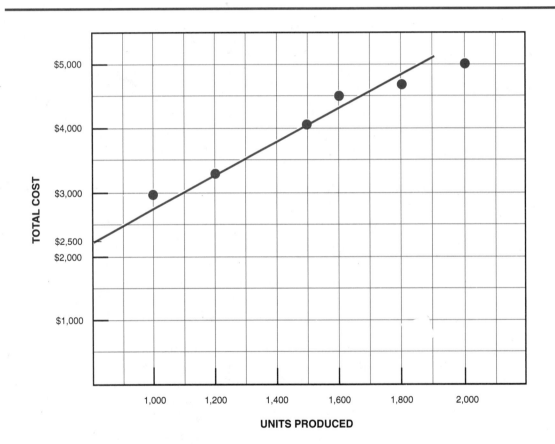

ber of data points lie above and below the line. The cost line in Figure 4-2 intersects the y-axis at $2,500. This is the estimate of the fixed cost portion of the semivariable cost. Subtract the fixed cost from the total cost at any volume level to determine the total variable cost at that level. For example, the total variable cost at a volume level of 1,500 units is $4,050 – $2,500 = $1,550. The variable cost per unit would then be $1.03 ($1,550 / 1,500 units).

LIMITATIONS OF HIGH-LOW AND STATISTICAL SCATTERGRAPH METHODS

The high-low and statistical scattergraph methods both use historic cost patterns to predict future costs and are, therefore, subject to the limitations that apply to all forecasting techniques. The use of mathematical techniques does not ensure accurate forecasts. To a great extent, the accuracy of a forecast depends on the validity of the data used with the chosen method.

Cost analysis is more useful for decision making when all costs are segregated into two categories: variable and fixed. Therefore, the semivariable costs should be analyzed and subdivided into the two categories. The high-low method bases its solution on two observations and assumes that all other unanalyzed relationships will fall along a straight line between these selected observations. Such an assumption may prove to be highly unrealistic because the two observations used may not be representative of the group from which the data were selected. The method may be considered reliable, however, if additional pairs of data are analyzed and the results approximate those obtained from the first observations.

The scattergraph method is an improvement over the high-low method because it uses all of the available data. Additionally, visual inspection of the graph enables nonrepresentative data points, called outliers, to be identified. The major disadvantage of the scattergraph method is that the cost line is drawn through the data points based on visual inspection rather than utilizing mathematical techniques. More sophisticated techniques of determining mathematically a line of best fit through a set of plotted points exist, but they are beyond the scope of this text.

Both methods stress the importance of the relationship of cost factors to volume; however, many other factors may affect cost behavior and should not be ignored. For example, consideration should also be given to price changes and changes in technology. Generalizations about cost patterns should be avoided because only a few costs have inherent characteristics. Management policies directly influence most costs.

> You should now be able to work the following: Questions 1–8,
> Exercises 1–3, and Problems 1 and 2.

BUDGETING FACTORY OVERHEAD COSTS

LEARNING OBJECTIVE
Prepare a budget for
factory overhead costs

Budgets are management's operating plans expressed in quantitative terms, such as units of production and related costs. After factory overhead costs have been classified as either fixed or variable, budgets can be prepared for expected levels of production. The segregation of fixed and variable cost components permits the company to prepare a **flexible budget**. A flexible budget is a budget that shows estimated costs at different production volumes.

Assume management desires to budget factory overhead costs at three levels of production—10,000, 20,000, and 40,000 units. Variable factory overhead cost is $5 per unit, and fixed overhead costs total $50,000. The budgeted costs at these volumes are as follows:

	10,000 units	20,000 units	40,000 units
Variable cost @ $5 per unit	$ 50,000	$100,000	$200,000
Fixed cost	50,000	50,000	50,000
Total factory overhead	$100,000	$150,000	$250,000
Factory overhead per unit	$10.00	$7.50	$6.25

As the volume increases, the factory overhead cost per unit decreases because the total fixed cost, $50,000, is spread over a larger number of units. For example, the fixed cost per unit will add $5 ($50,000 / 10,000 units) at the 10,000-unit level but only $1.25 ($50,000 / 40,000 units) when 40,000 units are produced. The variable cost remains constant at $5 per unit for the entire range of production.

Budgeting is a valuable management tool for planning and controlling costs. A flexible budget aids management in establishing realistic production goals and in comparing actual costs with budgeted costs.

ACCOUNTING FOR ACTUAL FACTORY OVERHEAD

LEARNING OBJECTIVE
Account for actual
factory overhead costs

Cost accounting systems are designed to accumulate, classify, and summarize the factory overhead costs actually incurred. The specific procedures used to account for actual factory overhead costs depend on the nature and organization of the manufacturing firm.

In a small manufacturing company having only one production department, factory overhead may be accounted for in much the same manner as selling and administrative expenses. All the factory overhead accounts may be kept in the general ledger. However, separate accounts should be kept for indirect materials, indirect labor, and for each of the other indirect manufacturing expenses.

Indirect materials and indirect labor costs are recorded first in the general journal. These entries are made from the summary of materials issued and returned and from the labor cost summary. Other factory overhead expenses also are recorded in the general journal from which they are posted to the appropriate accounts in the general ledger. The invoices that have been received are the sources for these entries. Schedules of fixed costs should be prepared and used as the source for general journal adjusting entries to record the amount of taxes, depreciation, insurance, and other similar expenses for the period.

A substantial modification must be made in the accounting system when the number of factory overhead accounts becomes sizeable. A factory overhead subsidiary ledger should be created and maintained, along with a control account in the general ledger. The subsidiary ledger is known as the **factory overhead ledger**, and the control account is entitled "Factory Overhead." At the end of each accounting period, the balance of the factory overhead control account is proved by comparing its balance to the total of the account balances in the subsidiary factory overhead ledger.

Accounts in the factory overhead ledger should have titles clearly descriptive of the nature of the expenditure. Examples of typical factory overhead accounts include the following:

Defective Work	Overtime Premium
Depreciation	Plant Security
Employee Fringe Benefits	Power
Fuel	Property Tax
Heat and Light	Rent
Indirect Labor	Repairs
Indirect Materials	Small Tools
Insurance	Spoilage
Janitorial Service	Supplies
Lubricants	Telephone
Maintenance	Water
Materials Handling	Workers' Compensation Insurance

DEPARTMENTALIZING FACTORY OVERHEAD

In manufacturing companies with several departments, the accounting system is designed to accumulate costs by department. Separate budgets are generally prepared for each department and then combined into a master budget for the company. The actual costs incurred can thus be readily compared with budgeted costs for each department.

Factory overhead expenses must be carefully analyzed before the expenses are assigned to departments. For example, total factory depreciation is analyzed to determine the distribution of depreciation charges among the departments. The accounting system should be designed to provide the necessary data promptly and accurately.

Factory Overhead Analysis Sheets. Instead of expanding the factory overhead ledger to include a separate account for each department's share of different expenses, factory overhead analysis sheets may be used to keep a subsidiary record of factory overhead expense. A separate analysis sheet may be used to record each type of expense, with individual columns for the departmental classification of the expense. Alternatively, a separate analysis sheet can be used for each department, with individual columns for the expense classification.

Figure 4-3 shows an example of an analysis sheet used to keep individual records for each kind of factory overhead expense. The **expense-type analysis sheet** provides a separate amount column for each department that makes it possible to distribute charges among departments as expenses are recorded. Each column represents a department; therefore, each analysis sheet replaces as many separate accounts as there are departments in the factory. In Figure 4-3, which illustrates the distribution of one month's depreciation to departments, the depreciation cost assignable to the various departments was determined by multiplying the plant and equipment valuation in each department (A:

FIGURE 4-3   Factory Overhead Analysis Sheet—Expense Type

Account No. 3111				Distribution Base: *Valuation of Plant and Equipment*						
Account *Depreciation*										
DEPARTMENTAL ANALYSIS				Date	Description	Post. Ref.	Debit	Credit	Balance	
Dept. A	Dept. B	Dept. C	Dept. D							
3 0 0 00	2 0 0 00	1 5 0 00	5 0 0 00	Jan. 31	Depreciation for January	GJ	1 1 5 0 00		1 1 5 0 00	

$36,000; B: $24,000; C: $18,000; D: $60,000) by the annual rate of depreciation (10%) applicable to the property. The estimated monthly depreciation (1/12 of the annual depreciation) was recorded in the general journal and became the source of posting to the analysis sheet.

The **department-type analysis sheet** in Figure 4-4 provides a separate amount column for each kind of expense. This makes it possible to distribute expenses on a departmental basis as they are recorded. Each column represents a different expense. Therefore, each analysis sheet replaces as many separate accounts as there are types of expenses in the factory. Figure 4-4 shows all expenses incurred for Department A, during January. Only the totals are entered. Expenses are posted from the books of original entry either in total or as of the date incurred. The fixed expenses are posted from the general journal at the end of the month.

Factory overhead analysis sheets, both expense and department types, serve as subsidiary ledgers and are controlled by the factory overhead account in the general ledger. The advantage of using an analysis sheet for each expense, classified by departments, is that it provides only

FIGURE 4-4   Factory Overhead Analysis Sheet—Department Type

FACTORY OVERHEAD—DEPARTMENT A

Indirect Materials No. 311.1	Indirect Labor No. 311.12	Power No. 311.13	Depreciation No. 311.18	Factory Property Tax No. 311.20	Insurance No. 311.30	General Factory Expenses No. 311.50
300 00	200 00	150 00	300 00	280 00	350 00	150 00

FACTORY OVERHEAD—DEPARTMENT A

Misc. Factory Expenses Account No.	Amount	Date	Description	Post. Ref.	Debit	Credit	Balance
		Jan. 31	Total expenses-January		1730 00		1730 00

as many amount columns as there are departments within the factory (see Figure 4-3). However, a summary should be prepared at the end of an accounting period to determine the total expenses incurred for each department.

The advantage of using an analysis sheet for each department, classified by expense, is that fewer sheets are required and the preparation of a summary is not required at the end of an accounting period (see Figure 4-4). When a factory is departmentalized, the factory overhead must be recorded departmentally to determine the total cost of operating each department.

Schedule of Fixed Costs. Fixed costs are assumed not to vary in amount from month to month. Some fixed costs, such as insurance and property taxes, are either prepaid or accrued expenses. Because these costs are considered very predictable, schedules for the periodic amount of fixed costs to be allocated to the various departments can be prepared in advance. A **schedule of fixed costs** similar to Figure 4-5 can be prepared for several periods. By referring to the schedule at the end of the period, a journal entry can be prepared to record the total fixed costs. The schedule can also be used as the source from which fixed costs can be posted to the departmental factory overhead analysis sheets.

In Figure 4-5, the schedule of fixed costs shows that for the month of January, the total depreciation expense for machinery, $1,150, is allocated to the departments as follows: A, $300; B, $200; C, $150; D, $500. Figure 4-5 also shows the monthly departmental fixed costs for property tax and insurance. At the end of the month, the accountant would post the amounts from the schedule of fixed costs to each department's analysis sheet.

General Factory Overhead Expenses. All factory overhead expenses are recorded in a regular, systematic manner so that at the end of an accounting period, all expenses chargeable to the period have already been distributed to the factory departments. The allocation of overhead to departments would have been made in proportion to the measurable benefits received from such expenses. However, for some items of factory overhead, the benefits cannot be measured departmentally. Instead, the factory as a whole is the beneficiary. An example is the salary of the plant manager, who has the responsibility to oversee all factory operations. Another example would be the wages of the company security guards.

General factory overhead expenses not identified with a specific department are charged to departments by a process of allocation. This allocation is usually made on a logical basis such as allocating heating

FIGURE 4-5   Schedule of Fixed Costs

Schedule of Fixed Costs

Item of Cost	January	February	March	April	May	June
Depreciation:						
Dept. A	$ 300.00	$ 300.00	$ 300.00	$ 300.00	$ 300.00	$ 300.00
Dept. B	200.00	200.00	200.00	200.00	200.00	200.00
Dept. C	150.00	150.00	150.00	150.00	150.00	150.00
Dept. D	500.00	500.00	500.00	500.00	500.00	500.00
Total	$1,150.00	$1,150.00	$1,150.00	$1,150.00	$1,150.00	$1,150.00
Property tax:						
Dept. A	$ 280.00	$ 280.00	$ 280.00	$ 280.00	$ 280.00	$ 280.00
Dept. B	270.00	270.00	270.00	270.00	270.00	270.00
Dept. C	250.00	250.00	250.00	250.00	250.00	250.00
Dept. D	200.00	200.00	200.00	200.00	200.00	200.00
Total	$1,000.00	$1,000.00	$1,000.00	$1,000.00	$1,000.00	$1,000.00
Insurance:						
Dept. A	$ 350.00	$ 350.00	$ 350.00	$ 350.00	$ 350.00	$ 350.00
Dept. B	325.00	325.00	325.00	325.00	325.00	325.00
Dept. C	300.00	300.00	300.00	300.00	300.00	300.00
Dept. D	425.00	425.00	425.00	425.00	425.00	425.00
Total	$1,400.00	$1,400.00	$1,400.00	$1,400.00	$1,400.00	$1,400.00
Grand Total	$3,550.00	$3,550.00	$3,550.00	$3,550.00	$3,550.00	$3,550.00

costs to departments based on the factory space devoted to each department. The allocation may be made for each item of expense as incurred and recorded, or expenses may be accumulated as incurred and the allocation of the total expenses made at the end of the accounting period. If the allocation is made at the end of the period, a separate analysis sheet is prepared to record each kind of general factory overhead expense incurred during the period. At the end of the period, the total is allocated and recorded on the departmental analysis sheets. The desirability of recording the overhead on a separate sheet depends on the frequency with which such expenses are incurred during the period.

Summary of Factory Overhead. All factory overhead expenses incurred during the accounting period, both variable and fixed, are recorded on factory overhead analysis sheets and in the factory overhead control account in the general ledger. After the posting is completed at the end of an accounting period, the balance of the control account is proved by preparing a **summary of factory overhead** (Figure 4-6) from the analysis sheets. This summary shows the items of expense by department and in total.

> **You should now be able to work the following: Questions 9 and 10, and Problem 3.**

DISTRIBUTING SERVICE DEPARTMENT EXPENSES

LEARNING OBJECTIVE
Distribute service department factory overhead costs to production departments

All job order and process cost systems are designed to accumulate the total cost of each job or unit of product. To include factory overhead as part of the total cost, the amount of factory overhead by each production department must be determined.

In a factory, the manufacturing process consists of a series of operations performed in departments or cost centers. Departments are divided into two classes: service departments and production departments. A **service department** is an essential part of the organization, but it does not work directly on the product. The function of a service department is to serve the needs of the production departments and other service

FIGURE 4-6   Summary of Factory Overhead

Summary of Factory Overhead
For the Month Ended January 31, 19—

Expenses	Dept. A	Dept. B	Dept. C	Dept. D	Total
Indirect materials	$ 100	$ 50	$ 40	$ 30	$ 220
Indirect labor	200	150	140	160	650
Power	150	140	120	100	510
Depreciation	300	200	150	500	1,150
Factory property tax	280	270	250	200	1,000
Insurance	350	325	300	425	1,400
General factory expenses	150	350	200	300	1,000
Total	$1,530	$1,485	$1,200	$1,715	$5,930

Departmental Classification

departments. The product indirectly receives the benefit of the work performed by the service department. Examples of service departments include a department that generates power for the factory, a building maintenance department that is responsible for maintaining the buildings, or the cost accounting department that maintains the factory accounting records.

A **production department** performs the actual manufacturing operations that physically change the units being processed. Because the production departments receive the benefit of the work performed by the service departments, the total cost of production must include not only the costs charged directly to the production departments but also a portion of the costs of operating the service departments. Therefore, the total product costs should include a share of service department costs.

The distribution of the service department costs to production departments involves an analysis of the service department's relationship to the other departments before an apportionment process can be developed. The cost of operating each service department should be distributed in proportion to the benefits received by the various departments. The apportionment of service department costs is complicated because some service departments render service to other service departments as well as to the production departments. For a distribution to be equitable, the cost of operating a service department should be divided among all departments that it serves, service and production alike.

The first requirement of the distribution process is to determine how a particular service department divides its services among the other departments. In some cases, the services performed for another department may be determined precisely; more often, however, the distribution must be based on approximations. For example, the power department may be furnishing power for the operation of the machines and for lighting the building and the surrounding grounds of the plant. If the power used in each department is metered, the meters can be read at the end of the period and the departments charged for the exact amount of power used. This type of charge to a department would be termed a **direct charge**.

On the other hand, a department such as building maintenance, which keeps the building clean and in repair, cannot measure exactly the benefits it provides to the other departments that it serves. The cost of operating the building maintenance department is therefore distributed on some equitable basis to the other departments.

Common bases for distributing service department costs include the following:

Service Departments	Basis for Distribution
Building Maintenance	Floor space occupied by other departments
Inspection and Packing	Production volume
Machine Shop	Value of machinery and equipment
Personnel	Number of workers in departments served
Purchasing	Number of purchase orders
Shipping	Floor space occupied by other departments
Stores	Units of materials requisitioned
Tool Room	Total direct labor hours in departments served

After the bases for distribution have been selected for the service departments, the next step is to distribute the total cost of each service department to the other departments. To illustrate the distribution process, assume the following conditions:

1. The maintenance department services the power plant building.

2. The power department furnishes power to the maintenance department for maintenance equipment.

3. The power department and the maintenance department service the personnel department facilities.

4. The personnel department services the power and maintenance departments through their functions of hiring personnel and maintaining the departments' personnel records.

The first step is to compute the total cost of any one of these overlapping departments. Three different methods are available for use:

1. The **direct distribution method**, which distributes service department costs directly to production departments.

2. The **sequential distribution or step-down method**, which distributes service department costs regressively to other service departments and then to production departments. The sequence of allocating service department costs usually is established on one of two bases:

    a. The number of other departments served,

    b. The magnitude of total costs in each service department.

3. The **algebraic distribution method** takes into consideration that some service departments not only may provide service to, but may also receive service from other service departments. A further explanation of this method is beyond the scope of this text.

The **direct distribution method** makes no attempt to determine the extent to which one service department renders its services to another service department. Instead, the service department's costs are allocated directly and only to the production departments| This method has the advantage of simplicity, but it may produce less accurate results than the other methods. Use of the direct method is justified if the costs allocated to the production departments do not differ materially from the costs that would be allocated using another, more precise method.

The **sequential distribution method** recognizes the interrelationship of the service departments. The power department costs are divided among the personnel, maintenance, and production departments. After the power department cost distribution, the personnel department's total costs—which now include a portion of the power department costs—will be allocated to the maintenance and the production departments. Finally, the maintenance department's costs will be distributed to the production departments.

The distribution sequence for allocating service department costs is a high priority decision when the sequential distribution method is used. The sequential procedure should first distribute the costs of the service department that services the greatest number of other departments. It should continue until all service department costs have been distributed to the production departments. The sequential distribution method can be long and laborious, but it has the advantage of being more accurate if the sequence established is based on a sound analysis of services rendered to the various departments. If a substantial degree of uncertainty exists as to which department's cost should be distributed first to other departments, and the uncertainty cannot be resolved, the department with the largest total overhead should be distributed first. This order of distribution is based on the assumption that the departments render services in direct proportion to the amount of expense they incur.

Figure 4-7 (direct distribution to production departments only) and Figure 4-8 (sequential distribution to service departments and production departments based on magnitude of total costs in service departments) show the direct and sequential methods of distributing service department costs to production departments. Note that the amount of costs in each service department is used as the criterion for determining the order of distribution because each service department services the same number of other departments. The organization and operational structure of a company is the determinant of which distribution method should be selected and used. If the variation from one method to another is insignificant, the direct distribution method would be suitable because it saves time and effort.

The completed distribution work sheets are the basis for a series of general journal entries. The following journal entries are based on the data shown in Figure 4-8.

FIGURE 4-7   Method 1—Direct Distribution of Service Department Costs to Production Departments

	Power	Personnel	Main-tenance	Dept. A	Dept. B	Dept. C	Dept. D	Total
Total from factory overhead analysis sheets	30,000 00	10,000 00	20,000 00	50,000 00	40,000 00	60,000 00	90,000 00	300,000 00
Power distribution— (kw. hours)								
A— 12,000 @ $.30*				3,600 00				
B— 18,000 @ .30					5,400 00			
C— 20,000 @ .30						6,000 00		
D— 50,000 @ .30							15,000 00	
100,000								
Personnel distribution (number of employees served)								
A— 30 @ $100**				3,000 00				
B— 10 @ $100					1,000 00			
C— 20 @ $100						2,000 00		
D— 40 @ $100							4,000 00	
100								
Maintenance distribution— (square feet)								
A— 5,000 @ $1.00**				5,000 00				
B— 6,000 @ 1.00					6,000 00			
C— 4,000 @ 1.00						4,000 00		
D— 5,000 @ 1.00							5,000 00	
20,000				61,600 00	52,400 00	72,000 00	114,000 00	300,000 00

*$30,000 ÷ 100,000 (kilowatt hours) = $.30 per kilowatt hour
**$10,000 ÷ 100 (number of employees served) = $100 per employee
***$20,000 ÷ 20,000 (square feet) = $1.00 per square foot

FIGURE 4-8 Method 2—Sequential Distribution of Service Department Costs Based on Magnitude of Total Costs in Service Departments

	Power	Maintenance	Personnel	Dept. A	Dept. B	Dept. C	Dept. D	Total
Total from factory overhead analysis sheets	30,000 00	20,000 00	10,000 00	50,000 00	40,000 00	60,000 00	90,000 00	300,000 00
Power distribution— (kw. hours)								
Maintenance— 10,000 @ $.25*		2,500 00						
Personnel— 10,000 @ .25			2,500 00					
A— 12,000 @ .25*				3,000 00				
B— 18,000 @ .25					4,500 00			
C— 20,000 @ .25						5,000 00		
D— 50,000 @ .25							12,500 00	
120,000								
Maintenance distribution— (square feet)		22,500 00						
Personnel— 5,000 @ $.90**			4,500 00					
A— 5,000 @ .90**				4,500 00				
B— 6,000 @ .90					5,400 00			
C— 4,000 @ .90						3,600 00		
D— 5,000 @ .90							4,500 00	
25,000								
Personnel distribution (number of employees served)			17,000 00					
A— 30 @ $170**				5,100 00				
B— 10 @ $170					1,700 00			
C— 20 @ $170						3,400 00		
D— 40 @ $170							6,800 00	
100				62,600 00	51,600 00	72,000 00	113,800 00	300,000 00

*$30,000 ÷ 120,000 (kilowatt hours) = $.25 per kilowatt hour
**$22,500 ÷ 25,000 (square feet) = $.90 per square foot
***$17,000 ÷ 100 (number of employees served) = $170 per employee

Factory Overhead—Power Department	30,000
Factory Overhead—Maintenance Department	20,000
Factory Overhead—Personnel Department	10,000
Factory Overhead—Department A	50,000
Factory Overhead—Department B	40,000
Factory Overhead—Department C	60,000
Factory Overhead—Department D	90,000
Factory Overhead	300,000

Closed factory overhead expenses to service and production departments.

The allocation of service department costs would be journalized as follows:

Factory Overhead—Maintenance Department	2,500
Factory Overhead—Personnel Department	2,500
Factory Overhead—Department A	3,000
Factory Overhead—Department B	4,500
Factory Overhead—Department C	5,000
Factory Overhead—Department D	12,500
Factory Overhead—Power Department	30,000

Closed factory overhead expenses of power department to service and production departments.

Factory Overhead—Personnel Department	4,500
Factory Overhead—Department A	4,500
Factory Overhead—Department B	5,400
Factory Overhead—Department C	3,600
Factory Overhead—Department D	4,500
Factory Overhead—Maintenance Department . . .	22,500

Closed factory overhead expenses of maintenance department to service and production departments.

Factory Overhead—Department A	5,100
Factory Overhead—Department B	1,700
Factory Overhead—Department C	3,400
Factory Overhead—Department D	6,800
Factory Overhead—Personnel Department	17,000

Closed factory overhead expenses of personnel department to production departments.

An accounting system can be designed to reduce the number of factory overhead accounts to be maintained for the service departments. In such a system, after the distribution work sheet in Figure 4-8 has been completed, a journal entry can be made to close the factory overhead control account. The charges are made directly to the production departments as follows:

Factory Overhead—Department A	62,600	
Factory Overhead—Department B	51,600	
Factory Overhead—Department C	72,000	
Factory Overhead—Department D	113,800	
Factory Overhead		300,000

Closed factory overhead to production departments. (The departmental totals include the apportioned costs of the service departments.)

After posting the journal entries to the general ledger, the total balances of the departmental factory overhead accounts will equal the balance of the factory overhead control account before it was closed. The journal entries have not affected the total of the factory overhead expenses. However, the general ledger now shows the amount of factory overhead expense being allocated to each of the production departments.

APPLYING FACTORY OVERHEAD TO PRODUCTION

In previous discussions, companies avoided estimating and applying factory overhead to production by charging the actual or incurred factory overhead costs to the work in process account. Companies used these procedures to emphasize the flow of costs and the basic techniques used in cost accounting without unduly complicating the fundamentals. However, factory overhead includes many different costs, some of which will not be known until the end of the accounting period. Because it is desirable to know the total cost of a job or process soon after completion, some method must be established for estimating the amount of factory overhead that should be applied to the finished product. Through the estimating procedure, a job or process will be charged an estimated amount of factory overhead expense. At the end of a period, the actual or incurred factory overhead costs can be compared to the estimated factory overhead applied. If the company encounters a difference, it can make an analysis and subsequent distribution to the appropriate accounts.

The advantages of estimating and charging factory overhead include billing customers on a more timely basis and preparing bids for new contracts more accurately. If it were not possible to bill a customer for a completed job until a month or more later because all factory overhead costs were not known, the extension of time in collecting such accounts would prove very costly to the company. Many companies rely heavily on a bidding process to obtain new jobs. If a company cannot include a fairly accurate factory overhead charge in the cost of a bid, the financial health of the enterprise can be detrimentally affected. If a company has underbid an awarded contract because of understating the actual factory overhead expenses, it could lose income as a result. On the other hand, overstating factory overhead on bids may lead to a lack of new work. Therefore, approximating the overhead charges assigned to bids and to completed jobs is important to a company's financial well-being and continued growth.

ESTABLISHING PREDETERMINED FACTORY OVERHEAD RATES

The flexible budget, which includes the expected departmental factory overhead costs at given levels of production, is used to establish **predetermined factory overhead rates**. The rates are computed by dividing the budgeted factory overhead cost by the budgeted production. The budgeted production may be expressed in terms of machine hours, direct labor hours, direct labor cost, units, and so on. The accuracy of the rate depends on the cost projections and production estimates forecast in the flexible budget. In budget projections, the fixed and variable cost components, historic cost behavior patterns, and possible future economic and operational differences must be considered carefully. Specifically, these factors include the anticipated volume of production, the variability of expenses, the fixed costs relevant to the production levels, the activity of the industry as forecast, and the possible price changes that may occur. Because of the many unknowns, absolute accuracy cannot be expected. Nevertheless, management should give a high priority to attaining the most accurate rate possible.

In a departmentalized company, factory overhead should be budgeted for each department. The procedures for distributing the budgeted departmental expenses are identical to those used to allocate the actual factory overhead expenses. The departmental overhead budgets should also include an allotment of budgeted fixed expenses, such as depreciation and a portion of the budgeted service department expenses.

Upon completing the factory overhead expense budget, the company must choose a method to use when applying the estimated expenses to the departments. The usual application methods require that data from the period's production budgets be obtained. The production budgets will provide information as to the estimated quantity of product, direct labor cost, direct labor hours, and machine hours.

From the production estimates for the plant or for each department, the company can select a method that will charge the product with a fair share of the factory overhead that is expected to be incurred. The departmental composition of human labor versus machines will influence the method of applying factory overhead to the product. A department with little mechanization will usually apply overhead using either the direct labor cost or direct labor hour method, whereas a highly mechanized production department will normally use the machine hour method.

DIRECT LABOR COST METHOD

The **direct labor cost method** uses the amount of direct labor cost that has been charged to the product as the basis for applying factory overhead. The overhead rate to be used is predetermined by dividing the estimated (budgeted) factory overhead cost by the estimated (budgeted) direct labor cost. The relationship of the overhead to the direct labor cost is expressed as a percentage of direct labor cost (the base).

For example, assume the budgeted factory overhead cost for Department A amounts to $100,000, and the estimated direct labor cost is expected to be $200,000. The predetermined rate would be 50% of direct labor dollars ($100,000 / $200,000).

Also, assume that during the first month of operations, Job 100 incurred $1,000 for direct materials and $3,000 for direct labor. The job is completed. Using the predetermined rate to estimate factory overhead, the total cost is computed as follows:

Job 100

Direct Materials	$1,000
Direct labor	3,000
Factory overhead (50% of direct labor $)	1,500
Total cost of completed job	$5,500

The direct labor cost method is appropriate in departments that require mostly human labor and in which the direct labor cost charges are relatively stable from one product to another. If a labor force generates direct labor cost that varies widely due to the hourly rate range of the employees or absenteeism, another method should be used. For example, a low-paid hourly employee could be replaced, due to absenteeism, with a higher-paid hourly employee. The higher-paid employee would increase the direct labor cost and thereby increase the amount of factory overhead charged to the department. Such increases in factory overhead charges to a department are usually unwarranted because the higher-paid employee does not normally increase the actual factory overhead expense incurred by the department. Any fluctuation in the department-al direct labor cost not accompanied by a proportional increase in actual factory overhead expenses will cause a distortion in the product's total cost. This can be detrimental to the company's ability to control costs and to make good production and marketing decisions.

DIRECT LABOR HOUR METHOD

The **direct labor hour method** overcomes the problem of varying wage rates by applying factory overhead using the number of direct labor hours worked on a job or process. The predetermined rate is computed by dividing the budgeted factory overhead cost by the estimated direct labor hours to be worked. For example, assume the budgeted factory overhead cost was $100,000, and it is expected that production will require 25,000 direct labor hours. The predetermined rate would be $4 per direct labor hour ($100,000 / 25,000 hours).

If factory overhead is applied to Job 100 using the direct labor hours method, the records must include the number of direct labor hours worked on each job. Assume it took 500 direct labor hours to complete Job 100, and the direct materials and direct labor costs were $1,000 and $3,000, respectively:

Job 100

Direct materials	$1,000
Direct labor (500 hours)	3,000
Factory overhead (500 hours @ $4)	2,000
Total cost of completed job	$6,000

An advantage of the direct labor hour method is that the amount of factory overhead applied is not affected by the mix of labor rates in the total direct labor cost. A disadvantage in using this method could be that the application base (the number of direct labor hours) could be substantially smaller than when direct labor cost is used. This application base would thereby be more affected by slight deviations in direct labor hours. Also, if factory overhead primarily consists of items that are more closely tied to labor dollars, such as employee fringe benefits, then the direct labor hour method may not be as accurate.

MACHINE HOUR METHOD

A highly mechanized department is normally best served by the **machine hour method**. In such a department, the factory overhead cost should be more proportionate to the machine hours generated by the equipment than the direct labor hours or costs incurred by the employees operating the machinery. It is common in mechanized departments for one employee to operate more than one piece of equipment. Therefore, one direct labor hour may generate, possibly, five machine hours. It is a complex method that requires substantial preliminary study before installation and an additional quantity of records to be maintained. However, the advantages to be gained by a more dependable factory overhead application rate may more than outweigh the additional effort and costs involved./The machine hour rate is determined by dividing the budgeted factory overhead cost by the estimated machine hours to be used by production/

For example, assume the factory overhead budget is $100,000, and it is expected that 10,000 machine hours will be required. The predetermined rate would be $10 per machine hour ($100,000 / 10,000 hours).

Assume that Job 100, now completed, used $1,000 for direct materials, $3,000 for direct labor, and required 300 machine hours.

Job 100

Direct materials	$1,000
Direct labor	3,000
Factory overhead (300 machine hours @ $10)	3,000
Total cost of completed job	$7,000

ACTIVITY-BASED COSTING METHOD

The preceding methods of applying overhead to products assumed that all overhead costs incurred were related to volume. For example, the amount of overhead costs incurred were solely a function of how many direct labor hours or machine hours were worked. In a modern factory that produces many products, a substantial portion of the overhead may be more a function of the complexity of the product being made rather than the number of units produced. **Activity-based costing (ABC)** considers non-volume-related activities that create overhead costs, such as the number of machine setups or product design changes required of a particular product line.

A product that is difficult to make may also be produced in small numbers, perhaps due to its unusual nature and the resulting lack of demand. If overhead were applied to products strictly on the basis of direct labor hours or machine hours, very little overhead would be charged to such a product due to its low production volume. Its complexity to produce, however, may have created a lot of additional overhead costs in the form of machine setups and design changes, even though the number of units in the production run was small.

To successfully employ an ABC system, a company must first identify activities in the factory that create costs. Examples of those would include design changes, inspections, materials movements, material requisitions, and machine setups. The cost of performing each of these activities in the coming period then must be determined. The next step is to decide upon the **cost driver**, or basis used to allocate each of the activity cost pools. For example, for machine setup costs the cost driver may be total estimated setup time for the coming period or the estimated number of setups to be performed. Lastly, the estimated cost of each activity pool is divided by the estimated number of cost driver units related to that pool to compute an overhead or activity rate that is used to charge each product or job based on its consumption of the resources required to sustain each activity.

For example, assume the factory overhead budget is $100,000. The allocation bases, expected levels of activity for each cost pool, and overhead rates follow:

Cost Pool	Expected Amount	Expected Level of Allocation Base	Overhead Rate
Direct labor usage	$ 30,000	10,000 labor hours	$3/direct labor hour
Machine usage	$ 40,000	5,000 machine hours	$8/machine hour
Machine setups	$ 20,000	100 setups	$200/setup
Design changes	$ 10,000	25 design changes	$400/design change
	$100,000		

Assume that Job 100, now completed, required $1,000 for direct materials, $3,000 for direct labor, 500 direct labor hours, 75 machine hours, two setups, and one design change. The cost of the job would be computed as follows:

Job 100

Direct materials	$ 1,000
Direct labor (500 hours)	3,000
Factory overhead related to:	
direct labor usage (500 hours × $3/direct labor hour)	1,500
machine usage (75 hours × $8/machine hour)	600
machine setups (2 setups × $200/setup)	400
design changes (1 change × $400/design change)	400
Total cost of complete job	$ 6,900

Note that the overhead charged to this job using activity-based costing and, thus, the total cost of the job are greater than they were under any of the other methods of charging overhead. Activity-based costing better reflects the additional costs of performing a job that requires a design change and more than one setup.

YES, ABC WORKS WITH PURCHASING, TOO.

The use of activity-based costing to determine better product costs is not limited to costs incurred on the factory floor. The authors of an article in *Management Accounting* explained how they applied ABC to the purchasing department costs of a midwestern company that was having costing problems.

Misallocating costs can devastate a business by making its pricing decisions no better than guesswork. While activity-based costing (ABC) has proven effective and increasingly popular in determining real costs in the manufacturing arena, the authors tested the feasibility of applying ABC to the purchasing function. The test showed the success of ABC as a way to analyze a purchasing department.

In allocating purchasing department costs by using a rate based on direct labor costs, management discovered the data provided were not useful, so it switched to a percentage-of-product cost system. This method was based on the assumption there was a relationship between the price of the component and the purchasing department's costs and that the price level of the component would remain constant.

While this method was better, significant errors remained: It either overallocated or underallocated department costs to the product by 24% to 79%. And purchase orders with expensive material were being charged with a much higher allocation than those with inexpensive material.

ABC resolved a number of purchasing problems. It identified the drivers that affected purchasing department costs, and it offered management several options for allocating costs. Most important, it provides management with accurate cost data in helping it determine a product's contribution to profit.

Specifically, the authors used the purchase order as the cost driver and developed a separate charging rate for each major category of materials being purchased. Because different products used differing types and amounts of materials, the ABC method enabled the purchasing costs to be charged to the products in proportion to their consumption of purchasing department activities that resulted in these costs.

Harper A. Roehm, Melissa A. Critchfield, and Joseph F. Castellano, "Yes, ABC Works with Purchasing, Too," *Journal of Accountancy,* November 1992, pp. 58–62.

You should now be able to work the following: Questions 11–20, Exercises 4–9, and Problems 4–8, 10, and 12.

APPLYING FACTORY OVERHEAD AT PREDETERMINED RATES

After selecting the application method and computing the predetermined rate to be used, all jobs or processes should be charged with the estimated overhead cost rather than the actual factory overhead costs being incurred. The estimated factory overhead is applied to production by a debit to Work in Process and a credit to an account entitled **Applied Factory Overhead**. Use of the separate applied factory overhead account rather than the credit side of the factory overhead control account avoids confusing the actual factory overhead charges, which are debited to the factory overhead control account, with the estimated charges that are debited to production. At the end of a period, the debit balance in Factory Overhead is compared to the credit balance in Applied Factory Overhead to determine the accuracy of the predetermined rates.

To illustrate the use of a predetermined rate, assume the company has estimated a rate of $5 per direct labor hour, and a production job required 1,000 direct labor hours to complete. Using the direct labor hour method, $5,000 of estimated factory overhead cost would be applied to the job as follows:

Work in Process	5,000	
Applied Factory Overhead		5,000
Applied factory overhead to job (1,000 hours @ $5).		

At the end of the period, the applied factory overhead account is closed to the factory overhead control account:

Applied Factory Overhead	5,000	
Factory Overhead		5,000
Closed applied factory overhead account to control account.		

After the above entries are posted, if a balance (debit or credit) remains in the factory overhead control account, it indicates that the actual factory overhead incurred did not equal the estimated factory overhead applied. A remaining debit balance in Factory Overhead indicates that a smaller amount of overhead was applied to production than was actually incurred during the period. The debit balance indicates that the factory overhead costs were **underapplied** or **underabsorbed**. In other words, the work in process account was undercharged for the costs of factory overhead incurred in the accounting period. If, on the other hand, a credit balance remains after the applied factory overhead account is closed to the control account, the credit balance would represent **overapplied** or **overabsorbed factory overhead**. This means that more overhead was applied to production than was actually incurred in the period. In order to begin each new month with a zero balance in Factory Overhead, the debit or credit balance in the account is usually transferred to an account entitled **Under- and Overapplied Factory Overhead**, as follows:

```
Under- and Overapplied Factory Overhead  . . . . . . .        xx
    Factory Overhead  . . . . . . . . . . . . . . . . . . . .       xx
        Closed debit balance (underapplied) in factory overhead control account.


Factory Overhead . . . . . . . . . . . . . . . . . . . .        xx
    Under- and Overapplied Factory Overhead  . . . . .          xx
        Closed credit balance (overapplied) in factory overhead control account.
```

The special account, Under- and Overapplied Factory Overhead, will accumulate the month-to-month differences. At the end of the year, the balance of the under- and overapplied account will be closed to Cost of Goods Sold or allocated on a pro rata basis to Work in Process, Finished Goods, and Cost of Goods Sold. The balance should be prorated if it would materially distort net income to charge the entire amount to Cost of Goods Sold.

The following table illustrates how under- and overapplied factory overhead costs typically offset each other over a given period of time as seasonal demands and production levels change:

Under- and Overapplied Factory Overhead

Month	Underapplied	Overapplied	Dr(Cr) Balance
January	$1,200		$1,200
February	800		2,000
March		$3,500	(1,500)
April		2,000	(3,500)
May		1,000	(4,500)
June		500	(5,000)
July	700		(4,300)
August	1,100		(3,200)
September	2,500		(700)
October	1,000		300
November	500		800
December		1,000	(200)
	$7,800	$8,000	

If a small balance, such as the $200 in the preceding example, remains in Under- and Overapplied Factory Overhead at year-end, it may be closed directly to Cost of Goods Sold because it will not materially affect net income. A large remaining balance, however, could distort the year's net income if it were closed entirely to Cost of Goods Sold when the company had material amounts of work in process and finished goods inventories. Therefore, an adjustment is required to restate the balances of the Work in Process, Finished Goods, and Cost of Goods Sold accounts.

To illustrate the proration (adjusting) procedure, assume a debit balance of $10,000 (underapplied factory overhead) remained in the under- and overapplied factory overhead account. The year-end balances, before adjustment, of the following accounts were as follows:

		Percent of Total
Work in Process	$ 10,000	10%
Finished Goods	30,000	30
Cost of Goods Sold	60,000	60
Total	$100,000	100%

The pro rata amount of underapplied factory overhead chargeable to each account would be computed as follows:

Work in Process ($10,000 × 10%)	$ 1,000
Finished Goods ($10,000 × 30%)	3,000
Cost of Goods Sold ($10,000 × 60%)	6,000
	$10,000

The journal entry to close the debit balance in Under- and Overapplied Factory Overhead would be as follows:

Work in Process	1,000	
Finished Goods	3,000	
Cost of Goods Sold	6,000	
Under- and Overapplied Factory Overhead		10,000
Closed debit balance in Under- and Overapplied Factory Overhead.		

The amount allocated to Cost of Goods Sold becomes a **period cost** that directly reduces the amount of net income for the current period. The amounts allocated to Work in Process and Finished Goods become part of the **product cost** of the inventories and will be deferred, along with the other inventory costs, to the next period when the inventory is sold.

ILLUSTRATION OF ACTUAL AND APPLIED FACTORY OVERHEAD

The preceding sections of this chapter have presented and illustrated the various aspects of accounting for factory overhead, including departmentalizing factory overhead costs, distributing service department costs, applying factory overhead to production using predetermined rates, and accounting for differences between actual and applied factory overhead. Figures 4-9 through 4-15 tie together these various aspects and show the flow of factory overhead costs through the accounting system.

Figure 4-9 shows actual factory overhead costs accumulated during the month and distributed at the end of the month using the same data and service department cost distribution method presented in Figure 4-8. Factory overhead was applied to the production departments as jobs were worked on throughout the month, as follows:

Department A	$ 66,000
Department B	56,000
Department C	70,000
Department D	110,000

Figure 4-9 also shows the under- or overapplied factory overhead by department and in total as follows:

	Actual Costs	Applied	Under/(Over)
Department A	$ 62,600	$ 66,000	$(3,400)
Department B	51,600	56,000	(4,400)
Department C	72,000	70,000	2,000
Department D	113,800	110,000	3,800
Total	$300,000	$302,000	$(2,000)

Figure 4-10 shows the flow of actual factory overhead expenses through the accounting records. The example assumes that the amounts posted to the factory overhead control account were originally recorded in the general journal. The total charge to the control account of $300,000 equals the sum of the actual factory overhead expenses incurred by the individual departments and recorded on the factory overhead analysis sheets.

In Figure 4-11, the $300,000 balance in the factory overhead control account is transferred to the factory overhead accounts for both the service and production departments. The factory overhead analysis sheets provide the data necessary for the distribution.

Figure 4-12 shows the distribution of the service department's costs to the production department's factory overhead accounts using the sequential distribution method of service department costs with the service department, with the greatest total cost being distributed first. Figure 4-13 shows the application of factory overhead, based on predetermined rates, to the individual production departments. In Figure 4-14, the applied factory overhead accounts are closed to the departmental factory overhead accounts. Finally, as shown in Figure 4-15, the balances in

FIGURE 4-9   Summary of Actual and Applied Factory Overhead

	Power	Maintenance	Personnel	Dept. A	Dept. B	Dept. C	Dept. D	Total
Total actual expenses from factory overhead analysis sheets	30,000 00	20,000 00	10,000 00	50,000 00	40,000 00	60,000 00	90,000 00	300,000 00
Power distribution— (kw. hours)								
Maintenance— 10,000 @ $.25		2,500 00						
Personnel— 10,000 @ .25			2,500 00					
A— 12,000 @ .25				3,000 00				
B— 18,000 @ .25					4,500 00			
C— 20,000 @ .25						5,000 00		
D— 50,000 @ .25							12,500 00	
120,000		22,500 00						
Maintenance distribution— (square feet)								
Personnel— 5,000 @ $.90			4,500 00					
A— 5,000 @ .90				4,500 00				
B— 6,000 @ .90					5,400 00			
C— 4,000 @ .90						3,600 00		
D— 5,000 @ .90							4,500 00	
25,000			17,000 00					
Personnel distribution (number of employees served)								
A— 30 @ $170				5,100 00				
B— 10 @ $170					1,700 00			
C— 20 @ $170						3,400 00		
D— 40 @ $170							6,800 00	
100				62,600 00	51,600 00	72,000 00	113,800 00	300,000 00
Applied factory overhead				66,000 00	56,000 00	70,000 00	110,000 00	302,000 00
(Over-) or underapplied factory overhead				(3,400 00)	(4,400 00)	2,000 00	3,800 00	(2,000 00)

FIGURE 4-10   Actual Factory Overhead Expenses •

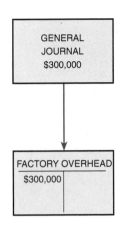

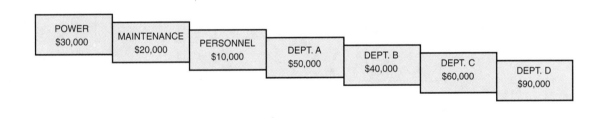

FIGURE 4-11   Distribution of Actual Factory Overhead to Service and Production Departments

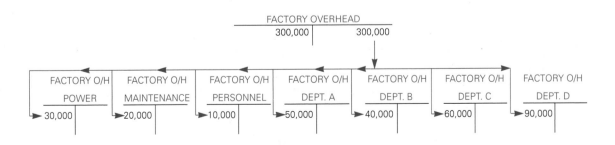

FIGURE 4-12   Distribution of Service Department Costs

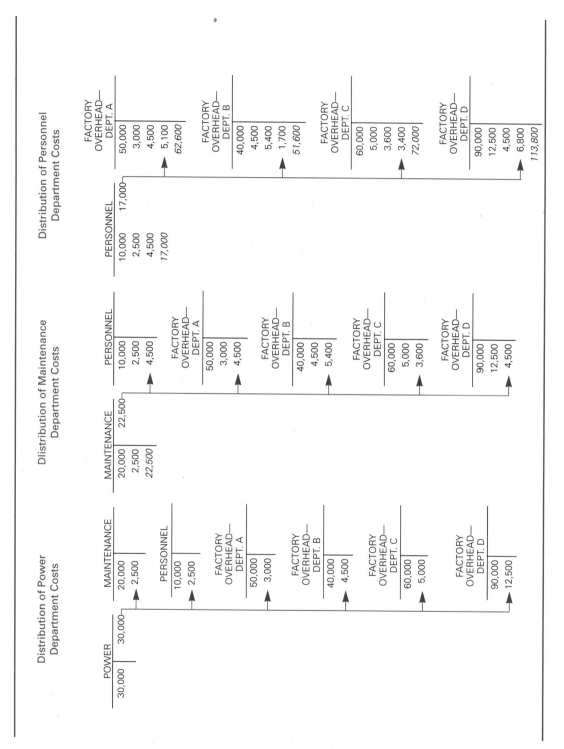

FIGURE 4-13   Departmental Applied Factory Overhead

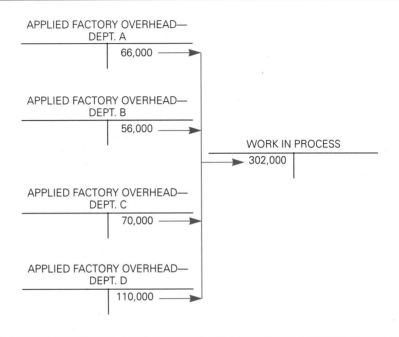

FIGURE 4-14   Closing Applied Factory Overhead Accounts to Departmental Factory Overhead Accounts

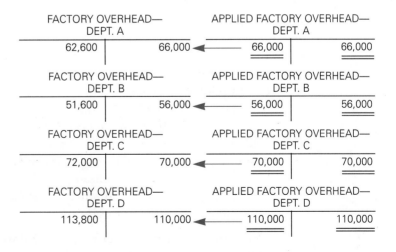

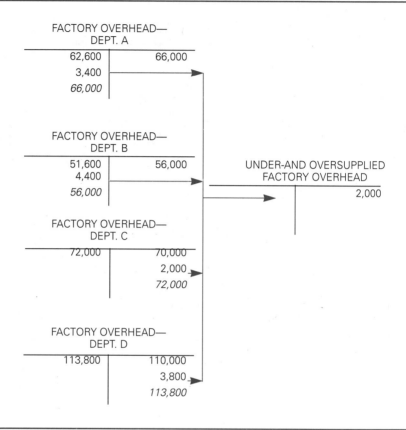

the departmental factory overhead accounts are closed to Under- and Overapplied Factory Overhead. The net amount of overapplied factory overhead, $2,000, is relatively small and would be closed entirely to Cost of Goods Sold rather than allocated (prorated) among Cost of Goods Sold and the inventory accounts. Chapter 9 includes an in-depth discussion of the reason why the actual factory overhead incurred may differ from the applied factory overhead.

Figure 4-16 shows in summary form the transactions involved in accounting for factory overhead.

You should now be able to work the following: Exercises 10–12 and Problems 9, 11, and 13.

FIGURE 4-16　　Summary of Factory Overhead Transactions　*Must know for Test*

ACCOUNTING FOR FACTORY OVERHEAD

Transaction	Source of Data	Book of Original Entry	General Ledger Entry	Subsidiary Cost Records
Indirect materials requisitioned from storeroom for factory use	Materials issued summary	General Journal or Requisition Journal	Factory Overhead Materials	Factory overhead analysis ledger sheets Stores ledger cards
Indirect labor employed in factory	Labor cost summary	General Journal	Factory Overhead Payroll	Factory overhead analysis ledger sheets
Payroll taxes imposed on the analysis ledger employer	Payroll record	General Journal	Factory Overhead FICA Tax Payable *employer share* FUTA Tax Payable State Unemployment Tax Payable	Factory overhead sheets
Vouchering factory overhead such as rent, power, and repairs	Invoices	Voucher Register	Factory Overhead Accounts Payable	Factory overhead analysis ledger sheets
Adjustments for factory overhead such as expired insurance, accrued property tax, and depreciation	Schedules	General Journal	Factory Overhead Prepaid Insurance Accrued Property Tax Payable Accumulated Depreciation	Factory overhead analysis ledger sheets
Distribution of factory overhead to service and production departments	Schedules	General Journal	Departmental Factory Overhead Accounts Factory Overhead	None
Distribution of service department expenses to production department expense accounts	Schedules	General Journal	Production Department Factory Overhead Accounts Service Department Expense Accounts	Factory overhead analysis ledger sheets
Application of factory overhead to jobs	Schedule of predetermined departmental application rates	General Journal	Work in Process Production Department Applied Factory Overhead Accounts	Job cost sheets
Close applied factory overhead accounts to factory overhead control	Applied factory overhead accounts	General Journal	Applied Factory Overhead Accounts Factory Overhead	None
Close factory overhead control balances to under- and overapplied factory overhead account	Factory overhead control accounts	General Journal	Under- and Overapplied Factory Overhead Factory Overhead (if underapplied) Factory Overhead Under- and Overapplied Factory Overhead (if overapplied)	None

KEY TERMS

SELF-STUDY PROBLEM

JOB COST SHEETS; JOURNAL ENTRIES; BUDGET AND CAPACITY VARIANCES

SEA BREEZE

On April 1, Sea Breeze Company, makers of custom-made pleasure boats, found that Job 500 was completed on March 31, and there were no jobs in process in the plant. Prior to April 1, the predetermined overhead application rate for April was computed, based on an estimate of 40,000 direct labor hours, from the following data:

Estimated variable factory overhead	$10,000
Estimated fixed factory overhead	20,000
Total estimated factory overhead	$30,000
Estimated variable factory overhead per hour	$ .25
Estimated fixed factory overhead per hour	.50
Predetermined overhead rate per direct labor hour	$ .75

The factory has one production department, and the direct labor hour method is used to apply factory overhead.

Three jobs are started during the month and postings are made daily to the job cost sheets from the materials requisitions and time tickets. The following schedule shows the jobs and amounts posted to the job cost sheets:

Job	Date Started	Direct Materials	Direct Labor	Direct Labor Hours
401	April 1	$10,000	$20,000	12,000
402	April 12	20,000	25,000	18,000
403	April 15	8,000	14,000	8,000
		$38,000	$59,000	38,000

The factory overhead control account was debited during the month for actual factory overhead expenses of $32,500. On April 11, Job 401 was completed and delivered to the customer at a markup of 50% on manufacturing cost. On April 24, Job 402 was completed and transferred to Finished Goods. On April 30, Job 403 was still in process.

Required:

1. Prepare job cost sheets for Jobs 401, 402, and 403 including factory overhead applied when the job was completed or at the end of the month for partially completed jobs.
2. Prepare journal entries as of April 30 for the following:
   a. Applying factory overhead to production.
   b. Closing the applied factory overhead account.
   c. Closing the factory overhead account.
   d. Transferring the cost of the completed jobs to Finished Goods.
   e. Recording the cost of sale and the sale of Job 401.

Suggestions:

1. When completing the job cost sheets, you must first determine how much overhead should be applied to each job.
2. When closing the factory overhead account, the balance will represent the under- or overapplied factory overhead.
3. The sum of the budget and capacity variances must equal the amount of the under- or overapplied factory overhead.

SOLUTION TO SELF-STUDY PROBLEM

Preparing the job cost sheets

1. On April 11, Job 401 was completed and factory overhead was applied as follows:

Job 401

Direct materials	$10,000
Direct labor	20,000
Applied factory overhead (12,000 hours × $.75)	9,000
Total cost	$39,000

On April 24, Job 402 was completed and factory overhead was applied as follows:

Job 402

Direct materials	$20,000
Direct labor	25,000
Applied factory overhead (18,000 hours × $.75)	13,500
Total cost	$58,500

On April 30, Job 403 is not completed; however, factory overhead is applied to the partially completed job to determine the total cost incurred during the month of April.

Job 403

Direct materials	$ 8,000
Direct labor	14,000
Applied factory overhead (8,000 hours × $.75)	6,000
Total cost (for month of April)	$28,000

Preparing the journal entries

2. a. The total factory overhead applied to the three jobs during April was $28,500. The general journal entry made on April 30 to apply factory overhead to production follows:

April 30	Work in Process	28,500	
	Applied Factory Overhead		28,500

The applied factory overhead of $28,500 has already been recorded on the job cost sheets. The above general journal entry brings the work in process control account into agreement with the subsidiary job cost ledger.

   b. & c. The next procedure is to close the applied factory overhead account to Factory Overhead. Then, transfer any remaining balance to the under- and overapplied factory overhead account.

April 30	Applied Factory Overhead	28,500	
	Factory Overhead		28,500
April 30	Under- and Overapplied Factory Overhead . .	4,000	
	Factory Overhead		4,000
	Closed factory overhead.		

   d. & e. During April, the following entries were made to transfer the cost of completed Jobs 401 and 402 to Finished Goods, and to record the cost of sales and sale of Job 401:

Finished Goods	97,500	
Work in Process		97,500
Completed Jobs 401 ($39,000) and 402 ($58,500) and transferred to finished goods.		

Accounts Receivable	58,500	
Sales		58,500
Delivered Job 401 to customer and billed at 50% markup.		

Cost of Goods Sold   39,000
    Finished Goods   39,000
    Recorded cost of Job 401 delivered to customer.

QUESTIONS

1. What are factory overhead expenses and what distinguishes them from other manufacturing costs? What other terms are used to describe factory overhead expenses?

2. What are three categories of factory overhead expenses? Give examples of each.

3. What are the distinguishing characteristics of variable, fixed, and semivariable factory overhead costs?

4. When a product's cost is composed of both fixed and variable costs, what effect does the increase or decrease in production have on total unit cost?

5. What effect does a change in volume have on total variable, fixed, and semivariable costs?

6. What is the basic premise underlying the high-low method of analyzing semivariable costs?

7. What are the advantages and disadvantages of the scattergraph method as compared to the high-low method?

8. How does accounting for factory overhead differ in small enterprises versus large enterprises?

9. What is the function and use of each of the two types of factory overhead analysis sheets?

10. What are two types of departments found in a factory? What is the function or purpose of each?

11. What are the two most frequently used methods of distributing service department costs to production departments?

12. What are the shortcomings of waiting until the actual factory overhead expenses are known before recording such costs on the job cost sheets?

13. What are the two types of budget data needed to compute predetermined overhead rates?

14. What are three methods traditionally used for applying factory overhead to jobs? Discuss the application of each method.

15. What factory operating conditions and data are required for each of the traditionally used methods for applying factory overhead to products? Discuss the strengths and weaknesses of each method.

16. Under what conditions would it be desirable for a company to use more than one method to apply factory overhead to jobs or products?

17. How does activity-based costing differ from traditional methods of applying overhead to products?

18. What steps must a company take to successfully employ activity-based costing?

19. If the factory overhead control account has a debit balance of $1,000 at the end of the first month of the fiscal year, has the overhead been under- or overapplied for the month? What are some probable causes for the debit balance?

20. What are two ways that an under- or overapplied factory overhead balance can be disposed of at the end of a fiscal period?

EXERCISES

E4-1
Classifying fixed and variable costs
Learning Objective 1

Classify each of the following items of factory overhead as either a fixed or a variable cost. (Include any costs that you consider to be semivariable within the variable category.)

a. Indirect labor
b. Indirect materials
c. Insurance on building
d. Overtime premium pay
e. Depreciation on building (straight-line)
f. Polishing compounds
g. Depreciation on machinery (based on hours used)
h. Employer's payroll taxes
i. Property taxes
j. Machine lubricants
k. Employees' hospital insurance (paid by employer)
l. Labor for machine repairs
m. Vacation pay
n. Patent amortization
o. Janitor's wages
p. Rent
q. Small tools
r. Plant manager's salary
s. Receiving clerk's wages
t. Product inspector's wages

E4-2
High-low methods
Learning Objective 2

The Upson Downs Company has accumulated the following data over a six-month period.

	Indirect Labor Hours	Indirect Labor Costs
January	400	$ 6,000
February	500	7,000
March	600	8,000
April	700	9,000
May	800	10,000
June	900	11,000
	3,900	$51,000

Separate the indirect labor into its fixed and variable components using the high-low method.

E4-3
Scattergraph method
Learning Objective 2

Using the data in E4-2 and a piece of graph paper

1. Plot the data points on the graph and draw a line by visual inspection indicating the trend shown by the data points.

2. Determine the variable cost per unit and the total fixed cost from the information on the graph.

E4-4
Computing unit costs at different levels of production
Learning Objective. 3

Morgan Manufacturing Company budgeted for 12,000 units of product x during the month of May. The unit cost of product x was $20, consisting of direct materials, $7; direct labor, $8; and factory overhead, $5 (fixed, $3 and variable, $2).

a. What would be the unit cost if 8,000 units were manufactured?
b. What would be the unit cost if 15,000 units were manufactured?
c. Explain why a difference occurs in the unit costs.

E4-5
Identifying basis for distribution of overhead to departments
Learning Objective 5

What would be the appropriate basis for distributing each of the following factory overhead expenses to departments?

a. Depreciation on buildings   ~~Square Ft~~
b. Depreciation on machinery   ~~Machine value~~   ~~Exam~~
c. Taxes on the buildings   ~~Square Ft~~
d. Insurance on the machinery   ~~Machine value~~
e. Heat   ~~Square ft   cubic ft~~
f. Light   ~~cubic ft   ,wattage used   whatever you~~
g. Indirect materials   ~~requisition materials - requisition~~
h. Indirect labor   ~~Time cards, time sheets~~
i. FICA taxes   ~~Payroll~~
j. Unemployment taxes   ~~payroll~~
k. Repairs to machinery   ~~work order~~

(handwritten note: payroll rate)

E4-6
Sequential distribution of service departments costs; computing factory overhead application rates—direct labor hour method
Learning Objective 5

A manufacturing company has two service and two production departments. Building maintenance and factory office are the service departments.

The production departments are assembly and machining. The following data have been estimated for next year's operations:

Direct labor hours: Assembly, 80,000; Machining, 40,000
Floor space occupied: Factory Office 10%; Assembly, 50%; Machining, 40%

The direct charges expected to be made to the departments are as follows:

Building maintenance	$ 90,000
Factory office	171,000
Assembly	378,000
Machining	328,000

The building maintenance department services all departments of the company and its costs are allocated using floor space occupied while factory office costs are allocable to assembly and machining on the basis of direct labor hours. The sequential distribution method is used with the department servicing the greatest number of other departments distributed first.

1. Distribute the service department costs using the sequential distribution method.
2. Determine the departmental direct labor hour application rate for each production department.

E4-7
Determining job cost using direct labor cost, direct labor hour, and machine hour methods
Learning Objective 6

a. If the direct labor cost method is used in applying factory overhead and the predetermined rate is 150%, what amount should be charged to Job 1776 for factory overhead? Assume the direct materials used totaled $5,000 and the direct labor cost totaled $3,200.
b. If the direct labor hour method is used in applying factory overhead and the predetermined rate is $2 an hour, what amount should be charged to Job 1776 for factory overhead? Assume the direct materials used totaled $5,000, the direct labor cost totaled $3,200, and the number of direct labor hours totaled 2,500.
c. If the machine hour method is used in applying factory overhead and the predetermined rate is $15 an hour, what amount should be charged to Job 1776 for factory overhead? Assume the direct materials used totaled $5,000, the direct labor cost totaled $3,200, and the number of machine hours totaled 295.

E4-8
Determining job costs using ABC method

Job 1107 required $5000 for direct materials, $2000 for direct labor, 200 direct labor hours, 100 machine hours, three setups, and two design changes. The cost pools and overhead rates for each pool follow:

Cost Pool	Overhead Rate
Direct labor usage	$5/Direct labor hour
Machine usage	$10/Machine hour
Machine setups	$250/setup
Design changes	$500/design change

Determine the cost of Job 1107.

E4-9
Determining actual factory overhead
Learning Objective 6

The books of Presto Products Company revealed that the following general journal entry had been made at the end of the current accounting period:

Factory Overhead	2,000	
Under- and Overapplied Factory Overhead		2,000

The total direct materials cost for the period was $40,000. The total direct labor cost, at an average rate of $10 per hour for direct labor, was one and one-half times the direct materials cost. Factory overhead was applied on the basis of $4 per direct labor hour. What was the total actual factory overhead incurred for the period?

E4-10
Determining labor and factory overhead costs
Learning Objective 6

The general ledger of Penguin Manufacturing Company contains the following control account:

Work in Process			
Materials	15,000	Finished goods	30,000
Labor	16,000		
Factory overhead	8,000		

If the materials charged to the one uncompleted job still in process amounted to $3,400, what amount of labor and factory overhead must have been charged to the job? (Assume overhead is applied on the basis of direct labor cost for the purpose of determining the individual amounts for labor and factory overhead.)

E4-11
General ledger account analysis
Learning Objective 6

The following form represents an account taken from the general ledger of Mojo Manufacturing Company:

Indirect materials	500	Work in Process	8,200
Supervisor's salary	1,200	(50% of $16,400 direct labor)	
Power	5,000		
Building expenses	1,000		
Miscellaneous overhead	1,400		
	———		
Bal. 900	9,100		

Answer the following questions:

a. What is the title of the account?
b. Is this a departmentalized factory?
c. What does the balance of the account represent?
d. How was the 50% rate determined?
e. What disposition should be made of the balance?

E4-12
Computing under- and overapplied overhead
Learning Objective 6

Hoyle Company had a remaining debit balance of $20,000 in its under- and over-applied factory overhead account at year-end. The balance was deemed to be large and, therefore, should be closed to Work In Process, Finished Goods, and Cost of Goods Sold. The year-end balances, before adjustment, of these accounts showed the following:

Work in Process	$ 25,000
Finished Goods	50,000
Cost of Goods Sold	100,000
Totals	175,000

a. Determine the prorated amount of the underapplied factory overhead that is changeable to each of the accounts.
b. Prepare the journal entry to close the debit balance in Under- and Overapplied Factory Overhead.

PROBLEMS

P4-1
Variable and fixed cost analysis; high-low method
Learning Objective 2

Virginia Company manufactures a product that requires the use of a considerable amount of natural gas to heat it to a desired temperature. The process requires a constant level of heat, so the furnaces are maintained at a set temperature for 24 hours a day. Although units are not continuously processed, management desires that the variable cost be charged directly to the product and the fixed cost to the factory overhead. The following data have been collected for the year:

	Units	Cost		Units	Cost
January . . .	2,400	$4,400	July	2,200	$4,400
February . . .	2,300	4,300	August	2,100	4,100
March	2,200	4,200	September	2,000	3,800
April	2,000	4,000	October	1,400	3,400
May	1,800	3,800	November	1,900	3,700
June	1,900	3,900	December	1,800	4,050

Required:

1. Separate the variable and fixed elements using the high-low method.
2. Determine the cost to be charged to the product for the year.
3. Determine the cost to be charged to factory overhead for the year.

P4-2
Scattergraph method
Learning Objective 2

Using the data in P4-1 and a piece of graph paper

1. Plot the data points on the graph and draw a line by visual inspection indicating the trend shown by the data points.
2. Determine the variable cost per unit and the total fixed cost from the information on the graph.
3. Determine the cost to be charged to the product for the year.
4. Determine the cost to be charged to factory overhead for the year.

P4-3
Variable and fixed
cost pattern analysis
Learning Objective 1

The cost behavior patterns below are lettered A through H. The vertical axes of the graphs represent total dollars of expense and the horizontal axes represent production. In each case, the zero point is at the intersection of the two axes. Each graph may be used more than once.

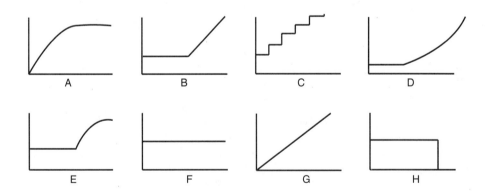

Required:

Select the graph that matches the lettered cost described below.

a. Depreciation of equipment—the amount of depreciation charged is computed by the machine hour method.
b. Electricity bill—flat fixed charge, plus a variable cost after a certain number of kilowatt hours are used.

c. City water bill—computed as follows:

First 1,000,000 gallons or less . . . . $1,000 flat fee
Next 10,000 gallons . . . .   .003 per gallon used
Next 10,000 gallons . . . .   .006 per gallon used
Next 10,000 gallons . . . .   .009 per gallon used
and so on.

d. Depreciation of equipment—the amount is computed by the straight-line method.
e. Rent on a factory building donated by the city—the agreement calls for a fixed fee payment unless 200,000 labor hours are worked, in which case no rent need be paid.
f. Salaries of repair workers—one repair worker is needed for every 1,000 hours of machine hours or less (i.e., 0 to 1,000 hours requires one repair worker, 1,001 to 2,000 hours requires two repair workers, etc.).
g. Cost of raw materials used.

(AICPA adapted)

P4-4
General journal entries for factory overhead
Learning Objectives 4, 6

Hubert Company uses a job order cost system. Selected transactions dealing with factory overhead for the month follow:

a. Requisitioned indirect materials from storeroom, $3,200.
b. Purchased, on account, factory supplies for future needs, $4,400.
c. Purchased parts, on account, for repairing a machine, $1,400.
d. Requisitioned factory supplies from storeroom, $900.
e. Returned defective factory supplies to vendor, $700.
f. Factory rent accrued for the month, $2,400.
g. Returned previously requisitioned factory supplies to storeroom, $350.
h. Depreciation of machinery and equipment, $2,800.
i. Payroll taxes liability for month, $3,200.
j. Heat, light, and power charges payable for the month, $6,400.
k. Expired insurance on inventories, $1,350.
l. Factory overhead applied to production, $36,400.
m. Indirect labor for the month, $2,600.
n. Goods completed and transferred to finished goods: materials, $14,400; labor, $40,400; factory overhead, $30,400.

Required:

Record the above transactions in general journal form. Assume that the records include a control account and a subsidiary ledger for factory overhead to which the entries will be posted at some later date.

P4-5
Distribution of service department costs to production departments
Learning Objective 5

Goode Manufacturing Company is divided into five departments, A, B, C, D, and E. The first three departments are engaged in production work. Departments D and E are service departments. During the month of June, the following factory overhead was incurred for the various departments:

Department A . . . . $21,000   Department D $9,000
Department B   18,000   Department E   6,400
Department C   25,000

The bases for distributing service department expenses to the other departments follow:

Department E—On the basis of floor space occupied by the other departments as follows: Department A, 10,000 sq. ft.; Department B, 4,500 sq. ft.; Department C, 10,500 sq. ft.; and Department D, 7,000 sq. ft.

Department D—Divided: Department A—30%; Department B—20%; Department C—50%.

Required:

Prepare schedules showing the distribution of the service departments' expenses for the following:

1. The direct distribution method.
2. The sequential distribution method in the order of number of other departments served.

P4-6
Determining total job costs using predetermined overhead rate
Learning Objective 6

Barkely Manufacturing Company uses the job order cost system of accounting. Shown below is a list of the jobs completed during the month of March showing the charges for materials requisitioned and for direct labor.

Job	Materials Requisitioned	Direct Labor
007	$ 300.00	$ 600.00
008	1,080.00	940.00
009	720.00	1,400.00
010	4,200.00	5,120.00

Assume that factory overhead is applied on the basis of direct labor costs and that the predetermined rate is 200%.

Required:

1. Compute the amount of overhead to be added to the cost of each job completed during the month.
2. Compute the total cost of each job completed during the month.
3. Compute the total cost of producing all the jobs finished during the month.

P4-7
Determining job cost—calculation of predetermined rate for applying overhead by direct labor cost and direct labor hour methods
Learning Objective 6

Spolle Manufacturing Company has its factory divided into three departments with individual factory overhead rates for each department. In each department, all the operations are sufficiently alike for the department to be regarded as a cost center. The estimated monthly factory overhead for the departments are as follows: Department A, $64,000; Department B, $36,000; and Department C, $10,080. The estimated production data include the following:

	Dept. A	Dept. B	Dept. C
Materials used	$20,000	$10,000	$10,000
Direct labor cost	$16,000	$15,000	$ 8,400
Direct labor hours	16,000	10,000	7,000

The job cost ledger shows the following data for Job 2525, which was completed during the month:

	Dept. A	Dept. B	Dept. C
Materials used	$12.00	$14.00	$12.00
Direct labor cost	$13.00	$13.50	$12.50
Direct labor hours	11	9	10

Required:

Determine the cost of Job 2525. Assume that the factory overhead is applied to production orders based on the following:
1. Direct labor cost
2. Direct labor hours

P4-8
Determining overhead rates using direct labor cost, direct labor hour, and machine hour methods; determining job cost; computing underapplied and overapplied overhead
Learning Objective 6

The Big-O Manufacturing Company is studying the results of applying factory overhead to production. The following data have been used: estimated factory overhead, $60,000; estimated materials costs, $50,000; estimated labor costs, $60,000; estimated direct labor hours, 40,000; estimated machine hours, 25,000; work in process at the beginning of the month, none.

The actual factory overhead incurred for the month of November was $54,000, and the production statistics on November 30 are as follows:

Job	Materials Costs	Direct Labor Costs	Direct Labor Hours	Machine Hours	Date Jobs Completed
101	$ 5,000	$ 7,200	5,000	3,000	Nov. 10
102	7,000	10,000	6,000	3,200	Nov. 14
103	8,000	11,000	6,500	4,000	Nov. 20
104	9,000	9,000	5,600	3,400	In process
105	10,000	15,000	10,500	6,500	Nov. 26
106	11,000	4,200	3,000	1,500	In process
Total	$50,000	$56,400	36,600	21,600	

Required:

1. Compute the predetermined rate based on the following:
   a. Direct labor cost
   b. Direct labor hours
   c. Machine hours
2. Using each of the methods, compute the total cost of each job at the end of the month.
3. Determine the under- or overapplied factory overhead, in total, at the end of the month under each of the methods.
4. Which method would you recommend? Why?

P4-9
Determining overhead rate; using direct labor cost, direct labor hour, and machine hour methods
Learning Objective 6

The following information was taken from the books of Keith Company and represents the operations for the month of January:

	Dept. A	Dept. B	Dept. C
Materials used	$20,000	$10,000	$10,000
Direct labor cost	$ 8,000	$ 5,000	$ 9,000
Direct labor hours	20,000	10,000	27,000
Machine hours	4,000	5,000	2,025
Factory overhead	$20,000	$10,000	$16,200

The job cost system is used, and the February cost sheet for Job 1812 shows the following:

	Dept. A	Dept. B	Dept. C
Materials	$2.00	$4.00	$2.00
Direct labor	$3.60	$3.00	$2.10
Direct labor hours	8	6	6
Machine hours	2	3	1

The following information was accumulated during February:

	Dept. A	Dept. B	Dept. C
Direct labor hours	15,000	9,800	20,000
Factory overhead	$14,000	$10,000	$11,800

Required:

1. Using the January data, ascertain the factory overhead application rates to be used during February based on the following:
   a. Direct labor cost
   b. Direct labor hours
   c. Machine hours
2. Prepare a schedule showing the total production cost of Job 1812 under each method of applying factory overhead.
3. Draft in general journal form the entries required to record the following for February operations:
   a. Payment of total factory overhead.
   b. Distribution of factory overhead to the departments.
   c. Application of factory overhead to the jobs using direct labor hours. (Use the predetermined rate calculated in 1. above.)
   d. Closing of the applied factory overhead accounts.
   e. Recording under- and overapplied factory overhead.

P4-10
Determining job costs using activity-based costing
Learning Objective 6

Modern Manufacturing Company uses activity-based costing. The factory overhead budget for the coming period is $500,000 consisting of the following:

Cost Pool	Budgeted Amount
Direct Labor usage	$150,000
Machine usage	$200,000
Machine setups	$100,000
Design changes	$ 50,000
TOTALS	$500,000

The potential allocation bases and their estimated amounts were as follows:

Allocation Base	Budgeted Amount
Number of design changes	50
Number of setups	200
Machine hours	10,000
Direct labor hours	20,000

Required:	1. Determine the overhead rate for each cost pool, using the most appropriate allocation base for each pool.
	2. Job 1267 required $25,000 for direct materials, $10,000 for direct labor, 1,000 direct labor hours, 500 machine hours, three setups, and five design changes. Determine the cost of Job 1267.

P4-11
Determining the
under- and
overapplied overhead
Learning Objectives
5, 6

Skippy Corporation has four departmental accounts: Building Maintenance, General Factory Overhead, Department A, and Department B. The direct labor hours method is used to apply factory overhead to the jobs being worked on in Departments A and B. The company expects each production department to use 30,000 direct labor hours during the year. The estimated overhead rates for the year include the following:

	Dept. A	Dept. B
Variable cost per hour	$1.10	$1.20
Fixed cost per hour	2.70	3.00
	$3.80	$4.20

During the year, both Departments A and B used 28,000 direct labor hours. Factory overhead costs incurred during the year follow:

Building maintenance	$30,000
General factory overhead	75,400
Department A	45,800
Department B	68,800

In determining application rates at the beginning of the year, cost allocations were made as follows:

Building Maintenance to General Factory Overhead, 10%; to Department A, 50%; to Department B, 40%.

General factory overhead was distributed according to direct labor hours.

Required:

Determine the under- or overapplied overhead for each production department.

P4-12
Job cost sheets,
journal entries
Learning Objectives
4, 6

On June 1, Manchu Manufacturing Company found that Job 2525 was completed on May 31, and there were no jobs in process in the plant. Prior to June 1, the predetermined overhead application rate for June was computed from the following data, based on an estimate of 5,000 direct labor hours:

Estimated variable factory overhead	$20,000
Estimated fixed factory overhead	10,000
Total estimated factory overhead	$30,000
Estimated variable factory overhead per hour	$4
Estimated fixed factory overhead per hour	2
Predetermined overhead rate per direct labor hour	$6

The factory has one production department, and uses the direct labor hour method to apply factory overhead.

Three jobs are started during the month and postings are made daily to the job cost sheets from the materials requisitions and time tickets. The following schedule shows the jobs and amounts posted to the job cost sheets:

Job	Date Started	Materials	Direct Labor	Direct Labor Hours
2526	June 1	$ 5,000	$10,000	1,600
2527	June 12	10,000	15,000	1,900
2528	June 15	4,000	7,000	1,300
		$19,000	$32,000	4,800

The factory overhead control account was debited during the month for actual factory overhead expenses of $25,500. On June 11, Job 2526 was completed and delivered to the customer at a markup of 50% on manufacturing cost. On June 24, Job 2527 was completed and transferred to Finished Goods. On June 30, Job 2528 was still in process.

Required:

1. Prepare job cost sheets for Jobs 2526, 2527, and 2528 including factory overhead applied when the job was completed or at the end of the month for partially completed jobs.
2. Prepare journal entries as of June 30 for the following:
   a. Applying factory overhead to production.
   b. Closing the applied factory overhead account.
   c. Closing the factory overhead account.
   d. Transferring the cost of the completed jobs to finished goods.
   e. Recording the cost of sale and the sale of Job 2526.

P4-13
Closing under- and overapplied overhead at year end
Learning Objective 6

Jackyl Company had a remaining credit balance of $10,000 in its under- and over-applied factory overhead account at year-end. It also had year-end balances in the following accounts:

Work in Process	$ 25,000
Finished Goods	$ 15,000
Cost of Goods Sold	$ 85,000
Totals	$125,000

Required:

1. Prepare the closing entry for the $10,000 of overapplied overhead, assuming that the balance is not considered to be material.
2. Prepare the closing entry for the $10,000 of overapplied overhead, assuming that the balance is considered to be material.

Comprehensive Application of Job Order Cost Accounting— Mountain Oak Office Interiors

LEARNING OBJECTIVES

After studying this chapter, you should be able to:

1. Apply the principles and procedures involved in accounting for materials, labor, and factory overhead by a manufacturing firm using a job order cost system.
2. Complete the Mountain Oak Office Interiors (MOOI) practice set.

The principles and procedures involved in accounting for materials, labor, and factory overhead have been discussed in the preceding chapters. This chapter integrates the information previously developed and illustrates the application of cost accounting procedures to the operations of a hypothetical manufacturing concern. The procedures illustrated are typical of those encountered in firms using the job order cost system.

To derive the maximum benefit, the chapter should be read carefully and thoughtfully. Each transaction should be followed through the accounting process, and each figure in the general ledger accounts should be analyzed in order to understand the origin of the figure and how it flows into the ledger account. Then the Mountain Oak Office Interiors practice set should be completed.

COMPREHENSIVE ILLUSTRATION OF JOB ORDER COST ACCOUNTING

LEARNING OBJECTIVE
Apply the principles and procedures involved in accounting for materials, labor, and factory overhead by a manufacturing firm using a job order cost system.

This comprehensive illustration covers the accounting procedures for the Mountain Oak Office Interiors (MOOI) for the month of August. Following a description of the company's factory organization and accounting system, a complete accounting cycle is presented from beginning-of-the-month balances through the recording of transactions for the month and end-of-month procedures, including preparation of the trial balance, the work sheet, schedules, and financial statements.

BACKGROUND

MOOI is a manufacturer of specialty office cabinets. Although the basic designs of the cabinets are essentially the same, each job is unique as the size and type of cabinets that MOOI produces for a particular job depend on the design provided by the customer or developed by the company's design department.

PRODUCTS

The raw materials used by the company consist of oak and fir plywood, oak lumber, formica (counter top covering), cabinet hardware, and consumable supplies such as screws, nails, adhesive, and wood finishes. The company produces several styles of cabinets with standard heights and depths, but which can be any length the customer needs. The styles include the following:

Counters	3' high × 30" deep × desired customer length (no shelf)
	3.5' high × 30" deep × desired customer length (one shelf)
Cupboards	3' high × 24" deep × desired customer length (2 shelves)
	2.5' high × 24" deep × desired customer length (1 shelf)
	7' high × 30" deep × 3' wide (3 or 4 shelves)

FACTORY ORGANIZATION

MOOI'S manufacturing process is organized into four departments:

Sawing and Planing Department (S & P). The sawing and planing department requisitions the necessary wood and plywood for an order, saws them into the required dimensions, and sands or planes the pieces as necessary.

Assembly and Finishing Department (A & F). After receiving the wood pieces from the sawing and planing department, the assembly and finishing department requisitions any formica or hardware, assembles the cabinets, glues on the formica, applies stain or other finish, and installs the hardware.

Development and Design Department (D & D). The design department is responsible for both continued design upgrading of the company's standard products and assisting customers in configuring their unique designs as necessary. The expenses of this service department are allocated on an arbitrary basis of three-fourths to the sawing and planing department and one-fourth to the assembly and finishing department. This allocation is based on the company's belief that approximately 75% of all design work impacts the sawing and planing department.

Clean-up and Repair Department (C & R). This service department is responsible for keeping the factory clean and keeping the equipment in good running order. The expenses of the clean-up and repair department are allocated to each department based on a combination of square footage and an adjustment factor to account for the machinery that must be maintained in each department as follows:

	Square Footage	Adjustment Factor	Adjusted Square Footage
Sawing and Planing Department	20,000	2.0	40,000
Assembly and Finishing Department	10,000	1.5	15,000
Development and Design Department	5,000	1.0	5,000
Total	35,000		60,000

CHART OF ACCOUNTS

The chart of general ledger accounts for Mountain Oak Office Interiors is reproduced here. Control accounts for subsidiary ledgers are maintained as described on the following pages.

MOUNTAIN OAK OFFICE INTERIORS
CHART OF ACCOUNTS

Current Assets:
  Cash
  1110 Cash
  1120 Petty Cash

Temporary Investments
  1200 Marketable Securities

Receivables
  1310 Notes Receivable

  1320 Interest Receivable
  1330 Accounts Receivable
  1331 Allowance for Doubtful Accounts

Inventories
  1410 Finished Goods
  1420 Work in Process
  1430 Materials

Prepayments
  1510 Prepaid Insurance

Property, Plant, and Equipment
  1610 Land
  1620 Buildings
  1621 Accumulated Depreciation—Buildings
  1630 Machinery
  1631 Accumulated Depreciation—Machinery
  1640 Furniture and Fixtures
  1641 Accumulated Depreciation—Furniture and Fixtures
  1650 Small Tools
  1651 Accumulated Depreciation—Small Tools

Intangibles
  1710 Organization Costs
  1720 Trademarks

Current Liabilities:
  2210 Notes Payable
  2220 Accounts Payable
  2230 FICA Tax Payable
  2240 Federal Unemployment Tax Payable
  2250 State Unemployment Tax Payable
  2260 Employees Income Tax Payable
  2271 Property Tax Payable
  2272 Estimated Income Tax Payable
  2273 Interest Payable
  2274 Wages Payable

Long-Term Liabilities
  2710 Long-Term Note Payable

Stockholders' Equity
  2910 Capital Stock
  2920 Paid in Capital in Excess of Par Value

  2980 Retained Earnings
  2990 Income Summary

Factory Overhead
  3100 Factory Overhead
  3140 Factory Overhead—Department S & P
  3150 Factory Overhead—Department A & F
  3160 Factory Overhead—Department D & D
  3170 Factory Overhead—Department C & R
  3180 Under- and Overapplied Overhead

Sales and Cost of Goods Sold
  4100 Sales
  4600 Cost of Goods Sold

Payroll and General Expenses
  5000 Payroll
  5100 Salaries
  5200 Payroll Tax Expense—Salaries
  5300 Office Expense
  5500 Public Relations Expense
  5600 Amortization Expense
  5800 Doubtful Accounts Expense
  5900 Miscellaneous General Expense

Additions to and Deductions from Operating Income:
Additions to Income
  6110 Purchase Discounts
  6120 Interest Income
Deductions from Income
  6220 Interest Expense
  6420 Provision for Income Tax

SELECTED ACCOUNT DESCRIPTIONS

1330 Accounts Receivable. Accounts Receivable is the control account for the accounts receivable ledger. The accounts receivable ledger is a loose-leaf ledger containing ledger sheets for the individual customer accounts. The accounts are kept in alphabetic order.

1410 Finished Goods. Finished Goods is the control account for the finished goods ledger. An account for each size counter or cupboard is maintained on a card. Because most of the work done by the company is on specific orders received from customers, the only items that will be recorded in the finished goods ledger will be counters and cupboards of popular sizes and styles, and jobs completed but not delivered. During slack seasons, the employees and facilities of the company may be profitably employed in building up the stock of popular counters and cupboards. The job cost sheets are the source of the information needed in recording the quantities and manufacturing costs of all counters and cupboards manufactured for stock.

1420 Work in Process. Work in Process is the control account for the job cost ledger. The job cost ledger is a loose-leaf ledger in which a job cost sheet is used to keep an account of the cost of completing each job.

1430 Materials. Materials is the control account for the stores ledger. Cards are used to keep track of the various types of materials and factory supplies carried in stock. Purchase invoices and receiving reports are the sources of the information needed to record the quantities and costs of materials and factory supplies received. Materials requisitions provide the source of the information needed to record the quantities and costs of materials and factory supplies issued.

2910 Capital Stock. Capital Stock is the control account for the stockholders ledger. A separate account for each stockholder is kept in the stockholders ledger. Mountain Oak Office Interiors has an authorized capital of $200,000 divided into 2,000 shares of common stock with par value of $100 per share. All stock has been issued and is outstanding.

3100 Factory Overhead. Factory Overhead is the control account for the factory overhead ledger. The factory overhead ledger is a loose-leaf ledger in which analysis sheets, similar to those on pages 213 and 214 are used. Following is a list of the individual accounts kept in the factory overhead ledger.

Fixed Costs	Variable Costs
3111 Depreciation	**3121** Indirect Materials
3112 Property Tax	**3122** Indirect Labor
3113 Insurance	**3123** Fuel Consumed
	3124 Water
	3125 Light
	3126 Power
	3127 Payroll Tax Expense
	3128 Miscellaneous Factory Expense

TRIAL BALANCE

The company operates on a fiscal year ending July 31. The post-closing trial balance as of July 31 is shown below.

Mountain Oak Office Interiors
Post-Closing Trial Balance
July 31, 19—

	Debit	Credit
Cash	15,700.00	
Petty Cash	200.00	
Marketable Securities	6,050.00	
Notes Receivable	10,000.00	
Interest Receivable	101.66	
Accounts Receivable	46,000.00	
Allowance for Doubtful Accounts		2,300.00
Finished Goods	14,000.00	
Work in Process	12,000.00	
Materials	23,000.00	
Prepaid Insurance	5,000.00	
Land	26,300.00	
Buildings	80,000.00	
Accumulated Depreciation—Buildings		12,000.00
Machinery	120,000.00	
Accumulated Depreciation—Machinery		24,000.00
Furniture and Fixtures	15,000.00	
Accumulated Depreciation— Furniture and Fixtures		5,480.00
Small Tools	16,500.00	
Accumulated Depreciation—Small Tools		9,020.00
Organization Costs	3,800.00	
Trademarks	1,500.00	
Notes Payable		7,000.00
Accounts Payable		10,500.00
FICA Tax Payable		1,800.00
Federal Unemployment Tax Payable		315.00
State Unemployment Tax Payable		1,215.00
Employees Income Tax Payable		1,500.00
Property Tax Payable		2,000.00
Estimated Income Tax Payable		15,700.00
Interest Payable		102.22
Long-term Note Payable		25,000.00
Capital Stock		200,000.00
Retained Earnings		77,219.44
	395,151.66	395,151.66

ACCOUNTING SYSTEM

208

Mountain Oak Office Interiors uses an ac<
rate journals and ledgers are kept to record
books of account and other records consist of .

LEDGERS

1. General ledger
2. Subsidiary ledgers:
   a. Accounts receivable ledger
   b. Stores ledger
   c. Job cost ledger
   d. Factory overhead ledger
   e. Finished goods ledger
   f. Stockholders ledger

JOURN

1. Gei
2. Vouci
3. Check ı
4. Sales jouı
5. Cash receip

AUXILIARY RECORDS

1. Clock card
2. Time ticket
3. Materials requisition
4. Petty cash disbursements record

Figure 5-1 illustrates the voucher register and check register used by
Mountain Oak Office Interiors.

NARRATIVE OF TRANSACTIONS

The following discussion examines the transactions MOOI completed
during August. The subsequent posting of the journal entries illustrated
in each of the following transactions is presented on pages 221 to 228.

(a) Materials Purchased. As each purchase transaction is completed, the
purchase invoice is verified and a voucher is prepared. The voucher is
recorded in the voucher register in the columns headed Materials and
Accounts Payable and is posted to the proper accounts in the stores
ledger. Because the voucher system is used, the file of unpaid vouchers
takes the place of a subsidiary accounts payable ledger.

At the end of the month when the summary posting from the
voucher register is completed, the total of the Materials column, $24,300,
is posted as a debit to Materials (Account No. 1430). At the same time,
the total of the Accounts Payable column is posted as a credit to
Accounts Payable (Account No. 2220). The entry, in general journal form,
to record these summary data appears as follows:

Materials	24,300	
Accounts Payable		24,300

FIGURE 5-1 Voucher Register and Check Register

VOUCHER REGISTER FOR MONTH OF 19 PAGE

	MATERIALS DR.	WAGES PAYABLE DR.	FACTORY OVERHEAD DR.	SUNDRY ACCOUNTS			DAY	VOU. NO.	TO WHOM ISSUED	TERMS	DISPOSITION		ACCOUNTS PAYABLE CR.	
				ACCT. NO.	AMOUNT DR.	AMOUNT CR.					DATE	CK. NO.		
1									AMOUNTS FORWARDED					1
2														2
3														3
4														4
5														5
6														6

CHECK REGISTER FOR MONTH OF 19 PAGE

	ACCOUNTS PAY. DR.		DAY	DRAWN TO THE ORDER OF	PURCHASE DISCOUNTS CR.	CASH CR.		
	NO.	AMOUNT				CK. NO.	AMOUNT	
1								1
2								2
3								3
4								4
5								5
6								6

(b) Factory Overhead. Invoices for factory overhead expenses are verified and vouchered, recorded in the voucher register in the columns headed Factory Overhead and Accounts Payable, and are posted to the proper accounts in the factory overhead ledger. The factory overhead ledger contains individual accounts for each type of overhead expense including indirect materials, indirect labor, and other indirect manufacturing expenses.

At the end of the month, the total of the Factory Overhead column is posted as a debit to Factory Overhead (Account No. 3100). The amounts recorded in the Accounts Payable column are included in the column total, which is posted as a credit to Accounts Payable. The entry, in general journal form, to record these summary data appears as follows:

Factory Overhead	3,750	
Accounts Payable		3,750

(c) Payroll. The wages of factory employees are paid weekly. The salaries of all other employees are paid semimonthly. On each payday, the payroll record serves as a subsidiary record for the preparation of a journal entry for the payroll. The entry, in general journal form, to record these summary data appears as follows:

Payroll	62,000	
FICA Tax Payable		4,960
Employees Income Tax Payable		9,300
Wages Payable		47,740

In a voucher system, a voucher first must be prepared for the amount due to the workers before they can be paid. The entry in the voucher register would be recorded as follows:

Wages Payable	47,740	
Accounts Payable		47,740

(d) Payroll Checks. The checks issued in payment of the payroll vouchers are recorded in the check register. At the end of the month, the total of the check register column headed Accounts Payable is posted as a debit to Accounts Payable, and the total of the Cash column is posted as a credit to Cash. These column totals include payments for materials, payroll, various factory overhead items, and all other expenditures made by check during the period. The entry, in general journal form, to record the payment of wages and salaries follows:

Accounts Payable	47,740	
Cash		47,740

(e) Materials Requisitioned. During the month, materials requisitions are posted to the proper accounts in the subsidiary stores ledger, job cost ledger, and factory overhead ledger. At the end of the month, a summary of the materials requisitions is prepared. The summary for August provides the following information:

Direct materials requisitioned:

For Job 707	$ 1,900
For Job 708	3,422
For Job 801	3,748
For Job 802	4,276
For Job 803	3,626
For Job 804	1,792
Total direct materials requisitioned	$ 18,764
Indirect materials requisitioned	3,500
Total materials requisitioned	$ 22,264

The entry, in general journal form, to record these summary data appears as follows:

Work in Process	18,764	
Factory Overhead	3,500	
Materials		22,264

Three control accounts are affected by this entry: Work in Process (Account No. 1420), the control account for the job cost ledger; Factory Overhead (Account No. 3100), the control account for the factory overhead ledger; and Materials (Account No. 1430), the control account for the stores ledger.

(f) Wages and Salaries Earned. The time tickets and schedule of fixed salaries are the sources of individual postings to the proper accounts in the subsidiary job cost ledger and factory overhead ledger. At the end of the month, the labor cost summary is prepared from the time tickets, which show the amount of labor applied directly to jobs in process and the amount of indirect labor. The labor cost summary and a schedule of the fixed salaries provide the information for drafting a general journal entry to distribute the total wages and salaries earned during the month.

In distributing the total wages and salaries earned during the month, two control accounts are affected. Work in Process (Account No. 1420) is debited for the total of the direct labor cost, and Factory Overhead (Account No. 3100) is debited for the total indirect labor cost. Also, Salaries (Account No. 5100) is debited for the total of the salaries paid to all other employees. Payroll (Account No. 5000) is credited for the total wages and salaries earned during the month. The following general journal entry distributes the total wages and salaries earned during the month:

Work in Process	47,500	
Factory Overhead	7,500	
Salaries	12,500	
Payroll		67,500

In the subsidiary job cost ledger, the detail for the direct labor in Work in Process follows:

Job 702	$ 4,500
Job 707	5,500
Job 708	6,800
Job 801	7,250
Job 802	7,650
Job 803	7,600
Job 804	8,200
Total direct labor	$ 47,500

Because some of the wages are paid on a weekly basis and the last payday for the month does not fall on the last day of the month, Mountain Oak Office Interiors must account for accrued wages. The amount of the accrued wages for August is $5,500, which is the credit balance of the payroll account.

If the payroll account is debited for the total wages and salaries paid during the month and is credited for the total wages and salaries earned during the month, the credit balance of the account should always represent the total amount of the wages and salaries accrued at the end of the month. This credit balance should be transferred to a liability account. Therefore, at the end of August, the following general journal entry is recorded:

Payroll	5,500	
Wages Payable		5,500

(g) Payroll Taxes Imposed on Employer. The payroll records provide the following information for the schedule of wages earned and payroll taxes. At the end of each payroll period, the payroll taxes imposed on the employer for FICA and federal and state unemployment taxes are recorded. At the end of August, the employer's payroll taxes on the accrued payroll are recorded.

Schedule of Earnings and Payroll Taxes
For the Month Ended August 31, 19—

Classification of Wages and Salaries	Total Earnings	FICA 8%	Unemployment Taxes Federal 1%	State 4%	Total Payroll Taxes
Direct labor	$47,500.00	$3,800.00	$475.00	$1,900.00	$6,175.00
Indirect labor	7,500.00	600.00	75.00	300.00	975.00
Total taxes on wages		$4,400.00	$550.00	$2,200.00	$7,150.00
Salaries	12,500.00	1,000.00	125.00	500.00	1,625.00
Total	$67,500.00	$5,400.00	$675.00	$2,700.00	$8,775.00

The combined general journal entry to record these summary data for August follows:

```
Factory Overhead . . . . . . . . . . . . . . . . . . . . .     7,150
Payroll Tax Expense—Salaries  . . . . . . . . . . . .     1,625
    FICA Tax Payable   . . . . . . . . . . . . . . . . . . .          5,400
    Federal Unemployment Tax Payable  . . . . . . . .            675
    State Unemployment Tax Payable . . . . . . . . . .          2,700
```

(h) **Fixed Expenses.** At the end of each month, the schedule of fixed costs is the source of a general journal entry debiting Factory Overhead (Account No. 3100) for the amount of all fixed manufacturing expenses, such as depreciation, property tax, and insurance applicable to the month. The schedule of fixed expenses is also the source of the posting of the proper amounts to the individual accounts in the subsidiary factory overhead ledger.

The depreciation of factory property is computed at the following annual rates:

Buildings—4.875%   Furniture and Fixtures—10%
Machinery—8.25%   Small Tools—20%

The following general journal entry records these fixed expenses:

```
Factory Overhead   . . . . . . . . . . . . . . . . . . . .   2,450.00
    Accumulated Depreciation—Buildings   . . . . . . .           325.00
    Accumulated Depreciation—Machinery . . . . . . .           825.00
    Accumulated Depreciation—Furniture and Fixtures .         125.00
    Accumulated Depreciation—Small Tools  . . . . . .          275.00
    Property Tax Payable   . . . . . . . . . . . . . . . . .        400.00
    Prepaid Insurance   . . . . . . . . . . . . . . . . . . .       500.00
```

(i) Factory Overhead Distributed to Departments. At the end of each month, a summary of factory overhead is prepared on a departmental basis. The summary for August follows:

Summary of Factory Overhead
For the Month Ended August 31, 19—

Acct. No.	Account	Dept. S & P	Dept. A & F	Dept. D & D	Dept. C & R	Total
3111	Depreciation	$ 645.00	$ 575.00	$ 125.00	$ 205.00	$ 1,550.00
3112	Property tax	150.00	120.00	80.00	50.00	400.00
3113	Insurance	250.00	190.00	10.00	50.00	500.00
3121	Indirect materials	1,540.00	1,350.00	360.00	250.00	3,500.00
3122	Indirect labor	2,300.00	2,400.00	1,000.00	1,800.00	7,500.00
3123	Natural Gas	200.00	150.00	45.00	55.00	450.00
3124	Water	20.00	35.00	20.00	150.00	225.00
3125	Light	400.00	300.00	150.00	50.00	900.00
3126	Power	850.00	450.00	100.00	150.00	1,550.00
3127	Payroll taxes	3,885.00	2,140.00	750.00	375.00	7,150.00
3128	Miscellaneous factory expenses	235.00	187.00	123.00	80.00	625.00
	Total	$10,475.00	$7,897.00	$2,763.00	$3,215.00	$24,350.00

The subsidiary factory overhead ledger accounts are the source of the information for this summary. The amounts charged to Payroll Taxes Expense (Account No. 3127) include the FICA tax of 8%, the federal unemployment tax of 1%, and the state unemployment tax of 4% imposed on employers. From the summary, a general journal entry is prepared as follows:

Factory Overhead—S & P Department	10,475	
Factory Overhead—A & F Department	7,897	
Factory Overhead—D & D Department	2,763	
Factory Overhead—C & R Department	3,215	
Factory Overhead		24,350

After this entry is posted, the factory overhead control account has a zero balance. The individual accounts in the subsidiary factory overhead ledger are also assumed to have zero balances.

(j) Distribution of Clean-up and Repair Department Expenses. At the end of each month, the service departments' expenses are distributed on the basis of service rendered to the other departments. Two service departments exist: The clean-up and repair department (C & R) and the development and design department (D & D). The following work sheet was prepared to distribute the expenses of both service departments. The clean-up and repair department expenses are distributed to the other departments on the basis of the number of adjusted square feet occupied by each department.

Department	Area Sq. Ft.	Adjustment Factor	Adjusted Area Sq. Ft.	Rate per Sq. Ft.*	Amount
S & P	20,000	2.0	40,000	$.0535833	$2,143.33
A & F	10,000	1.5	15,000	.0535833	803.75
D & D	5,000	1.0	5,000	.0535833	267.92
	35,000		60,000		$3,215.00

*$3,215 divided by 60,000 adj. sq. ft. = $. 0535833

Service Departments Expense Distribution Work Sheet
For the Month Ended August 31, 19—

Description	C & R Dept.	D & D Dept.	S & P Dept.	A & F Dept.	Total
Direct costs	$3,215.00	$2,763.00	$10,475.00	$7,897.00	$24,350.00
C & R Department—Distribution $.0535833 per adj. sq. ft.					
D & D Dept.—5,000 adj. sq. ft. ..		267.92			
S & P Dept.—40,000 adj. sq. ft. ..			2,143.33		
A & F Dept.—15,00 adj. sq. ft. ..				803.75	
		$3,030.92			
D & D Department—Distribution basis arbitrary					
Dept. S & P—3/4			2,273.19		
Dept. A & F—1/4				757.73	
Total			$14,891.52	$9,458.48	$24,350.00

The distribution is accomplished by the following general journal entry:

Factory Overhead—S & P Department	2,143.33	
Factory Overhead—A & F Department	803.75	
Factory Overhead—D & D Department	267.92	
Factory Overhead—C & R Department		3,215.00

(k) Distribution of Development and Design Department Expenses. The D & D department expenses are distributed to the production departments on the basis of three-fourths to the S & P department and one-fourth to the A & F department. This arbitrary distribution is based on the past experience of the company. The amount to be distributed includes both the direct expenses from the D & D department and the apportioned expenses from the C & R department. The distributed amounts are computed as follows:

S & P Department—3/4 times $3,030.92 = $2,273.19
A & F Department—1/4 times $3,030.92 = $ 757.73

The distribution is accomplished by the following general journal entry:

Factory Overhead—S & P Department 2,273.19
Factory Overhead—A & F Department 757.73
    Factory Overhead—D & D Department 3,030.92

(1) Distribution of the Production Departments' Expenses. During the month, direct materials and direct labor costs are charged to the proper accounts in the job cost ledger from the materials requisitions and time tickets. To ascertain the total cost of each job processed during the month, factory overhead must be added. The company has adopted the direct labor hour basis for applying factory overhead. To ascertain the current rates, the company prepared the following annual estimates at the beginning of the fiscal year, August 1:

Department	Estimated Direct Labor Hours	Estimated Factory Overhead	Application Rate per Hour
S & P	26,500	$174,900	$6.60
A & F	21,900	117,165	5.35
	48,400	$290,065	

During the month, departmental overhead expenses are added to the cost of the jobs in process by applying the predetermined application rates to the actual number of direct labor hours used on each job. The amount of overhead applicable to each job finished during the month is recorded at the time of completion. The amount of overhead applicable to the jobs still in process at the end of the month is recorded on the last day of the month. To determine the amount of overhead applied to jobs processed during August, the summary of applied factory overhead is prepared on August 31:

Summary of Applied Factory Overhead for August

	S & P Dept.			A & F Dept.			
Job	Direct Labor Cost	Direct Labor Hours	Applied Factory Overhead	Direct Labor Cost	Direct Labor Hours	Applied Factory Overhead	Total Applied Factory Overhead
702				$ 3,600	345	$1,845.75	$ 1,845.75
707	$ 2,250	177	$ 1,168.20	2,700	260	1,391.00	2,559.20
708	3,400	262	1,729.20	3,000	290	1,551.50	3,280.70
801	3,550	275	1,815.00	3,600	345	1,845.75	3,660.75
802	6,000	463	3,055.80	3,700	355	1,899.25	4,955.05
803	6,200	480	3,168.00	2,400	230	1,230.50	4,398.50
804	7,100	551	3,636.60				3,636.60
	$28,500	2,208	$14,572.80	$19,000	1,825	$9,763.75	$24,336.55

The summary is the basis for the following general journal entry:

Work in Process	24,336.55	
Factory Overhead—S & P Department		14,572.80
Factory Overhead—A & F Department		9,763.75
S & P—2,208 DLH times $6.60 = $14,572.80		
A & F—1,825 DLH times $5.35 = $ 9,763.75		

On August 1, there were three jobs in process, represented in the general ledger by a debit balance of $12,000 in the work in process control account, with three subsidiary accounts to which materials and labor costs have been posted during July and factory overhead has been applied on July 31. The following summary shows the jobs in process:

Work in Process, July 31

Job	Materials	Labor	Overhead	Total
702	$2,500	$2,000	$1,000	$ 5,500
707	500	1,500	750	2,750
708	1,500	1,500	750	3,750
	$4,500	$5,000	$2,500	$12,000

Job 702 is almost completed. The other two need considerable work before they will be completed. All three are worked on during August. In addition, work is started on Jobs 801, 802, 803, and 804. In all, seven jobs are being processed during August. In the case of the jobs in process on August 1, the costs incurred for their benefit during August are added to the costs already recorded in July. The following summary shows the jobs in process during August.

Summary of Factory Operations for August

Job	Materials	Applied Labor	Overhead	Charges to Work in Process in Total	Prior Periods	Total Charges to Work in Process
702		$ 4,500.00	$ 1,845.75	$ 6,345.75	$ 5,500.00	$ 11,845.75
707	$ 1,900.00	5,500.00	2,559.20	9,959.20	2,750.00	12,709.20
708	3,422.00	6,800.00	3,280.70	13,502.70	3,750.00	17,252.70
801	3,748.00	7,250.00	3,660.75	14,658.75		14,658.75
802	4,276.00	7,650.00	4,955.05	16,881.05		16,881.05
803	3,626.00	7,600.00	4,398.50	15,624.50		15,624.50
804	1,792.00	8,200.00	3,636.60	13,628.60		13,628.60
	$18,764.00	$47,500.00	$24,336.55	$90,600.55	$12,000.00	$102,600.55

The charges of $102,600.55 must be accounted for as costs assigned to jobs remaining to be completed and to completed jobs that have been transferred out of Work in Process.

(m) Under- and Overapplied Overhead. After the departmental overhead expenses are applied to the costs of the jobs in process at the predetermined application rates, Factory Overhead—S & P Department has a debit balance of $318.72 ($14,891.52 minus $14,572.80). The debit balance represents an underapplication of overhead to the jobs in process during the month. Factory Overhead—A & F Department has a credit balance of $305.27 ($9,458.48 minus $9,763.75). The credit balance represents an overapplication of overhead to the jobs in process during the month. It is common practice to transfer the balances of the departmental factory overhead accounts to an account entitled Under- and Overapplied Overhead. At the end of the year, this account is usually closed into Cost of Goods Sold, unless the balance of the account is unusually large.

The following general journal entry closes the departmental factory overhead accounts:

Under- and Overapplied Overhead	13.45	
Factory Overhead—A & F Department	305.27	
Factory Overhead—S & P Department		318.72

(n) Finished Goods. Jobs 702, 707, 708, and 801 are completed during August. The following information is prepared from the summary of Factory Overhead Operations.

Job	Total Cost
702	$11,845.75
707	12,709.20
708	17,252.70
801	14,658.75
Total cost of goods finished during August	$56,466.40

The following general journal entry transfers the cost applicable to jobs finished in August from Work in Process to Finished Goods:

Finished Goods	56,466.40	
Work in Process		56,466.40

After Finished Goods is debited and Work in Process is credited for the total cost of the jobs completed during August, the balance of the work in process account, $46,134.15, represents the amount of work in process on August 31.

(o) Sales. The sales for August follow:

Job	Manufacturing Cost	Selling Price
702	$11,845.75	$19,742.92
706	14,000.00	23,333.33
707	12,709.20	21,182.00
708	17,252.70	28,754.50
	$55,807.65	$93,012.75

Job 706 was completed during July at a total cost of $14,000, but it was not sold until August. Reference to the post-closing trial balance for July 31 shows that this amount was the inventory of finished goods and indicates that this job was the only job completed and not delivered by that date. The sales during August are recorded in a sales journal in which separate amount columns are provided for recording both the selling price and the cost of goods sold. At the end of the month, the amount of total sales is posted to the general ledger as a debit to Accounts Receivable (Account No. 1330) and a credit to Sales (Account No. 4100). The total cost of goods sold is posted to the general ledger as a debit to Cost of Goods Sold (Account No. 4600) and a credit to Finished Goods (Account No. 1410).

The entries, in general journal form, to record these summary data appear as follows:

Accounts Receivable	93,012.75	
Sales		93,012.75
Cost of Goods Sold	55,807.65	
Finished Goods		55,807.65

After the posting is completed, the finished goods account has a balance of $14,658.75. This amount represents the cost of Job 801, which is the only job completed but undelivered on August 31.

(p) Receipts from Customers. Cash received from customers to apply on account is recorded in the cash receipts journal. A separate amount column is provided for recording credits to Accounts Receivable. At the end of August, the total of this column, $93,077, is posted to the general ledger as a credit to Accounts Receivable. At the same time, the amount of cash received is included in the total deposits, which is posted as a debit to Cash.

The entry, in general journal form, to record these summary data follows:

```
Cash    . . . . . . . . . . . . . . . . . . . . .93,077
    Accounts Receivable    . . . . . . . . . . . . . . . . .            93,077
```

(q) Payments to Creditors. Checks issued to creditors in settlement of vouchers payable are recorded in the check register. A separate amount column is provided for recording debits to Accounts Payable. At the end of August, the total of this column is posted to the general ledger as a debit to Accounts Payable. At the same time, the total of the column headed Purchase Discounts is posted to the general ledger as a credit to Purchase Discounts (Account No. 6110). The total of the Cash column is posted to the general ledger as a credit to Cash.

The entry, in general journal form, to record these summary data appears as follows:

```
Accounts Payable    . . . . . . . . . . . . . . . . . . . . .    19,786
    Purchase Discounts . . . . . . . . . . . . . . . . . .                186
    Cash    . . . . . . . . . . . . . . . . . . . . . . . .             19,600
```

(r) Vouchering FICA Taxes and Employees' Income Taxes. Periodically, the amounts withheld for employee FICA and income taxes plus the employer's share of FICA tax are paid to a depository (bank). Therefore, after the entries for the employer's and employees' taxes are made, vouchers are prepared to pay the taxes.

During August, vouchers were prepared for the taxes that were recorded for the last week of July and the first three weeks of August. These vouchers were recorded in the voucher register as a debit to FICA Tax Payable, a debit to Employees Income Tax Payable, and a credit to Accounts Payable. The debits are posted individually to Account Nos. 2230 and 2260. The amount credited to Account No. 2220 is included in the total of the column headed Accounts Payable, which is posted at the end of the month.

The entry, in general journal form, to record these summary data appears as follows:

FICA Tax Payable	11,720	
Employees Income Tax Payable	9,700	
Accounts Payable		21,420

(s) Payment of FICA Taxes and Employees' Income Taxes. The check for $21,420, issued to the depository in payment of the taxes, is recorded in the check register as a debit to Accounts Payable and as a credit to Cash. At the end of the month, the total of the column headed Accounts Payable is posted as a debit to Account No. 2220. The total of the Cash column is posted as a credit to Account No. 1110.

The entry, in general journal form, to record the payment of these taxes appears as follows:

Accounts Payable	21,420	
Cash		21,420

(t) General Expenses. The general expenses incurred during the month include the following:

> Office expense, $2,250
> Miscellaneous general expense, $976
> Public relations expense, $2,865

Vouchers are issued for the expense invoices as they are received. The entry, in general journal form, to record these summary data appears as follows:

Office Expense	2,250	
Public Relations Expense	2,865	
Miscellaneous General Expense	976	
Accounts Payable		6,091

(u) Amortization of Intangible Assets. Organization costs and trademarks are expensed at the rate of $100 and $30 per month respectively. The total ($130) is debited to Account No. 5600 (Amortization Expense) and Account Nos. 1710 and 1720 are credited for the respective amount.

Amortization Expense	130	
Organization Costs		100
Trademarks		30

THE END OF THE MONTH

Following is the general ledger of Mountain Oak Office Interiors showing the balances of the accounts on August 31 (including adjustments from the work sheet).

General Ledger

Cash				Acct. No. 1110
19—			19—	
August	1 Balance	15,700.00	August 31 Payroll	(d) 47,740.00
	31 Deposit	(p) 93,077.00	31 Creditors	(q) 19,600.00
		108,777.00	31 Taxes	(s) 21,420.00
		20,017.00		*88,760.00*

Petty Cash			Acct. No. 1120
19—			
August	1 Balance	200.00	

Marketable Securities			Acct. No. 1200
19—			
August	1 Balance	6,050.00	

Notes Receivable			Acct. No. 1310
19—			
August	1 Balance	10,000.00	

Interest Receivable			Acct. No. 1320
19—			
August	1 Balance	101.66	
	31 Adjustment	48.34	
		150.00	

Accounts Receivable				Acct. No. 1330
19—			19—	
August	1 Balance	46,000.00	August 31 Receipts	(p) 93,077.00
	31 Sales	(o) 93,012.75		
		139,012.75		
		45,935.75		

Allowance for Doubtful Accounts			Acct. No. 1331
		19—	
		August	1 Balance	2,300.00
			31 Adjustment	930.00
				3,230.00

Finished Goods — Acct. No. 1410

19—				19—			
August	1	Inventory	14,000.00	August	31	Cost of goods	
	31	Goods completed (n)	56,466.40			sold (o)	55,807.65
			70,466.40				
			14,658.75				

Work in Process — Acct. No. 1420

19—				19—			
August	1	Inventory	12,000.00	August	31	Finished goods (n)	56,466.40
	31	Materials	(e) 18,764.00				
	31	Labor	(f) 47,500.00				
	31	Overhead	(l) 24,336.55				
			102,600.55				
			46,134.15				

Materials — Acct. No. 1430

19—				19—			
August	1	Inventory	23,000.00	August	31	Requisitions	(e) 22,264.00
	31	Purchases	(a) 24,300.00				
			47,300.00				
			25,036.00				

Prepaid Insurance — Acct. No. 1510

19—				19—			
August	1	Balance	5,000.00	August	31	Expired	(h) 500.00
			4,500.00				

Land — Acct. No. 1610

19—			
August	1	Balance	26,300.00

Buildings — Acct. No. 1620

19—			
August	1	Balance	80,000.00

Accumulated Depreciation—Buildings — Acct. No. 1621

				19—			
				August	1	Balance	12,000.00
					31	Addition	(h) 325.00
							12,325.00

Machinery						Acct. No. 1630
19—						
August	1	Balance	120,000.00			

Accumulated Depreciation—Machinery					Acct. No. 1631
			19—		
			August	1	Balance	24,000.00
				31	Addition	(h) 825.00
						24,825.00

Furniture and Fixtures						Acct. No. 1640
19—						
August	1	Balance	15,000.00			

Accumulated Depreciation—Furniture and Fixtures				Acct. No. 1641
			19—		
			August	1	Balance	5,480.00
				31	Addition	(h) 125.00
						5,605.00

Small Tools						Acct. No. 1650
19—						
August	1	Balance	16,500.00			

Accumulated Depreciation—Small Tools					Acct. No. 1651
			19—		
			August	1	Balance	9,020.00
				31	Addition	(h) 275.00
						9,295.00

Organization Costs						Acct. No. 1710
19—						
August	1	Balance	3,800.00	August	31 Amortization	(u) 100.00
			3,700.00			

Trademarks						Acct. No. 1720
19—						
August	1	Balance	1,500.00	August	31 Amortization	(u) 30.00
			1,470.00			

Notes Payable					Acct. No. 2210
			19—		
			August	1	Balance	7,000.00

Accounts Payable — Acct. No. 2220

19—				19—			
August	31	Payroll	(d) 47,740.00	August	1	Balance	10,500.00
	31	Creditors	(q) 19,786.00		31	Materials	(a) 24,300.00
	31	U.S. Depository	(s) 21,420.00		31	Overhead	(b) 3,750.00
			88,946.00		31	Payroll	(c) 47,740.00
					31	FICA taxes and employees income taxes	(r) 21,420.00
					31	Misc. general expense	(t) 6,091.00
							113,801.00
							24,855.00

FICA Tax Payable — Acct. No. 2230

19—				19—			
August	31	Vouchered	(r)11,720.00	August	1	Balance	1,800.00
					31	Employees	(c) 4,960.00
					31	Employer	(g) 5,400.00
							12,160.00
							440.00

Federal Unemployment Tax Payable — Acct. No. 2240

				19—			
				August	1	Balance	315.00
					31	Employer	(g) 675.00
							990.00

State Unemployment Tax Payable — Acct. No. 2250

				19—			
				August	1	Balance	1,215.00
					31	Employer	(g) 2,700.00
							3,915.00

Employees Income Tax Payable — Acct. No. 2260

19—				19—			
August	31	Vouchered	(r) 9,700.00	August	1	Balance	1,500.00
					31	Withheld	(c) 9,300.00
							10,800.00
							1,100.00

Property Tax Payable   Acct. No. 2271

	19—		
	August	1	Balance	2,000.00
		31	Accrued	(h) 400.00
				2,400.00

Estimated Income Tax Payable   Acct. No. 2272

	19—		
	August	1	Balance	15,700.00
		31	Adjustment	2,710.50
				18,410.50

Interest Payable   Acct. No. 2273

	19—		
	August	1	Balance	102.22
		31	Adjustment	31.53
				133.75

Wages Payable   Acct. No. 2274

August	31	Payroll	(d) 47,740.00	19—			
				August	31	Payroll	(c) 47,740.00
				August	31	Accrued	(f) 5,500.00
							53,240.00
						5,500.00	

Bonds Payable   Acct. No. 2710

	19—		
	August	1	Balance	25,000.00

Capital Stock   Acct. No. 2910

	19—		
	August	1	Balance	200,000.00

Retained Earnings   Acct. No. 2980

	19—		
	August	1	Balance	77,219.44
		31	Net income	6,723.31
				83,942.75

Income Summary   Acct. No. 2990

19—				19—		
August	31	Closing	75,783.28	August	31	Closing	82,506.59
		Retained Earnings	6,723.31			
			82,506.59			82,506.59

Factory Overhead — Acct. No. 3100

19—					19—				
August	31	Manufacturing expenses	(b)	3,750.00	August	31	Distributed	(i)	24,350.00
	31	Indirect materials	(e)	3,500.00					
	31	Indirect labor	(f)	7,500.00					
	31	Payroll taxes	(g)	7,150.00					
	31	Fixed expense	(h)	2,450.00					
				24,350.00					24,350.00

Factory Overhead—S & P Department — Acct. No. 3140

19—					19—				
August	31	Distributed	(i)	10,475.00	August	31	Applied	(l)	14,572.80
	31	Department C&R	(j)	2,143.33		31	Trans. to		
	31	Department D&D	(k)	2,273.19			Acct. No. 3180	(m)	318.72
				14,891.52					14,891.52

Factory Overhead—A & F Department — Acct. No. 3150

19—					19—				
August	31	Distributed	(i)	7,897.00	August	31	Applied	(l)	9,763.75
	31	Department C&R	(j)	803.75					
	31	Department D&D	(k)	757.73					
	31	Trans. to Acct. No. 3180	(m)	305.27					
				9,763.75					9,763.75

Factory Overhead—C & R Department — Acct. No. 3160

19—					19—				
August	31	Distributed	(i)	3,215.00	August	31	Distributed	(j)	3,215.00

Factory Overhead—D & D Department — Acct. No. 3170

August	31	Distributed	(i)	2,763.00	August	31	Distributed	(k)	3,030.92
	31	Department C&R	(j)	267.92					
				3,030.92					3,030.92

Under- and Overapplied Overhead — Acct. No. 3180

19—					19—				
August	31	Underapplied overhead	(m)	13.45	August	31	Cost of goods sold		13.45

Sales   Acct. No. 4100

19—					19—				
August	31	Income Summary		93,012.75	August	31	On account	(o)	93,012.75

Cost of Goods Sold   Acct. No. 4600

19—					19—				
August	31	Finished goods	(o)	55,807.65	August	31	Income Summary		55,821.10
	31	Under- and over-							
		applied overhead		13.45					
				55,821.10					55,821.10

Payroll   Acct. No. 5000

19—					19—				
August	31	Vouchered	(c)	62,000.00	August	31	Distributed	(f)	67,500.00
	31	Accrued	(f)	5,500.00					
				67,500.00					67,500.00

Salaries   Acct. No. 5100

19—					19—				
August	31		(f)	12,500.00	August	31	Income Summary		12,500.00

Payroll Tax Expense—Salaries   Acct. No. 5200

19—					19—				
August	31		(g)	1,625.00	August	31	Income Summary		1,625.00

Office Expense   Acct. No. 5300

19—					19—				
August	31		(t)	2,250.00	August	31	Income Summary		2,250.00

Public Relations Expense   Acct. No. 5500

19—					19—				
August	31		(t)	2,865.00	August	31	Income Summary		2,865.00

Amortization Expense   Acct. No. 5600

19—					19—				
August	31		(t)	130.00	August	31	Income Summary		130.00

Doubtful Accounts Expense   Acct. No. 5800

19—					19—				
August	31	Adjustment		930.00	August	31	Income Summary		930.00

	Miscellaneous General Expense			Acct. No 5900
19— August 31		(t) 976.00	19— August 31 Income Summary	976.00

	Purchase Discounts			Acct. No. 6110
19— August 31 Income Summary		186.00	19— August 31	(q) 186.00

	Interest Income			Acct. No. 6120
19— August 31 Income Summary	19—	48.34	August 31 Adjustment	48.34

	Interest Expense			Acct. No. 6220
19— August 31 Adjustment		31.53	19— August 31 Income Summary	31.53

	Provision for Income Tax			Acct. No. 6420
19— August 31 Adjustment		5,104.00	19— August 31 Income Summary	5,104.00

WORK SHEET

A work sheet, properly designed, is an aid in preparing monthly financial statements, as is shown in Figure 5-2, the work sheet for August.

Trial Balance. The first step in preparing the work sheet is to prepare a trial balance of the general ledger accounts as of August 31. This unadjusted trial balance appears in the first two amount columns.

   The balances of the accounts for work in process, accounts receivable, and accounts payable are verified by preparing schedules of the subsidiary work in process and accounts receivable accounts and a schedule of the unpaid vouchers. These schedules follow.

Schedule of Work in Process, August 31, 19—

Job	Name	Amount
802	LC Schools	$16,881.05
803	MAP & Associates	15,624.50
804	Guide Trust and Savings Bank	13,628.60
	Total	$46,134.15

FIGURE 5-2   MOOI Worksheet

Mountain Oak Office Interiors
Work Sheet
For the Month Ended August 31, 19—

Account	Acct. No.	TRIAL BALANCE DEBIT	TRIAL BALANCE CREDIT	ADJUSTMENTS DEBIT	ADJUSTMENTS CREDIT	INCOME STATEMENT DEBIT	INCOME STATEMENT CREDIT	BALANCE SHEET DEBIT	BALANCE SHEET CREDIT
Cash	1110	20,017.00						20,017.00	
Petty Cash	1120	200.00						200.00	
Marketable Securities	1200	6,050.00						6,050.00	
Notes Receivable	1310	10,000.00						10,000.00	
Interest Receivable	1320	101.66		48.34				150.00	
Accounts Receivable	1330	45,935.75						45,935.75	
Allowance for Doubtful Accounts	1331		2,300.00		930.00				3,230.00
Finished Goods	1410	14,658.75						14,658.75	
Work in Process	1420	46,134.15						46,134.15	
Materials	1430	25,036.00						25,036.00	
Prepaid Insurance	1510	4,500.00						4,500.00	
Land	1610	26,300.00						26,300.00	
Buildings	1620	80,000.00						80,000.00	
Accumulated Depreciation—Buildings	1621		12,325.00						12,325.00
Machinery	1630	120,000.00						120,000.00	
Accumulated Depreciation—Machinery	1631		24,825.00						24,825.00
Furniture and Fixtures	1640	15,000.00						15,000.00	
Accumulated Depreciation—Furniture and Fixtures	1641		5,605.00						5,605.00
Small Tools	1650	16,500.00						16,500.00	
Accumulated Depreciation—Small Tools	1651		9,295.00						9,295.00
Organization Costs	1710	3,700.00						3,700.00	
Trademarks	1720	1,470.00						1,470.00	
Notes Payable	2210		7,000.00						7,000.00
Accounts Payable	2220		24,855.00						24,855.00
FICA Tax Payable	2230		440.00						440.00
Federal Unemployment Tax Payable	2240		990.00						990.00
State Unemployment Tax Payable	2250		3,915.00						3,915.00
Employees Income Tax Payable	2260		1,100.00						1,100.00
Property Tax Payable	2271		2,400.00						2,400.00
Estimated Income Tax Payable	2272		15,700.00		5,104.00				20,804.00
Interest Payable	2273		102.22		31.53				133.75
Wages Payable	2274		5,500.00						5,500.00
Long-term Note Payable	2710		25,000.00						25,000.00
Capital Stock	2910		200,000.00						200,000.00
Retained Earnings	2980		77,219.44						77,219.44
Sales	4100		93,012.75				93,012.75		
Cost of Goods Sold	4600	55,821.10				55,821.10			
Salaries	5100	12,500.00				12,500.00			
Payroll Tax Expense—Salaries	5200	1,625.00				1,625.00			
Office Expense	5300	2,250.00				2,250.00			
Public Relations Expense	5500	2,865.00				2,865.00			
Amortization Expense	5600	130.00				130.00			
Doubtful Accounts Expense	5800			930.00		930.00			
Miscellaneous General Expense	5900	976.00				976.00			
Purchase Discounts	6110		186.00				186.00		
Interest Income	6120				48.34	-48.34			
Interest Expense	6220			31.53		31.53			
		511,770.41	511,770.41	6,113.87	6,113.87	77,080.29	93,198.75	435,651.65	424,637.19
Provision for Income Tax	6420			5,104.00		5,104.00			
						11,014.46			11,014.46
						93,198.75	93,198.75	435,651.65	435,651.65

Schedule of Accounts Receivable, August 31, 19—

Name	Amount
Storm Guard Roofing, Wiser Lake	$ 9,610.00
J. Calman Enterprises, Laurel	19,742.92
Moezie's Latte Shop, Moscow	970.00
Sportsworld Sporting Goods, Lynden	10,157.83
Spotted Cow Dairy Store, Custer	5,455.00
Total	$45,935.75

Schedule of Accounts Payable, August 31, 19—

Voucher No.	To Whom Issued	Amount
47	Vander Kooi Lumber	$ 4,256
83	Horne's Office Supplies	870
88	Sefton Hardwood Company	5,639
92	Synthetic Resins, Inc.	1,325
94	Lyncs Exotic Laminates	3,165
96	Paulson Hardware Sales	3,250
97	Z's Plywood	6,350
	Total	$24,855

Adjustments. It is usually necessary to adjust certain accounts before financial statements can be prepared. The adjustments required on August 31 follow:

a. Increase in accrued interest receivable, $48.34

b. Increase in accrued interest payable, $31.53

c. Increase in allowance for doubtful accounts, 1% of the account sales for August, $930

d. Provision for estimated income tax, $5104

The proper adjustments are entered in the third and fourth amount columns on the work sheet.

Income Statement. The adjusted balances of the temporary or nominal accounts are extended to the fifth and sixth amount columns on the work sheet. These columns provide the information for preparing the income statement for August.

Balance Sheet. The adjusted balances of the assets, liabilities, and capital, or real accounts, are extended to the seventh and eighth amount columns on the work sheet. These columns provide the information for preparing the balance sheet as of August 31.

FINANCIAL STATEMENTS

It is generally desirable to prepare monthly financial statements for the use of the company's principal executives. These statements can be prepared only if inventories are taken monthly or if a system of cost accounting is made a part of the company's accounting procedure. Ordinarily, it is impractical to take monthly physical inventories of materials, work in process, and finished goods. A properly developed cost accounting system, however, makes a monthly physical inventory unnecessary. It provides for recording the cost of work in process and finished goods and the maintenance of book inventories of materials, work in process, and finished goods.

Mountain Oak Office Interiors follows the practice of preparing a monthly manufacturing statement, income statement, and balance sheet. The statements prepared at the end of August are reproduced on pages 231 to 235.

Statement of Cost of Goods Manufactured. In preparing the manufacturing statement for August, the costs of materials, labor, and applied factory overhead are first determined. The work in process account is the source of the information for these costs. Because the application rates are based upon estimates made at the beginning of the fiscal year, it is not unusual that the amount of applied overhead may differ from the actual overhead incurred during any month of the year. It is to be expected that further fluctuations will occur during succeeding months. In preparing the man-

Mountain Oak Office Interiors
Statement of Cost of Goods Manufactured
For the Month Ended August 31, 19—

Direct materials used	$ 18,764.00
Direct labor	47,500.00
Applied factory overhead	24,336.55
Total manufacturing cost	$ 90,600.55
Add work in process inventory, August 1	12,000.00
Total	$102,600.55
Less work in process inventory, August 31	46,134.15
Cost of goods manufactured during the month at predetermined application rates	$ 56,466.40
Add underapplied factory overhead	13.45
Cost of goods manufactured during the month	$ 56,479.85

Mountain Oak Office Interiors
Income Statement
For the Month Ended August 31, 19—

Net sales		$93,012.75
Less cost of goods sold:		
Finished goods inventory, August 1	$14,000.00	
Add cost of goods manufactured	56,479.85	
Goods available for sale	$70,479.85	
Less finished goods inventory, August 31	14,658.75	
Cost of goods sold		55,821.10
Gross margin on sales		$37,191.65
Operating expenses:		
Salaries	$12,500.00	
Public relations expense	2,865.00	
Office expense	2,250.00	
Doubtful accounts expense	930.00	
Payroll tax expense—salaries	1,625.00	
Amortization expense	130.00	
Miscellaneous general expense	976.00	
Total operating expenses		21,276.00
Income from operations		$15,915.65
Other revenue:		
Purchase discounts	$ 186.00	
Interest income	48.34	234.34
		$16,149.99
Other expense:		
Interest expense		31.53
Income before provision for income tax	$16,118.46	
Less income tax (estimated)		5,104.00
Net income		$11,014.46

ufacturing statement for any part of the year, the amount of any under-applied overhead should be added in computing the actual cost of the goods manufactured during the period. Any overapplied overhead should be subtracted in computing the actual cost of the goods manufactured.

Income Statement. The income statement follows the traditional form. The gross margin on sales is shown first, followed by the income from operations, and finally the income both before and after deducting income tax. The provision for income tax is based on an estimate, because the actual amount of the tax cannot be computed until the income for the year is determined and the tax rates applicable to the year are known.

Balance Sheet. It should be noted that the accounts are listed in the balance sheet in the order of their arrangement in the chart of accounts. Thus, the current assets appear first in the assets section of the balance sheet, followed by plant assets and goodwill. In the liabilities section, the current liabilities are listed first, followed by the long-term liabilities and capital. In practice, the arrangement of items will depend on the uses for which the balance sheet is intended. If it is to be submitted to a bank with application for a loan, the form of balance sheet to which the particular bank is accustomed would be desirable. If it is prepared at the end of the year for inclusion in the report to stockholders, it should be arranged so as to be most informative to them. If it is prepared monthly for the use of the principal executives, the items may be expressed in more technical language than would be advisable if it were to be submitted to the stockholders.

ADJUSTING ENTRIES

After the financial statements have been prepared, the adjustments entered on the work sheet are journalized as follows and posted to the accounts to bring them into agreement with the statements.

Adjusting Entries, August 31

Interest Receivable	48.34	
Interest Income		48.34
Increase in accrued interest receivable.		
Interest Expense	31.53	
Interest Payable		31.53
Increase in accrued interest payable.		
Doubtful Accounts Expense	930.00	
Allowance for Doubtful Accounts		930.00
Increase in allowance for doubtful accounts.		
Provision for Income Tax	5,104.00	
Estimated Income Tax Payable		5,104.00
Provision for estimated income tax applicable to the income for August.		

Mountain Oak Office Interiors
Balance Sheet
August 31, 19—

Current assets:

Cash		$ 20,017.00	
Petty cash		200.00	
Marketable securities		6,050.00	
Notes receivable		10,000.00	
Interest receivable		150.00	
Accounts receivable	$ 45,935.75		
Less allowance for doubtful accounts	3,230.00	42,705.75	
Finished goods		14,658.75	
Work in process		46,134.15	
Materials		25,036.00	
Prepaid insurance		4,500.00	
Total current assets			$169,451.65

Property, plant, and equipment:

Land		$ 26,300.00	
Buildings	$ 80,000.00		
Less accumulated depreciation	12,325.00	67,675.00	
Machinery	$120,000.00		
Less accumulated depreciation	24,825.00	95,175.00	
Furniture and fixtures	$ 15,000.00		
Less accumulated depreciation	5,605.00	9,395.00	
Small tools	$ 16,500,00		
Less accumulated depreciation	9,295.00	7,205.00	
Total property, plant, and equipment			205,750.00

Intangibles:

Organization Costs	3,700.00
Trademarks	1,470.00
Total assets	$380,371.65

Liabilities

Current liabilities:

Notes payable	$ 7,000.00
Accounts payable	24,855.00
FICA tax payable	440.00
Federal unemployment tax payable	990.00
State unemployment tax payable	3,915.00
Employees income tax payable	1,100.00
Property tax payable	2,400.00
Estimated income tax payable	20,804.00
Interest payable	133.75
Wages Payable	5,500.00

Total current liabilities		$ 67,137.75
Long-term liability:		
Bonds payable		25,000.00
Total liabilities		$ 92,137.75
Stockholders' Equity		
Capital stock	$200,000.00	
Retained earnings, August 1 . . . $77,219.44		
Net income for month 11,014.46		
Retained earnings, August 31	88,233.90	
Total stockholders' equity		288,233.90
Total liabilities and stockholders' equity		$380,371.65

CLOSING ENTRIES

Mountain Oak Office Interiors prepares monthly financial statements but does not close the temporary accounts until the end of the fiscal year. However, to illustrate the procedure in closing the accounts of a manufacturing company, the closing entries that would be required if the accounts were to be closed at the end of August are journalized as follows and are posted to the accounts on pages 221 to 228.

Closing Entries, August 31

Cost of Goods Sold	13.45	
Under- and Overapplied Overhead		13.45
Underapplied overhead transferred to Cost of Goods Sold.		
Sales	93,012.75	
Purchase Discounts	186.00	
Interest Income	48.34	
Income Summary		93,247.09
Closing the income accounts to Income Summary.		
Income Summary	82,232.63	
Cost of Goods Sold		55,821.10
Salaries		12,500.00
Payroll Tax Expense—Salaries		1,625,00
Office Expense		2,250.00
Public Relations Expense		2,865.00
Amortization Expense		130.00
Doubtful Accounts Expense		930.00
Miscellaneous General Expense		976.00
Interest Expense		31.53
Provision for Income Tax		5,104.00
Closing the cost of goods sold and expense accounts to Income Summary.		

| Income Summary | . . . . | 11,014.46 | |
| Retained Earnings | . . . . | | 11,014.46 |

Balance of the income summary account transferred to Retained Earnings.

LEARNING OBJECTIVE
Complete the Mountain Oak Office Interiors (MOOI) practice set

The Mountain Oak Office Interiors practice set contains the transactions for the month of September.

QUESTIONS

This chapter reviews subjects discussed in previous chapters. These chapters should be referred to for answers to some of the following questions, exercises, and problems.

1. What is the relationship between planning and control? How does a cost accounting system contribute to the planning and control processes.

2. A manufacturer of an electronic component ran short of a part needed to complete an assembly. The shortage occurred because the purchasing department inaccurately estimated the materials requirements. The required parts were shipped by air freight at a cost of $4,000. When these materials are shipped by regular transportation methods, these items cost $3,600. How would you recommend recording the amount paid for these rush-order materials?

3. Due to an improperly adjusted machine, 50 of the 200 units produced during the day on a job order are damaged beyond repair. How should these units be accounted for?

4. A company that uses departmental predetermined rates is considering changing to a blanket predetermined rate for all departments. The controller believes the change will substantially reduce accounting costs because only one rate will have to be developed and applied to all production. Do you believe the "saving" is justifiable?

5. Mountain Oak Office Interiors is organized on a departmental basis. What are the names of the departments and which are service departments and which are production departments?

6. What subsidiary ledgers are maintained for Mountain Oak Office Interiors? What are the numbers and titles of their control accounts in the general ledger?

7. What are the names of the books of original entry used by Mountain Oak Office Interiors?

8. Are the deductions for FICA tax and employees' income tax entered in the voucher register at the time of recording the voucher or in the check register at the time of recording the payroll check?

9. What forms are used in accounting for materials? What is the purpose of each form?

10. What control accounts are affected and how are they affected by the general journal entry required at the end of each month to record materials requisitioned during the month?

11. What forms are used in accounting for labor and what is the purpose of each?

12. How is the control account for factory overhead closed at the end of each month?

13. Assume that the machine hour method is used to apply factory overhead and that the following estimates were made for each department:

	Total Machine Hours for the Year	Total Factory Overhead for the Year
Dept. A	170,400	$86,904
Dept. B	117,600	85,848
Dept. C	40,800	11,016

What amount should be charged to the work in process account for the month of August if the departments used the following number of machine hours?

Department A—15,100 hours
Department B—11,000 hours
Department C— 3,750 hours

14. Refer to the ledger of Mountain Oak Office Interiors. What are the balances of the Accounts Receivable, Prepaid Insurance, and Small Tools (net book value) at the end of August?

15. Refer to the ledger of Mountain Oak Office Interiors. What is the amount of the under- and overapplied overhead for each production department at the end of August?

16. Refer to the financial statements of Mountain Oak Office Interiors prepared at the end of August and ascertain the following:

   a. Cost of goods manufactured during August.
   b. Cost of goods sold during August.
   c. Net income for August.
   d. Current assets as of the end of August.

EXERCISES

E5-1
Journal entries and cost of goods manufactured statement

Certain selected accounts from the general ledger of the Browning Manufacturing Company follow:

Work in Process		
21,870.00	38,300.00	
25,210.00		
8,250.00		

Materials		
1/1	6,850.00	24,850.00
	........*	
1/3 Bal.	10,525.00	

Payroll	
27,400.00	27,400.00

Factory Overhead	
2,980.00	........*
2,190.00	
3,562.00	
........*	

Under- and Overapplied Overhead	
482	

*To be computed.

From an analysis of these accounts, complete the following requirements:
   a. Make all entries, in general journal form, that were made during the month to the various manufacturing accounts. (For recording payroll

taxes, use the arbitrary rates of: FICA, 8%; federal income tax, 10%; federal unemployment tax, 1%; and state unemployment tax, 4%.)

b. Prepare a statement of cost of goods manufactured.

c. If the ending work in process balance has the same proportion of materials, labor, and factory overhead as the goods processed during the month, how much of each cost is included in the ending balance?

d. If the average cost of direct labor per hour was $10, what is the overhead application rate based on direct labor hours, rounded to the nearest whole cent?

E5-2
Journal entry for factory overhead and worksheet and journal entries for distributing service department costs

The Nooksack Backpack Company uses the job order cost system of accounting. Following is a summary of the factory overhead incurred during the month of May. The information needed to prepare this summary was obtained from the accounts in the subsidiary factory overhead ledger.

Summary of Factory Overhead for May

Account	Dept. A Layout & Cutting	Dept. B Sewing	Dept. C Maintenance	Dept. D Pattern Making	Total
Depreciation	$1,400.00	$1,250.00	$ 700.00	$ 250.00	$ 3,600.00
Property tax	75.00	50.00	25.00	12.00	162.00
Insurance	100.00	75.00	20.00	10.00	205.00
Power	100.00	50.00	35.00	10.00	195.00
Indirect materials	2,000.00	1,600.00	590.00	440.00	4,630.00
Indirect labor	900.00	500.00	600.00	300.00	2,300.00
Heat, light, and power	200.00	150.00	85.00	25.00	460.00
Payroll taxes	245.00	110.00	95.00	70.00	520.00
Total	$5,020.00	$3,785.00	$2,150.00	$1,117.00	$12,072.00

Departments C and D of the Nooksack Backpack Company are service departments. Departments A and B are production departments. Department C expenses are distributed to Departments A, B, and D on the basis of the number of square feet occupied by each department, as follows:

Department	Area (Square Feet)
A	16,000
B	12,000
D	6,000

Department D expenses are distributed to the production departments on a basis of 65% to A and 35% to B.

a. Make an entry, in general journal form, to distribute the factory overhead expenses to the proper departments.

b. Prepare a work sheet showing the proper distribution of the service department expenses. Make the required entries, in general journal form, to record the distribution of the service department expenses to the production departments. (Round answers to the nearest whole cent.)

E5-3
Job cost, variances,
journal entry

Saguaro Corporation, using a job order cost system, has compiled the following data on work started during the week:

Job	Direct Materials	Direct Labor Hours
206	$ 2,750	220
207	3,100	240
208	2,500	180
209	1,500	110
210	1,850	130
211	2,100	150
212	800	70
213	1,000	50
214	600	30
	$16,200	1,180

The direct labor rate is $12 an hour. The overhead rate is $9 per direct labor hour. The actual factory overhead costs for the week were $11,127. Jobs 206, 207, 208, and 211 were completed.

a. Compute the total cost of each job for the week.
b. Compute the under- or overapplied factory overhead for the week.
c. Compute the work in process at the end of the week.
d. Make a general journal entry to transfer the completed jobs to finished goods.

E5-4
Scrap material

The Meridian Company manufactures a product that starts in Department A and is finished in Department B. All materials required for the product are issued in Department A. When the materials are introduced in Department A, about 10% are usually spoiled and have to be sold as scrap. The receipts from the sale of scrap are credited to the department.
    Meridian incurred the following costs for one month's production:

	Department A	Department B
Materials	$ 37,800	-0-
Direct labor	61,400	$20,400
Factory overhead	58,000	22,600
	$157,200	$43,000

Receipts from the sale of scrap during the month amounted to $1,200. Production data for the month were as follows:

	Department A	Department B
Units started or received from preceding department	13,000	11,500
Units spoiled (material only)	1,500	
Units completed and transferred	11,500	11,500

a. Prepare a schedule that shows the unit cost of production in Department A, Department B, and in total.
b. Suppose that Department B, at the point of final inspection before the goods are transferred to finished goods, discards 750 units as spoiled with no salvage value. How much will the total cost per unit increase if this spoilage is not charged to factory overhead?

PROBLEMS

P5-1
Effect of change in capacity on unit costs

Sailboards Unlimited has just negotiated a labor contract that increases direct labor costs by 10%. The company is already experiencing a serious decline in sales and profit. As a consequence, the CEO has requested production and sales statistics, which include the following:

a. The maximum capacity the plant can achieve is 20,000 units per year. At this capacity, the production costs will be as follows:

Materials		$ 550,000
Direct labor		3,000,000
Factory overhead:		
Fixed cost	$500,000	
Variable cost	800,000	1,300,000
Total		$4,850,000

b. Sales are not expected to exceed 18,000 units per year, nor can the units be sold for more than $400 per unit because of market competition.
c. To maintain its position in the industry, a 35% gross margin on sales should be realized on a volume of 16,000 units per year.
d. A cost study shows that at 16,000 units per year, fixed costs can be reduced by 60%, and the possibility exists of reducing the variable factory overhead costs.

Required:

1. What are the unit costs for materials, labor, and overhead at the 20,000 unit level? What is the gross margin per unit?
2. If direct labor costs increase by 10% but only 16,000 units are produced and sold, what is the gross margin per unit?
3. What unit cost will result if at the 20,000 unit capacity, the fixed costs are reduced by 60%, labor cost increases 10%, and 16,000 units are produced and sold?
4. At the 16,000 unit level for production and sales, with a 60% fixed cost reduction and 10% labor cost increase, how much per unit may variable factory overhead be increased while still achieving a 35% gross margin?

P5-2
Calculation of budget and capacity variances

The Van Zee Company has accumulated the following data pertaining to factory overhead costs for the year. Each department is budgeted for $17,000 of fixed costs for the year. The company uses the direct labor hour method of applying factory overhead to the jobs.

	Department A	Department B	Department C
Total budgeted factory overhead	$52,500	$76,000	$105,000
Budgeted direct labor hours	12,000	16,000	20,000
Total actual factory overhead	$47,000	$83,500	$105,000
Actual direct labor hours	10,500	17,800	20,000

Required:

1. Compute the predetermined overhead rate for each department.
2. Compute the variable and fixed portions of the predetermined overhead rate.
3. Compute the under- or overapplied factory overhead for each department.

(Hint: To successfully complete all parts of this problem, first compare the overhead application rate for each department and then divide it into its fixed and variable components.)

P5-3
Review of job order cost procedures

The Rosebud Manufacturing Company uses a job order cost system. The balances in the inventory accounts on September 1 were as follows:

Finished Goods	$265,650
Work in Process	114,280
Materials	115,540

The job cost sheets on September 1 contained the following data:

Job	Materials	Labor	Overhead	Total
1234	$ 1,150	$ 2,400	$ 3,600	$ 7,150
1235	3,150	3,500	4,900	11,550
1238	4,190	5,200	7,800	17,190
1244	2,560	3,850	5,390	11,800
1250	11,500	17,500	24,500	53,500
1251	3,850	3,850	5,390	13,090
Total	$26,400	$36,300	$51,580	$114,280

The transactions for September were as follows:

a. Materials purchased, $85,500.
b. Materials requisitioned by the factory were as follows:

Job 1234	$ 2,700
Job 1235	3,200
Job 1244	2,500
Job 1252	6,700
Job 1253	4,800
Job 1254	5,500
Job 1255	12,000
Indirect Materials—Dept. A	5,400
Indirect Materials—Dept. B	4,800
Indirect Materials—Dept. C	2,700
Total	$50,300

c. Actual labor costs incurred were as follows:

Job	Dept. A	Dept. B	Dept. C	Total
1234		$ 900	$ 600	$ 1,500
1235	$ 1,200	500	800	2,500
1238	1,000	1,600	2,700	5,300
1244	1,400	1,100	500	3,000
1250	1,500	3,200	1,300	6,000
1251	1,700	900	1,500	4,100
1252	2,100	2,200	700	5,000
1253	1,600	1,600	1,200	4,400
1254	1,300	1,400	900	3,600
1255	5,500	4,000	1,300	10,800
Indirect	7,000	3,200	4,300	14,500
Total	$24,300	$20,600	$15,800	$60,700

d. Other factory overhead costs were as follows:

	Dept. A	Dept. B	Dept. C	Total
Supervision	$ 1,500	$ 1,300	$ 900	$ 3,700
Heat, light, and water	1,600	1,200	2,100	4,900
Maintenance	800	500	1,100	2,400
Payroll taxes, vacation				
pay, etc.	8,800	8,300	6,500	23,600
Depreciation	4,200	2,800	3,700	10,700
Miscellaneous	700	500	800	2,000
Total	$17,600	$14,600	$15,100	$47,300

e. The direct labor cost method is used to apply factory overhead to the jobs. The rates for the departments are as follows:

Dept. A—150%
Dept. B—130%
Dept. C—180%

f. The jobs completed and transferred to finished goods were Jobs 1234, 1235, 1238, 1244, and 1251.

g. Finished goods sold totaled $247,600.

Required:

1. Set up individual job cost sheets, and record the September costs for each job.
2. Record the beginning balances in the inventory accounts. Record the September transactions in inventory, overhead, and cost of goods sold accounts. Each department has a factory overhead account.
3. Compute the under- or overapplied overhead for each department.
4. Prepare a statement of cost of goods manufactured.

P5-4
Service department allocations and determining overhead rates

The Duval Manufacturing Company has two production departments (grinding and shaping) and three service departments (general factory administration, factory maintenance, and factory cafeteria). A summary of overhead costs and other data for each department prior to allocation of service department costs follows:

	General Factory Admin.	Factory Mainte- nance	Factory Cafeteria	Grinding	Shaping	Total
Indirect labor	$90,000	$82,100	$87,000	$1,950,000	$2,050,000	$4,259,100
Indirect material		65,000	91,000	3,130,000	950,000	4,236,000
Other factory overhead	70,000	56,100	62,000	1,650,000	1,850,000	3,688,100
Direct labor hours				562,500	437,500	1,000,000
Number of employees	12	8	20	280	200	520
Square footage occupied . . .	1,750	2,000	4,800	88,000	72,000	168,550

The costs of the general factory administration department, factory maintenance department, and factory cafeteria are allocated on the basis of direct labor hours, square footage occupied, and number of employees, respectively.

Required:

1. Allocate the service departments' costs directly to production without inter-service department cost allocation and compute an overhead rate for each production department based on direct labor hours.
2. Allocate the service departments' costs sequentially, starting with the service department with the greatest total costs, to other service departments as well as to the production departments. Compute an overhead rate for each production department based on direct labor hours.
3. Explain which of the previous methods of service department cost allocation you would choose for this company.

(AICPA adapted)

P5-5
Comprehensive review of job order procedures

The Kooy Chrome Company manufactures special chromed parts made to the order and specifications of the customer. It has two production departments, stamping and plating, and two service departments, power and maintenance. In any production department, the job in process is wholly completed before the next job is started.

The company operates on a fiscal year which ends September 30. Following is the post-closing trial balance as of September 30:

Kooy Chrome Company
Post-Closing Trial Balance
September 30, 19—

Cash	22,500	
Accounts Receivable	21,700	
Finished Goods	8,750	
Work in Process	3,600	
Materials	15,000	
Prepaid Insurance	4,320	
Factory Building	64,000	
Accum. Depr.—Factory Building		22,500
Machinery and Equipment	38,000	
Accum. Depr.—Machinery and Equipment		16,000
Office Equipment	10,500	
Accum. Depr.—Office Equipment		7,500
Accounts Payable		2,500
FICA Tax Payable		3,120
Federal Unemployment Tax Payable		364
State Unemployment Tax Payable		1,404
Employees Income Tax Payable		5,200
Capital Stock		75,000
Retained Earnings		54,782
	188,370	188,370

Additional information:

1. The balance of the materials account represents the following:

Materials	Units	Unit Cost	Total
A	120	$25	$ 3,000
B	320	15	4,800
C	180	30	5,400
Factory Supplies			1,800
			$15,000

The company uses the FIFO method of accounting for all inventories. Material A is used in the stamping department and materials B and C in the plating department.

2. The balance of the work in process account represents the following costs that are applicable to Job 905. (The customer's order is for 1,000 units of the finished product.)

Direct materials	$1,500
Direct labor	1,200
Factory overhead	900
	$3,600

3. The finished goods account reflects the cost of Job 803, which was finished at the end of the preceding month and is awaiting delivery orders from the customer.
4. At the beginning of the year, factory overhead application rates were based on the following data:

	Stamping Dept.	Plating Dept.
Estimated factory overhead for the year . .	$145,000	$115,500
Estimated direct labor hours for the year . .	29,000	6,000

In October, the following transactions were recorded:
a. Purchased the following materials and supplies on account:

Material A	1,100 units @ $26
Material B	900 units @ $17
Material C	800 units @ $28
Factory Supplies	$3,200

b. The following materials were issued to the factory:

	Job 905	Job 1001	Job 1002
Material A		600 units	400 units
Material B		400 units	200 units
Material C	200 units	400 units	
Factory Supplies—$2,450			

Customers' orders covered by Jobs 1001 and 1002 are for 1,000 and 500 units of finished product, respectively.

c. Factory wages and office, sales, and administrative salaries are paid at the end of each month. The following data, provided from an analysis of labor time tickets and salary schedules, will be sufficient for the preparation of the entries to voucher the payroll. (Assume FICA and federal income tax rates of 8% and 10%, respectively.) Record the company's liability for state and federal unemployment taxes. (Assume rates of 4% and 1%, respectively.) Record the payroll distribution for the month of October.

	Stamping Dept.	Plating Dept.
Job 905	100 hrs. @ $9	300 hrs. @ $11
Job 1001	1,200 hrs. @ $9	300 hrs. @ $11
Job 1002	800 hrs. @ $9	

Wages of the supervisors, custodial personnel, etc., totaled $9,500; and administrative salaries were $18,300.

d. Miscellaneous factory overhead incurred during the month totaled $4,230. Miscellaneous selling and administrative expenses were $1,500. Vouchers were prepared for these items as well as for the FICA tax and federal income tax withheld for September. (See account balances on the post-closing trial balance for September 30.)

e. Annual depreciation on plant assets is calculated using the following rates:

Factory buildings—5%
Machinery and equipment—20%
Office equipment—20%

f. The balance of the prepaid insurance account represents a three-year premium for a fire insurance policy covering the factory building and machinery. It was paid on the last day of the preceding month and became effective on October 1.

g. The summary of factory overhead prepared from the factory overhead ledger is reproduced below:

Summary of Factory Overhead for October

Trans-action	Account	Stamping	Plating	Power	Mainte-nance	Total
b.	Factory supplies	$ 940.00	$ 750.00	$ 260.00	$ 500.00	$ 2,450.00
c.	Indirect labor	3,780.00	2,860.00	970.00	1,890.00	9,500.00
c.	Payroll taxes	2,948.40	1,229.80	126.10	245.70	4,550.00
d.	Miscellaneous	1,692.00	1,410.00	752.00	376.00	4,230.00
e.	Depreciation	360.00	270.00	90.00	180.00	900.00
f.	Insurance	48.00	40.00	16.00	16.00	120.00
	Total	$9,768.40	$6,559.80	$2,214.10	$3,207.70	$21,750.00

h. The total expenses of the maintenance department are distributed on the basis of floor space occupied by the power department (8,820 sq. ft.), stamping department (19,500 sq. ft.), and plating department (7,875 sq. ft.). The power department expenses are then allocated equally to the stamping and plating departments.

i. After the actual factory expenses have been distributed to the departmental accounts and the applied factory overhead has been recorded and posted, any balances in the departmental accounts are transferred to Under- and Overapplied Overhead.

j. Jobs 905 and 1001 were finished during the month. Job 1002 is still in process at the end of the month.

k. During the month, Jobs 803 and 905 were sold at a markup of 150% on cost.

l. Received $55,500 from customers in payment of their accounts.

m. Checks were issued during the month in the amount of $57,500 for payment of vouchers.

Required:

1. Set up the beginning trial balance in T-accounts.
2. Prepare materials inventory ledger cards and enter October 1 balances.
3. Set up job cost sheets as needed.
4. Record all transactions and related entries in general journal entry form for the month of October and post to T-accounts.
5. Prepare a service department expense distribution work sheet for October.

6. At the end of the month

   a. Analyze the balance in the materials account, the work in process account, and the finished goods account.
   b. Prepare the statement of cost of goods manufactured, income statement, and balance sheet for October 30.

6

Process Cost Accounting— General Procedures

Cost accounting provides management with accurate information about the cost of manufacturing a product. The type of cost accounting system a business uses depends on the nature of its manufacturing operations. The preceding chapters focused on the job-order cost system. Chapters 6 and 7 focus on procedures applicable in a process cost system.

As mentioned in Chapter 1, standard cost accounting procedures may be used with a process cost system. Chapters 8 and 9 cover standard costs.

COMPARISON OF BASIC COST SYSTEMS

As explained in Chapter 1, a **job-order cost system** is appropriate when products are manufactured on a special order basis. **Process cost** is used when goods of a similar or homogeneous nature are manufactured in a continuous production operation.

The focal point of a job-order cost system is the *job*, even in a departmentalized factory. The costs of materials, labor, and overhead are accumulated for each job and divided by the number of units produced to determine the unit cost for the job. The primary objective of the system is to determine the cost of producing each completed job during the accounting period and the cost that has been incurred on each unfinished job. Management uses this information for inventory valuation and also for planning, control, and measuring performance.

The focus of a process cost system is the **cost center**, which, as discussed in Chapter 1, is a unit within the factory to which costs are practically and equitably assigned. It is usually a department, but it could be a process or an operation. Costs accumulated by a cost center are divided by the number of units produced to compute the cost per unit. The primary objectives, like that of the job-order cost system, are to compute the unit cost of the products manufactured and the cost to be assigned to the units in process at the end of the period.

Many of the procedures utilized for job-order cost accounting also apply to process cost accounting. The main difference in the two methods is the manner in which costs are accumulated.

MATERIALS AND LABOR COSTS

Under the job-order cost system, the costs of materials and labor, as determined from the summaries of materials requisitions and time tickets, are charged to specific jobs or orders. Under the process cost system, the costs of materials and labor are charged directly to the departments where they are incurred. However, the indirect materials and indirect labor costs that cannot be directly associated with a particular department are charged to Factory Overhead, such as custodial supplies for the factory and the salary of a supervisor responsible for several departments.

A process system requires less clerical effort than a job-order cost system because some of the direct and indirect materials and labor are not separated and costs are charged to a few departments rather than to many jobs. For example, in a process cost system, detailed time tickets might be eliminated completely. In a job-order cost system, if a typical factory employee works on several different jobs, the total hours worked are allocated to those jobs. Whereas in a process cost system, the worker's time is generally assigned to the department where the work occurred.

Other than these limited differences, the procedures for acquiring, controlling, accounting for, and paying for materials and labor are similar in both systems. At the end of each month, the materials requisitions summary provides the data for the journal entry debiting Work in Process and Factory Overhead and crediting Materials. Similarly, the labor cost summary provides the data for the journal entry debiting Work in Process and Factory Overhead and crediting Payroll.

FACTORY OVERHEAD COSTS

In a process cost system, overhead costs are accumulated from the various journals in the same manner as in a job-order cost system. The actual costs for the period are collected in a general ledger control account to which postings are made from the general journal (for certain indirect materials, indirect labor, and fixed costs), from the voucher register, and from other appropriate journals. The control account is supported by a subsidiary ledger, which consists of factory overhead analysis sheets that show the detailed allocation of costs to the departments. At the end of the month, based on the data reflected in the analysis sheets, the total actual factory overhead is distributed to the departmentalized overhead accounts.

Service Departments. As with job-order cost accounting, the applicable factory overhead is charged to the service departments. Service department expenses are distributed to the production departments. A distribution work sheet is prepared showing the allocation of each service department's expenses to other service departments and to the production departments. A journal entry records the distribution of the service departments' expenses to the production departments and thus closes the service departments' accounts for factory overhead. Service department costs will not be considered in the following discussion because the fundamentals were developed in Chapter 4.

Application of Factory Overhead. In the job order cost system, overhead is applied to the jobs through predetermined rates. The use of predetermined rates is also common in a process cost system, but overhead is applied to departments rather than jobs. As in the job-order cost system, the amount of overhead applied is calculated by multiplying the predetermined rate by the selected base. The base may be direct labor cost,

"BATCH OF ONE" PROCESSING

Process cost accounting is suitable in manufacturing situations where all units of the final product are substantially identical. This type of operation produces a continuous output of homogeneous products. Industries of this type include those manufacturing automobiles, tires, chemicals, canned goods, lumber, paper, candy, foodstuffs, flour, glass, soap, toothpaste, and many other products.

Customers today demand variety in products. Businesses are faced with the challenge of producing products quickly and effectively while meeting this demand. An article in *Management Accounting* explains how industries that have produced products in large batches over long production runs are changing some of their production processes:

A combination of programmable automation and workers empowered to make decisions—"smart" technologies and "smart" people—provides an opportunity to break out of the dilemma of traditional mass production. A new "simple idea" is emerging and displacing the traditional model of economies of scale. It is the "batch of one" or "mass customization"—the ability to produce a customized batch, as small as a lot of one, at mass production prices.

This idea may seem to be an oxymoron. How could small to medium batch runs be more economical than continuous process?

The "economics of flexibility" are achieved through short cycle times, flexible automation, and the ability to do quick changeovers with little or no production stoppage or cost penalty. People are as important to the production as technology. Pushing down decision making to the line and empowering teams of employees allows the variety to be handled without cumbersome approvals and delays.

The result is variety at low cost. For example, different car models come down the line. The first may be a station wagon bound for Australia. The equipment reads a bar code and then locks into a certain pattern of steps. The next vehicle may be a sports car bound for North America. The bar code is read once again, and the software-drive equipment executes a different pattern. Changeover is instantaneous and virtually costless.

Gerald H. B. Ross, "Revolution in Management Control," *Management Accounting* (November 1990), pp. 23–27.

direct labor hours, machine hours, or any other method that will equitably distribute overhead to the departments in proportion to the benefit received by that department. Under- or overapplied overhead is treated in the same manner as discussed in Chapter 4.

PRODUCT COST IN A PROCESS COST SYSTEM

A basic principle established, in comparing the two cost systems, is that in a process cost system all costs of manufacturing are charged to production departments, either directly or indirectly. The unit cost in each department is calculated by dividing the total cost charged to the department by the number of units produced during the period. The total cost of each item finished equals the combined unit costs of all departments used in the manufacture of the product.

NONDEPARTMENTALIZED FACTORY

When the factory is operated as a single department producing a single product in a continuous output, the process cost system is relatively simple. The costs of operating the factory are summarized at the end of each accounting period. Then the total costs incurred are divided by the quantity of units produced to calculate the cost of each unit manufactured during the period.

The following cost of production summary illustrates this procedure:

Materials	$ 50,000
Labor	75,000
Factory overhead	35,000
Total cost of production	$160,000
Unit output for period	40,000 units
Unit cost for period	$4.00*

*$160,000 ÷ 40,000 units = $4

DEPARTMENTALIZED FACTORY

Generally, a company has several production and service departments. Products accumulate costs as they pass through each successive production department. Departments record costs according to the following procedure: (1) the costs of the service departments are allocated to the production departments; (2) the costs added by prior departments are carried over to successive departments; and (3) the costs of materials and labor directly identifiable with a department, as well as applied overhead, are charged to the department. The unit cost within a department is calculated by dividing the total costs by the number of units produced during the period.

WORK IN PROCESS INVENTORIES

If there is no work in process at the end of an accounting period, calculating the unit cost under the process cost system is a simple procedure: merely divide the total cost incurred for the period by number of units produced. However, each department will usually have work in process at the end of each accounting period. The calculation of unfinished work in process presents one of the most important and difficult problems in process cost accounting.

Normally, a factory will have units in varying stages of completion:

1. Units started and finished during the current period
2. Units started in a prior period and completed during the current period
3. Units started during the current period but not finished

Because materials, labor, and overhead may have been applied to each of the unfinished items, such charges cannot be ignored in computing the cost of all units. Therefore, consideration must be given to not only the number of items finished during the period but also the units in process at the beginning and at the end of the period. The primary problem is allocating total cost between (1) units finished during the period and (2) units still in process at the end of the period.

Two procedures are commonly used for assigning costs to the inventories: the **average cost method** and the **first-in, first-out (FIFO) method**. The average cost method is discussed and illustrated in the remainder of this chapter. Chapter 7 covers the first-in, first-out method.

AVERAGE COST METHOD

LEARNING OBJECTIVE
Assign costs to inventories using the average cost method

Under the **average cost method**, the cost of the work in process at the beginning of the period is added to the production costs incurred in the current period. Average unit cost for the period is then calculated by dividing the total costs (beginning inventory plus current costs) by the total equivalent production. **Equivalent production** represents the number of units that could have been completed during a period using the production costs incurred during the period. For example, if 1,000 units were 50% completed, they are considered in terms of "equivalents" as 500 units, 100% completed. Therefore, calculating equivalent production requires that the ending work in process be restated in terms of completed units. To illustrate, assume that the production costs of a department during a given period are as follows:

LEARNING OBJECTIVE
Explain and use the concept of equivalent production

Materials	$12,000
Labor	18,000
Factory overhead	6,000
Total cost of production	$36,000

If 18,000 units are produced during the period and no work in process exists, either at the beginning or end of the period, the unit cost of production is easily calculated to be $2 ($36,000 ÷ 18,000), and $36,000 would be transferred to Finished Goods in the general ledger.

Assume, instead, that the production report for the period shows no beginning work in process, 17,000 units are completed during the period, and the ending inventory consists of 2,000 units. The problem is to allocate the production cost for the period, $36,000, between the goods completed and the goods still in process. What portion of the total production cost was incurred during the month by the remaining 2,000 units in process?

If the 2,000 units are almost finished, more cost should be assigned to these unfinished units than would have been incurred if they had just been started in process. To make an accurate measurement, the stage of completion of the units still in process must considered. **Stage of completion** represents the fraction or percentage of materials, labor, and overhead costs of a completed unit that has been applied to goods that have not been completed. The department manager estimates the stage of completion. The possibility of error is minimized because the manager usually has the skills and the familiarity with the work to make reliable estimates.

At the end of the accounting period, the department manager submits a **production report** showing the following:

1. Number of units in the beginning work in process
2. Number of units completed
3. Number of units in the ending work in process and their estimated stage of completion

Assume 2,000 units in process are one-half completed. If materials, labor, and overhead are applied evenly throughout the process, one half of the total cost for completing 2,000 units can be applied to these units. Expressed in another way, the cost to bring these 2,000 units to the halfway point of completion is equivalent to the cost of fully completing 1,000 units. Therefore, in terms of equivalent production, 2,000 units one-half completed equal 1,000 units fully completed. Unit cost is calculated as follows:

Units finished during the period 17,000
Equivalent units of work in process at the end
　　of the period (2,000 units one-half completed) 1,000
Equivalent production for the period . . . . 18,000 units

$36,000 ÷ 18,000 = $2 unit cost for the month.

The inventory cost can now be calculated as follows:

Transferred to finished goods (17,000 units at $2) $34,000
Work in process (2,000 units × 1/2 × $2) 2,000
　　Total production costs accounted for $36,000

You should now be able to work the following: Exercises 1, 2, 3, 4 and Problems 1, 2.

LEARNING OBJECTIVE
Prepare a cost of production summary

Cost of Production Summary. In a process cost system, the reporting of production and related costs in each department involves the following:

1. Accumulating costs for which the department is accountable
2. Calculating equivalent production for the period
3. Computing the unit cost for the period
4. Summarizing the disposition of the production costs

These data are reported on a **cost of production summary**, which presents the necessary information for inventory valuation and serves as a source for summary journal entries. The procedures previously discussed are further developed through the four illustrative problems that follow.

LEARNING OBJECTIVE
Compute unit costs with and without beginning inventories when there is one department

Illustrative Problem No. 1—Computing the unit cost when there is no beginning inventory and only one department.

The Toy Factory manufactures a plastic toy on a continuous basis for inventory stock. The small factory operates as a single department and places finished goods in stock to be withdrawn as orders are received. At the end of January, the first month of operation for the company, the factory supervisor submits the January **production report**, Figure 6-1. The estimate of the stage of completion indicates that the units in process at the end of the month were, on the average, about one-half completed.

After receiving the production report, the accountant begins the cost of production summary by collecting the period's production costs

FIGURE 6-1   Production Report, January 31

PRODUCTION REPORT

For Month Ending <u>January 31, 19--</u>

In process, beginning of month <u>   none   </u>

Finished during the month <u>   4,900 units   </u>

In process, end of month <u>   200 units   </u>

Estimated stage of completion of work in process, end of month <u>1/2</u>

Remarks

<u>R.L.B.</u>
Supervisor

---

from summaries of materials requisitions, payroll, and factory overhead analysis sheets. The units in process are then converted to equivalent units. The estimate that the 200 units in process are one-half completed means that one-half the total cost of the materials, labor, and factory overhead needed to produce 200 units has been incurred. The equivalent of 200 units in process, one-half completed, is 100 units. Therefore, the costs incurred in partially completing 200 units is considered to be equivalent to the total cost of producing 100 units. The cost of producing 4,900 fully completed units and 200 units one-half completed during the month is equivalent to producing 5,000 fully completed units.

The Toy Factory
Cost of Production Summary
For the Month Ended January 31, 19—

Cost of production for month:
  Materials . . . . $ 5,000
  Labor   3,000
  Factory overhead   2,000
    Total costs to be accounted for **$10,000**

Unit output for month:
  Finished during month   4,900
  Equivalent units of work in process, end
    of month (200 units, one-half completed)   100
    Total equivalent production   5,000

Unit cost for month:
  Materials ($5,000 ÷ 5,000 units) $1.00
  Labor ($3,000 ÷ 5,000 units) 60
  Factory overhead ($2,000 ÷ 5,000 units) 40
    Total $2.00

Inventory costs:
  Cost of goods finished during month (4,900 × $2) . . . . . $ 9,800
  Cost of work in process, end of month:
    Materials (200 × 1/2 × $1) $100
    Labor (200 × 1/2 × $.60) 60
    Factory overhead (200 × 1/2 × $.40) 40   200
Total production costs accounted for **$10,000**

At the end of the month, the following journal entries record the factory operations for January:

Jan. 31 Work in Process   5,000
      Materials   5,000

    Work in Process *Applied*   3,000
      Payroll   3,000

Jan. 31 Factory Overhead   2,000
    Various accounts (Accumulated Depreciation,
    Prepaid Insurance, Accrued Taxes, Accounts
    Payable)   2,000

    Work in Process   2,000
      Factory Overhead   2,000

After preparing the cost of production summary, the accountant can make the following entry:

| Jan. 31 | Finished Goods | . . . . | 9,800 | |
| | Work in Process | . . . . | | 9,800 |

After posting these entries, the work in process account has a debit balance of $200, representing the valuation of the work in process on January 31, shown as follows:

Work in Process			
Jan. 31	5,000	Jan. 31	9,800
	3,000		
	2,000		
	10,000		
200			

The January statement of the cost of goods manufactured can now be prepared as follows:

The Toy Factory
Statement of Cost of Goods Manufactured
For the Month Ended January 31, 19—

Materials	$ 5,000
Labor	3,000
Factory overhead..	2,000
Total..	$10,000
Less work in process inventory, January 31	200
Cost of goods manufactured during the month..........................	$ 9,800

LEARNING OBJECTIVE
Compute unit costs with and without beginning inventories when there is one department

Illustrative Problem No. 2—Computing the unit cost when there is a beginning inventory and only one department.

At the end of February, the second month of operations for The Toy Factory, the factory supervisor submits the February production report, Figure 6-2.

FIGURE 6-2   Production Report, February 28

PRODUCTION REPORT
For Month Ending February 28, 19--

In process, beginning of month _____ 200 units

Finished during the month _____ 6,900 units

In process, end of month _____ 600 units

Estimated stage of completion of work in process, end of month 1/3

The cost of production summary for February is prepared as follows:

(handwritten: Study) *(handwritten: materials evenly)*

The Toy Factory
Cost of Production Summary
For the Month Ended February 28, 19—

Cost of work in process, beginning of month:*
Materials	$ 100	
Labor	60	
Factory overhead	40	$ 200

Cost of production for month:
Materials	$7,000	
Labor	4,200	
Factory overhead	2,800	14,000
Total costs to be accounted for		**$14,200**

Unit output for month:
Finished during month	6,900
Equivalent units of work in process, end of month (600 units, one-third completed)	200
Total equivalent production	7,100

Unit cost for month:
Materials [($100 + $7,000) ÷ 7,100]	$1.00
Labor [($60 + $4,200) ÷ 7,100]	.60
Factory overhead [($40 + $2,800) ÷ 7,100]	.40
Total	$2.00

Inventory costs:
Cost of goods finished during month (6,900 × $2)		$13,800
Cost of work in process, end of month:		
Materials (600 × 1/3 × $1)	$ 200	
Labor (600 × 1/3 × $.60)	120	
Factory overhead (600 × 1/3 × $.40)	80	400
Total production costs accounted for		**$14,200**

*The beginning inventory in February was the ending work in process inventory for the month of January.

All costs incurred or assigned must be accounted for. Therefore, the cost of the ending work in process in January, which is the beginning inventory in February, is added to the total costs incurred during the month of February. The calculation of unit output for the month includes the units finished during the month and the equivalent units in process at the end of the current month. The fact that one-half of the work had been completed on 200 units in the prior month does not have to be considered in this calculation because the cost of that work is added to the current month's costs for the purpose of calculating unit costs. This procedure is the identifying characteristic of the average costing method.

From the data developed on the cost of production summary, the following entry can now be made:

```
Feb. 28  Finished Goods . . . . . . . . . . . . . . . . . .   13,800
             Work in Process  . . . . . . . . . . . . . . . .          13,800
```

After posting this entry and the entries for the month's production costs, the work in process account has a debit balance of $400, as shown:

Work in Process			
Jan. 31	5,000	Jan. 31	9,800
	3,000		
	2,000		
	10,000		
	200		
Feb. 28	7,000	Feb. 28	13,800
	4,200		
	2,800		
	14,000		*23,600*
	400		

The following statement of the cost of goods manufactured can now be prepared:

The Toy Factory
Statement of Cost of Goods Manufactured
For the Month Ended February 28, 19—

Materials	$ 7,000
Labor	4,200
Factory overhead	2,800
Total	$14,000
Add work in process inventory, February 1	200
Total	$14,200
Less work in process inventory, February 28	400
Cost of goods manufactured during the month	$13,800

You should now be able to work the following: Exercises 4, 5, 6 and Problems 3, 4.

Illustrative Problem No. 3—Computing the unit cost when there are no beginning inventories and two or more departments.

The business of The Toy Factory continued to grow until management decided to departmentalize the factory and reorganize the cost records. Accordingly, on January 1 of the following year, the factory was divided into three departments as follows:

> Dept. A—Cutting
> Dept. B—Forming
> Dept. C—Painting

Separate control accounts are maintained in the general ledger to record the costs of operating each department. Departmental expense analysis sheets are used to record the manufacturing expenses incurred. Figure 6-3, 6-4, and 6-5 show the departmental production reports for January. Note there are no beginning inventories of work in process in any department.

After receiving the production reports from the department managers, the accountant prepares a cost of production summary for each department. Journal entries are then made from the cost of production summaries to record the operations of each department and to transfer costs.

FIGURE 6-3   Production Report, Dept. A—Cutting

PRODUCTION REPORT

For Month Ending January 31, 19--

Dept. A--Cutting

In process, beginning of period	none
Stage of completion	
Placed in process during period	3,700 unit
Received from dept. _____ during period	
Transferred to dept. B during period	2,700 units
Transferred to stockroom during period	none
In process, end of period	1,000 units
Stage of completion	1/2

Note the costs accumulated in the department are transferred to the next department along with the units completed during the period. Thus, costs follow the flow of goods through the manufacturing process.

The Toy Factory
Cost of Production Summary—Department A
For the Month Ended, January 31, 19—

Cost of production for month:		
Materials		$16,000
Labor		8,640
Factory overhead		7,360
Total costs to be accounted for		**$32,000**
Unit output for month:		
Finished and transferred to Dept. B during month		2,700
Equivalent units of work in process, end of month		
(1,000 units, one-half completed)		500
Total equivalent production		3,200
Unit cost for month:		
Materials ($16,000 ÷ 3,200 units)		$ 5.00
Labor ($8,640 ÷ 3,200 units)		2.70
Factory overhead ($7,360 ÷ 3,200 units)		2.30
Total		$10.00
Inventory costs:		
Cost of goods finished and transferred to Dept. B during		
month (2,700 × $10.00)		$27,000
Cost of work in process, end of month:		
Materials (1,000 × 1/2 × $5.00)	$2,500	
Labor (1,000 × 1/2 × $2.70)	1,350	
Factory overhead (1,000 × 1/2 × $2.30)	1,150	5,000
Total production costs accounted for		**$32,000**

After posting the usual end-of-month entries, the work in process account for Dept. A has a debit balance of $5,000. The balance represents the cost of the partially completed ending inventory.

Work in Process—Dept. A

Jan. 3		16,000	Jan. 31	27,000
		8,640		
		7,360		
		32,000		
	5,000			

FIGURE 6-4   Production Report, Dept. B—Forming

PRODUCTION REPORT

For Month Ending January 31, 19--

Dept. B-Forming

In process, beginning of period _____   none

Stage of completion   _____

Placed in process during period _____   none

Received from dept. ___A___ during period 2,700 units

Transferred to dept. ___C___ during period 2,200 units

Transferred to stockroom during period _____   none

In process, end of period _____   500 units

Stage of completion _____   2/5

The only difference in procedure between this problem and Illustrative Problem No. 1 is that the goods completed in Dept. A are transferred to Dept. B for further processing rather than being transferred to the stockroom as finished goods.

As the goods continue to flow through the manufacturing process, the units transferred and their related costs are treated as completed products in Dept. A but the units transferred to Dept. B are considered by Dept. B as raw materials that will be added at the beginning of Dept. B's processing operation. The transferred cost of the units includes the costs of materials, labor, and factory overhead incurred in Dept. A. However, the individual cost elements are combined and transferred in total to Dept. B.

In reviewing the cost of production summary for Dept. B, note that the calculation of unit cost for the month in Dept. B takes into consideration only those costs incurred for material, labor, and factory overhead during the month and the equivalent units produced in the department. The **transferred-in costs** and **units from the prior department** are not included in the computation.

However, in determining the cost transferred to Dept. C, the prior department costs, along with Dept. B's cost of work in process, must be considered. Also, in calculating the ending work in process valuation, the full cost of $10 per unit from Dept. A is attached to the 500 units still in process in Dept. B, because the transferred-in units have been fully completed by Dept. A, while only a fraction of cost of the additional work performed by Dept. B, based on the stage of completion, is considered.

The Toy Factory
Cost of Production Summary—Department B
For the Month Ended January 31, 19—

Cost of goods received from Dept. A during month			
(2,700 units × $10.00)			$27,000
Cost of production for month—Dept. B:			
Materials		$ 1,200	
Labor		3,000	
Factory overhead		1,800	6,000
Total costs to be accounted for			$33,000
Unit output for month:			
Finished and transferred to Dept. C during month			2,200
Equivalent units of work in process, end of month			
(500 units, two-fifths completed)			200
Total equivalent production			2,400
Unit cost for month—Dept. B:			
Materials ($1,200 ÷ 2,400 units)			$ .50
Labor ($3,000 ÷ 2,400 units)			1.25
Factory overhead ($1,800 ÷ 2,400 units)			.75
Total			$2.50
Inventory costs:			
Cost of goods finished and transferred to Dept. C			
during month:			
Cost in Dept. A (2,200 × $10.00)		$22,000	
Cost in Dept. B (2,200 × 2.50)		5,500	
(2,200 × $12.50)			$27,500
Cost of work in process, end of month:			
Cost in Dept. A (500 × $10.00)		$ 5,000	
Cost in Dept. B:			
Materials (500 × 2/5 × $.50)	$100		
Labor (500 × 2/5 × $1.25)	250		
Factory overhead (500 × 2/5 × $.75) . . .	150	500	5,500
Total production costs accounted for			$33,000

FIGURE 6-5   Production Report, Dept. C—Painting

PRODUCTION REPORT

For Month Ending January 31, 19--

Dept. C-Painting

In process, beginning of period _____ none

Stage of completion _____

Placed in process during period _____ none

Received from dept. ____B____ during period _2,200 units_

Transferred to dept. _____ during period _____

Transferred to stockroom during period _____ 2,000 units

In process, end of period _____ 200 units

Stage of completion _____ 1/2

After posting the end-of-month entries, the work in process account for Dept. B, has a debit balance of $5,500.

Work in Process—Dept. B			
Jan. 31	1,200	Jan. 31	27,500
	3,000		
	1,800		
	27,000		
	33,000		
5,500			

Data for Dept. C is shown in the following example. The cost of production is prepared in a manner similar to the Dept. B summary. As the cost of successive departments accumulate, it may be desirable in the *inventory costs* section of the report to show the *cost of goods finished and transferred to finished goods during the month* as follows:

Inventory costs:
  Cost of goods finished and transferred to finished goods:
    (2,000 units × $16.50) $33,000

The $16.50 represents the total unit cost of the goods through Dept. C. The detailed unit cost of completed goods, department-by-department, shows the accumulation of the total unit cost.

The Toy Factory
Cost of Production Summary—Department C
For the Month Ended January 31, 19—

Cost of goods received from Dept. B during month			
(2,200 units × $12.50)			$27,500
Cost of production for month—Dept. C:			
Materials		$ 3,150	
Labor		2,310	
Factory overhead		2,940	8,400
Total costs to be accounted for			**$35,900**
Unit output for month:			
Finished and transferred to finished goods			
during month			2,000
Equivalent units of work in process, end of			
month (200 units, one-half completed)			100
Total equivalent production			2,100
Unit cost for month—Dept. C:			
Materials ($3,150 ÷ 2,100 units)			$1.50
Labor ($2,310 ÷ 2,100 units)			1.10
Factory overhead ($2,940 ÷ 2,100 units)			1.40
Total			$4.00
Inventory costs:			
Cost of goods finished and transferred to finished goods during month:			
Cost in Dept. A (2,000 × $10.00)		$20,000	
Cost in Dept. B (2,000 × 2.50)		5,000	
Cost in Dept. C (2,000 × 4.00)		8,000	
(2,000 × $16.50)			$33,000
Cost of work in process, end of month:			
Cost in Dept. A (200 × $10.00)		$ 2,000	
Cost in Dept. B (200 × $ 2.50)		500	
Cost in Dept. C:			
Materials (200 × 1/2 × $1.50)	$150		
Labor (200 × 1/2 × $1.10)	110		
Factory overhead (200 × 1/2 × $1.40)	140	400	2,900
Total production costs accounted for			**$35,900**

After posting the end-of-month entries, the work in process account for Dept. C has a debit balance of $2,900.

Work in Process—Dept. C		
Jan. 31	3,150	Jan. 31	33,000
	2,310		
	2,940		
	27,500		
	35,900		
2,900			

As a means of classifying and summarizing the factory operations for January, the work sheet in Figure 6-6 provides the information for the following statement of cost of goods manufactured.

The Toy Factory
Statement of Cost of Goods Manufactured
For the Month Ended January 31, 19—

Materials	$20,350
Labor	13,950
Factory overhead	12,100
Total	$46,400
Less work in process inventories, January 31	13,400
Cost of goods manufactured during the month	$33,000

At the end of the month, the following general journal entries are made:

Jan. 31 Work in Process—Dept. A	16,000	
Work in Process—Dept. B	1,200	
Work in Process—Dept. C	3,150	
Factory Overhead*	1,000	
Materials		21,350

*The amount charged to Factory Overhead for indirect materials is an *arbitrary amount* chosen for this example to illustrate how the costs are collected and distributed. This amount represents the cost of various expenses and supplies issued that could not be charged directly to a department.

FIGURE 6-6   Worksheet, January 31

The Toy Factory Corp.
Departmental Cost Work Sheet
For the Month Ended January 31, 19—

Analysis	Cost per unit transferred	Units received in department	Units transferred or on hand	Amount charged to department	Amount credited to department
Dept. A—Cutting:					
Started in process		3,700			
Costs for month:					
Materials				16,000 00	
Labor				8,640 00	
Factory overhead				7,360 00	
Finished and transferred to Dept. B	10 00		2,700		27,000 00
Closing work in process			1,000		5,000 00
Total	10 00	3,700	3,700	32,000 00	32,000 00
Dept. B—Forming:					
Received during month from Dept. A		2,700		27,000 00	
Costs added during month:					
Materials				1,200 00	
Labor				3,000 00	
Factory overhead				1,800 00	
Finished and transferred to Dept. C	2 50		2,200		27,500 00
Closing work in process			500		5,500 00
Total	12 50	2,700	2,700	33,000 00	33,000 00
Dept. C—Painting:					
Received during month from Dept. B		2,200		27,500 00	
Costs added during month:					
Materials				3,150 00	
Labor				2,310 00	
Factory overhead				2,940 00	
Finished and transferred to stock	4 00		2,000		33,000 00
Closing work in process			200		2,900 00
Total	16 50	2,200	2,200	35,900 00	35,900 00

Analysis				Amount	Total
Summary:					
Materials:					
Dept. A				16,000 00	
Dept. B				1,200 00	
Dept. C				3,150 00	20,350 00
Labor:					
Dept. A				8,640 00	
Dept. B				3,000 00	
Dept. C				2,310 00	13,950 00
Factory overhead:					
Dept. A				7,360 00	
Dept. B				1,800 00	
Dept. C				2,940 00	12,100 00
Total production costs for January					46,400 00
Deduct work in process inventory, end of month: . .					
Dept. A				5,000 00	
Dept. B				5,500 00	
Dept. C				2,900 00	13,400 00
Cost of production, goods fully manufactured during January					33,000 00

Jan. 31	Work in Process—Dept. A	8,640	
	Work in Process—Dept. B	3,000	
	Work in Process—Dept. C	2,310	
	Factory Overhead	1,500	
	Payroll		15,450

Again, the amount charged to the factory overhead control account is an arbitrary amount chosen to illustrate payroll costs that could not be charged directly to any given department.

Jan. 31	Factory Overhead	9,000	
	Various accounts (Accumulated Depre-		
	ciation, Prepaid Insurance, Payroll Taxes) . .		9,000

The previous entry summarizes several entries made in the general journal and possibly other journals to reflect the current month's provision for depreciation, insurance, payroll taxes, and other expenses.

Jan. 31	Factory Overhead—Dept. A	6,600	
	Factory Overhead—Dept. B	2,100	
	Factory Overhead—Dept. C	2,800	
	Factory Overhead		11,500

The previous entry distributes the actual overhead for the period to the departments. The basis for this entry would be the *factory overhead analysis sheets*, which show in detail the allocation or apportionment of the actual expenses to the various departments. Note these actual amounts do not appear on the cost of production summaries, which contain the estimated amounts of factory overhead applied to production.

Jan. 31	Work in Process—Dept. A	7,360	
	Work in Process—Dept. B	1,800	
	Work in Process—Dept. C	2,940	
	Factory Overhead—Dept. A		7,360
	Factory Overhead—Dept. B		1,800
	Factory Overhead—Dept. C		2,940

The previous entry charges the applied factory overhead appearing on the cost of production summaries to the work in process control accounts. The amounts are calculated by multiplying a predetermined overhead application rate by the base used for applying overhead to each department, such as labor hours or machine hours. A different base might be used for different departments, so that overhead would be equitably applied according to the benefit each department has received.

The cost of production summary is used to develop the entries to record the transfer of costs from one department to another and to Finished Goods, follows.

Jan. 31	Work in Process—Dept. B	27,000	
	Work in Process—Dept. A		27,000
31	Work in Process—Dept. C	27,500	
	Work in Process—Dept. B		27,500
31	Finished Goods	33,000	
	Work in Process—Dept. C		33,000

These journal entries are reflected in the following T-accounts. The balances remaining in the work in process accounts are reflected in total on the statement of cost of goods manufactured. The balances in the departmental factory overhead accounts represent under- or overapplied overhead and would usually be carried forward to future months. However, these balances can be transferred to an under- and overapplied factory overhead account. As discussed in previous chapters, these amounts of under- and overapplied overhead would be analyzed to determine if they are expected normal or seasonal variances, or if they represent inefficiencies that should be corrected.

Work in Process—Dept. A

Jan. 31	16,000	Jan. 31	27,000
	8,640		
	7,360		
	32,000		
5,000			

Work in Process—Dept. B

Jan. 31	1,200	Jan. 31	27,500
	3,000		
	1,800		
	27,000		
	33,000		
5,500			

Work in Process—Dept. C

Jan. 31	3,150	Jan. 31	33,000
	2,310		
	2,940		
	27,500		
2,900			

Finished Goods

Jan. 31	33,000		

Factory Overhead			
Jan. 31	1,000	Jan. 31	11,500
	1,500		
	9,000		
	11,500		
-0-			

Materials		
	Jan. 31	21,350

Payroll		
	Jan. 31	15,450

Factory Overhead—Dept. A			
Jan. 31	6,600	Jan. 31	7,360
		760	

Factory Overhead—Dept. B			
Jan. 31	2,100	Jan. 31	1,800
300			

Factory Overhead—Dept. C			
Jan. 31	2,800	Jan. 31	2,940
		140	

LEARNING OBJECTIVE

Compute unit costs with and without beginning inventories when there are two or more departments

Illustrative Problem No. 4—Computing the unit cost when there are beginning inventories and two or more departments.

The February production reports, Figures 6-7, 6-8, and 6-9, submitted by the department supervisors for The Toy Factory differ from the January production reports. There are now inventories for work in process in each department at the beginning of the month. Note, the number of units in process at the beginning of the period *plus* the units placed in process or received from another department during the period equal the *total number of units* to be accounted for by department. After receiving the production reports for February, the accountant prepares a cost of production summary for each department and makes entries to record the operations of each department in the general ledger accounts.

It should be noted in the following cost of production summary that in determining unit cost, the cost of beginning work in process from the prior month is added to the total costs incurred during the

FIGURE 6-7   Production Report, Dept. A—Cutting, February 28

PRODUCTION REPORT

For Month Ending February 28, 19--

Dept. A-Cutting

In process, beginning of period _____ 1,000 units

Stage of completion _____ 1/2

Placed in process during period _____ 3,800 units

Received from dept. _____ during period ____ none

Transferred to dept. ___B___ during period 3,900 units

Transferred to stockroom during period _____ none

In process, end of period _____ 500 units

Stage of completion _____ 4/5

---

current month as in an earlier example. The prior month's cost of material is added to the current month's cost of material and the total material cost is divided by the equivalent production for material. The same procedure is followed for labor and factory overhead. The calculation of unit output for the month takes into consideration all units finished during the month, including those in process at the beginning and those in process at the end of the period. Although the total unit cost is the same as in January, the unit cost of labor has increased, and the unit cost of factory overhead has decreased. Management would likely investigate the causes for these changes and take whatever action necessary.

The Toy Factory
Cost of Production Summary—Department A
For the Month Ended February 28, 19—

Cost of work in process, beginning of month:		
Materials	$ 2,500	
Labor	1,350	
Factory overhead	1,150	$ 5,000
Cost of production for month:		
Materials	$19,000	
Labor	10,260	
Factory overhead	8,740	38,000
Total costs to be accounted for		**$43,000**
Unit output for month:		
Finished and transferred to Dept. B during month		3,900
Equivalent units of work in process, end of month		
(500 units, four-fifths completed)		400
Total equivalent production		4,300
Unit cost for month:		
Materials [($2,500 + $19,000) ÷ 4,300		$ 5.00
Labor [($1,350 + $10,260) ÷ 4,300]		2.70
Factory overhead [($1,150 + $8,740) ÷ 4,300] .		2.30
Total		$10.00
Inventory costs:		
Cost of goods finished and transferred to Dept. B		
during month: (3,900 × $10.00)		$39,000
Cost of work in process, end of month:		
Materials (500 × 4/5 × $5.00)	$ 2,000	
Labor (500 × 4/5 × $2.70)	1,080	
Factory overhead (500 × 4/5 × $2.30)	920	4,000
Total production costs accounted for		**$43,000**

At this time the following general journal entry can be made:

Feb. 28 Work in Process—Dept. B	39,000	
Work in Process—Dept. A		39,000

The work in process account for this department now appears as follows:

Work in Process—Dept. A			
Jan. 31	16,000	Jan. 31	27,000
	8,640		
	7,360		
	32,000		
5,000			
Feb. 28	19,000	Feb. 28	39,000
	10,260		
	8,740		
	70,000		*66,000*
4,000			

In calculating the unit cost in Dept. B at the end of February, the amounts considered include (a) the production costs incurred by the department during the month, *plus* (b) the departmental cost of work in process at the beginning of the month. The cost from Dept. A included in the beginning work in process valuation ($5,000) is *not used* in this calculation because it is a *prior department's cost.*

FIGURE 6-8   Production Report, Dept. B—Forming, February 28

PRODUCTION REPORT

For Month Ending February 28, 19--

Dept. B-Forming

In process, beginning of period	500 units
Stage of completion	2/5
Placed in process during period	none
Received from dept. A during period	3,900 units
Transferred to dept. C during period	4,100 units
Transferred to stockroom during period	none
In process, end of period	300 units
Stage of completion	1/3

The Toy Factory
Cost of Production Summary—Dept. B
For the Month Ended February 28, 19—

Cost of work in process, beginning of month—Dept. B:			
Cost in Dept. A		$ 5,000	
Cost in Dept. B:			
Materials	$100		
Labor	250		
Factory overhead	150	500	$ 5,500
Cost of goods received from Dept. A during month .			39,000
Cost of production for month—Dept. B:			
Materials	$ 1,664		
Labor	5,000		
Factory overhead	3,336	10,000	
Total costs to be accounted for			**$54,500**
Unit output for month:			
Finished and transferred to Dept. C during month .			4,100
Equivalent units of work in process, end of month			
(300 units, one-third completed)			100
Total equivalent production			4,200
Unit cost for month—Dept. B:			
Materials [($100 + $1,664) ÷ 4,200]			$ .42
Labor [($250 + $5,000) ÷ 4,200]			1.25
Factory overhead [($150 + $3,336) ÷ 4,200]			.83
Total			$2.50
Inventory costs:			
Costs of goods finished and transferred to Dept. C			
during month:			
Cost in Dept. A (4,100 × $10.00)		$41,000	
Cost in Dept. B (4,100 × 2.50)		10,250	
(4,100 × $12.50)			$51,250
Cost of work in process, end of month:			
Cost in Dept. A (300 × $10.00)		$ 3,000	
Cost in Dept. B:			
Materials (300 × 1/3 × $.42)	$ 42		
Labor (300 × 1/3 × $1.25)	125		
Factory overhead (300 × 1/3 × $.83)	83	250	3,250
Total production costs accounted for			**$54,500**

The following journal entry can now be made:

Feb. 28 Work in Process—Dept. C 51,250
              Work in Process—Dept. B   51,250

The general ledger account for work in process in Dept. B appears as follows:

Work in Process—Dept. B			
Jan. 31	1,200	Jan. 31	27,500
	3,000		
	1,800		
	27,000		
	33,000		
5,500			
Feb. 28	1,664	Feb. 28	51,250
	5,000		*78,750*
	3,336		
	39,000		
	82,000		
3,250			

FIGURE 6-9   Production Report, Dept. C—Painting, February 28

PRODUCTION REPORT

For Month Ending February 28, 19--

Dept. C-Painting

In process, beginning of period _____ 200 units

Stage of completion _____ 1/2

Placed in process during period _____ none

Received from dept. __B__ during period _4,100 units_

Transferred to dept. _____ during period _____

Transferred to stockroom during period _____ 3,900 units

In process, end of period _____ 400 units

Stage of completion _____ 1/2

**The Toy Factory
Cost of Production Summary—Department C
For the Month Ended February 28, 19—**

Cost of work in process, beginning of month—Dept. C:			
Cost in Dept. A		$ 2,000*	
Cost in Dept. B		500*	
Cost in Dept. C:			
Materials	$150		
Labor	110		
Factory overhead	140	400	$ 2,900
Cost of goods received from			
Dept. B during month			51,250
Cost of production for month—Dept. C:			
Materials		$ 5,713	
Labor		4,564	
Factory overhead		5,723	16,000
Total costs to be accounted for . . .			**$70,150**

Unit output for month:	
Finished and transferred to finished goods	
during month	3,900
Equivalent units of work in process, end of month	
(400 units, one-half completed)	200
Total equivalent production	4,100

Unit cost for month—Dept. C:	
Materials [($150 + $5,713) ÷ 4,100] . . .	$1.43
Labor [($110 + $4,564) ÷ 4,100]	1.14
Factory overhead [($140 + $5,723) ÷ 4,100]	1.43
Total	$4.00

Inventory costs:		
Cost of goods finished and transferred to finished		
goods during month:		
Cost in Dept. A (3,900 × $10.00) . . .	$39,000	
Cost in Dept. B (3,900 × 2.50) . . .	9,750	
Cost in Dept. C (3,900 × 4.00) . . .	15,600	
(3,900 × $16.50) . . .		$64,350

Cost of work in process, end of month:			
Cost in Dept. A (400 × $10.00)		$ 4,000	
Cost in Dept. B (400 × $ 2.50)		1,000	
Cost in Dept. C:			
Materials (400 × 1/2 × $1.43)	$286		
Labor (400 × 1/2 × $1.14)	228		
Factory overhead (400 × 1/2 × $1.43) .	286	800	5,800
Total production costs accounted for . .			**$70,150**

* Not to be considered in calculating February unit cost in Department C.

The following journal entry can now be made:

Feb. 28   Finished Goods   64,350
               Work in Process—Dept. C   64,350

The general ledger account for work in process in Dept. C appears as follows:

Work in Process—Dept. C

Jan. 31		3,150	Jan. 31	33,000
		2,310		
		2,940		
		27,500		
		35,900		
	2,900			
Feb. 28		5,713	Feb. 28	64,350
		4,564		*97,350*
		5,723		
		51,250		
		103,150		
	5,800			

The work sheet in Figure 6-10 can now be prepared. It summarizes the factory operations for February and provides the data needed for preparing the statement of cost of goods manufactured.

The Toy Factory
Statement of Cost of Goods Manufactured
For the Month Ended February 28, 19—

Materials	$26,377
Labor	19,824
Factory overhead	17,799
Total	$64,000
Add work in process inventories, February 11	3,400
	$77,400
Less work in process inventories, February 28	13,050
Cost of goods manufactured during the month	$64,350

Occasionally finished goods in a department at the end of the month may not be transferred to the next department until the following month.

FIGURE 6-10   Worksheet, February 28

The Toy Factory Corp.
Departmental Cost Work Sheet
For the Month Ended February 28, 19—

Analysis	Cost per unit transferred	Units received in department	Units transferred or on hand	Amount charged to department	Amount credited to department
Dept. A—Cutting:					
Opening inventory in process		600		5,000 00	
Started in process		3,800			
Costs for month:					
Materials				19,000 00	
Labor				10,260 00	
Factory overhead				8,740 00	
Finished and transferred to Dept. B .	10 00		3,900		39,000 00
Closing work in process			500		4,000 00
Total	10 00	4,400	4,400	43,000 00	43,000 00
Dept. B—Forming:					
Opening inventory in process		500		5,500 00	
Received during month from Dept. A		3,900		39,000 00	
Costs added during month:					
Materials				1,664 00	
Labor				5,000 00	
Factory overhead				3,336 00	
Finished and transferred to Dept. C .	2 50		4,100		51,250 00
Closing work in process			300		3,250 00
Total	12 50	4,400	4,400	54,500 00	54,500 00
Dept. C—Painting:					
Opening inventory in process		200		2,900 00	
Received during month from Dept. B		4,100		51,250 00	
Costs added during month:					
Materials				5,713 00	
Labor				4,564 00	
Factory overhead				5,723 00	
Finished and transferred to stock . .	4 00		3,900		64,350 00
Closing work in process			400		5,800 00
Total	16 50	4,300	4,300	70,150 00	70,150 00

Analysis	Cost per unit transferred	Units received in department	Units transferred or on hand	Amount charged to department		Amount credited to department	
				Amount		Total	
Summary:							
Materials:							
Dept. A				19,000	00		
Dept. B				1,664	00		
Dept. C				5,713	00	26,377	00
Labor:							
Dept. A				10,260	00		
Dept. B				5,000	00		
Dept. C				4,564	00	19,824	00
Factory overhead:							
Dept. A				8,740	00		
Dept. B				3,336	00		
Dept. C				5,723	00	17,799	00
Total production costs for February						64,000	00
Add work in process, beginning of month:							
Dept. A				5,000	00		
Dept. B				5,500	00		
Dept. C				2,900	00	13,400	00
Total						77,400	00
Deduct work in process, end of month:							
Dept. A				4,000	00		
Dept. B				3,250	00		
Dept. C				5,800	00	13,050	00
Cost of production, goods fully manufactured during February						64,350	00

Because these units are still on hand in the department at the end of the month, they cannot be considered transferred. They are accounted for as "goods completed and on hand" and their cost is shown at the full unit price. They are considered work in process for financial statement purposes. Although the goods are finished in the department, they are considered in process until they are officially transferred to finished goods.

CHANGES IN PRIOR DEPARTMENTS UNIT TRANSFER COSTS

In the preceding illustrations, it was assumed this month's unit cost from prior departments was the same transfer-in unit cost as last month. This assumption permitted the prior department's unit cost to be used without determining a *new average unit cost* for the goods transferred-in even though the transfers came from two different periods of production. However, often the prior departments transfers from two different periods will have different unit costs each month. Therefore, these previous department costs must be *averaged as a separate grouping* so that these transferred-in costs can be properly allocated to the products being produced in the department. The method resembles that used for the cost of material, labor, and factory overhead in the department when the cost of these elements represent two different periods of time.

To illustrate, assume that 2,000 units are in process in Dept. 2 at the beginning of the month with a transferred cost from Dept. 1 of $10,600. During the month, 10,000 units with a total cost of $50,000 are received from Dept. 1; 11,000 units are finished and transferred to Dept. 3; and 1,000 units are in process in Dept. 2 at the end of the month, one-half completed. Processing costs in Dept. 2 for the month for materials, labor, and overhead costs are $23,000, $16,000, and $11,500 respectively. Using these data the unit cost calculation on the cost of production summary would be shown as follows:

```
Unit cost for month:
  Cost from prior department:
    Beginning inventory      (  2,000 units x $5.30)  . . .    $10,600
    Transferred in this month (10,000 units x $5.00)  . . .     50,000
    Average unit cost        (12,000 units)  . . . . . . .     $60,600    $5.05

  Cost in Dept. 2:
    Materials ($23,000 ÷ 11,500)  . . . . . . . . . . . .                 $2.00
    Labor ($16,100 ÷ 11,500)  . . . . . . . . . . . . . .                  1.40
    Overhead ($11,500 ÷ 11,500)  . . . . . . . . . . . .                   1.00
                                                                         $4.40
```

The following schedule of costs and the complete cost of production summary illustrates how the change in unit costs from prior departments are adjusted and reported. Note the cost from preceding department's unit cost adjustment to $5.05.

Cost of Production Summary—Dept. 2

Cost of work in process, beginning of month:

Cost in Dept. 1	. . . .		$ 10,600
Cost in Dept. 2:			
Materials	$ 2,000		
Labor	1,400		
Overhead	1,000	4,400	$ 15,000
Cost of goods received from Dept. 1			50,000
Cost in Dept. 2:			
Materials	$21,000		
Labor	14,700		
Overhead	10,500	46,200	
Total costs to be accounted for			**$111,200**

Unit output for month:

Finished and transferred to Dept. 3	11,000
Equivalent production of work in process:	
(1,000 units, one-half completed)	500
Total equivalent production	11,500

Unit cost for month:

Cost from preceding department:			
Beginning inventory	(2,000 units)	$10,600	
Transferred in this month	(10,000 units)	50,000	
Average cost per unit	(12,000 units)	$60,600	$5.05

Cost in Dept. 2:	
Materials [($2,000 + $21,000) ÷ 11,500] . . .	$2.00
Labor [($1,400 + $14,700) ÷ 11,500]	1.40
Overhead [($1,000 + $10,500) ÷ 11,500] . . .	1.00
	$4.40

Inventory costs:

Cost of goods finished and transferred:			
Cost in Dept. 1	(11,000 × $5.05)	$55,550	
Cost in Dept. 2	(11,000 × 4.40)	48,400	
Total finished and transferred (11,000 × $9.45)			$103,950

Cost in work in process, end of month:

Cost in Dept. 1 (1,000 × $5.05)		$ 5,050	
Materials (1,000 × 1/2 × $2.00) . .	$1,000		
Labor (1,000 × 1/2 × $1.40)	700		
Overhead (1,000 × 1/2 × $1.00) .	500	2,200	7,250
Total production costs accounted for			**$111,200**

	Units	Unit Cost	Cost from Dept. 1	Costs in Dept. 2			Total Cost
				Materials	Labor	Overhead	
In process, beginning of month	2,000	$5.30	$10,600	$2,000	$1,400	$1,000	$15,000
Received from Dept. 1 during month	10,000	$5.00	50,000				50,000
Cost incurred this month				21,000	14,700	10,500	46,200
Total units and costs to be accounted for . .	12,000		$60,600	$23,000	$16,100	$11,500	$111,200
Average cost of units from Dept. 1 ($60,600 ÷ 12,000)		$5.05					$5.05
Unit cost for month in Dept. B with equivalent production of 11,500 units . .				$2.00	$1.40	$1.00	4.40
Unit cost for finished goods							$9.45
Assignment of costs:							
Transferred to Dept. 3	11,000	$5.05	$55,550	$22,000	$15,400	$11,000	$103,950
In process end of month (1/2 complete)	1,000	$5.05	5,050	1,000	700	500	7,250
Total units and costs accounted for	12,000	$5.05	$60,600	$23,000	$16,100	$11,500	$111,200

KEY TERMS

Average cost method, p. 253
Cost center, p. 249
Cost of production summary, p. 255
Equivalent production, p. 253
First-in, first-out (FIFO) method, p. 253
Job cost system, p. 249

Process cost, p. 249
Production report, p. 255
Stage of completion, p. 254
Transferred-in costs, p. 263
Units from prior departments, p. 263

abnormal cost = period cost

SELF-STUDY PROBLEM

SAMSYN, INC.; COST OF PRODUCTION SUMMARY, TWO DEPARTMENTS

Samsyn, Inc., which manufactures products on a continuous basis, had 800 units in process in Dept. 1, one-half completed, at the beginning of May. The costs in April for processing these units were as follows: materials, $1,200; labor, $900, and factory overhead, $1,000. During May, Dept. 1 finished and transferred 10,000 units to Dept. 2 and had 400 units in process at the end of May, one-half completed.

Dept. 2 had 200 units in process at the beginning of the month, one-half completed. April costs for these units were as follows: cost transferred from Dept. 1, $1,550; materials, $200; labor, $175; factory overhead, $225. During May, Dept.

2 completed 9,000 units and had 1,200 units in process at the end of the period, two-thirds completed.

Production costs incurred by the two departments during May were as follows:

	Dept. 1	Dept. 2
Materials	$29,400	$19,400
Labor	22,050	16,975
Factory overhead	24,500	21,825

REQUIRED: Prepare a cost of production summary for each department.

SOLUTION TO DEMONSTRATION PROBLEM

Suggestions:

Read the entire problem through thoroughly, keeping in mind what you are required to do: *Prepare a cost of production summary for each department.*

The specifics in the problem highlight the following facts:

1. There are two departments: Dept. 1 and Dept. 2.
2. Dept. 1 had 800 units in process, one-half completed, at the beginning of May. *This statement indicates that materials, labor, and factory overhead are being added uniformly to production.*
3. To prepare a cost of production summary:
   a. The total cost to be accounted for in the department must be determined.
   b. The equivalent production should be calculated.
   c. Using the beginning inventory costs and the costs incurred during the period, determine the total cost of materials, the total cost of labor, and the total cost of factory overhead. Then divide the total cost of materials by the equivalent production of materials to calculate the unit cost of materials for the period. Also, divide the total cost of labor and factory overhead by the equivalent production determined for them.
   d. Using the calculated unit costs for materials, labor, and factory overhead determine the following:
      1. The cost of goods finished and transferred
      2. The cost of the ending work in process inventory

Preparing the cost of production summaries

Samsyn, Inc.
Cost of Production Summary—Dept. 1
For the Month Ended, May 31, 19—

First—Account for the total cost charged to Dept. 1.

Cost of work in process, beginning of month:		
Materials	$ 1,200	
Labor	900	
Factory overhead	1,000	$ 3,100
Cost of production for month:		
Materials	$29,400	
Labor	22,050	
Factory overhead	24,500	75,950
Total costs to be accounted for		$79,050

Second—Determine equivalent production for month. Materials, labor, and factory overhead added uniformly. Method of costing—average cost.

Unit of output for month:
Finished and transferred to Dept. 2 10,000
Equivalent units of work in process, end of month:
400 units, one-half completed 200

Total equivalent production 10,200

Third—Determine unit cost, by elements, for the month. The average cost method requires that the beginning inventory's element cost be added to the current month's element cost. The total cost for each element is then divided by the equivalent production for that element.

Unit cost for month:
Materials ($1,200 + $29,400) ÷ 10,200 . . . . $3.00
Labor ($900 + $22,050) ÷ 10,200 . . . . 2.25
Factory overhead ($1,000 + $24,500) ÷ 10,200 . . . . 2.50

Total $7.75

Fourth—Using the unit costs, calculate the cost of goods transferred and the cost of the ending work in process.

Inventory costs:
Cost of goods finished and transferred to
Dept. 2 during the month (10,000 × $7.75) $77,500
Cost of work in process, end of month:
Materials (400 × 1/2 × $3.00) $600
Labor (400 × 1/2 × $2.25)   450
Factory overhead (400 × 1/2 × $2.50)   500   1,550

Total production costs accounted for $79,050

Prepare the cost of production for Dept. 2.

Samsyn, Inc.
Cost of Production Summary—Dept. 2
For the Month Ended, May 31, 19—

First—Account for all costs charged to Dept. 2.
Cost of work in process, beginning of month:
Cost in Dept. 1 (preceding department) . . . $ 1,550
Cost in Dept. 2:
Materials $200
Labor   175
Factory overhead   225   600 $ 2,150

Cost of goods received from Dept. 1 during month: 77,500
Cost of production for month:
Materials $19,400
Labor   16,975
Factory overhead   21,825   58,200

Total costs to be accounted for $137,850

Second—Determine the equivalent production.

Finished and transferred to finished goods during month	9,000
Equivalent units of work in process, end of month	
(1,200 units, two-thirds completed)	800
Total equivalent production	9,800

Third—Determine unit cost by element. Add beginning inventory element cost to current month element cost and divide total by the equivalent production for that element.

Unit cost for month:

Materials ($200 + $19,400) ÷ 9,800	$2.00
Labor ($175 + $16,975) ÷ 9,800	1.75
Factory overhead ($225 + $21,825) ÷ 9,800	2.25
Total unit cost for Dept. 2	$6.00

Fourth—Using the unit costs from Dept. 1 and Dept. 2, calculate the cost of goods transferred and the cost of ending work in process.

Inventory costs:
Cost of goods finished and transferred to finished goods during month:

Cost in Dept. 1 (9,000 × $ 7.75)		$69,750	
Cost in Dept. 2 (9,000 × $ 6.00)		54,000	
Total (9,000 × $13.75)			$123,750
Cost in work in process, end of month:			
Cost in Dept. 1 (1,200 × $7.75)		$ 9,300	
Cost in Dept. 2:			
Materials (1,200 × 2/3 × $2.00)	$1,600		
Labor (1,200 × 2/3 × $1.75)	1,400		
Overhead (1,200 × 2/3 × $2.25)	1,800	4,800	14,100
Total production costs accounted for			$137,850

Note that, in the above ending work in process inventory, the unit cost from Dept. 1 is multiplied by the full 1,200 units because all of those units are complete as to Dept. 1 processing.

(Note that Problem 6-3 is similar to this problem.)

QUESTIONS

1. What are the two basic systems of cost accounting and under what conditions may each be used advantageously?

2. Following is a list of manufactured products. For each product, would a job-order or a process cost system be used to account for the costs of production?

   a. lumber   e. cereal
   b. buildings   f. textbooks
   c. airplanes   g. paint
   d. gasoline   h. women's hats

3. Is there any situation in which a manufacturing company might use both the job-order cost system and the process cost system?

4. What is the primary difference between the two cost accounting systems regarding the accumulation of costs and the calculation of unit costs?

5. What is the difference between the term "unit cost" as commonly used in the process cost system and the term "job cost" as commonly used in the job-order system of cost accounting?

6. How do the two cost accounting systems differ in accounting for each of the following items?

    a. materials

    b. labor

    c. factory overhead

7. What is the primary objective in accumulating costs by departments?

8. What is meant by the term "equivalent production" as used in the process cost system?

9. Why is it necessary to estimate the stage or degree of completion of work in process at the end of the accounting period under the process cost system?

10. What would be the effect on the unit cost of finished goods if an inaccurate estimate of the stage of completion of work in process is made?

11. What information is reflected on a production report?

12. What are the four divisions of a cost of production summary?

EXERCISES

E6-1
Identifying cost flows in process cost system

List in columnar form the transactions and the accounts debited and credited to reflect the flow of costs through a process cost accounting system.

E6-2
Computing equivalent production
Learning Objective 3

Compute the equivalent production (unit output) for the month for each of the following situations:

	Units Completed During Month	Units in Process End of Month	Stage of Completion
a.	10,000	2,000	1/2
b.	32,000	4,000	3/4
c.	8,000	1,000	3/4
		500	2/5
d.	20,000	5,000	1/2
		5,000	3/4
e.	48,000	1,500	1/5
		4,000	3/4

E6-3
Computing units in process, units completed, and equivalent production
Learning Objective 3

Using the data presented on the following page, determine which figures should be inserted in the blank spaces.

	Beginning Units in Process	Units Started in Production	Units Transferred to Finished Goods	Ending Units in Process	Equivalent Units
a.	600	8,000	8,600	—	—
b.	900	6,500	—	400—1/2 completed	—
c.	1,500	—	12,900	1,200—1/4 completed	—
d.	—	7,250	7,200	150—1/2 completed	—
e.	—	8,400	8,200	200—1/2 completed	—
f.	400	6,200	6,200	—	6,300

E6-4
Computing unit cost
Learning Objective 5

During the month, a company with no departmentalization incurred costs of $45,000 for materials, $36,000 for labor, and $22,500 for factory overhead. There were no units in process at the beginning or at the end of the month, and 9,000 units were completed. Determine the unit cost for the month for materials, labor, and factory overhead.

E6-5
Computing unit cost
Learning Objective 5

The Camden Manufacturing Co. recorded costs for the month of $18,900 for materials, $44,100 for labor, and $26,250 for factory overhead. There was no beginning work in process, 9,000 units were finished, and 2,000 units were in process at the end of the period, one-half completed. Compute the month's unit cost for each element of manufacturing cost.

E6-6
Computing unit cost
Learning Objective 5

The records of Buster, Inc., reflect the following data:
Work in process, beginning of month—2,000 units one-half completed at a cost of $1,250 for materials, $675 for labor, and $950 for overhead.
Production costs for the month—materials, $99,150; labor, $54,925; factory overhead, $75,050.
Units completed and transferred to stock—38,500.
Work in process, end of month—3,000 units one-half completed.
Calculate the unit cost for the month for materials, labor, and factory overhead.

E6-7
Computing unit cost
for department and
for completed units
Learning Objective 6

Westview Company has two production departments. The nature of the process is such that no units remain in process in Dept. 2 at the end of the period. During the period, 8,000 units with a cost of $27,200 were transferred from Dept. 1 to Dept. 2. Dept. 2 incurred costs of $8,800 for materials, $7,200 for labor, and $8,800 for factory overhead, and finished 8,000 units during the month.
a. Determine the unit cost for the month in Dept. 2.
b. Determine the unit cost of the products transferred to finished goods.

E6-8
Computing unit cost
Learning Objective 6

The Middleton Manufacturing Co. had 500 units, three-fifths completed, in process at the beginning of the month. During the month 2,000 units were started in process and finished. There was no work in process at the end of the month. Unit cost of production for the month was $1.20. Costs for materials, labor, and factory overhead incurred in the current month totaled $2,655. Calculate the unit cost for the *prior* month.

PROBLEMS

P6-1
Cost of production
summary, one
department;
beginning and ending
work in process
Learning Objective 4

The Margo Products Co. produces a household cleansing liquid and uses the process cost system. The following information was obtained from the company's accounts at the end of February:

Production Costs

Work in process, beginning of period:		
Materials	$ 6,000	
Labor	7,500	
Factory overhead	9,500	$23,000
Costs incurred during month:		
Materials	$30,000	
Labor	22,500	
Factory overhead	22,500	75,000
Total		$98,000

Production Report	Units
Finished and transferred to stockroom during month	76,000
Work in process, end of period, one-fourth completed	16,000

Required: Prepare a cost of production summary for February.

P6-2
Cost of production
summary, one
department;
beginning and ending
work in process
Learning Objective 4

The George Company uses the process cost system. The following data taken from the organization's books reflect the results of manufacturing operations during the month of October:

Production Costs

Work in process, beginning of period:		
Materials	$ 2,600	
Labor	2,300	
Factory overhead	1,000	$ 5,900
Costs incurred during month:		
Materials	$10,000	
Labor	7,500	
Factory overhead	6,000	23,500
Total		$29,400

Production Report	Units
Finished and transferred to stockroom during month	13,000
Work in process, end of period, one-half completed	2,000

Required: Prepare a cost of production summary for October.

P6-3
Cost of production
summary, two
departments
Learning Objectives 4
& 6

The Olmsted Corporation uses a process cost system. The records for the
month of May show the following information:

Production Report	Dept. 1	Dept. 2
Units in process, May 1	5,000	10,000
Started during the month	20,000	—
Received from prior department	—	15,000
Finished and transferred	15,000	10,000
Finished and on hand	5,000	—
Units in process, May 31	5,000	15,000
Stage of completion	1/5	1/3

Production Costs

Work in Process, May 1:		
Cost in Dept. 1		$ 50,000
Materials	$ 5,000	
Labor	6,450	
Factory overhead	3,550	
Cost in Dept. 2:		
Materials		5,000
Labor		5,500
Factory overhead		3,500
Costs incurred during the month:		
Materials	37,000	40,000
Labor	45,000	44,000
Factory overhead	50,000	37,000
Total	$147,000	$185,000

Required:

Prepare a cost of production summary for each department.

P6-4
Change in unit cost
from prior department
and valuation of
inventory
Learning Objective 6

The King Products Co. has two departments: mixing and cooking. At the beginning of the month, the cooking department had 2,000 units in process with costs
of $8,600 from the mixing department, and its own departmental costs of $500
for materials, $1,000 for labor, and $2,500 for factory overhead. During the
month, 8,000 units were received from the mixing department with a cost of
$36,400. The cooking department incurred costs of $4,250 for materials, $8,500
for labor, and $21,250 for factory overhead, and finished 9,000 units. At the end
of the month, there were 1,000 units in process, one-half completed.

Required:

1. Determine the unit cost for the month in the cooking department.
2. Determine the new average unit cost for all units received from the mixing
   department.
3. Determine the unit cost of goods finished.
4. Determine the accumulated cost of the goods finished and of the ending
   work in process using a schedule similar to the illustration on page 283.

P6-5
Cost of production summary, three departments; change in unit cost from prior department; departmental cost work sheet; journal entries; manufacturing statement
Learning Objectives 4 & 6

The Columbus Manufacturing Co. uses the process cost system. The following information for the month of December was obtained from the company's books and from the production reports submitted by the department heads:

Production Report	Dept. A	Dept. B	Dept. C
Units in process, beginning of period	2,500	1,500	3,000
Started in process during month	12,500	—	—
Received from prior department	—	13,000	10,000
Finished and transferred	13,000	10,000	11,000
Finished and on hand	—	500	—
Units in process, end of period	2,000	4,000	2,000
Stage of completion	1/4	4/5	1/2

Production Costs	Dept. A	Dept. B	Dept. C
Work in process, beginning of period:			
Cost in Dept. A		$ 3,075	$ 6,150
Materials	$ 1,470		
Labor	650		
Factory overhead	565		
Cost in Dept. B			3,660
Material		240	
Labor		905	
Factory overhead		750	
Cost in Dept. C			
Materials			900
Labor			3,100
Factory overhead			3,080
Costs incurred during month:			
Materials	15,000	2,500	1,500
Labor	4,750	8,000	6,500
Factory overhead	5,240	6,100	7,000
Total	$27,675	$21,570	$31,890

Required:

1. Prepare cost of production summaries for Depts. A, B, and C.
2. Prepare a departmental cost work sheet.
3. Draft the journal entries required to record the month's operations.
4. Prepare a statement of cost of goods manufactured for December.

P6-6
Departmental cost work sheet analysis; cost of production summary, three departments; journal entries; manufacturing statement
Learning Objectives 4 & 6

The Wonder Manufacturing Co. uses the process cost system of accounting. A portion of the departmental cost work sheet prepared by the cost accountant at the end of July is reproduced on the next page.

Departmental Cost Work Sheet
For the Month Ended July 31, 19—

Analysis	Cost per unit transferred		Units received in department	Units transferred or on hand	Amount charged to department		Amount credited to department	
Dept. A:								
Started in process			6,600					
Costs for month:								
Materials					30,000	00		
Labor					16,000	00		
Factory overhead					14,000	00		
Completed and transferred to Dept. B	10	00		5,400			54,000	00
Closing inventory in process				1,200			6,000	00
Total	10	00	6,600	6,600	60,000	00	60,000	00
Dept. B:								
Received during month from Dept. A			5,400		54,000	00		
Costs added during month:								
Materials					1,200	00		
Labor					6,000	00		
Factory overhead					4,800	00		
Completed and transferred to Dept. C	2	50		4,400			55,000	00
Closing inventory in process				1,000			11,000	00
Total	12	50	5,400	5,400	66,000	00	66,000	00
Dept. C:								
Received during month from Dept. B			4,400		55,000	00		
Costs added during month:								
Materials					6,300	00		
Labor					4,200	00		
Factory overhead					6,300	00		
Completed and transferred to stock	4	00		4,000			66,000	00
Closing inventory in process				400			5,800	00
Total	16	50	4,400	4,400	71,800	00	71,800	00

Required:

1. Prepare a cost of production summary for each department. The stage of completion of ending units in process must be computed.
2. Draft the necessary entries, in general journal form, to record the manufacturing costs incurred during the month of July.
3. Prepare a statement of cost of goods manufactured for the month ended July 31.

P6-7
Ledger account analysis; cost of production summary

Analyze the information presented in the following general ledger account of the Younger Manufacturing Co.:

Work in Process—Dept. B

Mar. 1		10,250	Mar. 31	50,000
31	Materials	4,000		
31	Labor	8,000		
31	Factory overhead	6,000		
31	Dept. A	36,000		

Additional facts:

a. 2,000 units were in process at the beginning of the month, one-half completed.

b. 9,000 units were received from Dept. A during the month.

c. 8,000 units were transferred to Dept. C during the month.

d. Unit costs in Depts. A and B were the same for March as for the prior month.

e. The ratio of materials, labor, and factory overhead costs for Dept. B in the beginning and ending balances of Work in Process was in the same ratio as the costs incurred in Dept. B during the current month.

Required: Prepare a cost of production summary for March.

Process Cost Accounting— Additional Procedures

LEARNING OBJECTIVES

After studying this chapter, you should be able to:

1. Compute unit costs when materials are not added uniformly throughout the process
2. Account for units lost at the beginning or end of the production process
3. Account for abnormal losses in production
4. Account for units gained in the production process
5. Assign costs to inventories using the first-in, first-out method
6. Recognize the differences between average costing and first-in, first-out methods of production costing
7. Identify the nature of joint costs and the methods used to apportion these costs to joint products
8. Account for by-products

The illustrative problems presented in Chapter 6 were based on the assumption that materials, labor, and factory overhead were uniformly applied during the processing period. When the work in process at the end of the accounting period was considered to be one-half completed, it was assumed that one-half of the materials cost, one-half of the labor cost, and one-half of the factory overhead cost had been added.

EQUIVALENT PRODUCTION—MATERIALS NOT UNIFORMLY APPLIED

In industries that use the process cost system, the materials may be put into production in varying quantities and at different points in the processing cycle.

For example, before any manufacturing process can begin, materials must be introduced in the first production department. This material may be a sheet of metal that will be cut or trimmed to size, shaped, and formed through the application of labor and the use of machines. In this case, all of the material is added at the beginning of processing in the first department. Then, labor and factory overhead are used to convert the material into a finished product. The stage of completion of partially completed work at the end of a period is irrelevant to material because all material costs will have been added at the very beginning of production. Some labor and overhead costs will need to be applied to the unfinished units in the department during the next period.

In the second production department, this same material may be processed further through the application of other labor operations, such as buffing and polishing. At the end of the process in the second department, several coats of enamel are to be applied. In this case, the units uncompleted in the department at the end of the period would have had a part of the departmental labor and overhead costs applied to them, but no materials cost would have been added because the enamel is applied at the very end of production in the second department.

In the third department, other materials, such as a knob, a handle, or pads, are added to the unit at the start of production. Then, a final polish is applied, involving labor and equipment. After it is polished, the unit is placed in a plastic container, which is an added material, and the package is sealed, incurring more labor and overhead cost.

In the third department, the uncompleted units may have had the first items of material and some labor and overhead applied, or they may have had the first material, some labor and overhead, and the additional materials added. In any event, the stage of completion must be carefully determined to measure accurately how much of each element of cost to apply to these unfinished units.

Compared with the principles and procedures developed in the preceding chapter, the only new procedure presented here is that equivalent production must be computed for each element of production cost, rather than only one equivalent production quantity used for materials, labor, and overhead. In addition, the allocation of cost for each element must be carefully considered when valuing the ending work in process.

To illustrate the problems involved in calculating unit costs under these conditions, three problems using the average cost method are presented. In these examples, materials are added at different stages in the process. Labor and factory overhead are assumed to be applied evenly throughout the process. This situation is typical in that overhead is usually so closely related to labor costs or hours that overhead is generally thought of as being incurred or applied in the same ratio as labor expense.

ILLUSTRATIVE PROBLEM NO. 1

LEARNING OBJECTIVE

Compute unit costs when materials are not added uniformly throughout the process

Computing the unit cost in department A where all the materials are added at the beginning of processing—average cost method. The production report for the month submitted by the department head, Figure 7-1, resembles those studied in the previous chapter.

The cost of production summary, Figure 7-2, is similar to the ones previously discussed, but it has the added feature of determining equivalent production for materials separately from that of labor and factory overhead.

FIGURE 7-1   Production Report, Dept. A

PRODUCTION REPORT

For Month Ending <u>April 30, 19--</u>

Dept. <u>A</u>

In process, beginning of period	500 units
Stage of completion	2/5
Placed in process during period	2,500 units
Received from dept. _____ during period	_____
Transferred to dept. __B__ during period	2,600 units
Transferred to stockroom during period	_____
In process, end of period	400 units
Stage of completion	3/4

FIGURE 7-2   Cost of Production Summary, Dept. A

Milford Manufacturing Corp.
Cost of Production Summary—Dept. A
For the Month Ended April 30, 19—

Cost of work in process, beginning of month:		
Materials	$1,500	
Labor	250	
Factory overhead	150	$ 1,900
Cost of production for month:		
Materials	$7,500	
Labor	3,375	
Factory overhead	2,025	12,900
Total costs to be accounted for		**$14,800**
Unit output for month:		
Materials:		
Finished and transferred to dept. B during month		2,600
Equivalent units of work in process, end of month		
(400 units, three-fourths completed, all materials)		400
Total equivalent production		3,000
Labor and factory overhead:		
Finished and transferred to Dept. B during month		2,600
Equivalent units of work in process, end of month		
(400 units, three-fourths completed)		300
Total equivalent production		2,900
Unit cost for month:		
Materials ($1,500 + $7,500) ÷ 3,000		$3.00
Labor ($250 + $3,375) ÷ 2,900		1.25
Factory overhead ($150 + $2,025) ÷ 2,900		.75
Total		$5.00
Inventory costs:		
Cost of goods finished and transferred to Dept. B		
during month (2,600 × $5)		13,000
Cost of work in process, end of month:		
Materials (400 × $3)	$1,200	
Labor (400 × 3/4 × $1.25)	375	
Factory overhead (400 × 3/4 × $.75)	225	1,800
Total production costs to be accounted for		**$14,800**

In Dept. A, because all materials are added at the start of processing, it is easy to determine the equivalent units for materials. The production report from the factory indicates that 500 units were in process at the beginning of the month with all materials added, and 2,500 units were started in process. Therefore, the equivalent production for materials is 3,000 units. Another way to calculate the figure by the method used in this chapter is as follows: the 2,600 units finished during the month plus the 400 units in process at the end of the month have all of the materials added. The total equivalent production for materials, therefore, is 3,000 units (2,600 + 400).

The unit output for labor and factory overhead is calculated as shown in the preceding chapter: 2,600 completed units, plus the equivalent of 300 completed units (400 units three-fourths completed), gives a total of 2,900 for the unit output for the month for labor and factory overhead.

With the equivalent production figures calculated for materials, labor, and overhead, the unit cost for the month can now be calculated. The cost of each element in the beginning work in process is added to the cost for that element incurred in the current month. This total cost for the element is then divided by the appropriate equivalent production figure to determine the unit cost for each element. In this example, the unit cost of materials is $3.00, for labor $1.25, and for overhead $.75, giving a total unit cost of $5.00.

The 2,600 units transferred to Dept. B are costed at $5.00 each and amount to a total cost of $13,000. In costing the ending work in process, the stage of completion and the point at which materials were added must be considered. In this instance, because materials were put into production at the beginning of the manufacturing cycle, the 400 units in process at the end of the period have had all materials added and are, therefore, costed at the full unit cost of $3.00 for materials. Because the goods are three-fourths completed, and labor and factory overhead are added evenly throughout the process, the 400 units are costed at three-fourths of the month's unit cost for labor and overhead.

ILLUSTRATIVE PROBLEM NO. 2

Computing the unit cost in Dept. B where all the materials are added at the close of processing—average cost method. In Dept. B, because the materials are added at the end of the process, materials cost will be applied only to those units finished. Therefore, the equivalent production for the month for materials in Dept. B is 2,500 units. The labor and factory overhead adds the 2,500 finished units to the equivalent production of the ending work in process, 350 units two-fifths completed, or 140, giving a total of 2,640 units as the equivalent output for the month. Figure 7-3 shows the

FIGURE 7-3   **Production Report, Dept. B**

PRODUCTION REPORT

For Month Ending _April 30, 19--_

Dept. _B_

In process, beginning of period _____ 250 units

Stage of completion _____ 1/2

Placed in process during period _____

Received from dept. ___A___ during period _2,600 units_

Transferred to dept. ___BC___ during period _2,500 units_

Transferred to stockroom during period _____

In process, end of period _____ 350 units

Stage of completion _____ 2/5

---

production report for Dept. B. Figure 7-4 shows the cost of production summary.

As in Dept. A, the unit cost for each element is determined by adding the cost in the beginning work in process to the cost for that element incurred during the month and dividing this total by the unit output for the month. For Dept. B, these unit costs for materials, labor, and factory overhead are $4, $3, and $3, respectively.

The units finished and transferred to Dept. C are valued at the full unit cost of $5 (from Dept. A), plus the unit cost of $10 added in Dept. B, amounting to a total cost transferred of $37,500 (2,500 units × $15).

The cost of the units in process at the end of the period includes the full cost of $5 from Dept. A. There is no materials cost for Dept. B because no materials were added. Because the units are two-fifths completed, two-fifths of the current unit costs for labor and factory overhead is used in costing the units. The combination of these items results in a cost of $2,590 for the ending work in process.

ILLUSTRATIVE PROBLEM NO. 3

Computing the unit cost in Dept. C where 60 percent of the materials cost is added to production at the beginning of processing and 40 percent of the materi-

FIGURE 7-4   Cost of Production Summary, Dept. B

Milford Manufacturing Corp.
Cost of Production Summary—Dept. B
For the Month Ended April 30,19—

Cost of work in process, beginning of month—Dept. B:			
Cost in Dept. A		$ 1,250	
Cost in Dept. B:			
Materials	-0-		
Labor	$375		
Factory overhead	375	750	$ 2,000
Cost of goods received from Dept. A during month			13,000
Cost of production for month:			
Materials	$10,000		
Labor	7,545		
Factory overhead	7,545	25,090	
Total costs to be accounted for			**$40,090**
Unit output for month:			
Materials:			
Finished and transferred to Dept. C during month			2,500
Equivalent units of work in process, end of month			-0-
Total equivalent production			2,500
Labor and factory overhead:			
Finished and transferred to Dept. C during month			2,500
Equivalent units of work in process, end of month			
(350 units, two-fifths completed)			140
Total equivalent production			2,640
Unit cost for month—Dept. B:			
Materials ($10,000 ÷ 2,500)			$4.00
Labor ($375 + $7,545) ÷ 2,640			3.00
Factory overhead ($375 + $7,545) ÷ 2,640			3.00
Total			$10.00
Inventory costs:			
Cost of goods finished and transferred to Dept. C			
during month:			
Cost in Dept. A (2,500 × $ 5)		$12,500	
Cost in Dept. B (2,500 × $10)		25,000	
(2,500 × $15)			$37,500
Cost of work in process, end of month:			
Cost in Dept. A (350 × $5)		$ 1,750	
Cost in Dept. B:			
Materials	-0-		
Labor (350 × 2/5 × $3)	$420		
Factory overhead (350 × 2/5 × $3)	420	840	2,590
Total production costs accounted for			**$40,090**

als *when the processing is one-half completed—average cost method.* In Dept. C, the calculation of equivalent production is more difficult because materials are added at different points throughout the process. The stage of completion of units in process cannot be averaged but must be reported in separate groups of units at various points in the manufacturing operation as shown in the production report, Figure 7-5. In calculating the units of output for the period, the stage of completion of each element group must be carefully examined as shown in Figure 7-6.

The equivalent production for materials for the month is calculated as follows: 2,400 units were finished, which includes all the materials, and 200 units are one-fourth completed at the end of the period. Because they are not yet at the halfway point of the process, only 60 percent of the materials have been added to the uncompleted units, an equivalent of 120 units. The 400 units that are three-fourths completed have passed the halfway stage and have had all materials added, a total of 400 units. Combining these figures—2,400, 120, and 400—results in the equivalent output for materials of 2,920 units.

It is simpler to calculate the equivalency for labor and factory overhead: 2,400 completed units, plus the equivalent of 50 completed units (200 units one-fourth completed), plus the equivalent of 300 completed

FIGURE 7-5   Production Report, Dept. C

PRODUCTION REPORT

For Month Ending _April 30, 19--_

Dept. _C_

In process, beginning of period _____ 500 units

Stage of completion _____ 200 units 3/4 completed-300 units 1/3 completed

Placed in process during period _____

Received from dept. ___B___ during period _2,500 units_

Transferred to dept. _____ during period _____

Transferred to stockroom during period _____ 2,400 units

In process, end of period _____ 600 units

Stage of completion _____ 200 units 1/4 completed-400 units 3/4 completed

FIGURE 7-6   Cost of Production Summary, Dept. C

Milford Manufacturing Corp.
Cost of Production Summary—Dept. C
For the Month Ended April 30, 19—

Cost of work in process, beginning of month—Dept. C:			
Cost in Dept. A		$ 2,500	
Cost in Dept. B		5,000	
Cost in Dept. C:			
Materials	$665		
Labor	300		
Factory overhead	150	1,115	$ 8,615
Cost of goods received from Dept. B during month			$37,500
Cost of production for month:			
Materials		$ 4,445	
Labor		3,000	
Factory overhead		1,500	8,945
Total costs to be accounted for			**$55,060**
Unit output for month:			
Materials:			
Finished and transferred to finished goods during month			2,400
Equivalent units of work in process, end of month:			
200 units, one-fourth completed (60% of materials)			120
400 units, three-fourths completed (all materials)			400
Total equivalent production			2,920
Labor and overhead:			
Finished and transferred to finished goods during month			2,400
Equivalent units of work in process, end of month:			
200 units, one-fourth completed			50
400 units, three-fourths completed			300
Total equivalent production			2,750
Unit cost for month—Dept. C:			
Materials ($665 + $4,445) ÷ 2,920			$1.75
Labor ($300 + $3,000) ÷ 2,750			1.20
Factory overhead ($150 + $1,500) ÷ 2,750			.60
Total			$3.55

Inventory costs:
  Cost of goods finished and transferred to finished goods
  during month:
    Cost in Dept. A (2,400 × $ 5.00) $12,000
    Cost in Dept. B (2,400 × $10.00)   24,000
    Cost in Dept. C (2,400 × $ 3.55)   8,520
                     (2,400 × $18.55) $44,520

Cost of work in process, end of month:
  200 units, one-fourth completed:
    Cost in Dept. A (200 × $5) . . . . $ 1,000
    Cost in Dept. B (200 × $10)   2,000
    Cost in Dept. C:
      Materials (200 × 60% × $1.75) . . . . $ 210
      Labor (200 × 25% × $1.20)   60
      Factory overhead (200 × 25% × $.60)   30   300

  400 units, three-fourths completed:
    Cost in Dept. A (400 × $5)   2,000
    Cost in Dept. B (400 × $10)   4,000
    Cost in Dept. C:
      Materials (400 × $1.75) . . . . $ 700
      Labor (400 × 75% × $1.20)   360
      Factory overhead (400 × 75% × $.60)   180   1,240   10,540

Total production costs accounted for **$55,060**

---

units (400 units three-fourths completed) equals a total equivalent production for labor and overhead of 2,750 units.

   The unit costs for the month are calculated as previously illustrated
and are determined to be $1.75, $1.20, and $.60 for materials, labor, and
factory overhead, respectively, for a total unit cost in Dept. C of $3.55.
The cost of the units finished and transferred to the stockroom includes
the unit costs from Dept. A of $5, from Dept. B of $10, and from Dept. C
of $3.55, a total cost of $18.55.

   In calculating the cost to be assigned to the ending work in process,
the stage of completion must be considered. The 200 units that are
one-fourth completed will have all the costs from Dept. A and B assigned
to them because they were 100% completed by those departments. The
costs in Dept. C are determined as follows: 60 percent of the materials
cost has been added to the 200 units, an equivalent of 120 units. The cost
of the materials will be as follows: 200 units × 60% × $1.75 = $210. The
costs allocated for labor and overhead are one-fourth of this month's unit
cost for each, or 200 units × 25% × $1.20 = $60 for labor and 200 units ×
25% × $.60 = $30 for overhead.

The 400 units that are three-fourths completed are assigned all of the unit costs from Depts. A ($5) and B ($10). Although these units are still in process, all materials required by department C have been added. Therefore, they are charged for the full cost of materials in Dept. C, $700 (400 units × $1.75). Three-fourths of the cost for labor and factory overhead would also be included in the cost of these units: $360 for labor (400 units × 75% × $1.20), and $180 for overhead (400 units × 75% × $.60).

After the cost of production summaries have been prepared for each department, the journal entries can be made as illustrated in Chapter 6. Entries would be made to transfer costs from one department to next department and so on, ending at Finished Goods. The actual costs incurred during the month for materials, labor, and factory overhead would be recorded in the journals and ledgers. After all entries have been made, the work in process accounts in the general ledger should have balances that equal the cost assigned to work in process on the cost of production summaries. If desired, a departmental cost work sheet can be prepared as illustrated in Chapter 6.

> **You should now be able to work the following: Exercises 1, 2, 3, 4, 5, 6 and Problems 1, 2, 3, 4.**

UNITS LOST IN PRODUCTION

LEARNING OBJECTIVE
Account for units lost at the beginning or end of the production process

In many industries that have a process manufacturing operation, the process is of a nature that some units will always be lost due to evaporation, shrinkage, spillage, or other factors. The effect of such losses is that when the number of units completed in a given period is added to the number of units still in process at the end of the period, the total units calculated will be less than the number of units that should be accounted for.

Normal losses are expected in the manufacturing process and cannot be avoided. They represent a necessary cost of producing the marketable units. Usually, normal losses are treated as product costs; that is, the cost of the lost units are included as a part of the cost of all units finished or still in process. In other words, the good units absorb the cost of the units lost. The effect is that the unit cost of the remaining units is greater than if no losses had been incurred, because of the smaller number of units over which to spread the production costs for the period. The following examples illustrate the procedures involved.

ILLUSTRATIVE PROBLEM NO. 1

Units lost in the first department. Assume that materials, labor, and factory overhead are applied evenly throughout the process and the monthly production report for Dept. A reports the following data:

Units started in process		12,000
Units finished and transferred to the next department . . .	9,000	
Units still in process, one-half completed	2,000	11,000
Units lost in production		1,000

This report is significant to factory managers, who review these figures to determine whether they represent normal unavoidable losses or abnormal losses that will require a different type of action. From the production statistics and costs of production data for the month, a cost of production summary as shown in Figure 7-7 can be prepared.

FIGURE 7-7   Gallion Cost of Production Summary, Dept. A

Gallion Refining Corporation
Cost of Production Summary—Dept. A
For the Month Ended July 31, 19—

Cost of production for month:		
Materials		$20,000
Labor		10,000
Factory overhead		5,000
Total costs to be accounted for		**$35,000**
Unit output for month:		
Finished and transferred to Dept. B during month		9,000
Equivalent units of work in process, end of month		
(2,000 units, one-half completed)		1,000
Total equivalent production		10,000
Unit cost for month:		
Materials ($20,000 ÷ 10,000)		$2.00
Labor ($10,000 ÷ 10,000)		1.00
Factory overhead ($5,000 ÷ 10,000)		.50
Total		$3.50
Inventory costs:		
Cost of goods finished and transferred to Dept. B during		
month (9,000 × $3.50)		$31,500
Cost of work in process, end of month:		
Materials (2,000 × 1/2 × $2)	$2,000	
Labor (2,000 × 1/2 × $1)	1,000	
Factory overhead (2,000 × 1/2 × $.50)	500	3,500
Total production costs accounted for		**$35,000**

Notice on the cost of production summary that the lost units have not been considered; they have been ignored in the calculation of equivalent production and in the determination of inventory costs. If the units had not been lost but had been finished, equivalent production would have been 11,000 units, and the unit costs for materials, labor, and factory overhead would have been lower. In the case illustrated, there is a loss of units, which is absorbed by the good units produced during the month.

ILLUSTRATIVE PROBLEM NO. 2

Units lost in subsequent department. The July production report for Dept. B reflects the following data:

Units received from Dept. A		9,000
Units finished and transferred to finished goods	8,000	
Units still in process, two-thirds completed	750	8,750
Units lost in production		250

On the cost of production summary for Dept. B, Figure 7-8, the unit costs for the month are calculated in the same way as they were calculated in Dept. A. The 250 units lost in the department during the period are ignored in the computations so that the higher unit costs for the month reflect the absorption of the costs relating to the lost units.

An additional computation is required, however, to determine the cost of goods finished and the cost of the work in process at the end of the month. The 250 units lost in Dept. B were ignored in determining unit costs for material, labor, and overhead in Dept. B, but these units carried a cost of $3.50 each from Dept. A and this unit cost from Dept. A must now be adjusted because there are fewer units left of the units transferred in.

During the month, 250 of the 9,000 units transferred from Dept. A were lost in Dept. B. Therefore, the total cost transferred, $31,500, must now be spread over the remaining 8,750 units, creating a new unit cost of $3.60. This new cost is referred to in the cost of production summary as the adjusted unit cost. The adjustment of the unit cost does not affect Dept. A's cost of production summary, because the units were lost in Dept. B; therefore, Dept. B is completely responsible for any loss that may occur.

Another way of making this calculation is as follows:

Units from Dept. A lost in Dept. B	250
Multiplied by the unit cost from Dept. A	$ 3.50
Cost applicable to the units lost	$875.00
Number of units transferred from Dept. A	9,000
Number of units lost	250
Number of units remaining	8,750

FIGURE 7-8   Gallion Cost of Production Summary, Dept. B

Gallion Refining Corporation
Cost of Production Summary—Dept. B
For the Month Ended July 31, 19—

Cost of production for month:

Materials	$15,300	
Labor	10,200	
Factory overhead	6,375	
Total		$31,875
Cost of goods received from Dept. A during month		31,500
Total costs to be accounted for		**$63,375**

Unit output for month:

Finished and transferred to finished goods during month	8,000
Equivalent units of work in process, end of month	
(750 units, two-thirds completed)	500
Total equivalent production	8,500

Unit cost for month:

Materials ($15,300 ÷ 8,500)	$1.80
Labor ($10,200 ÷ 8,500)	1.20
Factory overhead ($6,375 ÷ 8,500)	.75
Total	$3.75

Inventory costs:

Cost of goods finished and transferred to finished goods:

Cost in Dept. A (8,000 × $3.60, adjusted unit cost)	$28,800	
Cost in Dept. B (8,000 × $3.75	30,000	
(8,000 × $7.35)		$58,800

Cost of work in process, end of month:

Cost in Dept. A (750 × $3.60, adjusted unit cost)		$ 2,700	
Cost in Dept. B:			
Materials (750 × 2/3 × $1.80)	$900		
Labor (750 × 2/3 × $1.20)	600		
Factory overhead (750 × 2/3 × $.75)	375	1,875	4,575
Total production costs accounted for			**$63,375**

The cost applicable to lost units must be spread over the remaining units:

$$\frac{\$875}{8,750} = \$.10 \text{ adjustment in unit cost}$$

Original unit cost	$3.50
Add adjustment in unit cost	.10
Adjusted unit cost	$3.60

ILLUSTRATIVE PROBLEM NO. 3

Units lost at the end of the process. In the previous illustrations, the units lost were treated as though they had never been put into production. Both finished goods and the units still in process absorbed the cost of the lost units. However, if the units are lost at the end of the process or are rejected at the final inspection, the cost of the lost units should be absorbed fully *only by the units completed.* In this case, no part of the loss is charged to the units remaining in process that still must be completed. The lost units are *included* in the number of units used to determine equivalent production. The unit costs are then calculated in the usual way, thus producing a lower unit cost than if the lost units had been ignored. This unit cost is applied to goods finished and transferred, units still in process, and to the units that were lost. The cost assigned to lost units is then *added only to the cost of the goods completed,* and this total cost is transferred to the next department or to Finished Goods. The *unit cost* of the goods transferred will, of course, be *higher than the calculated monthly unit cost* of production because the transferred units have absorbed the cost of the lost units. Figure 7-9 shows these calculations in a cost of production summary. The data used in this summary came from Illustration Problem No. 1 (units lost in the first department).

The preceding discussion has considered only normal losses, with the cost of lost units being treated as a product cost, that is, charged to the remaining good units. But **abnormal losses** may also occur. Such losses are not expected in the manufacturing process and should not happen under normal, efficient operating conditions. Units lost under abnormal circumstances are included in the calculation of equivalent production and unit costs are determined as if the units were lost at the end of the process. However, abnormal losses are not included as part of the cost of transferred or finished goods, but are treated as a **period cost**—that is, they are charged to a separate account and shown as a separate item of expense on the current income statement and not as a part of the manufacturing costs. If the number of units lost in the following example was considered to be abnormal, the cost transferred to the next department would be $32,812; $729 would be charged to Abnormal Loss of Units, and the cost of work in process would remain unchanged at $1,459.

FIGURE 7-9   Gallion Cost of Production Summary, Dept. A

Gallion Refining Corporation
Cost of Production Summary—Dept. A
For the Month Ended July 31, 19—

Cost of production for month:

Materials	$20,000
Labor	10,000
Factory overhead	5,000
Total costs to be accounted for	**$35,000**

Unit output for month:

Finished and transferred to Dept. B during month	9,000
Equivalent units of work in process, end of month (800 units, one-half completed)	400
Lost at end of process	200
Total equivalent production	9,600

Unit cost for month:

Materials ($20,000 ÷ 9,600)	$2.0833
Labor ($10,000 ÷ 9,600)	1.0417
Factory overhead ($5,000 ÷ 9,600)	.5208
Total	$3.6458

Inventory costs:

Cost of goods finished and transferred to Dept. B during month (9,000 × $3.6458)	$32,812	
Add cost of units lost (200 × $3.6458)	729	
Total cost of good units finished and transferred to Dept. B during month (9,000 × $3.7268*)		$33,541
Cost of work in process, end of month:		
Materials (800 × 1/2 × $2.0833)	$833	
Labor (800 × 1/2 × $1.0417)	417	
Factory overhead (800 × 1/2 × $.5208)	209	1,459
Total production costs accounted for		**$35,000**

*$729 ÷ 9,000 units completed = $.081 unit cost adjustment for lost units; $3.6458 + $.081 = $3.7268 adjusted unit cost of units completed.

ILLUSTRATIVE PROBLEM NO. 4

Abnormal loss of units at the beginning of the process. If an abnormal loss occurs at the beginning of processing in a department, only materials and/or transferred-in costs are affected. Because they are lost early in the process, no labor or overhead should be added to these lost units. Using the Dept. A data, Figure 7-10 shows the abnormal loss calculated and accounted for.

The journal entry to transfer costs would be as follows:

Work in Process—Dept. B	33,111	
Abnormal Loss of Units	317	
Work in Process—Dept. A		33,528

FIGURE 7-10   Gallion Cost of Production Summary, Dept. A

**Gallion Refining Corporation
Cost of Production Summary—Dept. A
For the Month Ended July 31, 19—**

Cost of production for month:	
Materials	$20,000
Labor	10,00
Factory overhead	5,000
Total costs to be accounted for	**$35,000**

Unit output for month:		
Materials:		
Finished and transferred to Dept. B during month .	9,000	
Equivalent units of work in process, end of month		
(800 units, one-half completed)		400
Lost in process		200
Total equivalent production		9,600

Labor and factory overhead:		
Finished and transferred to Dept. B during month .	9,000	
Equivalent units of work in process, end of month		
(800 units, one-half completed)		400
Total equivalent production		9,400

Unit cost for month:	
Materials ($20,000 ÷ 9,600)	$2.0833
Labor ($10,000 ÷ 9,400)	1.0638
Factory overhead ($5,000 ÷ 9,400)	.5319
Total	$3.6790

Inventory costs and abnormal loss:		
Cost of goods finished and transferred to Dept. B		
(9,000 × $3.6790)		$33,111
Cost of work in process, end of month:		
Materials (800 × 1/2 × $2.0833)	$833	
Labor (800 × 1/2 × $1.0638)	426	
Factory overhead (800 × 1/2 × $.5319)	213	1,472
Cost of abnormal loss (200 × $2.0833)		417
Total production costs accounted for		**$35,000**

UNITS GAINED IN PRODUCTION

LEARNING OBJECTIVE
Account for units gained in the production process

For some products, the addition of materials in any department after the first department may increase the number of units being processed. For example, assume a liquid product is being produced. In the first department, 1,000 gallons of various materials are put into production. In the next department, an additional 500 gallons of a different material is added, increasing the number of units being manufactured to 1,500. This increase in units has the opposite effect of lost units and requires an adjustment to the unit cost. The calculation of this adjusted unit cost is similar to that made when units are lost, except that the total cost for the original units must now be spread over a greater number of units in the subsequent department, thereby reducing the unit cost.

To illustrate, assume that a concentrated detergent, Mor-Glean, is manufactured. During the month, 10,000 gallons of the partially processed product are transferred to Dept. B at a cost of $15,000, with a unit cost of $1.50. In Dept. B, 5,000 gallons of additional materials are added to these units in process. As these materials are added, the mixing and refining of the liquid involves the equal application of materials, labor, and overhead. A production report shows that 13,000 gallons were completed and transferred to finished goods, leaving 2,000 gallons in process, one-half completed. The cost of production summary, Figure 7-11, shows that the cost transferred from Dept. A for 10,000 gallons was $15,000, at a unit cost of $1.50. The addition of 5,000 gallons in Dept. B increases the liquid in process to 15,000 units. The cost from Dept. A of $15,000 must now be spread over these 15,000 units, resulting in an adjusted unit cost of $1.00.

It is possible that in addition to increasing the number of units, some units will also be lost during processing in Dept. B. This factor presents no additional problem, because the equivalent production and unit costs are calculated as though the lost units had not existed, and the type of computation shown in the preceding example would be the same. As

Mor-Glean Manufacturing Company
Cost of Production Summary—Dept. B
For the Month Ended May 31, 19—

Cost of goods received from Dept. A during month		
(10,000 gallons × $1.50)		$15,000
Cost of production for month:		
Materials	$15,400	
Labor	3,500	
Factory overhead	2,800	21,700
Total costs to be accounted for . . . . ?		**$36,700**
Unit output for month:		
Finished and transferred to finished goods		13,000
Equivalent units of work in process, end of month		
(2,000 gallons, one-half completed)		1,000
Total equivalent production		14,000
Unit cost for month:		
Materials ($15,400 ÷ 14,000)		$1.10
Labor ($3,500 ÷ 14,000)		.25
Factory overhead ($2,800 ÷ 14,000)		.20
Total		$1.55

Inventory costs:

Cost of goods finished and transferred to finished goods:			
Cost in Dept. A (13,000 × $1.00*, adjusted			
unit cost)		$13,000	
Cost in Dept. B (13,000 × $1.55)		20,150	
(13,000 × $2.55)			$33,150
Cost of work in process, end of month:			
Cost in Dept. A (2,000 × $1.00, adjusted unit cost)	$ 2,000		
Cost in Dept. B:			
Materials (2,000 × 1/2 × $1.10)	$1,100		
Labor (2,000 × 1/2 × $.25)	250		
Factory overhead (2,000 × 1/2 × $.20)	200	1,550	3,550
Total production costs accounted for			**$36,700**

*$15,000 ÷ 15,000 gal. = $1 per gal.

mentioned previously in this chapter, if management wishes to have a dollar accounting for lost units, the number lost would be included in equivalent production as though no loss had occurred. The unit cost would be computed and a dollar cost assigned to lost units by multiplying the unit cost by the number of units lost.

EQUIVALENT PRODUCTION—-FIRST-IN, FIRST-OUT METHOD

LEARNING OBJECTIVE
Assign costs to inventories using the first-in, first-out method

The previous discussion and illustrations have used the average method of costing. As mentioned in Chapter 6, another method commonly used is the **first-in, first-out (FIFO) method**. This procedure assumes that the unit costs calculated for the current period are applied for a variety of reasons: first, to complete the beginning units of work in process; second, to start and fully complete an additional number of units; and finally, to start other units that will remain unfinished at the end of the period.

The two problems that follow illustrate the FIFO method and compare it to the average costing method. When studying these examples, note that FIFO costing differs from average costing only if there are units in process at the start of the period. If no beginning work in process exists, both methods will produce the same results.

Also note that under the FIFO method, if units are lost, management must decide whether these units are from the beginning inventory or from the units started during the period. Assuming that unit costs differ from one period to the next, this decision is necessary in order to determine which transferred in unit cost should be adjusted, the transferred in unit cost shown for the beginning inventory or the unit cost for the units transferred in this period. Suppose for example, that the loss occurs in the second department at the very beginning of operations. Because the beginning inventory in the department has had some work completed, the loss has already affected the beginning inventory units. The only units subject to the loss would, therefore, be units transferred in this period.

Whether using the FIFO or the average cost method, the first step in preparing the cost of production summary is to list the costs that must be accounted for; the beginning balance of work in process, the current period's costs of production, and the cost of units transferred from a prior department, if any. With the FIFO method, it is not necessary to break down the cost of the beginning work in process into its cost elements as the average cost method requires.

The second step under the FIFO method, as with the average cost procedure, is to determine the unit output for the month. If there were units in process at the start of the period, the total equivalent production figures for the FIFO method will differ from those for the average cost method because the unit output required to complete the beginning work in process must be calculated in the FIFO method.

ILLUSTRATIVE PROBLEM NO. 1

LEARNING OBJECTIVE
Recognize the differences between average costing and first-in, first-out methods of production costing

FIFO cost method compared with average cost method—materials added at start of process. Assume that in Dept. 1, materials are added at the start of processing. Labor and factory overhead are applied evenly throughout the process. The production report for March reflects the following data:

Units in process, beginning of month, two-thirds completed . . .	3,000
Units started in process	9,000
Units finished and transferred to Dept. 2	8,000
Units in process, end of month, one-half completed	4,000

Cost data are as follows:

Beginning work in process, prior month's cost:

Materials	$ 9,600
Labor	3,600
Factory overhead	2,800
Total	$16,000

Current month's production costs:

Materials	$27,000
Labor	16,000
Factory overhead	8,000
Total	$51,000

Using the FIFO method, a cost of production summary is prepared as presented in Figure 7-12. For comparative purposes, Figure 7-13 shows a cost of production summary using the average cost method.

There were 3,000 units in process at the beginning of the month. These units were complete as to materials and two-thirds complete as to labor and factory overhead.

In the current month, no materials had to be added to the beginning inventory. However, the equivalent of 1,000 units (3,000 × 1/3) of labor and overhead had to be applied to finish the units in Dept. 1.

Of the 8,000 units finished and transferred to Dept. 2 during the month, 3,000 were from the beginning units in process. Therefore, 5,000 units were started and fully completed during the month. Under the FIFO cost method, the beginning units in process *are not merged* with the units started and finished during the month.

The calculation of equivalent production for the *ending work in process* is the *same* under FIFO and the average cost method. These 4,000 units in ending inventory have had all materials added and only one half of the labor and overhead. Thus, the ending inventory equivalent

FIGURE 7-12   Cost of Production Summary, Dept. 1, FIFO Method

---

FIFO METHOD

Bold Manufacturing Company
Cost of Production Summary—Dept. 1
For the Month Ended March 31, 19—

Cost of work in process, beginning of month		$16,000
Cost of production for month:		
Materials	$27,000	
Labor	16,000	
Factory overhead	8,000	51,000
Total costs to be accounted for		**$67,000**

Unit output for month:

	Materials	Labor and Factory Overhead
To complete beginning units in process	-0-	1,000
Units started and finished during month	5,000	5,000
Ending units in process	4,000	2,000
Total equivalent production	9,000	8,000

Unit cost for month:		
Materials ($27,000 ÷ 9,000)		$3.00
Labor ($16,000 ÷ 8,000)		2.00
Factory overhead ($8,000 ÷ 8,000)		1.00
Total		$6.00

Inventory costs:		
Cost of goods finished and transferred to Dept. 2 during month:		
Beginning units in process:		
Prior month's cost	$16,000	
Current cost to complete:		
Materials	-0-	
Labor (3,000 × 1/3 × $2)	2,000	
Factory overhead (3,000 × 1/3 × $1)	1,000	$19,000
Units started and finished during month		
(5,000 × $6.00)		30,000
Total cost transferred (8,000 × $6.125*) . . .		$49,000
Cost of work in process, end of month:		
Materials (4,000 × $3)	$12,000	
Labor (4,000 × 1/2 × $2)	4,000	
Factory overhead (4,000 × 1/2 × $1)	2,000	18,000
Total production costs accounted for		**$67,000**

*$49,000 ÷ 8,000 = $6.125

FIGURE 7-13   Cost of Production Summary, Dept. 1, Average Cost Method

AVERAGE COST METHOD

Bold Manufacturing Company
Cost of Production Summary—Dept. 1
For the Month Ended March 31, 19—

Cost of work in process, beginning of month:			
Materials		$ 9,600	
Labor		3,600	
Factory overhead		2,800	$16,000
Cost of production for month:			
Materials		$27,000	
Labor		16,000	
Factory overhead		8,000	51,000
Total costs to be accounted for			**$67,000**
Unit output for month:			
Materials:			
Finished and transferred to Dept. 2 during month			8,000
Work in process, end of month			4,000
Total equivalent production			12,000
Labor and factory overhead:			
Finished and transferred to Dept. 2 during month			8,000
Work in process, end of month			2,000
Total equivalent production			10,000
Unit cost for month:			
Materials ($9,600 + $27,000) ÷ 12,000			$3.05
Labor ($3,600 + $16,000) ÷ 10,000			1.96
Factory overhead ($2800 + $8,000) ÷ 10,000			1.08
Total			$6.09
Inventory costs:			
Cost of goods finished and transferred to Dept. 2			
during month (8,000 × $6.09)			$48,720
Cost of work in process, end of month:			
Materials (4,000 × $3.05)		$12,200	
Labor (4,000 × 1/2 × $1.96)		3,920	
Factory overhead (4,000 × 1/2 × $1.08)		2,160	18,280
Total production costs accounted for			**$67,000**

production for materials is 4,000 units and for labor and overhead, 2,000 units (4,000 × 1/2).

The calculation of unit costs with the FIFO method takes into consideration only the current period's cost data. The total cost of each element—materials, labor, and factory overhead—is divided by the equivalent production for the period to determine the unit cost for each element. The cost elements of the beginning work in process is not merged with current costs elements, under the FIFO method, as it is in the average cost method.

When assigning costs to the units finished and transferred, the average cost approach charges the 8,000 units transferred with the total unit cost of $6.09. Under the FIFO method, however, two calculations are necessary to determine the cost assigned to units transferred. First, the 3,000 units in process at the beginning of the month were previously completed as to materials; therefore, no cost for materials is added. However, the units had been only two-thirds completed during the previous month as to labor and overhead and must be one-third completed this month. Thus, one-third of the current period's unit cost for labor and overhead is assigned to each of the 3,000 units. The cost to complete the beginning inventory then is added to the $16,000 beginning inventory cost carried over from the prior period to arrive at a completed cost for the beginning inventory of $19,000.

Second, the 5,000 units started and fully manufactured during the month are priced at the unit cost of $6 for the period. The total accumulated cost of the 3,000 units in process at the beginning of the month ($19,000) plus the cost of the 5,000 units started and finished during the month ($30,000) is then transferred to Dept. 2 ($49,000). Note that when making this transfer of cost, the cost and unit cost related to the beginning inventory units lose their identity because they are merged with the costs of units started and finished during the current period. Thus, the $49,000 of the total cost transferred to Dept. 2 is divided by the 8,000 units transferred to Dept. 2 to arrive at a single unit cost of $6.125. The costs assigned to the ending work in process inventory are determined in the same manner under the FIFO method and the average cost approach. The 4,000 units are complete as to materials and are charged with the full cost of material. They are one-half complete as to labor and overhead and are allocated one half of the labor and overhead cost. Although the method of calculation is the same, the total costs charged to the ending units in process differ between the FIFO and average cost methods because of the difference in unit costs determined by the two procedures.

ILLUSTRATIVE PROBLEM NO. 2

FIFO cost method compared with average cost method—materials added at end of process and units lost during process. Assume that in Dept. 2, materials are added at the end of the process and labor and factory overhead are applied evenly throughout the process. The production for March reflects the following information:

Units in process, beginning of month, three-fourths completed .	2,000
Units received from Dept. 1	8,000
Units finished	8,000
Units in process, end of month, one-half completed	1,000
Units lost	1,000

Cost data are as follows:
Beginning work in process, prior month's cost:

Prior department cost	$12,000
Materials	-0-
Labor	4,160
Factory overhead	3,000
Total	$19,160

Cost of units received from Dept. 1	$49,000

Current month's production costs:

Materials	$16,000
Labor	21,000
Factory overhead	14,000
Total	$51,000

Figure 7-14 shows the cost of production summary for Dept. 2 using the FIFO method and Figure 7-15 shows the summary using the average cost method. In the cost of production summary using the FIFO method, the costs to be accounted for are listed and then the unit output for the period is determined. In this department, materials are added at the end of the process. Therefore, in order to finish the 2,000 units in process at the beginning of the period, all materials have to be added—a total of 2,000 units. Three-fourths of the labor and factory overhead were applied to these beginning inventory units in the previous period, so one-fourth of the labor and overhead need to be applied in the current month to finish the 2,000 units—an equivalent of 500 units.

Of the 8,000 units completed during the period, 2,000 were from the beginning inventory; therefore, 6,000 new units were started and fully manufactured during the current month. The 1,000 units in process at the end of the month have had no materials added but are one-half complete as to labor and overhead—an equivalent of 500 units.

FIGURE 7-14   Cost of Production Summary, Dept. 2, FIFO Method

---

FIFO METHOD

Bold Manufacturing Company
Cost of Production Summary—Dept. 2
For the Month Ended March 31, 19—

Cost of work in process, beginning of month . . .		$ 19,160
Cost of goods received from Dept. 1 during month		49,000
Cost of production for month:		
Materials	$16,000	
Labor	21,000	
Factory overhead	14,000	51,000
Total costs to be accounted for		**$119,160**

Unit output for month:

	Materials	Labor and Factory Overhead
To complete beginning units in process	2,000	500
Units started and finished during month	6,000	6,000
Ending units in process	-0-	500
Total equivalent production	8,000	7,000

Unit cost for month:	
Materials ($16,000 ÷ 8,000)	$2.00
Labor ($21,000 ÷ 7,000)	3.00
Factory overhead ($14,000 ÷ 7,000)	2.00
Total	$7.00

Inventory costs:
  Cost of goods finished:

Beginning units in process:		
Prior month's cost	$19,160	
Current cost to complete:		
Materials (2,000 × $2)	4,000	
Labor (2,000 × 1/4 × $3)	1,500	
Factory overhead (2,000 × 1/4 × $2) . . .	1,000	$25,660
Units started and finished during month:		
Cost in Dept. 1 (6,000 × $ 7*)	$42,000	
Cost in Dept. 2 (6,000 × $ 7)	42,000	84,000
(6,000 × $14)		
Total [(2,000 units + 6,000 units) × $13.7075]**		$109,660

Cost of work in process, end of month:
   Cost in Dept. 1 (1,000 × $7*) . . . . $ 7,000
   Cost in Dept. 2:
      Materials . . . .   -0-
      Labor (1,000 × 1/2 × $3) 1,500
      Factory overhead (1,000 × 1/2 × $2) 1,000   9,500

Total production costs accounted for **$119,160**

*The adjusted unit cost is calculated as follows:
  Units received from Dept. 1 during
     the current month 8,000
  Units lost in Dept. 2 1,000

  Units remaining 7,000

Cost transferred from Dept. 1—$49,000 ÷ 7,000 units = $7 adjusted unit cost.
**$109,660 ÷ 8,000 units = $13.7075

Notice that with both the FIFO and average cost methods, the units lost in processing are ignored for purposes of calculating the unit output. This procedure is based on the assumption that the losses are normal and usual in the processing of the product. If the losses were incurred at the end of the process, or were abnormal, the lost units would be included in the determination of equivalent production and a separate dollar amount would be calculated for these units.

As in Dept. 1, unit cost for FIFO is calculated by dividing the current period's cost of each element by the equivalent production for that element. Under the average cost method, unit cost is calculated by dividing the merged element costs of the current period and work in process by the equivalent production for each element.

In FIFO, to calculate the total completed cost of the beginning inventory, the total cost balance of the beginning work in process from the previous period is added to the costs incurred to complete these units in the current period. The 2,000 units are charged for the full cost of materials and with one-fourth of the current costs for labor and overhead. The average cost method does not require a separate computation to complete the beginning inventory.

Under the FIFO method, when calculating the cost to be allocated to units fully manufactured during the month, the lost units must be considered because the total unit cost transferred in from the previous department must be adjusted. As mentioned previously, it must be deter-

FIGURE 7-15   Cost of Production Summary, Dept. 2, Average Cost Method

---

AVERAGE COST METHOD

Bold Manufacturing Company
Cost of Production Summary—Dept. 2
For the Month Ended March 31, 19—

Cost of work process, beginning of month:			
Cost in Dept. 1		$12,000	
Cost in Dept. 2:			
Materials	-0-		
Labor	$4,160		
Factory overhead	3,000	7,160	$ 19,160
Cost of goods received from Dept. 1 during month			48,720
Cost of production for month:			
Materials	$16,000		
Labor	21,000		
Factory overhead	14,000	51,000	
Total costs to be accounted for			**$118,880**
Unit output for month:			
Materials finished during month			8,000
Labor and overhead:			
Finished during month		8,000	
Work in process, end of month . . .		500	8,500

Unit cost for month:		
Materials ($16,000 ÷ 8,000)		$2.00
Labor [($4,160 + $21,000) ÷ 8,500] . .		2.96
Factory overhead [($3,000 + $14,000)÷ 8,500]		2.00
Total		$6.96

Inventory costs:		
Cost of goods finished:		
Cost in Dept. 1 (8,000 × $ 6.74667*)	$53,973**	
Cost in Dept. 2 (8,000 × $ 6.96)	55,680	
(8,000 × $13.70667)		$109,653**
Cost of work in process, end of month:		
Cost in Dept. 1 (1,000 × $6.74667*)	$ 6,747**	

Cost in Dept. 2:
  Materials . . . . -0-
  Labor (1,000 × 1/2 × $2.96) 1,480
  Factory overhead (1,000 × 1/2 × $2.00) 1,000   9,227

Total production costs accounted for .   **$118,880**

*The adjusted unit cost is calculated as follows:
Total units processed during the month that
  had been received from Dept. 1 . . *10,000*
Units lost *1,000*

Units remaining *9,000*

Total cost from Dept. 1—($12,000 + $48,720) ÷ 9,000 = $6.74667
adjusted unit cost.
**Rounded

---

mined whether the lost units came from the units in process at the beginning of the period or from the units received during the period. For example, if losses occur in the process at the very beginning of the manufacturing process, any units in the beginning inventory would have already experienced a loss in the previous period. Only the units started in the current period then would be affected by a loss. The units transferred into the department this period would require an adjustment for the loss of units.

In the case illustrated, 8,000 units were received but 1,000 units were lost in processing, leaving only 7,000 of the transferred in units for Dept. 2 to process. The cost transferred from Dept. 1 during the period, $49,000, is divided by the 7,000 units remaining, which results in an adjusted unit cost of $7 for the goods received from Dept. 1. The 6,000 units started and finished during the month are charged with the $7 adjusted unit cost from the prior department *plus* the $7 current unit cost generated by Dept. 2.

Under the average cost method, all of the units from Dept. 1, whether this month's or last month's units, must be considered in determining the adjusted unit cost. The 2,000 units in process at the beginning of the period and the 8,000 units received during the month are included in the calculation. The prior department cost of $12,000, carried over from the previous month, is added to the current month's cost ($48,720) transferred from Dept. 1. The total prior department cost of $60,720 is then divided by the 9,000 remaining units to produce an adjusted unit cost of

$6.74667. The 8,000 units completed during the period have a total unit cost for the period of $13.70667, which consist of the transferred in adjusted cost of $6.74667 plus the cost added by the Dept. 2 operations of $6.96.

The calculation of the costs to be charged to the units in process at the end of the month obtain different results although both, FIFO and average cost, use the same mathematical methods. The values of the ending work in process differ because of the procedures used to derive the prior department and current month unit costs.

In comparing the FIFO and the average cost methods, FIFO provides that units started within the current period are valued at the current period's costs and are not distorted by the merging of the current costs with costs from the preceding period, which could be considerably different. The units and costs in the beginning inventory in a processing department maintain their separate identity. This helps to control costs by having purely current unit costs each month to compare when analyzing month-to-month costs for deviations. Use of the FIFO method, however, means that the units in the beginning inventory are valued when completed at a cost that represents neither the prior period's cost nor the current period's cost, but a combination of the two. Also, the identity of the beginning units in process is typically not maintained when these units are transferred to the next department. The cost of these units is usually combined with the cost of units fully manufactured during the month at the time of transfer.

The average cost method has an advantage when compared to FIFO in that all units completed during the period will be assigned the same unit cost. This cost assignment procedure makes average cost a simpler method to use. In the final analysis, however, a manufacturer should choose the method that not only minimizes the clerical cost of application but also most accurately gages its cost of production so that its products can successfully compete in the marketplace.

JOINT PRODUCTS AND BY-PRODUCTS

LEARNING OBJECTIVE
Identify the nature of joint costs and the methods used to apportion these costs to joint products

In many industries, the manufacturing process originates with one or more raw materials started in process, from which two or more distinct products are derived. Examples of these industries are petroleum refineries, lumber mills, and meat packing plants. Petroleum yields gasoline, heating oils, and lubricants. Lumber mills produce various grades of lumber and salable sawdust. Meat packing processes result in a variety of different cuts of meat and other products. The several items obtained from a common process are divided into two categories: those that are

INVESTIGATING COSTS

Many companies are striving to improve profit margins by lowering costs. Some companies have found that overhead and materials costs are much more significant than labor costs.

Electroplating (or *plating*) is the term used for a process in which electricity passes through a solution of metal salts to deposit the metal on another conductive surface. The concept has been known for hundreds of years but did not reach much industrial importance until fewer than one hundred years ago. The process became popular when companies developed additives that improved the appearance and properties of these electrodeposits.

Over the last fifty years, novel plating processes have been developed. Plating companies supplied the plating processes to metal finishing companies. These plating processes have been responsible for much of the bright work on automobiles, appliances, and other consumer goods. Truly novel processes commanded premium prices, which resulted in very attractive profit margins. As plating technology developed more slowly, key patents expired, and competition increased, these margins have decreased significantly. Where seventy percent factory profits were the rule, companies now try for sixty percent and often accept fifty percent.

For many years, plating companies maintained their margins by simply raising prices. Competitive pressures have greatly reduced this option so that companies must search for other means of maintaining profit margins. Customers of this plating process also expect a high degree of customer service. When a plating customer buys a jug of additives, that customer is paying for and expects to receive technical education, technical service, analytical support, and twenty-four hour help in solving production problems relating to the process that the jug of additives provides.

Many companies assumed that high labor costs were the reason for lower margins. A closer investigation found that labor in many companies represented only five percent of product cost. Materials represented sixty-five percent and overhead thirty percent of product cost. Thus, labor is an almost insignificant factor in the cost of the products. Materials are a major portion of costs but offer slight possibilities of savings; specific compounds must be used in many products and, in some cases, these compounds are produced internally for company use only. Companies are now striving to originate substitutions in their research laboratories and to improve overhead costs.

the primary objectives of the process, called **joint products**, and secondary products with relatively little value, called **by-products**.

ACCOUNTING FOR JOINT PRODUCTS

The costs of materials, labor, and overhead incurred during the joint process are called **joint costs**. The separate products become identifiable at the **split-off point**. The manufacturing costs incurred up to this point usually cannot be specifically identified with any one of the individual products. A joint process may have one or more split-off points depending on the types of output produced. If a market exists for the product, it may be sold at the split-off point. However, some method must be adopted to equitably allocate the joint costs to each identifiable product. If further processing of any of the products is required after the split-off point, these additional costs will be applied directly to the specific products.

Typical bases for apportionment of joint costs to joint products follow:

1. A physical unit of measure such as volume, weight, size, or grade.
2. Relative sales value of each product (or adjusted sales value).
3. Chemical, engineering, or other types of analyses.

The allocation of joint costs according to **physical unit of measure** is a simple method of apportionment which assumes that each product has received similar benefits from the process and, therefore, is charged with a proportionate share of the total processing costs.

To illustrate, assume that the Chemx-alene Co. produces two liquid products from one process. In the manufacturing process, various materials are mixed in a huge vat and allowed to settle, so that a light liquid rises to the top and a heavier liquid settles to the bottom of the vat. The products, A and B, are drawn off separately and piped directly into tank cars for shipment. The costs of materials, labor, and overhead total $200,000, producing 30,000 gallons of A and 20,000 gallons of B. The allocation of costs would be as follows:

Product	Units (Gals.)	Percent of Total Quantity	Assignment of Joint Costs
A	30,000	60%	$120,000
B	20,000	40%	80,000
Total	50,000	100%	$200,000

This method is satisfactory if all of the units manufactured are similar in producing revenue. It would not be satisfactory if large variances in gross margins were created between the products. Also, it could conceivably allocate to a product costs that would exceed the sales value of the product.

The allocation of costs based on physical measure could, at times, be misleading. Therefore, the assignment of costs in proportion to the rela-tive sales value of each product is more commonly used. This method assumes a direct relationship between selling prices and joint costs. It fol-lows the logic that the greatest share of joint cost should be assigned to the product that has the highest sales value.

Assume the same facts as given for Chemx-alene Co. and assume that product A sells for $10.00 a gallon and product B for $25.00 a gallon. Using the relative sales value method, the joint costs of $200,000 would be allocated as follows:

Product	Units Produced		Unit Selling Price		Total Sales Value	Percent of Sales Value	Assignment of Joint Costs
A	30,000	×	$10.00	=	$300,000	37.5%	$ 75,000
B	20,000	×	25.00	=	500,000	62.5%	125,000
Total	50,000				$800,000	100.0%	$200,000

Some companies further refine this method by subtracting the esti-mated selling expenses for each product from its sales value to determine the net realizable value of the product. If a product is to be processed fur-ther after the point of separation, costs should not be assigned on the basis of ultimate sales value because the additional processing adds value to the product. In a case such as this, an adjusted sales value is used that takes into consideration the cost of the processing after split-off.

Assume that Chemx-alene Co. market researchers determine that product B would have a better market if it were sold in powder form in individual packages. After studying this proposition, the company decides to pipe product B into ovens to dehydrate it. The resulting pow-der is divided into one-pound packages that will sell for $80 each.

During the month of October, when the new process began, the costs of materials, labor, and factory overhead in the mixing and settling department were $127,500, $42,500, and $30,000, respectively, and 30,000 gallons of product A were transferred to tank cars. In the baking depart-ment, costs totaled $100,000 for baking and packaging the 20,000 gallons of product B received from mixing and settling, and 10,000 one-pound packages were produced.

The assignment of costs of $200,000 in the mixing and settling department, using the adjusted sales value method, follows:

Units Produced		Unit Selling Price		Ultimate Sales Value	Less Cost after Split-Off	Sales Value at Split-Off	Percent Sales Value	Assignment of Joint Costs
A—30,000 gal.	×	$10.00	=	$ 300,000	-0-	$ 300,000	30%	$ 60,000
B—10,000 lb.*	×	80.00	=	800,000	$100,000	700,000	70	140,000
Total				$1,100,000	$100,000	$1,000,000	100%	$200,000

20,000 gallons of liquid is further processed into 10,000 lbs. of powder.

The allocated cost of product A is transferred to a finished goods inventory account. The assigned cost of product B is transferred to a work in process account to which the additional costs of processing is charged. The total cost of product B is then transferred to a finished goods inventory account.

Occasionally, the makeup of the joint products is such that a chemical or engineering analysis, or some other type of examination of component parts, can be employed to determine the amount of raw materials present in each completed product. This procedure is complex and should be carried out by qualified experts. The accountant's allocation of costs can be based on these analyses and will follow the procedures previously discussed.

If the Chemx-alene Co. found, upon analysis, that 40% of the raw materials introduced into the process were present in the finished product A and 60% in product B and that labor and overhead were added evenly, the company could make the following allocation of costs:

October Processing Costs (A/B)			Allocated to Products	
			A	B
Materials	$127,500	(40/60)	$51,000	$ 76,500
Labor	42,500	(50/50)	21,250	21,250
Factory overhead	30,000	(50/50)	15,000	15,000
Total	$200,000		$87,250	$112,750

ACCOUNTING FOR BY-PRODUCTS

LEARNING OBJECTIVE
Account for
by-products

In accounting for by-products, the common practice is to make no allocation of the processing costs up to the split-off point. Costs incurred up to that point are chargeable to the main products. If no further processing is required to make the by-products marketable, they may be accounted for by debiting an inventory account, By-Products, and crediting Work in Process for the estimated sales value of the by-products recovered.

Under this procedure, the estimated sales value of the by-products reduces the cost of the main products. The reduction in costs, due to the by-product, is shown in the inventory costs section of the cost of production summary. If the by-products are sold for more or less than the estimated sales value, the difference may be credited or debited to Gain and Loss on Sales of By-Products.

Assume that the production management of the Chemx-alene Co. finds that nonusable residue at the bottom of the vat can be sold for

---

Chemx-alene Co.
Cost of Production Summary—Mixing and Settling Department
For the Month Ended November 30, 19—

Cost of production for month:

Materials	$127,500
Labor	42,500
Factory overhead	30,000
Total costs to be accounted for	**$200,000**

Unit output for month:

Finished and transferred to finished goods (product A)	30,000
Finished and transferred to baking department (product B)	20,000
Total	50,000

Unit cost for month:

Materials ($127,500 ÷ 50,000)	$2.55
Labor ($42,500 ÷ 50,000)	.85
Factory overhead ($30,000 ÷ 50,000)	.60
Total	$4.00

Total costs to split-off point	$200,000
Less market value of by-product	10,000
Total cost to be assigned to joint products finished and transferred	$190,000

Inventory costs:

Cost of goods finished (product A) and transferred to finished goods (30% × $190,000)	$ 57,000
Cost of goods finished (product B) and transferred to baking department (70% × $190,000)	133,000
Cost of by-product finished and transferred to by-product inventory	10,000
Total production costs accounted for	**$200,000**

$10,000 without further processing. Also assume that other data for the month of November are the same as for October. The following cost of production summary reflects the assignment of joint costs under the adjusted sales value method and uses the by-product value as a reduction in the cost of the joint products and as the cost assigned to the by-product.

In some instances, an unstable market will make the sales value of the by-product so insignificant or so uncertain that the cost of the main products will not be reduced. In this case, no entry for the by-product is made at the point of separation. When the by-product is sold, the transaction is recorded by debiting Cash or Accounts Receivable and crediting By-Product Sales or Miscellaneous Income. The revenue account will usually be treated as "other income" on the income statement. However, some companies, if the amount is significant, will show this revenue as sales income, as a deduction from the cost of the main products sold or as a reduction in the total cost of the main products manufactured.

If further processing is required to make the by-product salable, an account entitled By-Products in Process may be opened, and all subsequent processing costs are charged to that account. As with other products, when the processing is completed, an entry is made to transfer the costs from the in-process account to an inventory account.

KEY TERMS

SELF-STUDY PROBLEM

AVERAGE AND FIFO COST METHODS; LOSSES AT THE BEGINNING AND END OF PROCESSING

METCALF

Metcalf Production Company uses a process cost system. Its manufacturing operation is carried on in two departments: machining and finishing. The machining department uses the average cost method and the finishing department uses the FIFO cost method. Materials are added in both departments at the beginning of operations, and the added materials do not increase the number of units being processed. Units are lost in both departments. However, the units lost in the machining department are lost at the point of final inspection. In the finishing department, they are lost at the very beginning of operations. The lost units have no scrap value and are inherent to the processes.

Production statistics for May show the following data:

	Machining	Finishing
Units in process, May 1 (all material, 20% of labor and overhead)	10,000	
Units in process, May 1 (all material, 60% of labor and overhead)		20,000
Units started in production	70,000	
Units completed and transferred	50,000	
Units transferred from machining		50,000
Units completed and transferred to finished goods		50,000
Units in process, May 31 (all material, 40% of labor and overhead)	20,000	
Units in process, May 31 (all material, 20% of labor and overhead)		10,000
Units lost in production	10,000	10,000

Required:

Prepare a cost of production summary for each department.

SOLUTION TO SELF-STUDY PROBLEM

Suggestions:

Read the entire problem thoroughly, keeping in mind that you will *prepare a cost of production summary for each department.*

Highlight the following facts:

1. The company has two departments.
2. The machining department uses the average cost method while the finishing department uses the FIFO cost method.
3. Units are lost in both departments but at different points. In machining, the loss occurs at the end of processing; in finishing, the loss occurs at the beginning of processing.
4. The lost units have no scrap value and the losses are considered normal (inherent).
5. The materials are added at the beginning of operations in both departments, but the labor and overhead are added evenly. Therefore, the equivalent production for materials will differ from the labor and overhead equivalent production in each department.

Preparing a cost of production summary for the machining department

1. Account for the total cost charged to the department.
2. Calculate the equivalent production using the average cost procedures for (a) materials and (b) labor and factory overhead.

Because the lost units are discovered at the very end of production, they were completed just like the good units that which passed the final inspection. The lost units, therefore, should be added into the equivalent production total just like the good units that were transferred. The rejected units cost can then be accounted for separately.

3. Calculate the unit costs for materials, labor, and overhead.
4. Using the calculated unit costs determine the following:
   a. Cost of goods finished and transferred. (The cost of the lost units will be included in the transferred-out cost.)
   b. the cost of the ending work in process

The Metcalf Production Company
Cost of Production Summary—Machining Department
For the Month Ended May 31, 19—

First—Account for the total cost charged to the department.

Cost in work in process, beginning of month:

Materials	$ 20,000	
Labor	12,000	
Factory overhead	4,000	$ 36,000

Cost of production for month:

Materials	$140,000	
Labor	90,000	
Factory overhead	30,000	260,000
Total costs to be accounted for		**$296,000**

Second—Calculate the unit output (equivalent production).

Unit output for month:
Materials:

Finished and transferred during month	50,000
Equivalent units of work in process, end of month (20,000, 100% completed)	20,000
Units rejected at final inspection	10,000
Total equivalent production	80,000

Labor and factory overhead:

Finished and transferred during month	50,000
Equivalent units of work in process, end of month (20,000, 40% completed)	8,000
Units rejected at final inspection	10,000
Total equivalent production	68,000

Third—Calculate unit costs.

Materials ($20,000 + $140,000) ÷ 80,000	$2.00
Labor ($12,000 + $90,000) ÷ 68,000	1.50
Factory overhead ($4,000 + $30,000) ÷ 68,000	.50
Total	$4.00

Fourth—*Determine inventory costs using calculated unit costs.*

Inventory costs:
Cost of goods finished and transferred:
(50,000 × $4.00) $200,000
Add cost of units lost (10,000 × $4.00)   40,000

Total cost of good units transferred (50,000 × $4.80*)		$240,000
Cost of work in process, end of month:		
Materials (20,000 × $2.00)	$ 40,000	
Labor (20,000 × 40% × $1.50)	12,000	
Factory overhead (20,000 × 40% × $.50)	4,000	56,000
Total production costs accounted for		**$296,000**

*10,000 units lost × $4.00 = $40,000 ÷ 50,000 units completed = $.80; $4.00 + .80 = $4.80 adjusted unit cost of units completed and transferred.

Preparing a cost of production summary for the finishing department

Note: Use the same sequence of instructions as were given for the machining department.

Metcalf Production Company
Cost of Production Summary—Finishing Department
For the Month Ended May 31, 19—

Cost of work in process, beginning of month:			
Cost in machining department		$120,000	
Cost in finishing department:			
Materials	$55,000		
Labor	30,000		
Factory overhead	20,000	105,000	$225,000
Cost of goods received from machining during month			240,000
Cost of production for month:			
Materials		$120,000	
Labor		80,000	
Factory overhead		40,000	240,000
Total costs to be accounted for			**$705,000**

Note: When units are lost at the beginning of operations, the units lost are not added into the equivalent production of units. It is assumed that the good units produced will absorb the loss because the unit cost of materials, labor, and overhead will increase when the lost units are ignored. There will be an adjustment necessary for the unit cost of the goods transferred from the machining department, but this calculation does not affect the equivalent production of units.

Unit output for month:
  Materials:
    To complete beginning units in process   . . . .   -0-
    Units started and fully manufactured
      during month   30,000
    Ending units in process (10,000, all material)   . .   10,000
      Total equivalent production   40,000

  Labor and factory overhead:
    To complete beginning units in process
      (20,000, 40% completed)   8,000
    Units started and fully manufactured during month   30,000
    Ending units in process (10,000, 20% completed)   2,000
      Total equivalent production   40,000

Unit cost for month:
  Materials ($120,000 ÷ 40,000) $3.00
  Labor ($80,000 ÷ 40,000) 2.00
  Factory overhead ($40,000 ÷ 40,000) 1.00
    Total $6.00

Inventory costs:
  Cost of goods finished and transferred to finished goods during month:
    Beginning units in process:
      Prior month's cost $225,000
      Current cost to complete:
        Labor (20,000 × 40% × $2.00)   16,000
        Overhead (20,000 × 40% × $1.00) 8,000 $249,000

    Units started and finished during month:
      Cost in prior dept.   (30,000 × $ 6.00*) . . . $180,000
      Cost in finishing dept. (30,000 × $ 6.00) . . . 180,000
        Total cost transferred (30,000 × $12.00) . . .   360,000

    Cost of work in process, end of month:
      Cost in prior dept. (10,000 units × $6.00*) . . . $ 60,000
      Materials (10,000 units × $3.00)   30,000
      Labor (10,000 units × 20% × $2.00)   4,000
      Factory overhead (10,000 units × 20% × $1.00)   2,000   96,000
  Total production costs accounted for $705,000

*Calculation of adjusted cost:
  Method 1:
    Units received from machining dept. during month   50,000
    Units lost   10,000
    Units remaining   40,000

    Cost transferred from machining dept.—$240,000 ÷ 40,000 =$6.00
adjusted unit cost

Method 2:

Units lost	10,000
Units cost from machining dept.	× $4.80
Cost applicable to units lost	$48,000
Number of units from machining dept.	50,000
Number of units lost	10,000
Number of units remaining	40,000

Calculation of adjustment:

$48,000 ÷ 40,000 = $1.20 adjustment in unit cost

Original unit cost from machining dept.	$4.80
Add adjustment in unit cost	1.20
Adjusted unit cost	$6.00

QUESTIONS

1. Under what conditions may the unit costs of materials, labor, and overhead be computed by using only one equivalent production figure?

2. When is it necessary to use separate equivalent production figures in computing the unit costs of materials, labor, and overhead?

3. If materials are not put into process uniformly, what must be considered when determining the cost of the ending work in process?

4. In what way does the cost of production summary, Figure 7-2, differ from the cost of production summaries presented in Chapter 6? What is the reason for this difference in treatment?

5. Why might the total number of units completed during a month plus the number of units in process at the end of a month be less than the total number of units in process at the beginning of the month plus the number of units placed in process during the month.

6. What is the usual method of handling the cost of losses that occur normally during processing?

7. If some units are normally lost during the manufacturing process and all units absorb the cost, what effect does this have on the unit cost of goods finished during the period and to the cost of the work in process at the end of the period?

8. How is the cost of units normally lost in manufacturing absorbed by the unit cost for the period?

9. What computations must be made if units are lost in a department other than the originating one?

10. What method is used for handling the cost of units lost or rejected at the end of a process?

11. How would you describe the method used to treat the cost of abnormal processing losses?

12. What computations must be made if materials added in a department increase the number of units being processed in that department?

13. If materials added in a department increase the number of units being processed and units are also lost through evaporation in that same department, what calculations must be made, assuming the company follows the practice of letting all units absorb the cost of lost units?

14. What is the difference between the average cost method and the first-in, first-out cost method?

15. How would you define each of the following?
    a. joint products
    b. by-products
    c. joint costs
    d. split-off point

16. a. What are three methods of allocating joint costs?

    b. Under what conditions might each of the three methods be used?

17. How would you describe two ways of accounting for by-products for which no further processing is required?

EXERCISES

Note: Use the average cost method for E7-1 through E7-6.

E7-1
Computing equivalent units of production for materials, labor, and overhead

Using the data given for Cases 1–3, compute the separate equivalent units of production—one for materials and one for labor and overhead—under each of the following assumptions (labor and factory overhead are applied evenly during the process in each assumption):

a. All materials go into production at the beginning of the process.
b. All materials go into production at the end of the process.
c. At the beginning of the process, 75% of the materials go into production and 25% go into production when the process is one-half completed.

Case 1— Started in process 5,000 units; finished 3,000 units; work in process, end of period 2,000 units, three-fourths completed.

Case 2— Opening inventory 5,000 units, three-fifths completed; started in process 40,000 units; finished 39,000 units; work in process, end of period 6,000 units, one-fourth completed.

Case 3— Opening inventory 1,000 units, one-half completed, and 8,000 units, one-fourth completed; started in process 30,000 units; finished 29,000 units; closing inventory work in process 5,000 units, one-fourth completed, and 5,000 units, one-half completed.

E7-2
Computing equivalent production, unit costs, and costs for completed units and ending inventory
Learning Objective 1

Exact Time Company manufactures the Timekeeper Series of wrist watches on an assembly line. The work-in-process inventory as of May 1 consisted of 5,000 watches that were complete as to materials and 50% complete as to labor and overhead. The May 1 work in process costs were as follows:

Materials	$ 5,000
Labor	5,000
Overhead	8,000
Total	$18,000

During the month, 10,000 units were started and 9,500 units were completed. The 1,500 units of ending inventory were complete as to materials and 1/3 complete as to labor and overhead.
The costs for May were as follows:

Materials	$ 61,000
Labor	40,000
Overhead	97,000
Total	$198,000

Calculate:

a. Equivalent units for material, labor, and overhead
b. Units costs for material, labor, and overhead
c. Cost of the units completed and transferred
d. Detailed cost of the ending inventory
e. Accounting for all costs

E7-3
Computing unit costs;
cost of units finished;
cost of units in
process
Learning Objective 1

The following data appeared in the accounting records of Miller Manufacturing Company:

Started in process	12,000 units
Finished and transferred	10,500 units
Work in process, end of month	1,500 units (2/5 completed)
Materials	$36,000
Labor	$44,400
Factory overhead	$22,200

Case 1— All materials are added at the beginning of the process and labor and factory overhead are added evenly throughout the process.

Case 2— One half of the materials are added at the start of the manufacturing process and the balance of the materials are added when the units are one-half completed. Labor and factory overhead are applied evenly during the process.

Make the following computations for each case:

a. Unit cost of materials, labor, and factory overhead for the month
b. Cost of the units finished during the month
c. Cost of the units in process at the end of the month

E7-4
Calculating equivalent
units
Learning Objective 1

Bright Manufacturing Company uses an average cost processing system. All materials are added at the start of the production process. Labor and overhead are added evenly at the same rate throughout the process. Bright Manufacturing records indicate the following data for May:

Beginning work in process, May 1 (60% completed)	1,000 units
Started in May	5,000 units
Completed and transferred	4,000 units

Ending work in process, May 31 is 20% completed. Make the following calculations:

a. Equivalent units for direct materials
b. Equivalent units for labor and overhead

E7-5
Computing costs and
units
Learning Objective 1

Assuming that all materials are added at the beginning of the process and the labor and factory overhead are applied evenly during the process, compute the figures to be inserted in the blank spaces of the following data.

	Case 1	Case 2	Case 3
Units in process, beginning of period	300	None	—
Materials cost in process, beginning of period	$ 915	None	$ 568
Labor cost in process, beginning of period	$ 351	None	$ 200
Overhead cost in process, beginning of period	$ 300	None	$ 188
Units started in process	—	—	19,200
Units transferred	1,300	8,000	—
Units in process, end of period	200	—	1,400
Stage of completion	1/4	—	1/5
Equivalent units—materials	—	—	—
Equivalent units—labor and factory overhead	—	—	18,440
Materials cost current month	$3,660	$13,120	$ —
Labor and factory overhead current month	$5,100	$16,200	$ —
Materials unit cost for period	$ —	$ 1.60	$ .30
Labor and factory overhead unit cost for period	$ —	$ 2.00	$ .20

E7-6
Computing units for materials and labor

Gallant Manufacturing Company uses a process cost system to account for the costs of its only product, product D. Production begins in the fabrication department, where units of raw materials are molded into various connecting parts. After fabrication is complete, the units are transferred to the assembly department. No materials are added in the assembly department. After assembly, the units are transferred to the packaging department where packing materials are placed around the units. After the units are ready for shipping, they are sent to a shipping area.

At year end, June 30, Gallant has the following inventory of product D:

a. No unused raw materials or packing materials
b. Fabrication departments—1,200 units, 1/3 complete as to raw material and 1/2 complete as to direct labor
c. Assembly department—4,000 units, 2/5 complete as to direct labor
d. Packaging department—300 units, 3/4 complete as to packing materials and 1/4 complete as to direct labor
e. Shipping area—1,200 units

1. Compute the number of equivalent units of raw materials in all inventories at June 30.
2. Compute the number of equivalent units of fabrication department direct labor in all inventories at June 30.
3. Compute the number of equivalent units of packing materials in all inventories at June 30.

E7-7
Computing average unit costs

Beard Company manufactures shaving cream and uses an average cost system. In November, production is 14,800 equivalent units for materials and 13,300 units for labor and overhead. During the month, materials, labor and overhead cost were as follows:

Materials	$ 73,000
Labor	68,134
Overhead	77,200

Beginning work in process for November had a cost of $11,360 for material, $11,666 for labor, and $9,250 for overhead.

Compute the following:

a. Average cost per unit for material
b. Average cost per unit for labor
c. Average cost per unit for overhead
d. Total unit cost for the month

E7-8
Calculating unit costs; cost of units transferred and in process
Learning Objective 2

Muster Products Company manufactures a liquid product. Due to the nature of the product and the process, units are regularly lost at the beginning of production. Goods finished in the mixing department are transferred to the refining department. Material and conversion costs are added evenly throughout the process. The following summaries were prepared for the month of January.

	Units	
Production Summary	**Mixing Dept.**	**Refining Dept.**
Started in process or received from prior department	10,000	8,000
Finished and transferred to the next department or		
the stockroom	8,000	7,000
In process, end of the month	1,000	500
Stage of completion	1/4	1/2
Lost in process	1,000	500
Cost Summary		
Materials	$132,000	$58,000
Labor	33,000	18,125
Factory overhead	20,650	10,875

Calculate the unit cost for materials, labor, and factory overhead for January and show the costs of units transferred and in process for (a) the mixing department and (b) the refining department.

E7-9
Calculating unit costs; costs of units transferred and in process
Learning Objective 4

A company manufactures a liquid product called Ez-Go. The basic ingredients are put into process in Dept. 1. In Dept. 2, other materials are added that increase the number of units being processed by 50%. The factory has only two departments.

	Units	
Production Summary	**Dept. 1**	**Dept. 2**
Started in process	18,000	
Received from prior department		14,000
Added to units in process		7,000
Finished and transferred	14,000	15,000
In process, end of month	4,000	6,000
Stage of completion	1/4	1/2
Cost Summary		
Materials	$90,000	$36,000
Labor	30,000	13,500
Factory overhead	15,000	4,500

Calculate the following for each department: (a) unit cost for the month for materials, labor, and factory overhead, (b) cost of the units transferred, and (c) cost of the work in process.

E7-10
Computing equivalent units, FIFO method

Using the data given below for Cases 1-3 and the FIFO cost method, compute the separate equivalent units of production, one for materials and one for labor and overhead, under each of the following assumptions (labor and factory overhead are applied evenly during the process in each assumption):

a. All materials go into production at the beginning of the process.
b. All materials go into production at the end of the process.
c. At the beginning of the process, 75% of the materials go into production and 25% go into production when the process is one-half completed.

Case 1— Started in process 5,000 units; finished 3,000 units; work in process, end of period 2,000 units, three-fourths completed.
Case 2— Opening inventory 5,000 units, three-fifths completed; started in process 40,000 units; finished 39,000 units; work in process, end of period 6,000 units, one-fourth completed.
Case 3— Opening inventory 1,000 units, one-half completed, and 8,000 units, one-fourth completed; started in process 30,000 units; finished 29,000 units; closing inventory work in process 5,000 units, one-fourth completed, and 5,000 units, one-half completed.

Compare your answers with those from E7-1 on the average cost basis.

E7-11
Using partial information to construct a cost of production report

A fire in the cost department destroyed the cost of production report that you had partially completed. From the remaining data, you determine that the unit cost for material was $4.20 and that the conversion cost (labor and overhead) was $5.05 for the month. Also, from the remaining records you ascertain that the equivalent units were 2,100 for material and 1,950 for conversion costs. A total of 600 units was in the ending inventory, having all materials added but only 3/4 of their conversion cost. Last month's ending inventory consisted of $560 for material and $380 for conversion cost.

Prepare a cost of production report that shows the total costs that have to be accounted for and the disposition of those costs.

E7-12
Preparing a cost of production report
Learning Objective 1

Armstrong Paving Corporation manufactures highway paving materials. The process requires that all materials are introduced at the beginning of processing. During March, the following data is accumulated:

Production Data

Raw materials started in production	25,000 tons
Ending work in process (3/4 completed)	5,000 tons

Cost Data

Materials	$300,000
Direct labor	19,000
Overhead	23,750

Prepare a cost of production report for March.

E7-13
Computing equivalent units, FIFO and average cost methods

Assume each of the following conditions concerning the data given.

1. All materials are added at the beginning of the process.
2. All materials are added at the end of the process.
3. Half of the materials are added at the beginning of the process and the balance of the materials are added when the units are three-fourths completed.

In all cases, labor and factory overhead are added evenly throughout the process.

Production Summary

	Units		
	Dept. 1	Dept. 2	Dept. 3
Work in process, beginning of month	3,000	1,500	1,200
Stage of completion	1/2	3/5	4/5
Started in process	18,000	16,000	21,000
Finished and transferred	19,000	15,500	21,000
Work in process, end of month	2,000	2,000	1,200
Stage of completion	1/4	4/5	1/5

Compute separate equivalent units of production, one for materials and one for labor and factory overhead, for each of the conditions listed, using (a) the average cost method and (b) the FIFO cost method.

E7-14
Making a journal entry—joint products
Learning Objective 7

Builders Lumber Co. processes rough timber to obtain three grades of finished lumber, A, B, and C. The company allocates costs to the joint products on the basis of market value. During the month of May, Builders incurred total production costs of $104,000 in producing the following:

Grade	Thousand Board Feet	Selling Price per 1,000 Board Feet
A	100	$200
B	300	100
C	500	160

Make the general journal entry to transfer the finished lumber to separate inventory accounts.

E7-15
Calculating joint cost allocation
Learning Objective 7

Topco Company produces two products, Spin-Two and Slick-One, which are used as additives to gasoline. These products begin from a joint refining process in batches of 1,000 gallons of mixture. At split-off, one-fourth of the mixture is Spin-Two and three-fourths is Slick-One. Both products require further processing after split-off. The cost and production data for August shows the following:

Total joint costs per batch	$15,000
Cost of further processing of Spin-Two	5,000
Cost of further processing of Slick-One	10,000

a. Calculate the joint cost allocation per batch for each product using the physical quantity method.
b. Calculate the total cost per gallon for each product.

E7-16 Computing joint costs—relative sales value and physical units Learning Objective 7	Moon Company's joint cost of producing 1,000 units of product A, 500 units of product B, and 500 units of product C is $200,000. The unit sales values of the three products at the split-off point are product A—$20, product B—$200, and product C—$160. Ending inventories include 100 units of product A, 300 units of product B, and 200 units of product C. Compute the amount of joint cost that would be included in the ending inventory valuation of the three products on the basis of each of the following: a. Their relative sales value b. Physical units
E7-17 Making a journal entry—by-product Learning Objective 8	Queen Chemical Co. manufactures product X. During the process, a by-product, AX, is obtained and placed in stock. The estimated sales value of AX produced during the month of April is $1,020. Assume that the value of the by-product reduces production cost. Make the journal entry for April to record the following: a. Placing of AX in stock b. Sale of three-fourths of the AX for $800
E7-18 Making journal entries—by-product Learning Objective 8	Loudon Manufacturing Co. makes one main product, X, and a by-product, Z, which splits off from the main product when the work is three-fourths completed. Product Z is sold without further processing and without being placed in stock. During June, $1,200 is realized from the sale of the by-product. Make the entries to record the recovery and sale of the by-product on the assumption that the recovery is treated as one of the following: a. A reduction in the cost of the main product b. Other income

P R O B L E M S

Note: The average cost method is to be used with P7-1 through P7-7.

P7-1 Cost of production summaries, one department, two months; journal entries Learning Objective 1	Manufacturing data for the months of January and February in Dept. A of the Husky Manufacturing Co. follow:

	January	February
Materials used	$20,000	$28,400
Labor	$15,200	$23,000
Factory overhead	$11,400	$19,800
Finished and transferred to Dept. B	3,600	3,200
Work in process, end of month	400	600
Stage of completion	1/2	1/3

All materials are added at the start of the process. Labor and factory overhead are added evenly throughout the process. No units were in process at the beginning of January. Goods finished in Dept. A are transferred to Dept. B for further processing.

Required:

1. From an analysis of this information, prepare a cost of production summary for each month.
2. Make the general journal entries necessary to record each month's transactions.

P7-2
General journal entries for a manufacturer
Learning Objective 1

On December 1, Cobra Production Company had a work in process inventory of 1,200 units that were complete as to materials and one-third complete as labor and overhead. December 1 costs follow:

Materials	$6,000
Labor	2.000
Overhead	2,000

During December the following transactions occurred:

a. Purchased materials costing $50,000 on account.
b. Placed materials costing $49,000 into production.
c. Incurred production wages totaling $48,500. The Wages Payable for production employees was $4,000 on December 1 and $6,000 on December 31.

Incurred Overhead costs for December:

Depreciation	$20,000
Utilities	28,000 (Cash payment)
Salaries	11,000 (Cash payment)
Supplies	2,000 (From inventory)

d. Applied overhead to work in process at a predetermined rate of 100% of direct labor cost.
e. Completed and transferred 10,000 units to Finished Goods.

Cobra Company uses an average cost system. The ending inventory of work in process consisted of 1,000 units that were completed as to materials and 50% complete as to labor and overhead.

Required:

Prepare the general journal entries to record the above information for the month of December.

P7-3
Cost of production summaries, three departments; departmental cost work sheet; journal entries; statement of cost of goods manufactured
Learning Objective 1

Franklin Manufacturing Company manufactures a cement sealing compound called Patchtite. The process requires that the product pass through three departments.

In Dept. 1, all materials are put into production at the beginning of the process; in Dept. 2, materials are put into production evenly throughout the process; and in Dept. 3, all materials are put into production at the end of the process. In each department, it is assumed that the labor and factory overhead are applied evenly throughout the process.

At the end of January, the production reports for the month show the following:

	Dept. 1	Dept. 2	Dept. 3
Started in process	50,000	—	—
Received from prior department	—	40,000	30,000
Finished and transferred	40,000	30,000	28,000

Finished and on hand	—	5,000	—
Work in process, end of month	10,000	5,000	2,000
Stage of completion	1/2	1/4	3/4

The cost summary for January shows the following:

	Dept. 1	Dept. 2	Dept. 3
Materials	$22,500	$23,200	$19,600
Labor	7,200	14,500	11,800
Factory overhead	10,800	14,500	8,850
	$40,500	$52,200	$40,250

Required:

1. Prepare a cost of production summary for each department for January.
2. Prepare a departmental cost work sheet for January.
3. Make the required general journal entries to record the January operations.
4. Prepare a statement of cost of goods manufactured for the month ended January 31.

P7-4
Cost of completed units and ending inventory
Learning Objective 1

Queen Island Company cans green beans and uses an average cost system. For the month of August the company showed the following:

Green Beans completed and canned	245,000 pounds
Green Beans in process at the end of August:	
100% complete as to beans, 70% complete as to labor and overhead, 0% complete as to cans	16,500 pounds
Cost data:	
Green Beans	$.05 per equivalent pound
Labor	$.25 per equivalent pound
Overhead	$.15 per equivalent pound
Cans	$.07 per can

Each can contains 16 oz. or one pound of Green Beans

Required:

1. Calculate the cost of the completed production for November.
2. Show the detailed cost of the ending inventory for November.

P7-5
Equivalent production; unit costs; cost of work in process
Learning Objective 1

Cebo Company manufactures a single product, a mechanical device known as "Klebo." The company maintains a process cost type of accounting system. A description of the manufacturing operation follows:

Material K, a metal, is stamped to form a part that is assembled with one of the purchased parts X. The unit is then machined and cleaned, after which it is assembled with two units of part Y to form the finished device known as a "Klebo." Spray priming and enameling is the final operation,

Time and motion studies indicate that of the total time required to manufacture a unit, the first operation required 25% of the labor cost, the first assembly an additional 25%, machining and cleaning 12.5%, the second assembly 25%, and painting 12.5%. Factory overhead is considered to follow the same pattern by operations as does labor.

Cebo collected the following data on October 31, the end of the first month of operation:

Material K purchased—100,000 lbs.	$25,000
Part X purchased—80,000 units	16,000
Part Y purchased—150,000 units	15,000
Primer and enamel used	1,072
Direct labor cost	45,415
Factory overhead	24,905

	Units
Units finished and sent to finished goods warehouse	67,000
Units assembled but not painted	5,000
Units ready for the second assembly	3,000
Inventories at the end of the month:	
Finished units	7,500
Material K (lbs.)	5,800
Part X (units of part X)	5,000
Part Y (units of part Y)	6,000
Klebos in process (units)	8,000

Required:

1. Prepare a schedule of equivalent units of production for labor.
2. Prepare a schedule of total and unit costs incurred in production for (a) each kind of material, (b) labor cost, (c) factory overhead, and (d) total cost of production.
3. Prepare a schedule of detailed materials, labor, and factory overhead costs assigned to the units left in process.

(AICPA adapted)

P7-6
Lost units; cost of production summaries
Learning Objective 2

High Products Co. uses the process cost system. A record of the factory operations for the month of October follows:

Production Summary

	Units
Started in process	12,500
Finished and transferred to stockroom	9,500
In process, end of month, one-half completed	1,000

Cost Summary

Materials	$30,000
Labor	12,000
Factory overhead	18,000

Required:

Prepare a cost of production summary for each of the following conditions.

1. The cost of lost units is absorbed by all units.
2. The cost of lost units is charged only to units completed.
3. The cost of lost units is charged to an expense account.

P7-7
Lost units; cost of
production
summaries
Learning Objective 2

Lowry Manufacturing Company manufactures a single product that passes through two departments: extruding and finishing-packing. The product is shipped at the end of the day in which it is packed. The production in the extruding and finishing-packing departments does not increase the number of units started. The company uses the average cost method.

The cost and production data for January follows:

Cost Data	Extruding Department	Finishing-Packing Department
Work in process, January 1:		
Cost from preceding department	—	$60,200
Materials	$ 5,900	—
Labor	1,900	1,500
Factory overhead	1,400	2,000
Costs added during January:		
Materials	20,100	4,400
Labor	10,700	7,720
Factory overhead	8,680	11,830
Percentage of completion of work in process:		
January 1:		
Materials	70%	0%
Labor	50	30
Factory overhead	50	30
January 31:		
Materials	50	0
Labor	40	35
Factory overhead	40	35

Production Data

	Extruding	Finishing-Packing
Units in process, January 1	10,000	29,000
Units in process, January 31	8,000	6,000
Units started or received from preceding department	20,000	22,000
Units completed and transferred or shipped	22,000	44,000

In the extruding department, materials are added at various phases of the process. All lost units occur at the end of the process when the inspection operation takes place.

In the finishing-packing department, the materials added consist only of packing supplies. These materials are added at the midpoint of the process when the packing operation begins. Cost studies have disclosed that one-half of the labor and overhead costs apply to the finishing operation and one-half to the packing operation. All lost units occur during the finishing operation. All of the work in process in this department at January 1 and January 31 was in the finishing operation phase of the manufacturing process.

Required:

1. Compute the units lost, if any, for each department during January.

2. Prepare a cost of production summary for each department for January. The report should disclose the equivalent units of production for the calculation of unit costs for each department for January, the departmental total cost, and cost per unit (for materials, labor, and overhead) of the units transferred to the finishing-packing department and for units shipped. Assume that January production and costs were normal. (Submit all supporting computations in good form.)

(AICPA adapted)

P7-8
Units gained and lost; cost of production summaries
Learning Objective 4

August Manufacturing Co., which uses the process cost system, has three departments: A, B, and C. In Dept. A, all of the materials are put into production at the beginning of the process; in Dept. B, no materials are added to the process; in Dept. C, all of the materials are put into production at the beginning of the process. The materials added in Dept. C increase the number of units being processed by 25%. Labor and factory overhead are incurred uniformly throughout the process in all departments. Losses of units in any department are considered unavoidable due to the nature of the manufacturing process and can occur at any time during the process.

A record of the factory operations for May follows:

Cost Summary	Dept. A	Dept. B	Dept. C
Materials	$25,000		$ 7,500
Labor	10,800	$6,910	10,150
Factory overhead	8,100	6,910	7,250

Production Summary	Units		
	Dept. A	Dept. B	Dept. C
Started in process	11,000		
Received from prior department		8,500	6,000
Added to units in process			1,500
Finished and transferred	8,500	6,000	7,000
Units in process, end of month	1,500	1,820	500
Stage of completion	1/3	1/2	1/2

Required:

Prepare a cost of production summary for each department for the month of May.

P7-9
FIFO cost method; cost of production summary

Lobo Products Co. uses the FIFO cost method and adds all materials, labor, and factory overhead evenly to production. A record of the factory operations for the month of October follows:

Production Summary	Units
Work in process, beginning of month, one-fourth completed	5,000
Started in process	13,000
Finished and transferred to stockroom	11,000
Work in process, end of month, three-fourths completed	7,000

Cost Summary

Work in process, beginning of month	$10,000
Materials	45,000
Labor	30,000
Factory overhead	15,000

Required: Prepare a cost of production summary for the month.

P7-10
Cost of units completed and ending inventory
Learning Objective 1

Plain Center Company had a cost per equivalent unit for the month of $4.56 for materials, $1.75 for labor, and $1.00 for overhead. During the period, 10,250 units were completed and transferred to finished goods. The 3,200 units in ending work in process were 100% complete as to materials and 60% complete as to labor and overhead. At the beginning of the month, 1,500 units were in process, 100% complete as to materials and 50% complete as to labor and overhead. The beginning inventory had a cost of $8,775. Plain Center uses FIFO costing.

Required:

1. Calculate the cost of the units completed and transferred.
2. Calculate the cost of ending work in process.

P7-11
FIFO cost method, lost units; cost of production summary
Learning Objective 2

Victor Company manufactures hobblees in three steps or departments. The finishing department is the third and last step before the product is transferred to finished goods inventory.

All materials needed to complete the hobblees are added at the beginning of the process in the finishing department, and lost units, if any, occur only at this point. The company uses the FIFO cost method in its accounting system and has accumulated the following data for July for the finishing department:

Production of Hobblees:	Units
In process, July 1 (labor and factory overhead three-fourths complete)	10,000
Transferred from preceding department during July	40,000
Finished and transferred to finished goods inventory during July	35,000
In process, July 31 (labor and factory overhead one-half complete)	10,000

Cost of work in process inventory, July 1:	
Cost from preceding departments	$ 38,000
Cost added in finishing department prior to July 1:	
Materials	21,500
Labor	39,000
Factory overhead	42,000
Total	$140,500

Hobblees transferred to the finishing department during July had costs of $280,000 assigned from preceding departments.

During July, the finishing department incurred the following production costs:

Materials	$ 70,000
Labor	162,500
Factory overhead	130,000
Total	$362,500

Required:

1. Calculate the number of hobblees lost in production during July.
2. Prepare a cost of production summary for July.

(AICPA adapted)

P7-12
FIFO cost method;
equivalent production;
units gained and lost
Learning Objective 2
& 4

Chemallo, Inc., produces a chemical compound by a unique chemical process which Lakeland has divided into two departments, A and B, for accounting purposes. The process functions as follows:

a. The formula for the chemical compound requires one pound of chemical X and one pound of chemical Y. In the simplest sense, one pound of chemical X is processed in Dept. A and transferred to Dept. B for further processing where one pound of chemical Y is added when the process is 50% complete. When the processing is complete in Dept. B, the finished chemical compound is transferred to finished goods. The process is continuous, operating twenty-four hours a day.
b. Normal processing losses occur in Dept. A. Five percent of chemical X is lost in the first few seconds of processing.
c. No processing losses occur in Dept. B.
d. In Dept. A, conversion costs are incurred uniformly throughout the process and are allocated to good pounds produced because processing losses are normal.
e. In Dept. B, conversion costs are allocated equally to each equivalent pound of output.
f. Lakeland's unit of measure for work in process and finished goods inventories is pounds.
g. The following data are available for the month of October:

	Dept. A	Dept. B
Work in process, October 1	8,000 pounds	10,000 pounds
Stage of completion of beginning inventory (one batch per department)	3/4	3/10
Started or transferred in	50,000 pounds	?
Transferred out	46,500 good pounds	?
Work in process, October 31	?	?
Stage of completion of ending inventory (one batch per department)	1/3	1/5
Total equivalent pounds of material added in Dept. B		44,500 pounds

Required:

1. Determine the amounts indicated by the question marks.
2. Prepare schedules computing equivalent "good" pounds of production (materials and conversion costs) for Depts. A and B for the month of October, using the first-in, first-out method for inventory cost.

(AICPA adapted)

P7-13
Joint cost
allocations—three
methods

Byson Corporation specializes in chicken farming. Chickens are grown, packaged, and sold mostly to grocery chains. Chickens are accounted for in batches of 50,000. At the end of each growing period, the chickens are separated and sold by grades. Grades AA and A are sold to large grocery chains, and B and C are sold to other buyers. For costing purposes, Byson treats each batch of chicks as a joint product. The cost data for a batch of 50,000 chicks follows:

Grade	Number of Chickens	Average Pounds per Chicken	Selling Price per Pound
AA	25,000	5	$.70
A	15,000	4	.50
B	6,000	2	.40
C	4,000	1	.30

Total joint costs for the batch was $50,000.

Required:

1. Compute the cost allocations for each product using the physical quantity number of chickens.
2. Compute the cost allocations for each product using physical quantity if measured in pounds per chicken.
3. Compute the cost allocations for each product using the relative sales value method.

P7-14
Allocation of joint costs

Hilawn Manufacturing Company buys zeon for $.80 a gallon. At the end of processing in Dept. 1, zeon splits off into products A, B, and C. Product A is sold at the split-off point with no further processing. Products B and C require further processing before they can be sold; product B is processed in Dept. 2 and product C is processed in Dept. 3. Following is a summary of costs and other related data for the year ended December 31.

	Dept. 1	Dept. 2	Dept. 3
Cost of zeon	$ 76,000	—	—
Direct labor	14,000	$45,000	$ 65,000
Factory overhead	10,000	21,000	49,000
Total	$100,000	$66,000	$114,000

	Product A	Product B	Product C
Gallons sold	20,000	30,000	45,000
Gallons on hand at December 31	10,000	—	15,000
Sales in dollars	$30,000	$96,000	$141,750

No inventories were on hand at the beginning of the year, and no zeon was on hand at the end of the year. All gallons on hand at the end of the year were complete as to processing. Hilawn uses the relative sales value method of allocating joint costs.

Required:

1. Calculate the allocation of joint costs.
2. Calculate the cost of product B sold.

P7-15
Allocation of joint costs
Learning Objectives 7 & 8

Michelli Corporation produces three products: Alpha, Beta, and Gamma. Alpha and Gamma are joint products, while Beta is a by-product of Alpha. No joint cost is to be allocated to the by-product. The production processes for a given year follow:

a. In Dept. 1, 110,000 pounds of raw material, Rho, are processed at a total cost of $120,000. After processing in Dept. 1, 60% of the units are transferred to Dept. 2 and 40% of the units (now Gamma) are transferred to Dept. 3.

b. In Dept. 2, the material is further processed at a total additional cost of $38,000. Seventy percent of the units (now Alpha) are transferred to Dept. 4 and 30% emerge as Beta, the by-product, to be sold at $1.20 per pound. Selling expenses related to disposing of Beta are $8,100,

c. In Dept. 4, Alpha is processed at a total additional cost of $23,660. After this processing, Alpha is ready for sales at $5 per pound.

d. In Dept. 3, Gamma is processed at a total additional cost of $165,000. In this department, a normal loss of units of Gamma occurs that equals 10% of the marketable output of Gamma. The remaining marketable output of Gamma is then sold for $12 per pound.

Required:

1. Prepare a schedule showing the allocation of the $120,000 joint cost between Alpha and Gamma using the relative sales value approach. The net realizable value of Beta should be treated as an addition to the sales value of Alpha.

2. What is the cost of Alpha transferred to finished goods, assuming that the net realizable value of Beta available for sale is to be deducted from the cost of producing Alpha?

Standard Cost Accounting— Materials and Labor

LEARNING OBJECTIVES

After studying this chapter, you should be able to:

1. Recognize the procedures and techniques involved in standard cost accounting
2. Describe the different standards used in determining standard costs
3. Use the proper procedures for recording standard costs for materials and labor
4. Explain the meaning of variances and how they are analyzed
5. Give examples of how to dispose of variances
6. Recognize the specific features of a standard cost system

The discussions of cost control in previous chapters emphasized the comparison of current costs with historical costs—costs of yesterday, last week, last month, or last year. When current costs differed unfavorably from earlier costs, it was suggested that management immediately investigate the cause of the deviation and try to eliminate it before the change became too costly. Management was also advised not only to watch for these fluctuations and attempt to correct them but to consider all possible ways to control costs.

While these previous methods of cost control are useful, management may tend to become complacent if the costs of manufacturing do not differ significantly from period to period. Managers may feel that the manufacturing operation is efficient because unit and overall costs have stabilized at a certain level. But stability of costs does not necessarily indicate efficiency when the earlier costs with which current costs are being compared may have built-in inefficiencies. Also, it may be possible to utilize current costs more effectively.

The purpose of **standard cost accounting** is to control costs and promote efficiency. This system is not a third cost accounting method for accumulating manufacturing costs but is used in conjunction with either a job-order or process manufacturing operation. Standard cost accounting is based on a predetermination of what it should cost to manufacture a product and a subsequent comparison of the actual costs with the established standard. Any deviation from the standards set can be quickly detected and responsibility pinpointed so that the company can take appropriate action to eliminate inefficiencies or take advantage of efficiencies.

Standard costs are usually determined for a period of one year and should be revised annually. However, if cost analyses during the year indicate that a standard is incorrect, or if a significant change has occurred in costs or other related factors, management should not hesitate to adjust the standard to remedy an adverse situation.

TYPES OF STANDARDS

A **standard** is a norm against which the actual performance can be measured. The objective of setting standards is to measure efficiency and to monitor costs by assigning responsibility for deviations from the standards. Also, a standard can motivate employees by providing a goal for achievement. But a question that often arises is "What is the proper standard to use?" A company can estimate materials, labor, and factory overhead usage and costs, but what about the unforeseen costs, such as spoilage, lost time, and equipment breakdowns? Should these items be considered in determining the standard cost to manufacture a product?

Some companies set their standards at the maximum degree of efficiency. Using such an **ideal standard**, costs are determined by considering estimated materials, labor, and overhead costs, the condition of the factory and machinery, and time for rest periods, holidays, and vacations; but no allowances are made for inefficient conditions such as lost time, waste, or spoilage. This ideal standard can be achieved only under the most efficient operating conditions; therefore, it is practically unattainable, generally giving rise to unfavorable variances. Companies using this type of utopian standard feel that it provides a maximum objective for which to strive in the attempt to improve efficiency. There is, however, a psychological disadvantage—the factory personnel may become discouraged and lose their incentive to meet standards that are usually impossible to attain except under perfect operating conditions.

Recognizing this potential problem, most companies set **attainable standards** that include such factors as lost time, spoilage, or waste. These companies realize that some inefficiencies cannot be completely eliminated, and so they design a standard that can be met or even bettered in efficient production situations. The primary concern of the manufacturer should be to set a standard that is high enough to provide motivation and promote efficiency, yet not so high that it is unreasonable and thus unattainable.

STANDARD COST PROCEDURES

LEARNING OBJECTIVE
Use the proper procedures for recording standard costs for materials and labor

Standard cost accounting is based on the following procedures:

1. Standard costs are determined for the three elements of cost—direct materials, direct labor, and factory overhead.

2. The standard costs, the actual costs, and the variances between the actual and standard costs are recorded in appropriate accounts.

3. All variances are analyzed and investigated and appropriate action taken.

DETERMINATION OF STANDARD COSTS FOR MATERIALS AND LABOR

The first step, the determination of standard costs for a product, is a complex task that requires considerable experience and familiarity with manufacturing operations as well as the cooperation of the departmental employees. The accounting department is often consulted to help determine historical costs, to point out prevalent trends, and to assist in establishing the standards. A **materials cost standard** is based on estimates of the **quantity** of materials required for a unit of product and the **unit cost** of the materials used. In setting a materials cost standard, management may consult the production engineering department to determine the amounts and types of materials needed, and the purchasing agent should supply knowledge of suppliers' prices to calculate the cost of these materials.

A **labor cost standard** is based on estimates of the **labor hours required** to produce a unit of product and the **cost of labor per unit**. In establishing a labor cost standard, the heads of various departments contribute their knowledge of the processing operations. The manufacturer may use services of time-study engineers to establish the time necessary to perform each operation, and the personnel manager should be consulted regarding prevailing wage rates for the various types of labor needed.

Historical costs and processes are studied to gain familiarity with these items, but the individuals who set the standards should also consider the prevailing trends that may cause changes in the company's future operations. In setting standards for materials and labor, a variety of factors may be considered:

1. The trend of prices for raw materials.

2. The use of different types of materials due to new processing or market developments.

3. The effect of negotiations with labor unions on labor rates.

4. The possible saving of labor time due to the use of more modern machinery and equipment.

The following table illustrates a simple standard cost summary for a product:

Fine Products, Inc.
Standard Cost Summary
Product X

Materials—1 lb. @ $4 per lb	$ 4.00
Labor —1/2 hr. @ $10 per hr	5.00
Factory overhead	2.00
Standard cost per unit	$11.00

The development of factory overhead standards will be discussed in the following chapter.

RECORDING STANDARD COSTS FOR MATERIALS AND LABOR

Once the standard cost for manufacturing a product has been determined, the second phase of the system can be put into effect: the standard costs, the actual costs, and the variances are recorded in journals and transferred to the general ledger. The journalizing and posting may occur weekly or monthly depending on the needs of management for current information.

LEARNING OBJECTIVE
Explain the meaning of variances and how they are analyzed

Determination of Variances. A **variance** represents the difference between the actual and the standard costs of materials, labor, and overhead. The variances measure efficiencies or inefficiencies in **usage** (quantity of materials used or number of labor hours worked) and **price** (cost of materials and wage rates).

Assume that the production report of Fine Products, Inc., whose standard cost summary is shown above, indicates that equivalent production for the month, calculated as discussed in previous chapters, was 10,000 units. The standard cost of this production is computed as follows:

Materials cost (10,000 units × $4.00)	$ 40,000
Labor cost (10,000 units × $5.00)	50,000
Factory overhead cost (10,000 units × $2.00)	20,000
Total standard cost of manufacturing 10,000 units	$110,000

Assume that the materials requisitions, the time tickets or payroll records, and the factory overhead records indicate the following actual costs of manufacturing these units:

Cost of direct materials used (11,000 lbs. @ $3.80)	$ 41,800
Cost of direct labor (4,500 hrs. @ $11.00)	49,500
Factory overhead applied	20,000
Total actual cost of manufacturing 10,000 units	$111,300

The standards can now be compared to the actual costs to determine whether any variances exist. This analysis is performed as follows:

	Standard Cost	Actual Cost	Net Variances— Favorable or (Unfavorable)
Materials	$ 40,000	$ 41,800	$(1,800)
Labor	50,000	49,500	500
Factory Overhead	20,000	20,000	—
Total	$110,000	$111,300	$(1,300)

The information presented by these comparative figures is significant because it shows that the total actual manufacturing costs have exceeded the standards previously established. The variances indicate that the cost of materials was $1,800 higher than it should have been and that the cost of labor was $500 less than the established standards, resulting in an overall unfavorable variance of $1,300. These figures can be of more value to cost control, however, if a further breakdown of the variances is made.

The accounts used to indicate the materials and labor variances follow:

Materials Price Variance reflects the actual unit cost of materials above or below the standard unit cost, multiplied by the actual quantity of materials used.

(Actual unit cost of materials minus standard unit cost) times
actual quantity of materials used = Materials Price Variance

Materials Quantity (Usage) Variance represents the actual quantity of direct materials used above or below the standard quantity allowed for the actual level of production at standard price.

(Actual quantity used minus standard quantity allowed) times standard price of material = Material Quantity Variance

Labor Rate (Price) Variance represents the average of the actual hourly rates paid above or below the standard hourly rate, multiplied by the actual number of hours worked.

(Actual labor rate per hour minus standard labor rate per hour) times actual number of labor hours worked = Labor Rate Variance

Labor Efficiency (Usage) Variance indicates the number of actual direct labor hours worked above or below the standard hours allowed for the actual level of production at standard price.

(Actual number of labors worked minus standard number of labor hours allowed) times standard cost per labor hour = Labor Efficiency Variance

The standard quantity for the actual level of production used for the material quantity variance and the labor efficiency variance represents the equivalent production determined for each of these elements. The equivalent production is calculated in exactly the same way as was used to determine the equivalent units in process costing. However, an additional calculation may be necessary when **each equivalent unit** requires **several pieces** of material or **number of hours** to complete. For example, assume that a calculation of the materials equivalent production determines that 1,000 units were produced during the period. The standard set for the material allows five pieces of material for each completed unit; therefore, the standard quantity allowed for the actual production would be 5,000 units of material (1,000 units × 5 pieces).

A **debit balance** in a variance account indicates an **unfavorable variance**; that is, actual costs have exceeded the established standard cost. A credit balance reflects a **favorable variance** indicating that actual costs were less than the standard cost. In management terminology, an unfavorable variance means that a charge (debit) has been added that increases the cost beyond the standard established, thereby reducing the expected profitability of the product. A favorable variance (credit) would add to a products anticipated profitability because it reduces the standard cost set for the product. When a company uses a standard cost system, it usually considers the product's standard cost to be the cost for setting its selling price. Therefore, any movement of cost above or below the standard will have a direct effect on the revenue earned.

Figure 8-1 shows the formulas commonly used to calculate the materials and labor variances, using the data previously presented for materials and labor.

This analysis shows the specific variances as quantity and price deviations from the established standards. The manufacturing effort exceeded the established materials standard for 10,000 units, which, at a standard price of $4.00 per pound, created an unfavorable materials quantity variance of $4,000 (1,000 pounds used in excess of standard allowed × $4.00). This variance was partially offset by the fact that the 11,000 pounds of materials used were obtained at a below-standard cost of $3.80 per pound, thereby creating a favorable price variance of $2,200 (11,000 pounds used at a saving of $.20 per pound).

The calculation of labor variances indicates a favorable labor efficiency variance of $5,000 because the number of hours worked was 500 hours below the standard allowed for the production of 10,000 units (500 hours times the standard rate of $10.00). However, during the period, the company paid a labor rate that at $11.00 per hour was higher than standard, creating an unfavorable rate variance of $4,500 (4,500 hours at a rate of $1.00 over standard).

Another method of calculating the variances, which displays the specific deviations from standard but does not provide enough data for making general journal entries, is shown on page 359.

	Standard Cost	−	Actual Cost	=	Difference	×	Actual Quantity or Hours	=	Variance
Materials Price Variance	$4.00 lb.		$3.80 lb.		$.20 (fav.)		11,000 lbs.		$2,200 (fav.)
Labor Rate Variance	$10.00 hr.		$11.00 hr.		$1.00 (unf.)		4,500 hrs.		$4,500 (unf.)

	Standard Quantity or Hours	−	Actual Quantity or Hours	=	Difference	×	Standard Cost	=	Variance
Materials Quantity Variance	10,000 lbs.		11,000 lbs.		1,000 lbs. (unf.)		$4.00 lb.		$4,000 (unf.)
Labor Efficiency Variance	5,000 hrs.		4,500 hrs.		500 hrs. (fav.)		$10.00 hr.		$5,000 (fav.)

FIGURE 8-1   Formulas for Calculating Variances

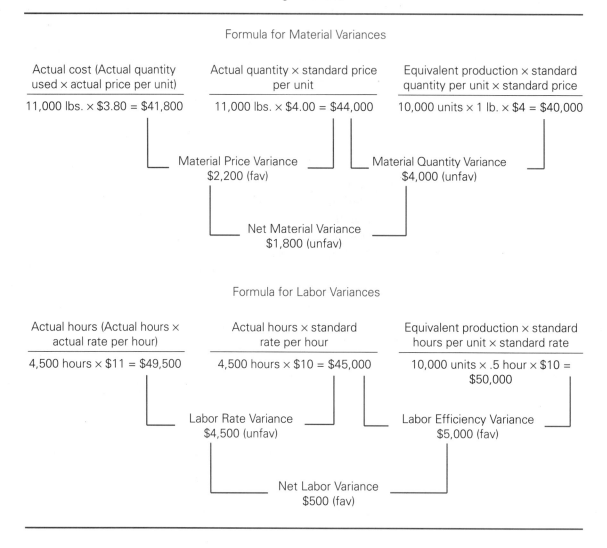

Formula for Material Variances

Actual cost (Actual quantity used × actual price per unit)	Actual quantity × standard price per unit	Equivalent production × standard quantity per unit × standard price
11,000 lbs. × $3.80 = $41,800	11,000 lbs. × $4.00 = $44,000	10,000 units × 1 lb. × $4 = $40,000

Material Price Variance
$2,200 (fav)

Material Quantity Variance
$4,000 (unfav)

Net Material Variance
$1,800 (unfav)

Formula for Labor Variances

Actual hours (Actual hours × actual rate per hour)	Actual hours × standard rate per hour	Equivalent production × standard hours per unit × standard rate
4,500 hours × $11 = $49,500	4,500 hours × $10 = $45,000	10,000 units × .5 hour × $10 = $50,000

Labor Rate Variance
$4,500 (unfav)

Labor Efficiency Variance
$5,000 (fav)

Net Labor Variance
$500 (fav)

It is important to understand that the terms *favorable* and *unfavorable* indicate only a deviation of the actual cost below or above standard. Further analysis and investigation may indicate that the unfavorable variance is not necessarily reflecting an inefficiency, nor is the favorable variance always indicating a desirable situation. An apparently unfavorable condition may be offset completely by a favorable situation. For example, a favorable materials price variance that results from buying less expensive materials than the standards call for may more than offset an unfavorable materials quantity variance that results from additional spoilage due to the use of cheaper materials. In any event, all variances, favorable or unfavorable, should be analyzed to determine the cause for and the effect of the deviations. Appropriate action should then be taken to improve the problem areas.

Accounting Procedure. The work in process account is always debited with the standard cost (standard quantity times standard price) determined for the period's equivalent production. The materials inventory account is credited for the actual cost of materials issued to the factory as indicated by materials requisitions and inventory ledger cards if an alternate method of recording material cost is not used. The payroll account is credited with the actual cost of labor incurred for the period. The differences between the debits (at standard costs) and the credits (at actual costs) are debited (unfavorable variances) or credited (favorable variances) to the variance accounts. The standard cost of units finished is transferred from Work in Process to Finished Goods.

To illustrate, use the figures previously presented for materials and labor costs.

1. To record the entry for direct materials cost:

Work in Process	40,000	
Materials Quantity Variance	4,000	
Materials Price Variance		2,200
Materials		41,800

2. To record the entry for direct labor cost:

Work in Process	50,000	
Labor Rate Variance	4,500	
Labor Efficiency Variance		5,000
Payroll		49,500

3. To record the entry applying factory overhead to work in process (assuming no variances):

Work in Process	20,000	
Factory Overhead		20,000

4. To record the entry for finished goods at standard cost (assuming no beginning or ending inventory of work in process, 10,000 units @ $11.00):

Finished Goods	110,000	
Work in Process		110,000

The balance sheet of Fine Products, Inc., using a standard cost system, would reflect inventories for work in process and finished goods at standard cost, while the materials inventory account would be shown at actual cost. This procedure will be followed in this text. The materials inventory account, however, may also be shown at standard cost, as explained in the following section.

Alternative Method of Recording Materials Cost. Some companies recognize materials price variances at the time materials are purchased by recording a **purchase price variance**, which represents the deviation of the purchase cost above or below the standard cost. The rationale for recording this variance at the time of purchase is that the difference between actual and standard cost is known at this time, so there is no reason for delaying the recognition of this variance until the materials are used.

Using the previous price figures and assuming that 12,000 pounds are purchased, the purchase entry under this method is as follows:

Materials (12,000 lbs. @ $4.00 standard price)	48,000	
Materials Purchase Price Variance		2,400
Accounts Payable (12,000 lbs. @ $3.80 actual price)		45,600

Under these conditions, the materials inventory account on the balance sheet would reflect standard cost. At the time the materials are used, there would be no price variance to record, and the quantity variance would be recorded as follows:

Work in Process (10,000 lbs. @ $4.00 standard price) .	40,000	
Materials Quantity Variance	4,000	
Materials (11,000 lbs. @ $4.00)		44,000

Another benefit of using the purchase price variance method is that the individual materials inventory accounts are maintained at standard cost. This saves recordkeeping expense because it is necessary to keep track only of the quantities purchased, issued, and on hand. It is not necessary to post individual materials costs nor to calculate continuously dollar amounts on the inventory ledger cards. Because the materials inventory account is kept at standard cost, the balance, in dollars, can be determined at any time by multiplying the standard price times the quantity on hand.

LEARNING OBJECTIVE
Give examples of how to dispose of variances

Disposition of Standard Cost Variances. At the end of the accounting period, the variances of actual cost from standard must be reflected in some appropriate manner on the financial statements. Different approaches for handling these items exist:

1. Some companies prorate these variances to Cost of Goods Sold, Work in Process, and Finished Goods. The net effect of this method is

that these accounts are adjusted to actual or historical cost. The rationale is that standard costs are important for management's evaluation of operations but are not proper for external financial reports. Therefore, the variances, being a part of actual manufacturing cost, should be included in inventory costs. When this method is followed, the allocation of materials, labor, and overhead variances will be in proportion to the standard materials, labor, and overhead costs included in cost of goods sold, work in process, and finished goods.

2. A more common approach, however, is to show the unfavorable net variance as an addition to the cost of goods sold for the period and the favorable net variance as a deduction. This is shown in the partial income statement that follows.

This approach is based on the fact that these variances result from favorable or unfavorable conditions or inefficiencies during the period. Therefore, they should be charged or credited to the period. These items should not be charged to future periods by including them in inventory costs.

Sales			$100,000
Cost of goods sold at standard		$80,000	
Add unfavorable variance:			
Materials quantity variance		800	
. . . .		$80,800	
Less favorable variances:			
Materials price variance	$410		
Labor efficiency variance	100		
Labor rate variance	105	615	
Cost of goods sold (actual cost)			80,185
Gross margin on sales (actual cost)			$ 19,815

3. If the variances are significant or have been caused by the use of an incorrect standard, the variances should be allocated to Inventory and to Cost of Goods Sold, and the standard cost adjusted accordingly.

4. If production is seasonal, with extreme peaks and valleys during the year, variances should be shown as deferred charges or credits on interim balance sheets, using the logic that they would be mostly offset in future periods. At the end of the year, however, some disposition of these variances, as described previously, must be made and the variance accounts closed.

5. If the variances are due to abnormal or unusual circumstances, such as strikes, fires, storms, or floods, there is justification for charging off these items as extraordinary losses on the income statement.

The material in this text will, unless indicated otherwise, use the more common approach of reflecting the materials and labor variances as adjustments to the standard cost of goods sold, as illustrated in Item 2. Variances of factory overhead costs, to be discussed in the next chapter, would also be reflected in the statements in a similar manner. Figure 8-2 provides an aid to understanding cost flow through a standard cost system.

ANALYSES OF VARIANCES

In analyzing materials and labor variances, two components are investigated: usage (quantity) and price. The analysis looks closely at the quantity of materials used, the cost per unit of each type of material, the number of direct labor hours worked, and the cost of each labor hour. When the usage and/or price differ from the established standards, the reason for the variance is examined, and whatever action can be taken to correct any deficiency before the loss becomes significant.

In analyzing the materials cost variance, the usage of materials may be above, below, or at standard, or the cost per unit of the materials used might be above, below, or at standard. Management requires this analyzed data to make corrective decisions if deemed necessary. Consider the following three possibilities in the manufacture of 10,000 units:

Example 1:

Standard cost, 10,000 lbs. of materials @ $4.00	$40,000
Actual cost, 10,000 lbs. of materials @ $4.18	41,800
Unfavorable materials price variance (10,000 × $.18)	$ (1,800)

This analysis shows that the factory usage of materials is at standard, but the price set for the materials has been exceeded. The variance is caused by the fact that the company used materials costing $.18 more than the standard price. With 10,000 pounds used, this $.18 per unit variance causes a total variance of $1,800.

Management now has the data with which to investigate why the materials cost per unit is higher than the standard of $4.00 per pound. Several possibilities exist, including the following:

1. Inefficient purchasing methods
2. Use of a slightly different material as an experiment
3. Increase in market price

Inefficient purchasing can be corrected by better planning and by careful selection of suppliers. If different material, which will be higher priced, is selected for use in manufacturing operations, the standard cost

FIGURE 8-2   Cost Flow Through a Standard Cost System

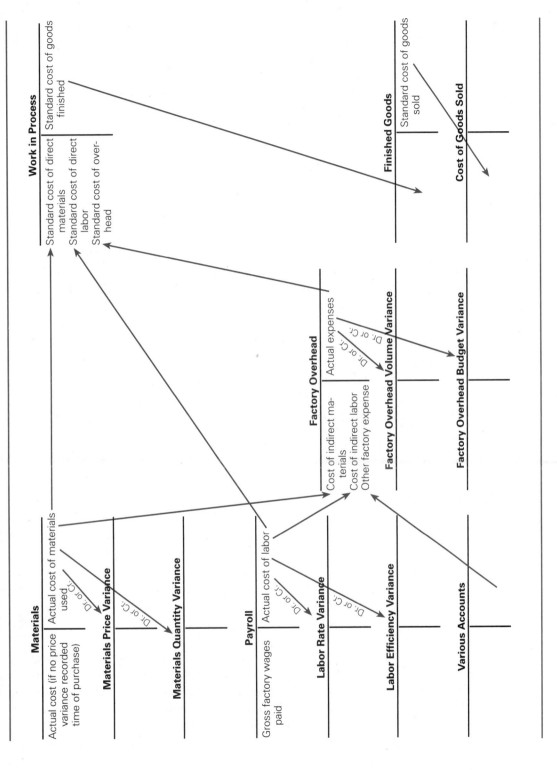

per unit of materials will have to be increased. The standard cost would also have to be increased if there is an increase in market price that is considered to be permanent.

The example illustrates the principle that management should carefully investigate any variance, favorable or unfavorable, so that corrective action can be taken. Such a decision may involve eliminating inefficiencies or changing the standard cost of the product.

Example 2:
Standard cost, 10,000 lbs. of materials @ $4.00	$40,000
Actual cost, 10,450 lbs. of materials @ $4.00	41,800
Unfavorable materials quantity variance (450 × $4.00)	$ (1,800)

In this case, the cost of the materials is at standard but the materials usage is excessive. The manufacturing operation used 450 pounds of materials more than it should have, as indicated by the standard. This additional 450 pounds at a cost of $4.00 per pound created the variance of $1,800 over standard cost.

As with the previous example, management must now determine why the extra materials were used. Again, various circumstances might have created this situation:

1. Materials were spoiled or wasted. This loss could have been due to a different type of material being used, careless workers, or lax supervisory personnel. If possible, the cause of the loss should be eliminated.

2. More materials were deliberately used per manufactured unit as an experiment to determine if the product's quality could be increased. If management decides to continue this usage, the standard cost per unit must be changed.

An analysis of the cause of this variance might also result in the elimination of inefficiencies or in a change in the standard cost.

Example 3:
Standard cost, 10,000 lbs. of materials @ $4.00	$40,000
Actual cost, 11,000 lbs. of materials @ $3.80	41,800
Unfavorable net materials variance	$ (1,800)

In this example, a combination of usage and price variances causes the overall unfavorable variance. The factory has used 1,000 pounds of materials over standard but has purchased these materials at a cost that is $.20 below standard. Once again, management should know why the additional materials were used and take appropriate action. It is important to recognize that the price variance of $.20 will also require investigation. The fact that this variance is favorable, below standard cost, is no reason for production personnel to be complacent and ignore it. This "better" price may have been created by more efficient buying techniques, a bargain purchase, or a general price reduction. On the other hand, materials of a lesser quality could have been purchased, thereby reducing the quality of the product and possibly causing an unfavorable effect on marketing.

It is also possible that the greater usage of materials may be related to the lower price. Waste and spoilage might be created by (1) the use of cheaper materials or (2) the production workers' unfamiliarity in the use of a different material. Further investigation may reveal that the standard was not properly determined and should be revised.

The following important points have been illustrated by the three examples with identical net variances:

1. The total variance between standard and actual cost must be broken down by usage and price.

2. The variances in usage and price, whether unfavorable or favorable, must be analyzed as to cause and effect. Variances may be stated in dollar amounts or in terms of units such as pounds or hours. The method chosen should be that which provides the greatest benefit in determining the cause of the variances.

3. Appropriate action must be taken. This action may include a change in methods of manufacturing, supervision, or purchasing, or a change in the standard cost of the product. It may involve taking advantage of efficient operations or functions. If the standard cost is changed, the units in inventory are often revalued at the new figure.

The same principles of analysis apply to the labor cost variances. Three similar examples are presented below.

Example 1:
Standard cost, 5,000 hrs. @ $10.00 per hr $50,000
Actual cost, 5,000 hrs. @ $9.90 per hr 49,500

Favorable labor rate variance (5,000 × $.10) . . . . $ 500

Example 2:
Standard cost, 5,000 hrs. @ $10.00 per hr $50,000
Actual cost, 4,950 hrs. @ $10.00 per hr 49,500

Favorable labor efficiency variance (50 × $10.00) . . . . $ 500

Example 3:
Standard cost, 5,000 hrs. @ $10.00 per hr $50,000
Actual cost, 4,500 hrs. @ $11.00 per hr 49,500

Favorable net labor variance . . . . $ 500

In the first example, it is apparent that the number of actual labor hours was at standard, but the cost per hour was lower than the standard of $10.00. Although this result appears to be favorable, the reason and the possible effect should still be determined. It may be that the personnel department is doing a more efficient job in hiring qualified employees and should be commended; or it may be that less-than-qualified workers are being hired at a lower rate, possibly reducing the quality of the work on the product. This second condition would not be acceptable.

The second example indicates that the labor rate is at standard, but the time required was 50 hours below standard. Again, the question is, why? It is possible that the speed of production has been increased, and the employees are working too fast to do top-quality work. This situation could have an adverse effect on sales. Again, of course, the possibility exists that the manufacturing and/or supervisory functions have become more efficient so that more work is done in less time.

In the third example, a saving of 500 hours is indicated, but there has been a payment per hour of $1.00 in excess of standard. These two factors could be related. The hiring of more highly skilled and higher-paid personnel quite often results in a reduction in the number of hours worked. But, as with the other examples, management should investigate to determine the cause and the effect of the variances in usage and price. If the labor efficiency variance is unfavorable, it may have been caused by the use of unskilled workers or it may be due to time lost because of machine breakdowns, improper production scheduling, or an inefficient flow of materials to the production line.

The analyses of materials and labor variances are not isolated from each other. It is very possible that a difference above or below standard of one is directly related to a variance of the other. For example, the hiring of more highly skilled personnel at a higher labor rate does not always reduce the number of hours worked, but it may reduce the amount of materials lost through spoilage. Conversely, the use of less skilled workers at a lower rate may cause greater materials loss. In examining any variance, management should look closely at the relationship of that variance to other variances.

FEATURES OF STANDARD COST ACCOUNTING

LEARNING OBJECTIVE
Recognize the specific features of a standard cost system

Some features of standard cost accounting must be emphasized. First, the company does not determine the actual unit cost of manufacturing a product. Only the total actual costs and the total standard costs are gathered.

Second, the fact that standards are based on estimates does not make them unreliable. A close examination and analysis of variances will quickly indicate whether the manufacturing operation is inefficient or whether the standards are reasonable.

Third, standards will change as conditions change. Permanent changes in prices, processes, or methods of operating may indicate the need for the standards to be adjusted.

Fourth, the purpose of using a standard cost accounting system is to provide continual incentive for factory personnel to keep costs and performance in line with predetermined management objectives. As mentioned earlier in the chapter, comparisons between actual costs and the predetermined standards are much more effective than comparisons between current actual costs and actual costs of prior periods.

Fifth, a standard cost accounting system, through the recording and analysis of manufacturing cost variances, helps focus management's attention on these questions:

1. Were materials purchased at prices above or below standard?
2. Were materials used in quantities above or below standard?
3. Is labor being paid at rates above or below standard?
4. Is labor being used in amounts above or below standard?

Finally, although the discussion in this text suggests that variances are determined at the end of the month, most manufacturing companies calculate variances on a weekly, or even daily, basis to allow for more timely action in correcting inefficiencies or taking advantage of efficiencies. The variances for the month, however, are still recorded in the accounts at the end of the month.

You should now be able to work the following: Exercises 1, 2, 3, 4, 5.

ILLUSTRATION OF STANDARD COST IN A DEPARTMENTALIZED FACTORY

The following example demonstrates standard cost accounting procedures in a factory having two departments.

Standard Cost Summary

		Dept. A	Dept. B	Total
Materials:	5 lbs. @ $1.00 lb.	$ 5		
	1 lb. @ $2.00 lb.		$ 2	$ 7
Labor:				
	1 hour @ $8.00	8		
	2 hours @ $10.00		20	28
Factory overhead:				
	Per unit	1	2	3
Standard costs per unit		$14	$24	$38

Production Report for the Month

	Dept. A	Dept. B
Beginning units in process	None	None
Units finished and transferred	2,200	1,800
Ending units in process	None	400
Stage of completion		1/2

Units pass through Dept. A to Dept. B. In both departments, materials, labor, and overhead are added evenly throughout the process. Actual costs for the month, as determined from materials requisitions, payroll records, and factory overhead records, follow:

	Dept. A		Dept. B		Total
Direct materials:					
12,000 lbs. @ $ .95	$11,400				
1,900 lbs. @ $2.10				$ 3,990	$15,390
Direct labor:					
2,000 hrs. @ $8.10	16,200				
4,100 hrs. @ $9.90				40,590	56,790
Factory overhead:					
Indirect materials	$ 400		$1,000		
Indirect labor	600		1,000		
Other items	1,200	2,200	2,000	4,000	6,200
		$29,800		$48,580	$78,380

From the data given on the standard cost summary, the standard costs of production can be determined. To facilitate the comparison of these figures with actual costs and the determination of variances, a form similar to Figure 8-3 can be used.

Using the data given in Figure 8-3, the specific variances for materials and labor can be computed as follows:

Materials—Dept. A

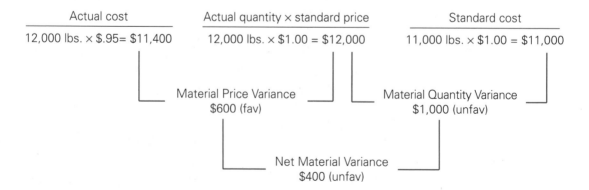

One thousand pounds of materials in excess of standard were used in Dept. A, which, at the standard cost of $1.00, caused an unfavorable variance of $1,000. If prices had not changed, there would have been no other variances. But price did change—12,000 pounds of materials at a cost of $.05 below standard resulted in a favorable price variance of $600. The combined variances resulted in a net unfavorable materials cost variance of $400 in Dept. A.

UPDATING STANDARD COST SYSTEMS

An article in the *Journal of Accountancy* discusses how standard cost systems should be updated to make them more useful today.

Standard cost systems need revisions to make them more useful in the new manufacturing environment. Traditional production-driven systems focus exclusively on inputs, which can lead to bad decisions, such as producing large amounts of unneeded inventories. A revised system should focus on both inputs and outputs and encourage managers to use the just-in-time concept of production, which results in small batches. This is accomplished by calculating four variances.

1. Quality variances indicate the production costs of defective units. They focus attention on the resources invested in units that must be reworked, scrapped, or sold as seconds.
2. Production variances indicate excess investment in inventories. Tracking them follows the just-in-time philosophy of minimizing inventories at all stages.
3. Price variances are based on materials used in production rather than materials purchased. Calculating them results in a better evaluation of the trade-offs between price and efficiency or quality. For example, buying high-priced materials may result in unfavorable price variances but in favorable efficiency and quality variances.
4. Efficiency variances detect waste that occurs during the production process. Costs expended on units that eventually are rejected are moved to the quality variance.

Carole Cheatham, "Updating Standard Cost Systems" *Journal of Accountancy* (December 1990), pp. 57–60.

FIGURE 8-3 Calculation of Variances

	Dept. A Equivalent Production of 2,200 Units			Dept. B Equivalent Production of 2,000 Units			Total		
	Standard Cost	Actual Cost	Favorable (Unfavorable) Variance	Standard Cost	Actual Cost	Favorable (Unfavorable) Variance	Standard Cost	Actual Cost	Favorable (Unfavorable) Variance
Materials:									
11,000 lbs. @ $1.00	$11,000								
12,000 lbs. @ $ .95		$11,400	$(400)						
2,000 lbs. @ $2.00				$4,000					
1,900 lbs. @ $2.10					$ 3,990	$ 10	$15,000	$15,390	$(390)
Labor:									
2,200 hrs. @ $ 8.00	17,600								
2,000 hrs. @ $ 8.10		16,200	1,400						
4,000 hrs. @ $10.00				40,000					
4,100 hrs. @ $ 9.90					40,590	(590)	57,600	56,790	810
Factory overhead:									
Standard cost per unit $1.00	2,200								
Actual cost		2,000	—						
Standard cost per unit $2.00				4,000					
Actual cost					4,000	—	6,200	6,200	—
Total	$30,800	$29,800	$1,000	$48,000	$48,580	$(580)	$78,800	$78,380	$ 420

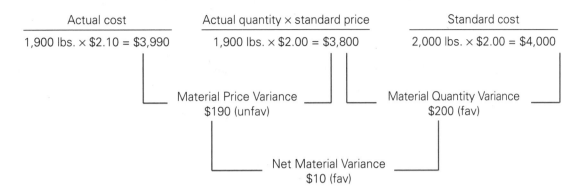

Materials—Dept. B

Actual cost	Actual quantity × standard price	Standard cost
1,900 lbs. × $2.10 = $3,990	1,900 lbs. × $2.00 = $3,800	2,000 lbs. × $2.00 = $4,000

Material Price Variance
$190 (unfav)

Material Quantity Variance
$200 (fav)

Net Material Variance
$10 (fav)

In this case, Dept. B used 100 pounds of materials less than standard. At a standard cost of $2.00 per pound, the favorable quantity variance was $200. But this variance was partially offset by the unfavorable price variance created by the increase in the cost per unit of the materials of $.10. With 1,900 pounds being used, the price variance was $190 above standard. The two variances resulted in a net favorable materials cost variance of $10 in Dept. B.

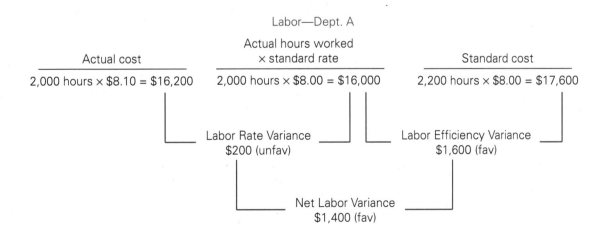

Labor—Dept. A

Actual cost	Actual hours worked × standard rate	Standard cost
2,000 hours × $8.10 = $16,200	2,000 hours × $8.00 = $16,000	2,200 hours × $8.00 = $17,600

Labor Rate Variance
$200 (unfav)

Labor Efficiency Variance
$1,600 (fav)

Net Labor Variance
$1,400 (fav)

During the month, Dept. A saved 200 hours by working fewer hours than the number established as a standard for the number of units produced. At a standard cost of $8.00 per hour, a favorable efficiency variance of $1,600 was realized. The average hourly rate of pay, however, was $.10 above standard so there was also an unfavorable rate variance. The company paid $.10 more per hour than the standard rate for 2,000 hours of work, or a total of $200.

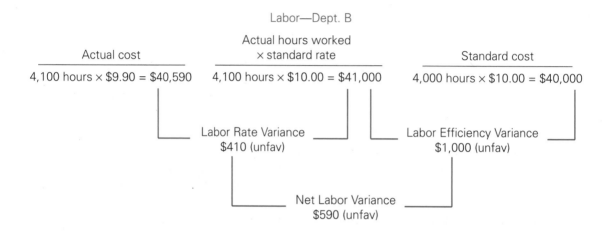

Dept. B used 100 hours more than the standard. Therefore, at the standard rate of $10.00, it had an unfavorable efficiency variance of $1,000. Because the actual rate was $.10 below standard, a favorable rate variance of $410 resulted, determined by multiplying the 4,100 hours worked by the $.10 rate differential. (For the purposes of discussion in this chapter, no variances have been shown for factory overhead. This variance will be discussed in the next chapter.)

The following journal entries can now be prepared:

Work in Process—Dept. A	11,000	
Work in Process—Dept. B	4,000	
Materials Quantity Variance—Dept. A	1,000	
Materials Price Variance—Dept. B	190	
Factory Overhead (Indirect Materials)	1,400	
Materials Price Variance—Dept. A		600
Materials Quantity Variance—Dept. B		200
Materials		16,790

Note that the accounts for work in process are charged for the standard cost of direct materials, the factory overhead account is debited for the actual cost of indirect materials used, the materials account is credited at actual cost for all direct and indirect materials used, and the variance accounts are debited if the variance is unfavorable and credited if it is favorable. (If this company followed the practice of recording the materials price variance at time of purchase, no price variances would be recorded at this time because the material purchase price variance would have been determined when the goods were received.)

Work in Process—Dept. A	17,600	
Work in Process—Dept. B	40,000	
Labor Rate Variance—Dept. A	200	
Labor Efficiency Variance—Dept. B	1,000	
Factory Overhead (Indirect Labor)	1,600	
Labor Efficiency Variance—Dept. A		1,600
Labor Rate Variance—Dept. B		410
Payroll		58,390

As with materials, only standard costs for direct labor are charged to Work in Process; the factory overhead account is debited for the actual cost of the indirect labor used; the payroll account is credited for the actual cost of direct and indirect labor during the month; and the variances are debited or credited to the appropriate accounts.

During the month and at the end of the month, there would be the usual entries in the journals to record the factory overhead other than indirect materials and indirect labor. These entries are summarized as follows:

Factory Overhead	3,200	
Various credits (Accounts Payable, Accumulated		
Depr., Prepaid Insurance)		3,200

Factory overhead would be applied to work in process by the following entry:

Work in Process—Dept. A (2,200 units × $1)	2,200	
Work in Process—Dept. B (2,000 units × $2)	4,000	
Factory Overhead		6,200

The entries are then made to transfer the standard cost of units finished in Dept. A to Dept. B and from Dept. B to finished goods.

Work in Process—Dept. B	30,800	
Work in Process—Dept. A		30,800
(2,200 units @ $14)		
Finished Goods	68,400	
Work in Process—Dept. B		68,400
(1,800 units @ $38)		

After these entries have been posted, the general ledger accounts would reflect the data as shown in T-account form.

Materials		Work in Process—Dept. A	
	16,790	11,000	30,800
		17,600	
		2,200	
		30,800	

Work in Process—Dept. B		Finished Goods	
4,000	68,400	68,400	
40,000			
4,000			
30,000			
78,800			
10,400			

Materials Quantity Variance—Dept. A		Materials Quantity Variance—Dept. B	
1,000			200

Materials Price Variance—Dept. A		Materials Price Variance—Dept. B	
	600	190	

Labor Efficiency Variance—Dept. A		Labor Efficiency Variance—Dept. B	
	1,600	1,000	

Labor Rate Variance—Dept. A		Labor Rate Variance—Dept. B	
200			410

Factory Overhead		Payroll	
1,400	6,200		58,390
1,600			
3,200			
6,200			

The work in process account for Dept. A has no balance because all work has been completed and transferred to Dept. B. The work in process account for Dept. B has a balance of $10,400 accounted for as follows:

Cost in Dept. A—400 units @ $14 . . . . $ 5,600
Cost in Dept. B—400 units @ $12 (one-half completed)   4,800

. . . . $10,400

Not included in the previous example are the additional entries that would have been made during the month for purchases of materials, vouching and payment of payrolls, and recording of cost of goods sold.

MIX AND YIELD VARIANCES

It is common for more than one material to be required in a production process. The proportion or ratio of one material to another material is called the **mix**. Often, in industries such as petroleum manufacturing, textiles, chemicals, foundries, rubber goods, and food processing, the mix of materials is deliberately changed from the standard formula. This may occur for such reasons as (1) achieving economy, (2) an experimental change in the quality of the product, or (3) because a given material is in short supply or is not available. Sometimes a change in mix will affect the **yield**, which is the number of units produced from a standard amount of materials introduced into the process. For example, if the standard calls for 2 gallons of material X and 1 gallon of material Y to produce 3 gallons of product Z, the mix ratio is 2/3 of X to 1/3 of Y. The yield is three units of Z. If the ratio of 2/3 material X to 1/3 material Y is altered in the production process, then the mix has been changed. If the ratio of 3 gallons of input materials to 3 gallons of output product is different, then the yield has been changed.

As discussed earlier, the materials quantity variance measures the cost of the actual quantity of direct materials used above or below the standard quantity for the actual level of production. If the mix has been changed, further analysis should be made to determine the effect of this change. This involves breaking down the materials quantity variance into a mix variance and a yield variance.

A **mix variance** shows the change in cost that results from changing the proportions of materials added to the production mix. It measures the effect of using a different combination of materials. In the previous example, if materials X and Y were used in equal proportions, the standard mix has changed, and a mix variance would be calculated. This variance is calculated by measuring the difference in cost, at standard prices, between the actual mix of quantities used and the standard mix of the total quantity used.

A **yield variance** measures whether a change in mix affected the yield and shows the difference in cost that results if the actual yield (output) varies from the standard quantity of yield determined for a given input of materials. In the previous example, if the mix was changed and 3 gallons of direct materials did not produce 3 gallons of product, the yield has also changed and a yield variance should be determined. This variance is calculated by measuring the difference between the actual quantity of materials used, at standard mix and prices, and the standard quantity of materials allowed for the actual amount of production, at standard prices.

To illustrate, assume that the standards for materials are as follows:

Material		Quantity		Price per Pound	Total Cost
A		60 lbs.	×	$1	$ 60
B		40	×	$3	120
		100 lbs.			$180

Standard yield = 100 lbs. of finished product; mix ratio = 60% A, 40% B.

Also assume that the production records for the month show that 100 pounds of finished product were manufactured at the following cost:

Material		Quantity		Price per Pound	Total Cost
A		90 lbs.	×	$1	$ 90
B		20	×	$3	60
		110 lbs.			$150

The materials quantity variance would be calculated as follows for 100 finished units:

Material	Actual Quantity	Standard Quantity	Quantity Difference		Standard Price	Quantity Variance
A ...	90 lbs.	60 lbs.	(30 lbs.) (U)	×	$1	$(30) (U)
B ...	20	40	20 (F)	×	$3	60 (F)
	110 lbs.	100 lbs.	(10 lbs.) (U)			$ 30 (F)

The mix variance is then calculated:

Material	Actual Quantity	Actual Quantity Converted to Standard Mix	Quantity Difference		Standard Price	Mix Variance
A	90 lbs.	66 lbs. (60% × 110 lbs.)	(24) lbs. (U)	×	$1	$(24)(U)
B	20	44 (40% × 110 lbs.)	24 (F)	×	$3	72 (F)
	110 lbs.	110 lbs.	-0-			$ 48 (F)

The mix variance is favorable because the actual mix of materials cost less than the standard mix. This resulted from the use of more lower cost material A and less use of the higher priced material B.

The yield variance is determined as follows:

Material	Actual Quantity Converted to Standard Mix	Standard Quantity (100 units)	Quantity Difference	Standard Price	Yield Variance
A	66 lbs.	60 lbs.	(6) lbs. (U)	$1	$ (6) (U)
B	44	40	(4) (U)	$3	(12) (U)
	110 lbs.	100 lbs.	(10) lbs. (U)		$(18) (U)

The analysis indicates that 110 pounds of input materials were used, rather than the standard 100 pounds, to produce 100 finished units. This creates an unfavorable yield variance, which may have been caused by (1) the use of an inferior grade of materials, (2) loss of units due to the different mix, or (3) rejection of units of poorer quality.

Note that the total of the mix and yield variances equals the quantity variance.

Mix variance	$48	(F)
Yield variance	(18)	(U)
Quantity variance	$30	(F)

These variances may be developed for internal use only, then only the materials quantity variance would be recorded in a journal entry, as discussed earlier in the chapter. However, if the mix and yield variances are to be recorded in the accounts in lieu of a materials quantity variance, the journal entry is as follows (assuming no price variance):

Work in Process	180	
Materials Yield Variance	18	
Materials Mix Variance		48
Materials		150

This same type of analysis can be applied to determine labor mix and yield variances. A change in labor mix would result if the relative proportions of skilled (higher-paid) and unskilled (lower-paid) workers were changed due to (1) cost-cutting, (2) absentee workers, (3) a shortage of one type of labor, or (4) problems in scheduling. In this case, the company would determine a mix variance. Because this type of variation from the standard labor mix usually would affect hours worked and unit yield, a yield variance would also be calculated.

Assume that the direct labor standard for manufacturing a unit of product is as follows:

Class 1 labor—1 hour @ $10	$10
Class 2 labor—1 hour @ $ 5	5
Total direct labor cost per unit	$15

Due to a shortage of skilled laborers, it was necessary to hire additional unskilled workers to complete the production process. The production data follow:

Number of units manufactured	1,000
Direct labor cost:	
Class 1 labor—900 hours @ $10	$9,000
Class 2 labor—1,300 hours @ $ 5	$6,500

The labor variances would first be calculated in the usual way:

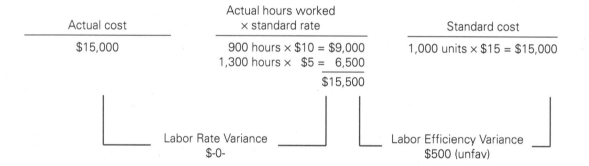

Actual cost	Actual hours worked × standard rate	Standard cost
$15,000	900 hours × $10 = $9,000 1,300 hours × $5 = 6,500 $15,500	1,000 units × $15 = $15,000

Labor Rate Variance $-0-

Labor Efficiency Variance $500 (unfav)

No labor rate variance exists because the two classes of workers were paid standard hourly rates for their classification. The labor efficiency variance is $500 and is unfavorable. This variance resulted because the number of hours worked (2,200) exceeded the standard number of hours (2,000) allowed for the production of 1,000 units. However, the breakdown of the efficiency variance into labor mix and yield variances will provide a more definitive analysis. The calculation of the mix variance follows:

Labor Class	Actual Hours	Actual Hours Converted to Standard Mix	Quantity Difference	Standard Price	Mix Variance
1	900	1,100 (50%)	200 hrs. (F)	$10	$2,000 (F)
2	1,300	1,100 (50%)	(200) hrs. (U)	5	(1,000) (U)
	2,200	2,200	-0-		$1,000 (F)

The mix variance is favorable because more lower-paid workers were used in place of higher-paid workers, but when this type of variance arises, management must be concerned as to whether the quality of the product and the yield were affected.

The yield variance is determined next:

Labor Class	Actual Hours Converted to Standard Mix	Standard Hours (1,000 units)	Quantity Difference	Standard Price	Yield Variance
1	1,100 (50%)	1,000	(100) hrs. (U)	$10	$(1,000) (U)
2	1,100 (50%)	1,000	(100) (U)	5	(500) (U)
	2,200	2,000	(200) hrs. (U)		$(1,500) (U)

The yield variance is unfavorable because 2,200 hours of labor produced only 1,000 units, rather than 1,100 units as prescribed by the standards. The total of the mix variance ($1,000 favorable) and the yield variance ($1,500 unfavorable) equals the amount of the efficiency variance ($500 unfavorable). Because a change in materials and/or labor mix can affect yields, costs, and quality of the product, management should carefully study these variances to determine the potential effect of nonstandard mix.

Diagrams of Formulas for Mix and Yield. Formulas that summarize the calculations required for determining variances for material and labor as well as for mix and yield are diagramed below:

Materials—Price, Mix, and Yield Variances

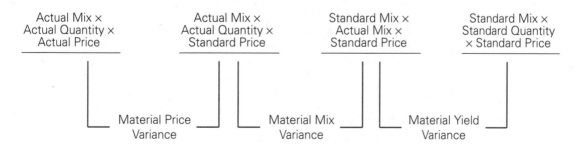

Labor—Rate, Mix, and Yield Variances

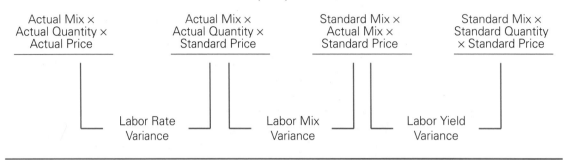

Actual Mix × Actual Quantity × Actual Price	Actual Mix × Actual Quantity × Standard Price	Standard Mix × Actual Mix × Standard Price	Standard Mix × Standard Quantity × Standard Price

Labor Rate Variance   Labor Mix Variance   Labor Yield Variance

KEY TERMS

Attainable standard, p. 353
Favorable variance, p. 356
Ideal standard, p. 352
Labor cost standard, p. 353
Labor efficiency (usage) variance, p. 356
Labor rate (price) variance, p. 356
Materials cost standard, p. 353
Materials price variance, p. 355
Materials quantity (usage) variance, p. 356
Mix, p. 375
Mix variance, p. 375
Price, p. 354

Purchase price variance, p. 360
Standard, p. 352
Standard cost accounting, p. 352
Standard quantity of material per unit, p. 353
Standard unit cost of material, p. 353
Standard labor hours required per unit, p. 353
Standard labor cost per unit, p. 353
Unfavorable variance, p. 356
Usage, p. 354
Variance, p. 354
Yield, p. 375
Yield variance, p. 376

SELF-STUDY PROBLEM

MATERIALS AND LABOR VARIANCE ANALYSES

Thomas Company

Thomas Company manufactures one product and uses a standard cost system. The established standards for materials and labor follow:

Material A: 3 lbs. @ $6 per lb. $18
Labor: 4 hours @ $4.50 per hour $18

The operating data for the month of May follow:

Work in process, May 1: 200 units, all materials, 20% complete as to labor.
Work in process, May 31: 600 units, all materials, 80% complete as to labor.
Completed during the month: 6,400 units.
All materials are added at the beginning of processing in the department.
    20,900 pounds of materials were used in production during the month, at a total cost of $123,310. Direct labor amounted to $127,370, which was at a rate of $4.70 per hour.

Required:

Using the FIFO method of costing, calculate the following variances:
1. Materials quantity variance
2. Materials price variance

3. Labor efficiency variance
4. Labor rate variance

SOLUTION TO DEMONSTRATION PROBLEM

The specifics in the problem highlight the following facts:

In addition to the usual procedures used to solve standard cost problems, equivalent production (FIFO) must be calculated. The equivalent production determined by the FIFO method will be used to calculate the standard materials and standard labor allowed. Two variances (price and quantity) must be determined for materials, and two variances (rate and efficiency) must be determined for labor.

Calculating equivalent production for materials and labor by the FIFO method

	Units
Materials:	
Work in process, May 1: 200 units (all material added last period)	-0-
Units started and finished during May	6,200
Work in process, May 31: 600 units (all materials added)	600
Total equivalent production—materials	6,800
Labor:	
Work in process, May 1: 200 units (80% of labor required)	160
Units started and finished during May	6,200
Work in process, May 31: 600 units (80% labor added)	480
Total equivalent production—labor	6,840

Determining the materials variances

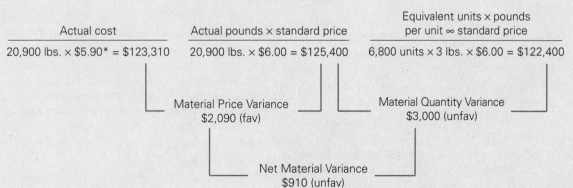

Materials Variances

Actual cost	Actual pounds × standard price	Equivalent units × pounds per unit ∞ standard price
20,900 lbs. × $5.90* = $123,310	20,900 lbs. × $6.00 = $125,400	6,800 units × 3 lbs. × $6.00 = $122,400

Material Price Variance
$2,090 (fav)

Material Quantity Variance
$3,000 (unfav)

Net Material Variance
$910 (unfav)

*$123,310/20,900 = $5.90 per pound

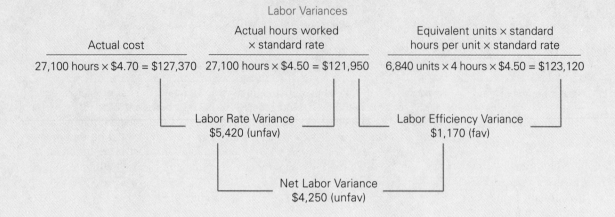

Labor Variances

Actual cost	Actual hours worked × standard rate	Equivalent units × standard hours per unit × standard rate
27,100 hours × $4.70 = $127,370	27,100 hours × $4.50 = $121,950	6,840 units × 4 hours × $4.50 = $123,120

Labor Rate Variance
$5,420 (unfav)

Labor Efficiency Variance
$1,170 (fav)

Net Labor Variance
$4,250 (unfav)

QUESTIONS

1. What are the function and objectives of standard cost accounting?

2. What is the difference between standard cost and actual cost of production?

3. What is a "standard"?

4. What are the specific procedures upon which a standard cost accounting system is based?

5. How are how standards for materials and labor costs determined?

6. What is a "variance"?

7. When are variances usually recorded in the journals?

8. How do price and quantity variances relate to materials costs?

9. How do rate and efficiency variances relate to labor costs?

10. Is a favorable variance "good" or an unfavorable variance "bad"? Explain.

11. Are actual costs or standard costs charged to Work in Process?

12. When a company uses a standard cost system are the inventory accounts—Finished Goods, Work in Process, and Materials—valued at actual cost or standard cost?

13. What two factors must be considered when breaking down a variance into its components? Explain.

14. What might cause the following variances?

    a. An unfavorable materials price variance.

    b. A favorable materials price variance.

    c. An unfavorable materials quantity variance.

    d. A favorable materials quantity variance.

    e. An unfavorable labor rate variance.

    f. A favorable labor rate variance.

    g. An unfavorable labor efficiency variance.

    h. A favorable labor efficiency variance.

15. Is it possible that a variance of one type might be partially or fully offset by another variance? Explain.

16. If, in a given period, the total actual cost of all materials used is exactly the same as the standard cost so that no net variance results, should the data be further analyzed? Explain.

17. What is a mix variance?

18. What is a yield variance?

EXERCISES

E8-1 through E8-5 use the following data:
The standard operating capacity of the Perfecto Manufacturing Co. is 1,000 units. A detailed study of the manufacturing data relating to the production of one product revealed the following:

1. Two pounds of materials are needed to produce one unit.
2. Standard unit cost of materials is $8 per pound.
3. It takes one hour of labor to produce one unit.
4. Standard labor rate is $10 per hour.
5. Standard overhead for this volume is $4,000.

Each case in E8-1 through E8-5 requires the following:

1. Set up a standard cost summary showing the standard unit cost.
2. Analyze the variances and make general journal entries to record the transfer to Work in Process of
   a. materials costs
   b. labor costs
   c. overhead costs

When making these entries, indicate the types of variances, and state whether each variance is favorable or unfavorable.

3. Prepare the general journal entry to record the transfer of costs to the finished goods account.

E8-1
Standard unit cost;
variance analysis;
journal entries

1,000 units were started and finished.
Case 1. All prices and quantities for the cost elements are standard, except for materials cost, which is $7.70 per pound.
Case 2. All prices and quantities for the cost elements are standard, except that 2,100 pounds of materials were used.

E8-2
Standard unit cost;
variance analysis;
journal entries

1,000 units were started and finished.
Case 1. All prices and quantities are standard, except for the labor rate, which is $10.20 per hour.
Case 2. All prices and quantities are standard with the exception of labor hours, which totaled 900.

E8-3
Computing standard
unit cost; variance
analysis; journal
entries

All of the deviations listed in E8-1 and E8-2 took place, and 1,000 units were started and finished.

E8-4
Standard unit cost;
variance analysis;
journal entries

All of the deviations listed in E8-1 and E8-2 took place, and 950 units were started and finished.

E8-5
Standard unit cost;
variance analysis;
journal entries

All of the deviations listed in E8-1 and E8-2 took place, and 1,050 units were started and finished.

E8-6
Computing material
variances
Learning Objective 3

Landscape Calendar Company specializes in manufacturing calendars that depict landscape pictures from around the world. The company uses a standard cost system to control it costs. During one month of operations, the direct materials costs and the quantities of paper used showed the following:

Actual purchase price	$.165 per page
Standard quantity allowed production	170,000 pages
Actual quantity purchased during month	200,000 pages
Actual quantity used during month	185,000 pages
Standard price per page	$.17 per page

Calculate the following:

1. Total cost of purchases for the month
2. Materials price variance
3. Materials quantity variance
4. Net material variance

E8-7
Computing labor
variances
Learning Objective 3

Superior Doors Company manufactures steel doors for homes and apartments. The standard quantity of direct labor to manufacture a door is 4.5 hours. The standard hourly wage in this department is $12.50 per hour. During August, 6,100 doors were produced. The payroll records indicate that 31,110 hours were worked at a total cost for payroll of $405,985.50.
    Calculate the following:

1. Labor rate variance
2. Labor efficiency variance
3. Net labor variance

E8-8
Standard cost
summary; materials
and labor cost
variances
Learning Objective 3

SS

A manufacturing plant produces an average of 10,000 units each month. The factory standards are 20,000 hours of direct labor and 10,000 pounds of materials for this volume. The standard cost of direct labor is $9.00 per hour, and the standard cost of materials is $4.00 per pound. The standard factory overhead at this level of production is $10,000.
    During the current month the production and cost reports reflected the following information:

Beginning units in process	None
Units finished	9,500
Units in process, end of month	None
Direct labor hours worked	20,000
Pounds of materials used	9,400
Cost of direct labor	$178,000
Cost of materials used	$ 39,480

On the basis of the above information:

1. Prepare a standard cost summary.
2. Calculate the materials and labor cost variances and indicate whether they are favorable or unfavorable using formulas in Figure 8-1.
3. Calculate the materials and labor cost variances, using a schedule similar to that shown on page 357.

E8-9
Computing labor variances

Fill in the missing figures for each of the following independent cases:

	Case 1	Case 2
Units produced	1,200	?
Std. hrs. per unit	2	.6
Std. hrs. allowed	?	1,200
Std. rate per hour	$5	?
Actual hours used	2,460	1,160
Actual labor cost	?	?
Labor rate variance	$123 U	$290 U
Labor Efficiency var.	?	80 F

E8-10
Preparing a standard cost summary and making journal entries
Learning Objective 3

The normal capacity of a manufacturing plant is 40,000 direct labor hours and 20,000 units per month. A finished unit requires 6 pounds of materials at an estimated cost of $2 per pound. The estimated cost of labor is $10.00 per hour. The plant estimates that overhead for a month will be $40,000.

During the month of March, the plant totaled 34,800 direct labor hours at an average rate of $9.50 an hour. The plant produced 18,000 units, using 105,000 pounds of materials at a cost of $2.04 per pound.

1. Prepare a standard cost summary showing the standard unit cost.
2. Make a general journal entries to charge materials and labor to Work in Process. Indicate variances, favorable or unfavorable.

E8-11
Making journal entries
Learning Objective 3

Assume that during the month of April the production report of the company in E8-7 revealed the following information:

Units produced during the month	21,000
Direct labor hours for the month	41,000
Materials used (in pounds)	130,000
Labor rate per hour	$10.04
Materials cost per pound	$1.98

Make general journal entries to charge materials and labor to Work in Process. Indicate variances, favorable or unfavorable.

E8-12
Determining actual quantities and costs for materials and labor
Learning Objective 3

From an analysis of the data presented below, determine the actual quantity of materials used and the actual price per pound as well as the actual direct labor hours incurred and the actual cost per hour.

Materials	Standard Quantity or Hours (pounds)	Standard Price or Rate	Variances Materials Quantity	Materials Price
A	2,200	$2.05	$205 Unf.	$115 Fav.
B	800	11.00	110 Fav.	79 Fav.
C	10,000	3.00	1,200 Unf.	520 Unf.

Labor	(hours)		Labor Efficiency	Labor Rate
D	5,600	10.00	$500 Unf.	$565 Fav.
E	8,800	9.00	900 Fav.	435 Unf.
F	11,500	10.50	1,575 Fav.	1,135 Unf.

E8-13
Using variance
analysis and
interpretation
Learning Objective 3

Last year Tuxedo Corporation adopted a standard cost system. Labor standards were set on the basis of time studies and prevailing wage rates. Materials standards were determined from materials specifications and the prices then in effect.

On June 30, the end of the current fiscal year, a partial trial balance revealed the following:

	Debit	Credit
Materials Price Variance		25,000
Materials Quantity Variance	9,000	
Labor Rate Variance	30,000	
Labor Efficiency Variance	7,500	

Standards set at the beginning of the year have remained unchanged. All inventories are priced at standard cost. What conclusions can be drawn from each of the four variances shown in Tuxedo's trial balance?

PROBLEMS

P8-1
Materials and labor
variance analyses
Learning Objective 3

The standard cost summary of Brunt Manufacturing Company is shown below, together with production and cost data for the period.

Standard Cost Summary

Materials:		
2 gallons A @ $2.00	$4.00	
2 gallons B @ $3.00	6.00	$10.00
Labor:		
1 hour @ $12.00		12.00
Factory overhead:		
$1.00 per direct labor hour		1.00
Total standard unit cost		$23.00

Production and Cost Summary

Units completed during the month	9,000
Ending units in process (one-fourth completed)	2,000
Gallons of material A used	21,000
Gallons of material B used	20,000
Direct labor hours worked	10,000
Cost of material A used	$ 41,160
Cost of material B used	$ 60,000
Cost of direct labor	$117,000

One gallon each of materials A and B are added at the start of processing. The balance of the materials are added when the process is two-thirds complete. Labor and overhead are added evenly throughout the process.

Required:

1. Calculate equivalent production.
2. Calculate materials and labor variances and indicate whether they are favorable or unfavorable, using the formulas shown in Figure 8-1.
3. Explain all variances by preparing a schedule similar to the one on page 357.
4. Determine the cost of materials and labor in the work in process account at the end of the month.
5. Prove that all materials and labor costs have been accounted for.

P8-2
Material and labor variances
Learning Objective 3

A housing inspection company specializes in determining whether a building or house's drain pipes are properly tied into the city's sewer system. The company pours colored chemical through the pipes and collects an inspection sample from each outlet, which is then analyzed. Each job should take 15 hours for each of 4 inspectors who are paid $18 per hour. Each job uses 5 gallons of Detecto (a colored chemical), which costs $25 per gallon. Data from the company's most recent job (a building) follow:

5 men worked a total of 80 hours and were paid $20 per hour	$1,600.00
3.5 gallons of Detecto was used and cost $27.50 per gallon	96.25
Total cost of the job	$1,696.25

Required:

1. Compute the material price and quantity variances.
2. Compute the labor rate and efficiency variances.

P8-3
Material and labor variances
Learning Objective 3

Steeple Company uses a standard cost to account for its single product. The standards established for the product include the following:

Materials	8 lbs. @ $.05 per lb.
Labor	6 hours @ $5.60 per hour

The following operating data came from the records for the month:

In process, beginning inventory, none.
In process, ending inventory 800 units, 75% complete as to labor; material is
    issued at the beginning of processing.
Completed during the month, 5,600 units.

Material issued to production was 51,680 pounds @ $.045 per pound.
Direct labor was $215,840 at the rate of $5.68 per hour.

Required:

Calculate the following variances:

1. Material price
2. Material quantity
3. Net material variance
4. Labor rate
5. Labor efficiency
6. Net labor variance

P8-4
Variance analysis,
journal entries, other
analyses
Learning Objectives 3
& 5

Cost and production data for the Derrick Products Company are presented below.

Standard Cost Summary

	Dept. I	Dept. II	Total
Materials:			
4 units @ $.50	$ 2		
1 unit @ $1.00		$ 1	$ 3
Labor:			
1 hour @ $ 8.00	8		
1 hour @ $10.00		10	18
Factory overhead:			
Per unit	1	2	3
	$11	$13	$24

Production Report

	Dept. I	Dept. II
Beginning units in process	None	None
Units finished and transferred	6,000	5,000
Ending units in process	2,000	1,000
Stage of completion	1/2	1/2

Cost Data

	Dept. I	Dept. II		
Direct materials:				
30,000 units @ $ .52		$15,600		
5,500 units @ $ .95			$5,225	
Direct labor:				
6,800 hours @ $ 8.00		54,400		
5,600 hours @ $10.20			57,120	
Factory overhead:				
Indirect materials	$ 500		$1,000	
Indirect labor	2,000		5,000	
Other	4,500	7,000	5,000	11,000

Required:	1. Calculate net variances for materials, labor, and factory overhead.

1. Calculate net variances for materials, labor, and factory overhead.
2. Calculate specific materials and labor variances by department.
3. Make all general journal entries to record production costs in Work in Process and Finished Goods.
4. Prove balances of Work in Process for both departments.
5. Prove that all costs have been accounted for. *Note:* Assume that materials, labor, and overhead are added evenly throughout the process.
6. Assume 4,000 units were sold at $40 each.
   a. Calculate the gross margin based on standard cost.
   b. Calculate the gross margin based on actual cost.

P8-5
Journal entries for material and labor variances
Learning Objective 3

Allgood Corporation has established the following standard cost per unit:

Materials—6 lbs. @ $2 per lb.	$12
Labor—2 hours @ $6.00 per hour	12

Although 10,000 units were budgeted, only 8,800 units were produced.

The purchasing department bought 55,000 pounds of material at a cost of $123,750. Actual pounds of material used were 54,305. Direct labor cost was $127,400 for 18,200 hours worked.

Required:

1. Make general journal entries to record the material transactions assuming that the material price variances were taken at the time of purchase.
2. Make general journal entries to record the labor variances.

P8-6
Analysis of materials and labor variances
Learning Objective 3

Americo Products Company manufactures a variety of products made of plastic and aluminum components. During the winter months, substantially all of the production capacity is devoted to the production of lawn sprinklers for the following spring and summer seasons. Other products are manufactured during the remainder of the year.

The company has developed standard costs for its several products. Standard costs for each year are set in the preceding October. The standard cost of a sprinkler for the current year is $3.70, computed as follows:

Direct materials:	
Aluminum—0.2 lb. @ $.40 per lb.	$ .08
Plastic—1.0 lb. @ $.38 per lb.	.38
Production labor—0.3 hr. @ $8.00 per hr.	2.40
Factory overhead	.84
Total	$3.70

During February, Americo manufactured 8,500 good sprinklers. The company incurred the following costs, which it charged to production:

Materials requisitioned for production:	
Aluminum—1,900 lbs. @ $.40 per lb.	$ 760
Plastic—Regular grade—6,000 lbs. @ $.38 per lb.	2,280
Low grade—3,500 lbs. @ $.38 per lb.	1,330
Production labor—2,700 hrs.	23,220
Factory overhead	7,140
Costs charged to production	$34,730

Materials price variations are not determined by usage but are charged to a materials price variation account at the time the invoice is entered. All materials are carried in inventory at standard prices. Materials purchases for February were as follows:

Aluminum—1,800 lbs. @ $.48 per lb. .... $ 864
Plastic—Regular grade—3,000 lbs. @ $.50 per lb. 1,500
    Low grade*—6,000 lbs. @ $.29 per lb. 1,740

*Due to plastic shortages, the company was forced to purchase lower grade plastic than called for in the standards. This increased the number of sprinklers rejected on inspection.

Required:

Calculate price and usage variances for each type of material and for labor.

P8-7
Materials and labor variances analyses
Learning Objective 3

Tuffco Company manufactures a fuel additive that has a stable selling price of $44 per drum. The company has been producing and selling 80,000 drums per month.

In connection with your examination of Tuffco's financial statements for the year ended September 30, management has asked you to review some computations made by Tuffco's cost accountant. Your working papers disclose the following about the company's operations:
    Standard costs per drum of product manufactured:

Materials:
    8 gallons of Miracle Mix @ $2 .... $16
    1 empty drum 1 $17

Direct labor—1 hour .... $ 8
Factory overhead .... $ 6

Costs and expenses during September:

Miracle Mix: 600,000 gallons purchased at a cost of $1,140,000; 645,000 gallons used
Empty drums: 94,000 purchased at a cost of $94,000; 80,000 used
Direct labor: 81,000 hours worked at a cost of $654,480
Factory overhead: $768,000

Required:

Prepare a schedule computing the following variances for September:

1. Materials quantity variance
2. Materials price variance (determined at time of purchase)
3. Labor efficiency variance
4. Labor rate variance

(AICPA adapted)

P8-8
Calculation of materials and labor variances
Learning Objective 3

Sudo Corporation manufactures and sells a single product. The company uses a standard cost system. The standard cost per unit of product follows:

Materials—one pound plastic @ $3.00	$ 3.00
Direct labor—1.6 hours @ $10.00	16.00
Factory overhead	4.45
Total	$23.45

The charges to the manufacturing department for November, when 5,000 units were produced, follow:

Materials—5,300 pounds @ $3.00	$ 15,900
Direct labor—8,200 hours @ $10.20	83,640
Factory overhead	23,815
Total	$123,355

The purchasing department normally buys about the same quantity as is used in production during a month. In November, 5,200 pounds were purchased at a price of $3.10 per pound.

Required: Calculate the following variances from standard costs for the data given:

1. Materials quantity
2. Materials price (at time of purchase)
3. Labor efficiency
4. Labor rate

**P8-9
Allocation of variances
Learning Objectives 5 & 6**

Elmona Manufacturing Corporation uses a standard cost system that records raw materials at actual cost, records materials price variances at the time that raw materials are issued to work in process, and prorates all variances at year end. Variances associated with direct materials are prorated based on the direct materials balances in the appropriate accounts, and variances associated with direct labor are prorated based on the direct labor balances in the appropriate accounts. The following information is available for Elmona for the year ended December 31.

Raw materials inventory at December 31	$ 65,000
Finished goods inventory at December 31:	
Direct materials	87,000
Direct labor	130,500
Applied factory overhead	104,400
Cost of goods sold for the year ended December 31:	
Direct materials	348,000
Direct labor	739,500
Applied factory overhead	591,600
Materials quantity variance (favorable)	15,000
Materials price variance (unfavorable)	10,000
Labor efficiency variance (favorable)	5,000
Labor rate variance (unfavorable)	20,000
Factory overhead applied	696,000

There were no beginning inventories and no ending work in process inventory.

Required: Calculate the following:

1. Amount of materials price variance to be prorated to finished goods inventory at December 31
2. Total amount of direct materials cost in the finished goods inventory at December 31, after all variances have been prorated
3. Total amount of direct labor cost in the finished goods inventory at December 31, after all variances have been prorated
4. Total cost of goods sold for the year ended December 31, after all variances have been prorated

(AICPA adapted)

P8-10
Analysis of materials and labor variances
Learning Objective 3

Stewart Manufacturing Company uses a standard cost system in accounting for the cost of production of its only product, product A. The standards for the production of one unit of product A follow:

> Direct materials: 10 feet of item 1 at $.75 per foot and 3 feet of item 2 at $1.00 per foot.
> Direct labor: 4 hours at $8.00 per hour.
> Factory overhead: applied at 150% of standard direct labor costs.

There was no beginning inventory on hand at July 1. Following is a summary of costs and related data for the production of product A during the following year ended June 30.

> 100,000 feet of item 1 were purchased at $.78 per foot.
> 30,000 feet of item 2 were purchased at $.90 per foot.
> 8,000 units of product A were produced that required 78,000 feet of item 1; 26,000 feet of item 2; and 31,000 hours of direct labor at $8.20 per hour.
> 6,000 units of product A were sold.

On June 30, there are 22,000 feet of item 1; 4,000 feet of item 2; and 2,000 completed units of product A on hand. All purchases and transfers are "charged in" at standard.

Required:

Calculate the following:

1. Materials quantity variance for item 1
2. Materials quantity variance for item 2
3. Materials price variance for item 1 (recorded at purchase)
4. Materials price variance for item 2 (recorded at purchase)
5. Labor efficiency variance
6. Labor rate variance

(AICPA adapted)

P8-11
Material price, mix, and yield variances

Purr Company produces kitty litter. Two materials are used: A and B. The following data are available:

> Standard quantities and costs per 20 pound bag:
> Material A—12 lbs. at $.30 per lb. = $3.60
> Material B—8 lbs. at $.10 per lb. = .80
> Actual quantities and costs for the month in which 10,000 20 pound bags were produced:

Material A—125,488 lbs. at $.29 per lb.
Material B—70,587 lbs. at $.08 per lb.

Required:

Compute the material price, mix, and yield variances.

P8-12
Materials mix and
yield variances

Using the data presented in P8-6, calculate materials mix and yield variances.

P8-13
Materials mix and
yield variances

Using the data given in P8-10, calculate materials mix and yield variances.

P8-14
Labor rate, mix, and
yield variances

Acme Company has a production department in which the employees have different pay rates. A standard department hour consists of 50 worker-hours distributed as follows:

Pay Grade	Hours	Standard Rate	Standard Cost
SP-1	20	$ 3	$ 60
SP-2	23	4	92
SP-3	5	8	40
SP-4	2	15	30
	50		$222

The standard output is 100 tons.

Charges to the department during the month were 1,300 hours of SP-1 at a total cost of $4,550; 1,250 hours of SP-2, costing $4,875; 310 hours of SP-3, costing $2,526.50; and 125 hours of SP-4, costing $1,812.50. The company produced 6,000 tons during the period.

Required:

1. Compute a labor rate, a labor mix, and a labor yield variance.
2. Make the journal entry to record these variances.

P8-15
Labor efficiency, rate,
mix, and yield
variances
Learning Objective 4

The direct labor standard for the Reed Company follows:

Class A labor—2 hours @ $12	$24
Class B labor—3 hours @ $6	18
Standard direct labor cost per unit	$42

During the month, Reed manufactured 2,000 units. Actual labor costs follow:

Class A labor—4,200 hours @ $12.00	$50,400
Class B labor—6,000 hours @ $5.75	34,500

Required:

1. Calculate the following:
   a. Labor efficiency variance
   b. Labor rate variance

      c. Labor mix variance

      d. Labor yield variance

2. Explain what might have caused the mix and yield variances.

Standard Cost Accounting—Factory Overhead

LEARNING OBJECTIVES

After studying this chapter, you should be able to:

1. Explain the general principles involved in the budgeting process
2. Recognize the different types of budgets prepared by businesses
3. Make an evaluation of budgets by the use of performance reports
4. Explain the appropriate procedures to determine standard amounts of factory overhead at different levels of production
5. Recognize the commonly used methods for analyzing overhead variances

A standard cost system is a good control procedure because it provides a method of data comparison essential for precision planning and control. Also, the study of changing volumes is an important factor in controlling factory overhead costs because certain costs vary with changes in activity while other costs do not.

To determine proper standards for the comparison of predetermined costs with actual costs at different activity levels, factory overhead must be accumulated in a manner that allows the relationship of cost to the volume of activity to be readily determined. Therefore, in addition to being classified by function, costs must be further classified as to behavior when an associated activity changes. **Cost behavior** is determined through the process of distinguishing whether a cost remains fixed or varies with changes that occur in activities.

Factory overhead costs are first grouped by department and then by behavior, fixed or variable. Then, overhead costs are further reduced to a predetermined or standard cost basis for each unit of product—either units of product, per direct labor hour, per machine hour, or per direct labor cost dollar. Because factory overhead cost per unit will increase as volume or activity decreases and vice versa, control of factory overhead costs can best be established by using a sliding or flexible budget. The development and use of *flexible budgets* facilitate more effective cost control and improved management planning.

BUDGETED FACTORY OVERHEAD

The standard amount of factory overhead allowed, or budgeted, at different levels of production requires that the dollar amounts be predetermined for the expected levels of production. That is, the expense is estimated at the beginning of the year, before production is started, for varying levels of production. Using these predetermined figures, the factory overhead variances can be determined by converting the production report data into standard costs and then comparing these costs with the actual costs that have been charged to the overhead accounts. The purpose of the following section is to discuss the procedures by which the accountant determines in advance what these standard amounts of factory overhead will be at different levels of production.

BUDGETS

Most successful companies today use operating budgets to help them in their constant effort to analyze and control operations, keep costs in line, and reduce expenses. **A budget** is a planning device that helps a company set goals and that serves as a gauge against which actual results can be measured. Many heads of households are familiar with the basic aspects of budgeting whereby they estimate their income for the following year, determine what their living expenses will be, and then, depending on the figures, reduce unnecessary spending, set up a savings plan, or possibly determine additional ways to supplement their income. During the year, they compare their budget with their actual income and expenditures to be sure that expenses do not exceed income and cause financial difficulties.

Budgeting in business and industry is a formal method of detailed financial planning. It encompasses the coordination and control of every significant item in the balance sheet and income statement. Budgeting is used to help the company reach its long-term and short-term objectives. If the principles of budgeting are carried out in a proper manner, the company can be assured that it will efficiently use all of its resources and achieve the most favorable results possible in the long run.

Basically, the primary objective of any company is to maximize its net income or attain the highest volume of sales at the lowest possible cost. Planning and control are absolutely essential in achieving this goal, and budgeting produces the framework within which the organization can reach this objective. The budget then becomes a road map that guides managers along the way and lets them know when the company is straying from its planned route. It is a chart of the course of operations, and in addition to forecasting costs and profits as a means of controlling costs, it requires those in authority in all areas of the business to analyze carefully all aspects of their responsibility for costs and also to analyze company strengths and weaknesses.

LEARNING OBJECTIVE
Explain the general principles involved in the budgeting process

Principles of Budgeting. The general principles of budgeting have several requirements:

1. Management must clearly define its objectives.

2. Goals must be realistic and possible to attain.

3. Because the budgeting process involves looking to the future, the budget must carefully consider economic developments, the general business climate, and the condition of the industry, as well as changes and trends that may influence sales and costs. Historical data should be used only as a stepping-off point for projections into the future.

4. There must be a plan, which is consistently followed, to constantly analyze the actual results as compared with the budget.

5. The budget must be flexible enough so that it can be modified in the light of changing conditions; it must not be so restrictive that changes cannot be made where more favorable results are foreseeable.

6. Responsibility for forecasting costs must be clearly defined, and accountability for actual results must be enforced. This principle encourages careful analysis and precise evaluation.

LEARNING OBJECTIVE
Recognize the different types of budgets prepared by businesses

Preparing the Budget. The following discussion is not intended to be an exhaustive survey of budgeting but is principally concerned with the preparation of the production plan and the manufacturing expense budget. However, a brief presentation of other budgets is appropriate, so that you can see how all budgets are interrelated and how the budget for the factory is influenced by the other budgets.

Forecast of Sales. In preparing a budget, management must consider all the items of income and expense. The usual starting point in the budgeting process is a forecast of sales, followed by a determination of inventory policy, a production plan, a budget of manufacturing costs, and a budget for all administrative and selling expenses. The final product is the amount of net income budgeted for the year. A balance sheet forecast should also be prepared, concerned primarily with cash, receivables, and capital additions.

Although all of the aforementioned budgets are important, the forecast of sales is especially significant, because management must use this information as a basis for preparing all other budgets. This forecast is concerned with projecting the volume of sales both in units and dollars. In estimating the sales for the forthcoming year, the sales department must take into consideration present and future economic situations. It should research and carefully analyze market prospects for its products and give consideration to the development of new products and the discontinuance of old products. It should make these analyses by territory, by type of product, and possibly by type of customer. Marketing researchers should also carefully survey and evaluate consumer demand. After this detailed examination, the mix of the products to be sold can be determined, as well as the volume and the sales price.

Inventory and Production Planning. After the sales mix and volume plans have been made, the factory can proceed with the determination of production requirements. In a simple situation, assuming one product, stable production throughout the year, and an ending inventory 2,000 units greater than the beginning inventory, the number of units to be produced can be calculated as follows:

Units to be sold	100,000
Ending inventory required	4,500
Total	104,500
Beginning inventory	2,500
Units to be manufactured	102,000
Units per month (102,000 / 12)	8,500

In actual practice, this computation is more complex. Management must try to achieve a satisfactory balance between production, inventory, and the timely availability of goods to be sold. For example, if the company's sales are seasonal rather than evenly distributed throughout the year, stable production might produce the following situation:

Number of Units

	Produced	Sold	On Hand
Beginning balance			2,500
January	8,500	1,000	10,000
February	8,500	2,000	16,500
March	8,500	3,000	22,000
April	8,500	10,000	20,500
May	8,500	15,000	14,000
June	8,500	15,000	7,500
July	8,500	12,000	4,000
August	8,500	9,000	3,500
September	8,500	9,000	3,000
October	8,500	8,000	3,500
November	8,500	8,000	4,000
December	8,500	8,000	4,500
Total	102,000	100,000	

The company must have enough storage facility to handle as many as 22,000 units. However, most of this space would be unused during several months of the year, resulting in a waste of invested capital for inventory and storage facilities and expenditures for upkeep, insurance, and taxes that provide no direct benefit. In this situation, a manufacturing concern might lease some storage facilities during the peak months, thereby requiring a much smaller company-owned facility. However, leasing may present problems of inconvenience, expense, and unavailability of the facilities at the right time and in the right place. In addition, during some months the company would have a considerable amount of capital tied up in finished goods that could be threatened by obsolescence.

Another solution is for management to schedule different levels of production each month in order to maintain a stable inventory and to minimize the number of units stored. The following table shows this approach:

Number of Units

	Produced	Sold	On Hand
Beginning balance			2,500
January	1,500	1,000	3,000
February	2,500	2,000	3,500
March	3,000	3,000	3,500
April	10,000	10,000	3,500
May	15,000	15,000	3,500
June	15,000	15,000	3,500
July	12,000	12,000	3,500
August	9,500	9,000	4,000
September	9,500	9,000	4,500

October	8,000	8,000	4,500
November	8,000	8,000	4,500
December	8,000	8,000	4,500
Total	102,000	100,000	

This alternative requires minimum storage space and related expenses, but it creates a new problem; the factory must have enough facilities to handle the peak production of 15,000 units, but these facilities would be from 50 percent to 90 percent idle during some months. A possible solution is to establish a smaller facility and to engage two or three shifts of employees during the busier months. Although the facility investment problem is reduced, a bigger problem is created because the working force can vary by 1,000 percent from the slowest period to the most active. This condition would require hiring new employees in the earlier months as production is climbing, with the problem of the high cost of recruiting and training as well as the problem of quality production with new, possibly inexperienced employees. In the later months, as production drops, many workers would be laid off, creating considerable additional expense for unemployment compensation as well as hardship for the employees and a feeling of ill-will toward the company.

Management is often faced with the problem of determining which course to follow—whether to maintain stable production, with the necessity of providing for storage capacity, the tie-up of capital funds in inventory, and the possibility of obsolescence; or to maintain a stable inventory, with all of the ensuing expenses of personnel and facilities. Most companies will carefully analyze the alternatives and arrive at a plan that represents a reasonable compromise between the two alternatives.

Budgets for Manufacturing Costs and Administrative and Selling Expenses. Once the production schedule has been determined, the budget for manufacturing costs can be prepared, which involves determining the costs of materials, labor, and factory overhead for each month (or week, or day) of the coming year. After standard costs have been determined, this calculation, whether for one or for several products, is relatively simple for direct materials and direct labor, involving the extension of the number of units to be produced times the standard cost per unit. However, the forecast of the factory overhead is more involved and will be considered in detail later in this section. When a company has determined its level of activity for sales and production, it can prepare its budgets for administrative, selling, and other expenses. As with other forecasts, the planners should take into consideration not only the planned volume for the company but also economic conditions, trends for local and national wages and salaries, and other expenses.

Other Budgets. Completing these budgets permits the company to determine its **budgeted income statement** for the year. Keep in mind that, although this discussion has centered around units and dollars, these forecasts could also be used to plan the hiring (or laying off) of personnel, to schedule the purchases of materials, to arrange for necessary facilities, to develop sales promotion, and other appropriate functions.

The company can now prepare its balance sheet budgets. The **cash budget** shows the anticipated flow of cash and the timing of receipts and disbursements based on projected revenues, the production schedule, and expenses. Using this budget, management can plan for necessary financing or for temporary investment of surplus funds. The **budget for receivables**, based on anticipated sales, credit terms, the economy, and other relevant factors, will influence the cash budget by showing when cash can be expected from the turnover of inventory and receivables. A **liabilities budget** is also necessary, reflecting how the company's cash position will be affected by paying these items.

The company may prepare a **capital additions budget**, which is a plan for the timing of acquisitions of buildings, equipment, or other significant assets during the year. This plan ties in with the sales and production plans and may influence the cash budget for expenditures to the extent that additional financing may be necessary.

Teamwork and cooperation in preparing the budgets are absolutely essential. The sales, engineering, manufacturing, and accounting divisions of the company must work together to produce meaningful forecasts, because many of the estimates depend on the plans of other departments. Also, a considerable amount of coordination is required. For example, the sales goal must be compatible with the production that can be attained with the facilities available; at the same time, the amount and scheduling of production relies heavily on the needs of the marketing department. As mentioned previously, some budgets can be prepared only after certain others have been completed, and they will be influenced by these other plans.

An important factor in the budgeting process is that the budgets are not necessarily prepared sequentially. After the sales forecast in units is made, the manufacturing division can begin working on the production schedule and the manufacturing expense budget; the sales department can start preparing its budget for selling expenses; and the administrative expense forecast can begin. The receivables turnover schedule can also be made at this point, and possibly the capital expenditures budget can be prepared. The cash budget and the schedule of liabilities and payments cannot be considered until all of the aforementioned items are completed.

LEARNING OBJECTIVE
Make an evaluation of
budgets by the use of
performance reports

Evaluating Budget Performance. If a budget is to be used successfully as a management tool for control, the actual results should be periodically compared with the budgeted figures and the differences thoroughly analyzed. Without this constant follow-up and analysis, the budget is a useless item. This principle has been discussed previously in connection with standard costs, and it also applies to the other planned amounts, both by unit and by dollar volume. If variances are found to exist in the number of units sold or manufactured, or in the dollar amounts of sales or expenses, or in other budgeted items, the planners must carefully evaluate the variances and determine responsibility.

Typically, performance reports are prepared and distributed to the people who are accountable for the actual results. For example, all supervisors and department heads receive reports for their respective departments. The vice president in charge of production receives information on all elements of manufacturing involving the production and service departments. The president of the company receives reports on all functions of the business—manufacturing, sales, and administrative. These reports should clearly reflect the variances from the budget in all areas so that appropriate action can be taken.

LEARNING OBJECTIVE
Explain the appropriate
procedures to
determine standard
amounts of factory
overhead at different
levels of production

Flexible Budgeting. The comparison of actual results with the budget to see if the planned objectives are being met leads to the use of **flexible budgeting**. This concept, introduced in Chapter 4, will be discussed from the standpoint of the factory overhead budget, but the principles are applicable to any item of expense that involves fixed and variable elements.

To implement a flexible budget, a company must plan how it will respond to varying sets of conditions, for example, the sale of 10,000 units per month rather than 9,000, the production of 15,000 units per month rather than 17,000, the addition or replacement of a machine in a department, or the development of new products or the discontinuance of the old. In other words, the company plans in advance what the effect will be on revenue, expense, and profit if sales or production differ from the budget. To illustrate, if budgeted sales for a month are $100,000 and the budgeted selling expense is $25,000, it is reasonable to assume that if actual sales are $80,000, the actual selling expense would be less than $25,000. If production volume was 10,000 units rather than the budgeted 9,000 units, the cost of production should logically be greater than the amount budgeted for the 9,000 units.

The flexible budget is influenced by the presence of fixed and variable costs as discussed in Chapter 4. Fixed costs have been previously defined as those costs that do not change as production changes over a given range. They are a function of time and generally will be incurred regardless of the level of production. These expenses, such as straight-line depreciation, insurance, taxes, supervisory salaries, and others, will remain the same in dollar total, except in the extreme case of a major change in production that requires more or fewer machines, facilities, and supervisory personnel.

Many costs do vary in total dollar amount in proportion to any change in production. These **variable costs**, which are a function of activity, include direct labor, direct materials, indirect labor, and maintenance costs. It is because of these variable elements that the total cost differs from amounts originally budgeted when the level of production is different. If the manufacturer has budgeted production of 5,000 units for the month at a cost of $50,000 and the actual production is more or less than 5,000 units, there would be little value in comparing the actual cost of production with the items making up the $50,000 of a fixed budget—that is, a budget where the costs are shown for only one level of activity. Under such operating conditions, however, a flexible budget is useful because it shows the planned expenses at various levels of production. Thus, management can quickly determine variances by comparing the actual costs with what the costs of production should have been at the actual level of production.

Preparing the Flexible Budget for Factory Overhead. Determining the standard overhead cost per unit and preparing the flexible budget for factory overhead follow the basic principles suggested for determining standards for materials and labor costs. All costs that might be incurred should be carefully considered. Prior costs, as adjusted, must be studied as well as the effect of new costs, future economic conditions, changes in processes, and trends. As with other standards, the individuals responsible for setting factory overhead standards should have considerable experience and familiarity with manufacturing operations.

Because costs are affected by the level of production, the first step is to determine what should be the standard volume of production. **Standard production** is the volume on which the initial calculation of costs is based. Several approaches are used to determine this figure and there are several related definitions of manufacturing capacity. These types of capacity include the following:

1. **Theoretical capacity** represents the maximum number of units that can be produced with the completely efficient use of all available facilities and personnel. Generally, this production level is almost impossible to attain. It represents a rigid standard for the factory

because it requires maximum production with no allowance for inefficiencies of any kind.

2. **Practical capacity** is the level of production that provides complete utilization of all facilities and personnel, but allows for some idle capacity due to operating interruptions, such as machinery breakdowns, idle time, and other inescapable inefficiencies.

3. **Normal capacity** is the level of production that will meet the normal requirements of ordinary sales demand over a period of years. Although it conceivably can be equal to or greater than practical capacity, normal capacity usually does not involve a plan for maximum usage of manufacturing facilities but allows for some unavoidable idle capacity and some inefficiencies in operations. Most manufacturing firms use this level of capacity for budget development because it represents a logical balance between maximum production capacity and the capacity that is demanded by actual sales volume. Furthermore, over a period of years, all factory overhead expense will normally be absorbed by production. The following discussion will assume the use of normal capacity for planning purposes.

To illustrate the flexible budget, the following figures were determined to be the factory overhead costs at the normal or standard volume of 1,000 units. (To simplify the illustration, only a few overhead classifications are used. In actual practice, many types of expenses would be broken down into fixed and variable categories.)

Standard production—1,000 units
Standard direct labor hours—2,000
Fixed cost:

Depreciation of building and equipment	$4,000	
Property tax and insurance	1,000	
Supervisory salaries	4,000	
Total fixed cost		$ 9,000

Variable cost:

Maintenance	$2,000	
Supplies	1,000	
Total variable cost		3,000
Total factory overhead cost		$12,000

Standard factory overhead application rate per direct labor hour:

Fixed cost ($9,000 / 2,000 hours)	$ 4.50
Variable cost ($3,000 / 2,000 hours)	1.50
Total factory overhead rate ($12,000 / 2,000 hours) . . .	$ 6.00
Standard overhead cost per unit ($12,000 / 1,000 units) .	$12.00

As discussed in Chapter 4, factory overhead can be applied to work in process using different bases, such as direct labor hours, direct labor cost, or machine hours. One of the most commonly used bases—direct labor hours method—applies overhead in relation to the standard number of direct labor hours allowed for the current actual production.

In the preceding schedule, both standard units and standard hours are given, because production may be expressed in terms of units or the standard number of direct labor hours allowed for the actual production. Whichever base for measuring production is chosen, the results are not affected. Based on the preceding budget, if 900 units are manufactured, Work in Process would be charged with $ 10,800 (900 × $ 12) for factory overhead. If production is expressed in terms of standard direct labor hours, in this case 1,800 (900 units × 2 hours), Work in Process would still be charged with $10,800 (1,800 hours × $6).

Figure 9-1 shows the flexible budget for this illustration. The individuals responsible for the work have determined what the fixed and variable costs will be at various levels of production. Notice that the factory overhead per direct labor hour decreases as volume increases, because the fixed factory overhead is being spread over more production. Also,

FIGURE 9-1   Factory Overhead Cost Budget

Percent of Normal Capacity	80%	90%	100%	110%	120%
Number of units	800	900	1,000	1,100	1,200
Number of standard direct labor hours	1,600	1,800	2,000	2,200	2,400
Budgeted factory overhead:					
Fixed cost:					
Depreciation of building and equipment	$ 4,000	$ 4,000	$ 4,000	$ 4,000	$ 4,000
Property taxes and insurance	1,000	1,000	1,000	1,000	1,000
Supervisory salaries	4,000	4,000	4,000	4,000	4,000
Total fixed cost	$ 9,000	$ 9,000	$ 9,000	$ 9,000	$ 9,000
Variable cost:					
Maintenance	$ 1,600	$ 1,800	$ 2,000	$ 2,200	$ 2,400
Supplies	800	900	1,000	1,100	1,200
Total variable cost	$ 2,400	$ 2,700	$ 3,000	$ 3,300	$ 3,600
Total factory overhead cost	$11,400	$11,700	$12,000	$12,300	$12,600
Factory overhead per direct labor hour	$7.125	$6.50	$6.00	$5.59	$5.25

notice that the standard volume of production is expressed as being 100% of capacity. This production level is not necessarily the maximum capacity of the manufacturing facility; but it does represent, considering sales demand, the most efficient use of the present facilities under normal operating conditions, with some allowance for operating interruptions. A factory can always produce more than the normal volume by working overtime, adding a shift, or squeezing in more machinery and workers; but these conditions are not normal. Because it is not uncommon to operate above or below normal, the flexible budget shows expense amounts for production above and below normal capacity of 100%.

Using the Flexible Budget. If actual production for a given period is exactly 1,000 units, a comparison of total or individual factory overhead costs incurred with these budgeted figures can be made and variances determined as follows:

Factory Overhead Cost Variances

Normal production . . . .   1,000 units (or 2,000 direct labor hours)
Actual production   . . . .   1,000 units (or 2,000 direct labor hours)

	Budget	Actual	Variances Favorable (Unfavorable)
Fixed cost:			
Depreciation of building and equipment	$ 4,000	$ 4,000	
Property taxes and insurance	1,000	1,000	
Supervisory salaries	4,000	4,000	
Total fixed cost	$ 9,000	$ 9,000	
Variable cost:			
Maintenance	$ 2,000	$ 2,500	$(500)
Supplies	1,000	900	100
Total variable cost	$ 3,000	$ 3,400	$(400)
Total factory overhead cost	$12,000	$12,400	$(400)

The net unfavorable variance is considered a budget, or controllable, variance because production was at normal capacity, eliminating the possibility of a volume variance, which would result from a volume differing from the normal capacity.

Usually, however, factory activity will not be exactly at the normal level. The volume of production invariably fluctuates to a certain extent from the standard level because it is affected by such factors as vacations, holidays, absentee employees, work interruptions, and equipment breakdowns. If a seasonal factor is involved, the fluctuation from one month to the next could be significant. Under these circumstances, the flexible budget provides the budgeted figures for the actual levels of production rather than the established normal level.

Upon receiving the report on actual volume for the period, the factory overhead costs that should have been incurred at that volume can be compared with the actual costs to determine variances. If the volume of production falls between two of the amounts shown in the budget, an approximation of budgeted cost can be interpolated.

```
Actual production 850 units (85%)
Budgeted cost at 90%  . . . . . . . . . . . . . . . . . . . . .   $11,700
Budgeted cost at 80%  . . . . . . . . . . . . . . . . . . . . .    11,400
Difference  . . . . . . . . . . . . . . . . . . . . . . . . . .   $   300

Range between volume levels  . . . . . . . . . . . . . . . . .       10%
```

Dividing the difference of $300 by 10 determines an additional cost of $30 for each percentage point increase.

```
Next lower budgeted volume   . . . . . . . . . . . . . . . . .       80%

Costs at 80% volume   . . . . . . . . . . . . . . . . . . . . .   $11,400
Plus (5 × $30) . . . . . . . . . . . . . . . . . . . . . . . . .      150
Budgeted costs at 85% volume   . . . . . . . . . . . . . . . .   $11,550
```

Semifixed and Semivariable Costs. The preceding method of determining the budgeted amount of factory overhead at a level of production different from that given in the budget is satisfactory if the overhead increases evenly throughout each range of activity, as would be the case if all costs were either fixed or variable. However, if significant semifixed or semivariable costs exist, then this method would not always be accurate enough for a meaningful evaluation.

Semifixed, or step, costs are those that tend to remain the same in dollar amount through a certain range of activity but increase when production exceeds certain limits. For example, the salary of a department head is generally considered a fixed cost, because no other department head will be employed through a given range of activity, and the salary cost will not change as the volume fluctuates. But if the production level exceeds a given number of units, an assistant department head might have to be employed to aid in supervising the greater number of workers that would be necessary. In this case, the fixed expense for supervisory personnel would increase, as illustrated in the following table.

Percent of Normal Capacity	80%	90%	100%	110%	120%	130%
Fixed cost	$20,000	$20,000	$20,000	$20,000	$28,000	$28,000
Variable cost	24,000	27,000	30,000	33,000	36,000	39,000
Total factory overhead	$44,000	$47,000	$50,000	$53,000	$64,000	$67,000

In this case, if the actual volume of production falls into the range between 110% and 120%, the use of interpolation to determine budgeted expense would probably not be satisfactory. A careful analysis of the expenses would need to be made, without the use of interpolation, to determine whether more supervisory personnel would be needed at 119% of capacity or 111% of capacity, for example.

Semivariable costs are those that may change with production but not necessarily in direct proportion. For example, if a company incurs expense to train new employees before they go into the factory, this expense will increase as production increases and new employees are hired. But if the volume of production decreases and no new employees are hired, no training expense will be incurred.

The existence of semifixed or semivariable costs indicates an even greater need for careful analysis and evaluation of the costs at each level of production. Semivariable expenses were discussed in Chapter 4. The approach in this chapter, however, assumes that fixed costs remain constant and variable costs vary evenly throughout the ranges of activity given unless stated otherwise.

SERVICE DEPARTMENT BUDGETS AND VARIANCES

Preparing a budget for a service department follows the same procedure as that for production departments. Expenses at different levels of production are estimated, and a standard rate for application of service department expenses to production departments is determined based on the type of service provided and the estimated usage by the production departments. The production departments will take these expenses into consideration in setting up their budgets.

During the period, the production departments are charged with service department expenses at the standard rate using their actual activity base, such as kilowatt hours or hours of maintenance labor. At the end of the period, the service department's actual expenses are compared with the amount charged to the production departments to determine the variances.

SUMMARY

Figure 9-2 summarizes the budgeting process for the factory, the determination of standard costs, and the segregation of the variances.

FIGURE 9-2   Summarization of the Budgeting Process

1 **A Sales Forecast** in units, considering the

2 **Inventory Policy**, minimum-maximum and stable or fluctuating, helps in developing the

3 **Production Plan** in units and by periods.

This information aids in developing the

4(a)	4(b)	4(c)
Requirements for Direct Materials	Requirements for Direct Labor	Requirements for Indirect Costs, Facilities, and Supplies
(quantities and prices)	(hours and rates)	(fixed and variable costs)

From this information is developed the

5(a)	5(b)	5(c)
Direct Materials Budget	Direct Labor Budget	Factory Overhead Budget

From these budgets are developed the

6(a)	6(b)	6(c)
Standard Unit Cost for Direct Materials	Standard Unit Cost for Direct Labor	Standard Unit Cost for Factory Overhead

(These combined figures determine the **Standard Unit Cost for the Product.**)

7 These unit costs, when multiplied by the equivalent production for the period, determine the amount to be charged to Work in Process for each element of production cost. The costs in 6(a) and 6(b) above are

8(a)	8(b)	8(c)
multiplied by the actual quantity of direct materials used.	multiplied by the actual direct labors hours worked.	From the flexible budget is determined the budgeted factory overhead cost, using the standard hours allowed at the actual level of production.

9(a)	9(b)	9(c)
Materials Quantity Variance	Labor Efficiency Variance	Factory Overhead Volume Variance

The comparison of 8 above with the actual cost for the period determines the

10(a)	10(b)	10(c)
Materials Price Variance*	Labor Rate Variance	Factory Overhead Controllable Variance

Unless the materials price variance is recognized at the time of purchase.

ANALYSIS OF FACTORY OVERHEAD STANDARD COST VARIANCES

LEARNING OBJECTIVE
Recognize the commonly used methods for analyzing overhead variances

Determining the **standard unit cost for factory overhead** involves estimating factory overhead cost at the standard, or normal, level of production, considering historical data (adjusted for distorting items in the past such as strikes or fire losses), and future changes and trends. The estimated factory overhead cost is divided by the standard number of hours expected for the planned units to be produced. For example, assume that the budgeted production is 1,000 units, which will require 2,000 direct labor hours. At this level of activity, the standard factory overhead is determined to be as follows:

Depreciation on building and machinery	$ 4,000
Taxes and insurance on building and machinery	1,000
Supervisory salaries	4,000
Maintenance costs	2,000
Supplies	1,000
Total standard factory overhead	$12,000

Dividing the standard factory overhead cost of $12,000 by the 2,000 direct labor hours results in a standard per direct labor hour cost of $6 per hour, and because each unit requires two direct labor hours, a standard cost per unit is $12. If equivalent production during the period is exactly 1,000 units, which used 2,000 direct labor hours, Work in Process will be charged with $12,000 of estimated factory overhead (1,000 units × 2 hours per unit × $6 per hour). As illustrated in the following journal entry and T-accounts, if the actual factory overhead were $12,000, all of this cost would be applied to the work in process account, and no over- or underapplied factory overhead would exist.

Work in Process	12,000
Factory Overhead	12,000
Applied factory overhead to work in process.	

Work in Process		Factory Overhead	
12,000		12,000	12,000
		(actual costs)	(standard cost
		recorded from	applied to Work
		various journals)	in Process)

If the actual factory overhead was greater than $12,000, Factory Overhead would have a debit balance after $12,000 of standard cost had been applied to Work in Process. This balance would reflect the amount of factory overhead cost not charged to the goods produced. An underapplied (unabsorbed) cost represents the amount of overhead incurred over and above the standard cost allowed for attained level of production. The balance in the account would be considered an unfavorable variance.

The following sections of this chapter analyze, in detail, what could cause an overhead variance. Although the two-variance method of factory overhead analysis is favored by many companies, the three-variance method is also used. The four-variance method, which is actually a derivative of the two-variance method, is often encountered in many managerial-type textbooks because it more clearly indicates the cost behavior patterns of factory overhead costs. Because the four-variance method is somewhat related to the two-variance method, it is discussed sequentially after the two-variance method.

TWO-VARIANCE METHOD OF ANALYSIS

The method a company chooses to analyze factory overhead variances depends on the benefits the company derives from the detailed analysis. The cost incurred in applying the standard factory overhead to production, maintaining the necessary accounts, and analyzing the results also plays a part in the process of selecting a method. Recently, many textbooks, cost and managerial, give extensive coverage to the four-variance method (discussed in the appendix) but ignore the added cost of maintaining the method if it were used in actual practice.

The four-variance method requires separating the variable and fixed cost elements as does the two-variance method. However, when the four-variance method is used, the separated elements are recorded in individual accounts established for overhead variable costs and overhead fixed costs. The two-variance method combines the variable and fixed elements into one-rate for factory overhead application and records all actual factory overhead costs in one factory overhead control account.

CONTROLLABLE VARIANCE

In **controllable variance** analysis, the actual factory overhead and the standard amount of overhead allowed the actual (equivalent) production for the period are compared. The difference results from the behavior of the fixed and variable cost items. As discussed previously, fixed cost items tend to remain the same in total dollars despite normal fluctuations in production volume, while total variable costs tend to vary proportionately with changes in production.

In the previous example, depreciation, taxes, insurance, and supervisory salaries are common items of fixed expense, while maintenance costs and supplies are usually listed in the category of variable cost.

Assume that the actual level of production given previously was 900 units—or 90% of the planned production of 1,000 units—and the 900 units are allowed 1,800 standard direct labor hours (900 units × 2 hours per unit). The actual amount of factory overhead for this period follows:

Depreciation on building and machinery (fixed)	$ 4,000
Taxes and insurance on the above (fixed)	1,000
Supervisory salaries (fixed)	4,000
Maintenance costs (variable)	1,800
Supplies (variable)	1,000
	$11,800

The fixed cost remains the same as budgeted at 1,000 units of production, but the variable costs are lower. Because 900 units were produced and each unit is allowed 2 direct labor hours at $6 per hour, the work in process was debited and factory overhead credited for $10,800. The factory overhead account shows a $1,000 underapplied (debit) balance.

Factory Overhead

11,800	10,800
(actual cost)	(applied 900 units × 2
	standard hours per unit
(*1,000* underapplied)	× $6)

Using the variable and fixed cost rates per unit calculated previously at $1.50 for variable cost and $4.50 for fixed cost, the calculation of controllable variance follows:

Standard factory overhead budgeted for *actual* level of production:	
Variable cost:	
900 units × 2 hours per unit × $1.50	$ 2,700
Fixed cost:	
As budgeted (total from budget)	9,000
Flexible budget at *actual* production level	$11,700
Actual factory overhead incurred	11,800
Controllable variance (unfavorable)	$ 100

VOLUME VARIANCE

The volume variance calculation uses the same flexible budget amount as determined in the previous calculation ($11,700) and compares the budget amount to the overhead applied to the production for the period.

Flexible budget at *actual* production level	$11,700
Factory overhead applied:	
900 units × 2 hours per unit × $6	10,800
Volume variance (unfavorable)	$ 900

In summary, the controllable and volume variance explain the under-applied $1,000 in the factory overhead account as follows:

Controllable variance (unfavorable)	$ 100
Volume variance (unfavorable)	900
Underapplied factory overhead	$1,000

The budget for the year anticipated the fixed cost of $9,000 would be spread over 2,000 direct labor hours and would be used to produce 1,000 units of product. Because only 900 units were produced, only $8,100 (1,800 direct labor hours × $4.50 fixed cost per hour) was applied. The result was an unfavorable variance of $900.

The following illustration shows this effect:

Actual Level of Production—900 units

	Budget	Applied	Volume Variance
Fixed cost applied:			
900 units × 2 hours × $4.50	$ 9,000	$ 8,100	$900
Variable cost applied:			
900 units × 2 hours × $1.50	2,700	2,700	-0-
Total applied (900 × 2 hours × $6)	$11,700	$10,800	$900

The volume variance is a significant factor because it indicates the degree that production was below the established standard. If management feels that 1,000 units should have been produced during the period, it will be concerned that only 900 units were produced and will investigate to determine the cause. This reduced production may result from inefficiencies in labor or supervision, machine breakdowns due to faulty maintenance, or from any number of unfavorable conditions. On the other hand, this level of production may indicate a normal seasonal fluctuation that will be offset by higher than normal production in other periods. If the reduction in production is not seasonal, it may have occurred because sales were not as high as predicted, in which case the marketing department could then be held accountable.

Whatever the circumstances, a factory that is producing below its normal capacity has idle and possibly wasted excess capacity. If it is producing above its normal capacity, the higher volume may create inefficient operating conditions and excessive costs. Such situations should be scrutinized by management, who is ultimately responsible for planning and implementing the most efficient production methods and schedules.

The formula for calculating factory overhead variances using the **two-variance method** is illustrated in the following example.

Formula for Calculating Factory Overhead Variances Using Two-Variance Method

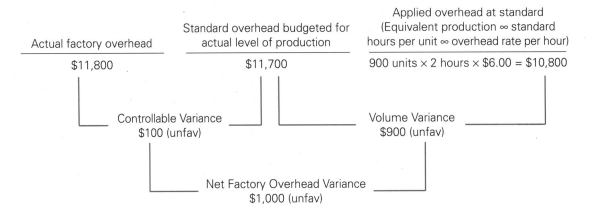

The amount of overhead applied to production is $900 less than the factory overhead calculated for the actual level of production by the flexible budget. This variance is unfavorable because the fixed overhead budgeted at the beginning of the period was not completely charged to production due to an insufficient number of units produced. It is referred to as a *volume variance* because it is created by the excess or lack of actual units produced compared to the planned production quantity.

The *controllable variance* originated because the actual factory overhead for the period exceeded the amount of overhead allowed for the level of production. The controllable variance is favorable when the actual expenditures are less than the flexible dollar amount calculated for the attained level of production; it is unfavorable when the actual factory overhead costs exceed the calculated budget.

After the variance analysis, the following journal entry can be made:

Factory Overhead—Volume Variance	900	
Factory Overhead—Controllable Variance	100	
Factory Overhead		1,000

The journal entry closes out the account for factory overhead and records the variances in individual accounts.

The journal entries to apply overhead and to record the variances may be combined in the following manner:

Work in Process	10,800	
Factory Overhead—Volume Variance	900	
Factory Overhead—Controllable Variance	100	
Factory Overhead		11,800

Production below the standard number of units will always cause an unfavorable volume variance. Conversely, production greater than the standard number of units will always produce a favorable volume variance. Assume the following facts for the period:

Standard overhead cost per unit (2 direct labor hours × $6)	$ 12
Number of units actually produced	1,200
Number of units expected to be produced (budgeted)	1,000
Actual factory overhead	$15,000

Standard factory overhead budgeted for actual level of production:

Fixed costs: (as budgeted)	$ 9,000
Variable Costs:	
1,200 units × 2 hours per unit × $1.50	3,600
Flexible budget for actual production level	$12,600

Under these circumstances, the work in process account would be charged with $14,400 applied factory overhead (1,200 units × 2 hours per unit × $6). The factory overhead account would have a debit balance of $600, as shown in the following T-account. The debit balance represents a net unfavorable variance.

Factory Overhead

15,000	14,400
(actual costs	(standard cost
recorded from	applied to work
various journals)	in process)
Bal. *600*	

The breakdown of the net variance shows a favorable volume variance because factory overhead was overabsorbed when the actual volume of production was higher than the established standard. The unfavorable controllable variance indicates that the actual overhead costs exceeded the amount allowed for the actual level of production.

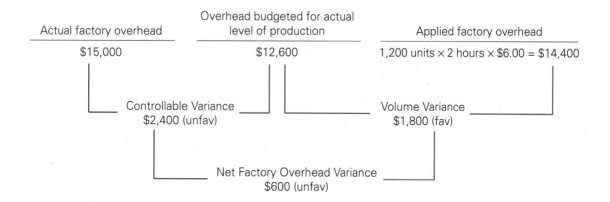

Both variances should be investigated for cause and effect. The *favorable volume variance* may be due to an anticipated seasonal fluctuation, and it may offset all or part of the previous unfavorable volume variances that arose during periods of low production. However, this level of production may have occurred because the company received more orders for goods than it had anticipated. From the standpoint of increased profits, this factor is favorable; however, if the factory worked beyond an established efficient capacity of production, the quality of the product may have suffered.

The *unfavorable controllable variance* should be examined to determine why the costs were higher than expected, where the responsibility for this condition lies, and what steps can be taken to keep these costs under control in the future. This variance could result from several factors, such as laxity in purchasing, inefficiency in supervision, or weak control of expenditures. However, some portion of the controllable variance may result from additional machine maintenance and repair costs, which are attributable to the increased use of facilities at the higher level of production.

On the financial statements, the overhead variances can be treated as additions to or deductions from the standard cost of goods sold. If the variances are material (sizable) in amount, seasonal, or due to unusual circumstances, they will be treated as discussed in Chapter 8.

> **You should now be able to work the following: Exercises 1, 2, 3, 4, 5 and Problems 1, 2, 3.**

APPENDIX 9A FOUR-VARIANCE AND THREE-VARIANCE METHODS OF ANALYSIS

FOUR-VARIANCE METHOD OF ANALYSIS

A refined management view of the two-variance method isolates the fixed and variable components that comprise the factory overhead cost and calculates separate variances for the variable costs and the fixed costs. The **four-variance method** recognizes *two* variable cost variances and *two* fixed cost variances. The cost variances are identified as a *spending variance* and an *efficiency variance*. For fixed cost, a *budget variance* and a *volume variance* is determined.

The four-variance method has two important aspects, (1) separate actual factory overhead accounts must be maintained for variable costs and fixed costs and (2) actual direct labor hours worked must be known.

Variable Factory Overhead Variances:

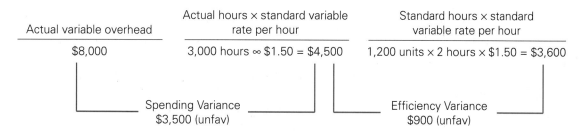

Actual variable overhead	Actual hours × standard variable rate per hour	Standard hours × standard variable rate per hour
$8,000	3,000 hours ∞ $1.50 = $4,500	1,200 units × 2 hours × $1.50 = $3,600

Spending Variance
$3,500 (unfav)

Efficiency Variance
$900 (unfav)

Fixed Factory Overhead Variances:

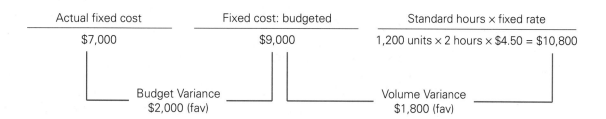

Actual fixed cost	Fixed cost: budgeted	Standard hours × fixed rate
$7,000	$9,000	1,200 units × 2 hours × $4.50 = $10,800

Budget Variance
$2,000 (fav)

Volume Variance
$1,800 (fav)

Using the same data for factory overhead as shown in the previous illustration (except recognizing that the actual factory overhead of $15,000 was composed of $8,000 of variable overhead costs and $7,000 of fixed overhead costs and that 3,000 direct labor hours were used in production), the four-variance calculations would be as follows:

Net factory overhead variance:
Spending	$3,500 (unfavorable)
Efficiency	900 (unfavorable)
Budget	2,000 (favorable)
Volume	1,800 (favorable)
Net overhead variance	$ 600 (unfavorable)

After analyzing the variances, the following journal entry can be made:

Factory Overhead—Spending Variance	3,500	
Factory Overhead—Efficiency Variance	900	
Factory Overhead—Budget Variance		2,000
Factory Overhead—Volume Variance		1,800
Factory Overhead		600

To close the factory overhead account.

COMPARISON OF THE TWO-VARIANCE AND FOUR-VARIANCE METHODS

Four-Variance Method		Two-Variance Method	
Variable cost:			
Spending variance—unfavorable	$3,500		
Efficiency variance—unfavorable	900	Controllable variance—unfavorable	$2,400
Fixed cost:			
Budget variance—favorable	2,000		
Volume variance—favorable	1,800	Volume variance—favorable	1,800
Net variance (unf.)	$ 600		$ 600

Both methods reach the same conclusion—the net factory overhead variance is $600 unfavorable. However, although the four-variance method identifies the fixed cost (budget variance as originating from the differences between actual fixed cost expenditures and the amount of fixed cost budgeted), the controllable variance (two-variance method) considers the budget variance to be a variable cost and includes it as part of the total controllable variance. The controllable variance encompasses the spending, efficiency, and budget variances in one total variance. The volume variance amount is shown as a single, separate item by both methods.

Most companies use the two-variance method of analysis for factory overhead and apply the factory overhead to production using a single rate that combines both the fixed and variable components. These companies consider it too costly from a clerical standpoint to apply separate fixed and variable rates to completed products and also maintain separate factory overhead accounts for fixed and variable elements. However, the most valuable use of the four-variance method is that it demonstrates the cost behavior patterns of fixed and variable costs when production volumes fluctuate. It is an excellent exercise in the study of cost behavior because it demonstrates the behavior patterns important in making management cost decisions that affect profitability.

THREE-VARIANCE METHOD OF ANALYSIS

The **three-variance method** of factory overhead analysis, although not as common as the two-variance method, is frequently used by manufacturers. This method separates actual and applied overhead into three variances: (1) budget (spending),(2) capacity, and (3) efficiency.

The **budget, or spending, variance** reflects the difference between the actual costs of overhead and the budgeted amount calculated for the actual hours worked. The saving or overspending is chargeable to the manager or a departmental supervisor responsible for the costs.

These budget variances should not be confused with those for the two-variance method; the calculations are different and result in a sharper distinction in variances. The primary difference between the two methods of variance analysis is that the three-variance method determines the budget allowances based on actual hours worked rather than on the standard number of hours allowed for the units produced.

The **capacity variance** indicates that the volume of production was more or less than normal. It reflects an under- or overabsorption of fixed costs and measures the difference between actual hours worked, multiplied by the standard overhead rate, and the budget allowance based on actual hours worked. This variance is considered the responsibility of management and can be due to expected seasonal variations or changes in the volume of production (caused by poor scheduling, improper use of labor, strikes, or other factors).

The **efficiency variance** measures the difference between the overhead applied (standard hours at the standard rate) and the actual hours worked multiplied by the standard rate. It shows the effect on fixed and variable overhead costs when the actual hours worked are more or less than standard hours allowed for the production volume. Unfavorable variances may be caused by inefficiencies in the use of labor or an excessive use of labor hours; favorable efficiency variances indicate a more effective use of labor than was anticipated by the standards.

Many accountants feel that the budget allowance for overhead is more appropriate when the base used reflects actual labor hours rather than standard labor hours. They believe a more definitive relationship exists between actual hours worked and factory expense involved and feel that the three-variance method provides a more precise analysis of overhead costs.

Whether the two-, three-, or four-variance method is used, the overhead applied to production is the same because the application is based on the standard number of labor hours allowed for the actual production multiplied by the standard rates established for overhead. Also, the actual overhead incurred would be similar in all cases. Therefore, the calculated net factory overhead variance would also be the same in all methods.

The budget variance illustrated is unfavorable because the actual overhead exceeded the budget allowance. Again, the amount differs from the two-variance method because actual rather than standard hours are used to determine the budget amount. Note that a budget variance is calculated for the four-variance method but it is specifically used to com-

Formula for Calculating Factory Overhead Variances

Using Three-Variance Method

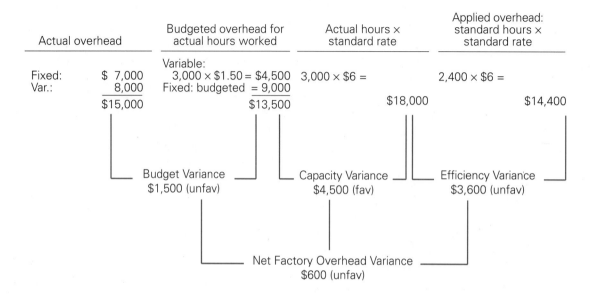

pare the fixed costs actually incurred for the period to the previously budgeted fixed cost. It is unfortunate that these variances have similar designations. The designations were not changed because both are widely accepted by accountants. These terms are rarely confused because they refer to different types of factory overhead analyses.

The efficiency variance, as illustrated, is unfavorable because the labor hours worked were more than the standard hours allowed for the level of production. In this case, the excess 600 hours times the standard overhead application rate of $6 equals the variance of $3,600 and reflects the underabsorption of fixed and variable costs.

The new budget for overhead, based on the actual hours worked, is calculated by multiplying the actual hours worked times the variable rate for overhead (3,000 hours × $1.50 per hour) amounting to $4,500 and adding the expected fixed cost for the period of $9,000. The new budget, for the hours worked, totals $13,500. The capacity variance theoretically reflects the cost of unused plant facilities and involves mostly fixed costs. At 3,000 actual labor hours worked, $13,500 (3,000 × $4.50) of fixed cost was absorbed in Work in Process, $4,500 more than was budgeted. This variance is similar to the volume variance under the two-variance method, but the amount differs because it is based on actual hours worked rather than on the standard hours allowed for 1,200 units.

For comparison purposes, the two-variance method would produce the following results:

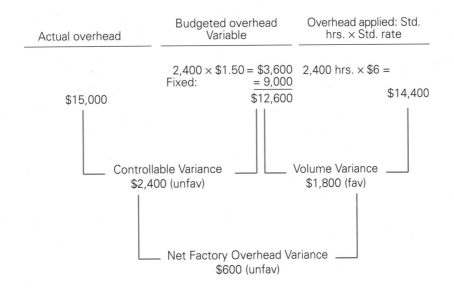

Actual overhead	Budgeted overhead Variable	Overhead applied: Std. hrs. × Std. rate
$15,000	2,400 × $1.50 = $3,600 Fixed: = 9,000 $12,600	2,400 hrs. × $6 = $14,400

Controllable Variance
$2,400 (unfav)

Volume Variance
$1,800 (fav)

Net Factory Overhead Variance
$600 (unfav)

K E Y   T E R M S

SELF-STUDY PROBLEM

FLEXIBLE BUDGETS; TWO-, THREE-, AND FOUR-VARIANCE METHODS OF FACTORY OVERHEAD ANALYSIS

Hensom Company
— ❖ —

Hensom Company manufactures a single product and uses a standard cost system. The factory overhead is applied on a basis of direct labor hours. A condensed version of the company's flexible budget follows:

Direct labor hours		20,000	25,000	40,000
Cost per hour	$2			
Factory overhead costs:				
Variable costs		$ 40,000	$ 50,000	$ 80,000
Fixed costs		200,000	200,000	200,000
Total		$240,000	$250,000	$280,000

The product requires 3 pounds of material at a standard cost per pound of $7 and 2 hours of direct labor at a standard cost of $6 per hour.

For the current year, the company planned to operate at the 25,000 direct-labor-hour level and to produce 12,500 units of product. Actual production and costs for the year follow:

Number of units produced	14,000
Actual direct labor hours worked	30,000
Actual variable overhead costs incurred	$ 52,000
Actual fixed overhead costs incurred	$208,000

Required:

1. Compute the factory overhead rate for the current year that will be used for production. Show the variable and fixed components that make up the total predetermined rate to be used.
2. Prepare a standard cost card for the product. Show the individual elements of the overhead rate as well as the total rate.
3. Compute (a) standard hours allowed for production and (b) under- or overapplied factory overhead for the year.
4. Determine the reason for any under- or overapplied factory overhead for the year by computing all variances using each of the following methods:
   a. two-variance method
   b. three-variance method (appendix)
   c. four-variance method (appendix)

SOLUTION TO SELF-STUDY PROBLEM

Compute the factory overhead rate by variable and fixed elements.

1. Show the total predetermined rate that will be used during the current year.

			Per DLH
Variable rate:			
Variable costs	$50,000	=	$2.00
Direct labor hours	25,000		
Fixed rate:			
Fixed costs	$200,000	=	$8.00
Direct labor hours	25,000		

Total rate:

Variable costs	$ 50,000	
Fixed costs	200,000	
Total	$250,000 =	$10.00
Direct labor hours	25,000	

2. Prepare a standard cost card for each unit of product

Direct material: 3 lbs. @ $7 per lb.		$21.00
Direct labor: 2 hours @ $6 per hour		12.00
Factory overhead:		
Variable cost: 2 hrs. @ $2	$ 4.00	
Fixed cost: 2 hrs. @ $8	16.00	20.00
Standard cost per unit		$53.00

3. (a) Compute the standard hours allowed production for the year.

Actual units produced	14,000
Number of hours allowed by standard established for each unit of product	× 2
Total standard hours allowed	28,000

(b) Compute the under or overapplied factory overhead for the year.

Actual factory overhead incurred:	
Variable costs	$ 52,000
Fixed costs	208,000
Total actual overhead costs	$260,000
Factory overhead costs applied:	
Standard hours allowed × Standard rate:	
28,000 hours × $10.00	280,000
Overapplied factory overhead	$ 20,000

4. Calculate the reason for the overapplied factory overhead by:
    a. Two variance method:

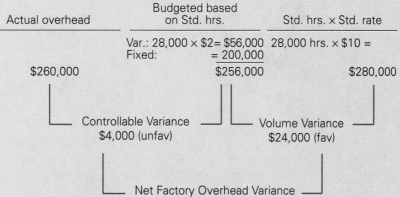

b. Three variance method: (Appendix)

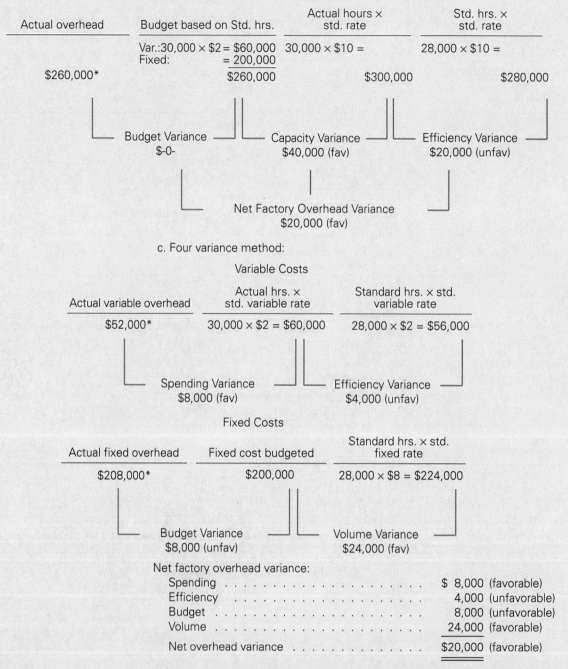

Actual overhead	Budget based on Std. hrs.	Actual hours × std. rate	Std. hrs. × std. rate
	Var.:30,000 × $2 = $60,000 Fixed: = 200,000	30,000 × $10 =	28,000 × $10 =
$260,000*	$260,000	$300,000	$280,000

Budget Variance $-0-

Capacity Variance $40,000 (fav)

Efficiency Variance $20,000 (unfav)

Net Factory Overhead Variance $20,000 (fav)

c. Four variance method:

Variable Costs

Actual variable overhead	Actual hrs. × std. variable rate	Standard hrs. × std. variable rate
$52,000*	30,000 × $2 = $60,000	28,000 × $2 = $56,000

Spending Variance $8,000 (fav)

Efficiency Variance $4,000 (unfav)

Fixed Costs

Actual fixed overhead	Fixed cost budgeted	Standard hrs. × std. fixed rate
$208,000*	$200,000	28,000 × $8 = $224,000

Budget Variance $8,000 (unfav)

Volume Variance $24,000 (fav)

Net factory overhead variance:

Spending	$ 8,000	(favorable)
Efficiency	4,000	(unfavorable)
Budget	8,000	(unfavorable)
Volume	24,000	(favorable)
Net overhead variance	$20,000	(favorable)

*These total costs represent actual hours × actual rates per hour. When the total cost is given, it is not necessary to determine the specific components which make up the total cost unless you do it to understand the formulas being used.

QUESTIONS

1. How is the standard cost per unit for factory overhead determined?
2. How is factory overhead cost applied to work in process in a standard cost accounting system?
3. What is a budget variance?
4. Why is it important to determine budget variances?
5. What is he difference between fixed and variable costs? Give examples of each.
6. What is a volume variance?
7. What is the significance of a volume variance?
8. If production is more or less than the standard volume, is it possible that no controllable or volume variances would exist? Explain.
9. What is a budget?
10. What is the advantage of using budgets for business and industry?
11. What are the six principles of good budgeting?
12. Which budget must be prepared before the others? Why?
13. If the sales forecast estimates that 50,000 units of product will be sold during the following year, should the factory plan on manufacturing 50,000 units in the coming year? Explain.
14. What are the advantages and disadvantages of each of the following?

    a. A stable production policy
    b. A stable inventory policy for a company that has greatly fluctuating sales during the year

15. After budgets have been prepared in units and dollars, what other activities can be planned?
16. What is a flexible budget?
17. How would you define the following?

    a. Theoretical capacity
    b. Practical capacity
    c. Normal capacity

18. Is it possible for a factory to operate at more than 100% of capacity?
19. If a factory operates at 100% of capacity one month, 90% of capacity the next month, and at 105% of capacity the next month, will a different cost per unit be charged to Work in Process each month for factory overhead?
20. At the end of the current fiscal year, the trial balance of Crowley Corporation revealed the following debit balances:

    Budget (Controllable) Variance—$2,000

    Volume Variance—$75,000

    What conclusions can be drawn from these two variances?

EXERCISES

E9-1
Calculating factory overhead
Learning Objective 4

The normal capacity of a manufacturing plant is 5,000 units per month. Fixed overhead at this volume is $2,500, and variable overhead is $7,500. Additional data follow:

	Month 1	Month 2
Actual production (units)	5,200	4,500
Actual factory overhead	$9,900	$9,400

Calculate the following:

1. Amount of factory overhead allowed for the actual levels of production

2. Variances for each month for factory overhead (indicate whether favorable or unfavorable)

**E9-2
Calculating factory overhead
Learning Objective 5**

The standard capacity of a factory is 8,000 units per month. Cost and production data follow:

Standard application rate for fixed overhead	$ .50 per unit
Standard application rate for variable overhead	$1.50 per unit
Production—Month 1	7,200 units
Production—Month 2	8,400 units
Actual factory overhead—Month 1	$14,500
Actual factory overhead—Month 2	$17,600

a. Calculate the amount of factory overhead allowed for the actual volume of production each month.
b. Calculate the variances for factory overhead (indicate whether favorable or unfavorable).
c. Explain the significance of the variances.

**E9-3
Calculating factory overhead:
two-variances
Learning Objective 5**

Morrow Manufacturing Company normally produces 10,000 units of product X each month. Each unit requires 2 hours of direct labor, and factory overhead is applied on a direct labor hour basis. Fixed costs and variable costs in factory overhead at the normal capacity are $5 and $3 per unit, respectively. Cost and production data for the month of May follow:

Production for the month	9,000 units
Direct labor hours used	18,500 hours
Factory overhead incurred for:	
Variable costs	$28,500
Fixed costs	$52,000

a. Calculate the controllable variance.
b. Calculate the volume variance.
c. Was the total factory overhead under or overapplied? By what amount?

**E9-4
Making journal entries for factory overhead and variances; analysis of variances
Learning Objective 5**

The normal capacity of a manufacturing plant is 30,000 direct labor hours or 20,000 units per month. Standard fixed costs are $6,000 and variable costs are $12,000. Data for two months follow:

	March	April
Units produced	18,000	21,000
Factory overhead incurred	$16,500	$19,000

For each month, make journal entries to charge overhead to Work in Process and to record variances. Indicate the types of variances and state whether each is favorable or unfavorable.

**E9-5
Calculating amount of factory overhead applied to work in process**

The overhead application rate for a company is $2.50 per unit, made up of $1.00 for fixed overhead and $1.50 for variable overhead. Normal capacity is 10,000 units. In one month, there was an unfavorable controllable variance of $200. Actual overhead for the month was $27,000. What was the amount of factory overhead applied to Work in Process?

E9-6
Preparing production budget and materials budget
Learning Objective 2

SS

The sales department of your company has forecast sales in March to be 20,000 units. Additional information follows:

Finished goods inventory, March 1 . . . . 1,000 units
Finished goods inventory required, March 31 . . . . 3,000 units

Materials used in production:

	Inventory March 1	Required Inventory March 31	Standard Cost
A (one gallon per unit)	500 gal.	1,000 gal.	$2 per gal.
B (one pound per unit)	1,000 lbs.	1,000 lbs.	$1 per lb.

Prepare the following:

a. A production budget for March (in units)
b. A materials budget for the month (in units and dollars)

E9-7 (APPENDIX 9A)
Calculating factory overhead: three-variances
Learning Objective 5

Using the data shown in E9-3, calculate the following overhead variances:

a. Budget variance
b. Capacity variance
c. Efficiency variance
d. Was the factory overhead under- or overapplied? By what amount?

E9-8 (APPENDIX 9A)
Calculating four-variance overhead analysis
Learning Objective 5

Alum-Valve Company budgets 8,000 direct labor hours for the year. The total overhead budget is expected to amount to $20,000. The standard cost for a unit of the company's product estimates the variable overhead as follows:

Variable factory overhead (3 hours @ $2) . . . . $6 per unit

The actual data for the period follow:

Actual completed units 2,500
Actual direct labor hours 7,640
Actual variable overhead $16,100
Actual fixed overhead 3,920

Using the four-variance method, calculate the overhead variances.

PROBLEMS

P9-1
Overhead application rate; calculation of all variances— two-variance overhead method
Learning Objective 5

Clinton Manufacturing Company uses a job-order cost system and standard costs. It manufactures one product, whose standard cost follows:

Materials, 20 yards @ $.90 per yard $18
Direct labor, 4 hours @ $9.00 per hour 36
Total factory overhead (the ratio of variable costs
 to fixed costs is 3 to 1) 32

Total unit cost $86

The standards are set based on normal activity of 2,400 direct labor hours. Actual activity for the month of October follows:

Materials purchased, 18,000 yards @ $.92 . . . . $16,560
Materials used 9,500 yards
Direct labor, 2,100 hours @ $9.15   19,215
Total factory overhead, 500 units actually produced   17,760

Required:

1. Compute the variable factory overhead rate per direct labor hour and the total fixed factory overhead based on normal activity.
2. Prepare a schedule computing the following variances for the month of October (indicate whether favorable or unfavorable):
   a. Materials quantity variance
   b. Materials purchase price variance
   c. Labor efficiency variance
   d. Labor rate variance
   e. Overhead budget (controllable) variance
   f. Overhead volume variance

(AICPA adapted)

P9-2
Journal entries;
variance analysis;
other analyses
Learning Objective 5

Cost and production data for the Paxton Products Company follow:

Standard Cost Sheet
(Normal capacity—1,000 units)

	Dept. A	Dept. B	Total
Materials:			
I—2 lbs.@ $2	$ 4		
II—2 lbs.@ $1		$ 2	$ 6
Labor:			
2 hours @ $5	10		
1 hour @ $6		6	16
Factory overhead: (per standard labor hour)			
Fixed Variable			
$2 $1	6		
1 3		4	10
Total	$20	$12	$32

Production Report

	Dept. A	Dept. B
Beginning units in process	None	None
Units finished and transferred	1,000	900
Ending units in process	200	100
Stage of completion	1/2	1/2

Cost Data

	Dept. A		Dept. B	
Direct materials used:				
I—2,300 lbs	$ 4,715			
II—1,850 lbs				$1,813
Direct labor:				
2,150 hours	10,965			
1,000 hours				5,900
Factory overhead:				
Indirect materials	$ 1,000		$ 500	
Indirect labor	1,300		1,000	
Other (fixed costs)	4,400	6,700	2,250	3,750
Total		$22,380		$11,463

During the month, 850 units were sold at $50 each.

Note: Materials, labor, and overhead are added evenly throughout the process.

Required:

1. Make general journal entries to record all transactions and variances. (Use the two-variance method for overhead variance analysis.)
2. Prove balances of Work in Process in both departments.
3. Prove that all costs have been accounted for.
4. Calculate the gross margin
   a. At standard cost
   b. At actual cost

P9-3
Material, labor, and overhead variances; two-variance overhead analysis
Learning Objective 5

The standard specifications for an electric motor manufactured by the Excel Motor Corporation follow:

EXL-Grade AA1

Standard cost per unit:
Material (2 lbs. × $5 per lb.) $10
Labor (4 hours × $6 per hour) 24
Factory overhead (4 hours × $3.50* per hour) 14

Total standard cost $48

*Variable—$1.00 + Fixed—$2.50 = $3.50

Factory overhead rates are based on a normal 70% capacity and use the following flexible budget:

	Normal		
	70%	85%	100%
Motors to be produced	2,000	2,500	3,000
Variable overhead	$ 8,000	$10,000	$12,000
Fixed overhead	20,000	20,000	20,000

The actual production was 2,500 motors and following costs were incurred:

Material (4,880 lbs.)	$25,856
Labor (11,800 hours @ $6.15 per hour)	72,570
Factory overhead	30,305

Required:

Calculate the material, labor, and factory overhead variances. Use the two-variance method for overhead.

P9-4
Flexible budget;
overhead variance
analysis
Learning Objectives 2
& 5

Presented below are the monthly factory overhead cost budget (at normal capacity of 5,000 units or 20,000 direct labor hours) and the production and cost data for a month.

Factory Overhead Cost Budget

Fixed cost:		
Depreciation on building and machinery	$1,200	
Taxes on building and machinery	500	
Insurance on building and machinery	500	
Superintendent's salary	1,500	
Supervisors' salaries	2,300	
Maintenance wages	1,000	$7,000
Variable cost:		
Repairs	$ 400	
Maintenance supplies	300	
Other supplies	200	
Payroll taxes	800	
Small tools	300	2,000
Total standard factory overhead		$9,000

Production and Cost Data

Number of units produced	4,000	
Factory overhead:		
Depreciation on building and machinery	$1,200	
Supervisors' salaries	2,300	
Insurance on building and machinery	480	
Maintenance supplies	200	
Maintenance wages	1,050	
Other supplies	150	
Payroll taxes	650	
Repairs	275	
Small tools	170	
Superintendent's salary	1,500	
Taxes on building and machinery	525	

Required:

Use the factory overhead cost budget for instructions (1) through (4).

1. Assuming that variable costs will vary in direct proportion to the change in volume, prepare a flexible budget for production levels of 80%, 90%, and 110%. Also determine the rate for application of factory overhead to work in process at each level of volume.

2. Prepare a flexible budget for production levels of 80%, 90%, and 110%, assuming that variable costs will vary in direct proportion to the change in volume, but with the following exceptions:
   a. At 110% of capacity, an assistant department head will be needed at a salary of $10,500 annually.
   b. At 80% of capacity, the repairs expense will drop to one half of the amount at 100% capacity.
   c. Maintenance supplies expense will remain constant at all levels of production.
   d. At 80% of capacity, one part-time maintenance worker, earning $6,000 a year, will be laid off.
   e. At 110% of capacity, a machine not normally in use and on which no depreciation is normally recorded will be used in production. Its cost was $12,000 and it has a ten-year life.
3. Using the flexible budget prepared in (1), determine the budgeted cost at 92% of capacity using interpolation.
4. Using the flexible budget prepared in (1), determine the budgeted cost at 104% of capacity using a method other than interpolation.
5. Using the production and cost data for a month and the flexible budget prepared in (1):
   a. Determine the variances by the two-variance method.
   b. Explain the meaning of the variances.
   c. Prepare a schedule comparing the actual and budgeted items and show the variance for each item of factory overhead. Indicate unfavorable variances in parentheses.

P9-5
Variance analysis
Learning Objective 5

Texo Shirts, Inc., manufactures men's sport shirts for large stores. Texo produces a single quality shirt in lots of a dozen according to each customer's order and attaches the store's label. The standard costs for a dozen shirts include the following:

Direct materials	24 yards @ $ .55	$13.20
Direct labor	3 hours @ $7.35	22.05
Factory overhead	3 hours @ $2.00	6.00
Standard cost per dozen		$41.25

During October, Texo worked on three orders for shirts. Job cost records for the month disclose the following:

Lot	Units in Lot	Materials Used	Hours Worked
30	1,000 dozen	24,100 yards	2,980
31	1,700 dozen	40,440 yards	5,130
32	1,200 dozen	28,825 yards	2,890

The following information is also available:

a. Western purchased 95,000 yards of materials during the month at a cost of $53,200. The materials price variance is recorded when goods are purchased and all inventories are carried at standard cost.
b. Direct labor incurred amounted to $81,400 during October. According to payroll records, production employees were paid $7.40 per hour.

c. Overhead is applied on the basis of direct labor hours. Factory overhead totaling $22,800 was incurred during October.

d. A total of $288,000 was budgeted for overhead for the year based on estimated production at the plant's normal capacity of 48,000 dozen shirts per year. Overhead is 40% fixed and 60% variable at this level of production.

e. There was no work in process at October 1. During October, Lots 30 and 31 were completed, and all materials were issued for Lot 32, which was 80% completed as to labor.

Required:

1. Prepare a schedule computing the standard cost for October of Lots 30, 31, and 32.
2. Prepare a schedule computing the materials price variance for October and indicate whether it is favorable or unfavorable.
3. For each lot produced during October, prepare schedules computing the following (indicate whether favorable or unfavorable):
   a. Materials quantity variance in yards
   b. Labor efficiency variance in hours
   c. Labor rate variance in dollars
4. Prepare a schedule computing the total controllable and volume overhead variances for October and indicate whether they are favorable or unfavorable.

(AICPA adapted)

P9-6
Material, labor, and overhead variances—two-variance method
Learning Objective 5

Ole Kooler Company manufactures products in batches of 100 units per batch. The company uses a standard cost system and prepares budgets that call for 500 of these batches per period. Fixed overhead is $60,000. The standard costs per batch follow:

Material (80 gallons)	$ 32
Labor (60 hours)	216
Factory overhead	252
Standard cost per batch	$500

During the period, 503 batches were manufactured and the following costs were incurred:

Material used (40,743 gallons)	$ 15,482.34
Labor (29,677 hours at $3.65 per hour)	108,321.05
Actual variable overhead	67,080.00
Actual fixed overhead	60,500.00

Required

Calculate the variances for material, labor, and overhead. For overhead use the two-variance method.

P9-7
Schedule of production and standard cost; variance analysis; mix and yield variances
Learning Objective 5

Pullom Product Company processes one compound product known as CLEAN and uses a standard cost accounting system. The process requires that three materials be prepared and blended in large batches with a variation from the standard mixture sometimes necessary to maintain quality. Pullom's cost accountant became ill at the end of October and you were engaged to determine standard costs of October production and explain any differences between actual and standard costs for the month. The following information is available for the blending department:

a. The standard cost ledger for a 500-pound batch shows the following standard costs:

	Quantity	Price	Total	Cost
Materials:				
Compound #1	250 lbs.	$.14	$35	
Compound #2	200 lbs.	.09	18	
Other ingredients	50 lbs.	.08	4	
Total per batch	500 lbs.			$57
Labor:				
Preparation and blending	10 hours	$6.00		60
Factory Overhead:				
Variable	10 hours	$1.00	$10	
Fixed	10 hours	.30	3	13
Total standard cost per 500-pound batch				$130

b. During October, 410 batches of 500 pounds each of the finished compound were completed and transferred to the packaging department.
c. Blending department inventories totaled 6,000 pounds at the beginning of the month and 9,000 pounds at the end of the month (assume both inventories were completely processed but not transferred and consisted of materials in their standard proportions). Inventories are carried in the accounts at standard cost prices.
d. During the month of October, the following materials were purchased and put into production:

	Pounds	Price	Total Cost
Compound #1	114,400	$.17	$19,448
Compound #2	85,800	.11	9,438
Other ingredients	19,800	.07	1,386
Total	220,000		$30,272

e. Wages paid for 4,212 hours of direct labor at $6.25 per hour amounted to $26,325.
f. Actual overhead costs for the month totaled $5,519.
g. The standards were established for a normal production volume of 200,000 pounds (400 batches) of CLEAN per month. At this level of production, variable factory overhead was budgeted at $4,000 and fixed factory overhead was budgeted at $1,200.

Required:

1. Prepare a schedule for the blending department presenting computations of the following:
   a. October production in both pounds and batches.

    b. Standard cost of October production itemized by components of materials, labor, and overhead

2. Prepare schedules computing the differences between actual and standard costs and analyzing the differences as each of the following:
    a. Materials variances (for each material) caused by
       (1) Quantity difference
       (2) Price difference
    b. Labor variances caused by
       (1) Efficiency difference
       (2) Rate difference
    c. Factory overhead variances caused by
       (1) Controllable factors
       (2) Volume factors

3. Calculate materials mix and yield variances.

(AICPA adapted)

P9-8
Analyses
Learning Objective 5

On May 1, Hatton Company began the manufacture of a new mechanical device known as Handy. The company installed a standard cost system in accounting for manufacturing costs. The standard costs for a unit of Handy follow:

Raw materials (5 lbs. @ $1 per lb.)	$ 5
Direct labor (1 hour @ $8 per hour)	8
Overhead (50% of direct labor costs)	4
	$17

The following data came from Hatton's records for the month of May:

	Units
Actual production	4,000
Units sold	2,500

	Debit	Credit
Sales		$50,000
Purchases (22,000 pounds)	$23,300	
Materials price variance	1,300	
Materials quantity variance	1,000	
Direct labor rate variance	770	
Direct labor efficiency variance		1,200
Manufacturing overhead total variance	500	

The amount shown above for materials price variance is applicable to raw materials purchased during May.

Required:

Compute each of the following items for Hatton for the month of May. Show computations in good form.
1. Standard quantity of raw materials allowed (in pounds)
2. Actual quantity of raw materials used (in pounds)
3. Standard hours allowed
4. Actual hours worked

5. Actual direct labor rate
6. Actual total overhead

(AICPA adapted)

P9-9 (APPENDIX 9A)
All variances;
four-variances for
factory overhead
Learning Objective 5

Anderson Manufacturing Company manufactures a small electric motor that is a replacement part for the more popular gas furnaces. The standard cost card shows the product requirements as follows:

Direct material—2 lbs. @ $4 per lb.	$ 8.00
Direct labor—5 hours @ $8 per hour	40.00
Factory overhead:	
Variable cost—5 hours @ $2 per hour	10.00
Fixed cost—5 hours @ $4 per hour	20.00
Total standard cost per unit	$78.00

Factory overhead rates are based on normal 100% capacity and the following flexible budgets:

	90%	Normal 100%	110%
Units produced	2,500	3,000	3,500
Factory overhead—variable	$25,000	$30,000	$35,000
Factory overhead—fixed	60,000	60,000	60,000

The company produced 3,500 units and incurred the following costs:

Materials (6,820 lbs.)	$27,962
Labor (18,375 hours @ $9)	165,375
Factory overhead—fixed	61,950
Factory overhead—variable	33,710

Required:

Calculate the following variances:

1. Materials price and quantity variances
2. Labor rate and efficiency variances
3. Factory overhead: spending, efficiency, budget and volume variances
4. Does the net variance represent under or overapplied factory overhead?

P9-10 (APPENDIX 9A)
Material, labor, and
overhead variances—
four-variance method
Learning Objective 5

Bird Corporation uses a standard cost system and manufactures one product. The variable costs per product follow:

Material (4 parts)	$ 2
Labor (2 hours)	6
Overhead	3
	$11

Budgeted fixed costs for the month are $4,000, and Bird expected to manufacture 2,000 units. Actual production, however, was only 1,800 units. Material prices were 5% over standard, and labor rates were 10% over standard. Of the factory overhead expense, only 80% was used and fixed overhead was $100 over the budgeted amount. In material usage, 8% more parts were used than were allowed for actual production by the standard and 6% more labor hours were used than were allowed.

Required:

1. Calculate the material and labor variances.
2. Calculate the variances for overhead by the four-variance method.

P9-11 (APPENDIX 9A)
Labor variances and
four-variance
overhead analysis
Learning Objective 5

EZ-GO Manufacturing Company estimates the following labor and overhead costs for the period:

Variable Overhead	$44,200
Fixed Overhead	50,050
Total estimated overhead	$94,250
Estimated direct labor cost	$65,000
Standard direct labor rate per hour	$5

Each unit will require 26 hours of labor.
Estimated production for the period . . . . .   500 units

Production statistics for the period:

Actual production	510 units
Actual direct labor hours used	13,015 hours
Actual direct labor cost	$66,116.20
Actual overhead costs:	
Variable costs	$45,009
Fixed costs	50,125

Required:

Use the four-variance method for overhead analysis. Calculate the variances for direct labor and overhead. Prove that the overhead variances equal over- or underapplied factory overhead for the period.

P9-12 (APPENDIX 9A)
Calculating overhead
rates—four-variance
analysis
Learning Objective 5

EZ-GO brought in a consultant from an independent accounting firm to help determine the fixed and variable components of departments. A committee consisting of personnel from production, engineering, and accounting was established to study and make suggestions. The results of the research on the standard overhead for two service and two production departments showed the following:

	Service Departments		Production Departments	
	Maintenance	Factory Adm.	Milling	Finishing
Standard overhead:				
Variable	$1,000	$3,000	$15,000	$30,000
Fixed	500	600	7,375	5,025
	$1,500	$3,600	$22,375	$35,025

Other estimated data:

Maintenance hours estimated	275	225
Employees	700	500
Direct labor hours	2,000	
Machine hours		5,000
Estimated units to be produced	500	1,000

The actual service department costs, after production is completed, is allocated to the production departments. The total actual production departmental costs follow:

	Milling	Finishing
Actual variable overhead	$17,000	$32,000
Actual fixed overhead	$ 7,750	$ 5,800
Actual direct labor hours	1,950	
Actual machine hours		5,040
Actual units produced	480	1,020

Required:

1. Using the direct method of allocating service departments to production departments, calculate the standard variable and fixed overhead rates for the production departments.
2. Prepare an overhead analysis for each production department, using the four-variance method.

P9-13 (APPENDIX 9A)
Three-variance
overhead analysis
Learning Objective 5

Using the data provided in P9-2, calculate the overhead cost variances under the three-variance method.

P9-14 (APPENDIX 9A)
Variance analysis
using the
three-variance
method for overhead
costs
Learning Objective 5

Ashwood Furniture Company uses a standard cost system in accounting for its production costs. The standard cost of a unit of furniture follows:

Lumber, 100 feet @ $150 per 1,000 feet		$15.00
Direct labor, 4 hours @ $10 per hour		40.00
Factory overhead:		
Fixed (15% of direct labor)	$ 6.00	
Variable (30% of direct labor)	12.00	18.00
Total unit cost		$73.00

The following flexible monthly overhead budget applies:

Direct Labor Hours	Estimated Overhead
5,200	$21,600
4,800	20,400
4,400	19,200
4,000 (normal capacity)	18,000
3,600	16,800

The actual unit costs for the month of December follow:

Lumber used (110 feet @ $120 per 1,000 feet)	$13.20
Direct labor (4 1/4 hours @ $10.24 per hour)	43.52

Factory overhead:

Variable costs	$ 7,400	
Fixed costs	13,720	
	($21,120/1,200 units)	17.60
Total actual unit cost		$74.32

Required:

Prepare a schedule using the three-variance method for overhead costs.

P9-15 (APPENDIX 9A)
Journal entries;
three-variance
analysis; income
statement
Learning Objective 5

Oakwood Company uses a standard cost system. The standards are based on a budget for operations at the rate of production anticipated for the current period. The company records in its general ledger variations in materials prices and usage, wage rates, and labor efficiency. The accounts for manufacturing costs reflect variations in activity from the projected rate of operations, variations of actual expense from amounts budgeted, and variations in the efficiency of production. Current standards follow:

Direct materials:

Material A	$1.20 per unit
Material B	2.60 per unit
Direct labor	6.05 per hour

	Special Widgets	Deluxe Widgets
Finished products (content of each unit):		
Material A	12 units	12 units
Material B	6 units	8 units
Direct labor	14 hours	20 hours

The general ledger does not include a finished goods inventory account; costs are transferred directly from Work in Process to Cost of Goods Sold at the time finished products are sold.

The budget and operating data for the month of March are summarized as follows:

Budget:

Projected direct labor hours	9,000
Fixed factory overhead	$ 4,500
Variable factory overhead	13,500
Selling expense	4,000
Administrative expense	7,500

Operating data:
Sales:

500 special widgets	$85,000
100 deluxe widgets	25,000

Purchases:

Material A—8,500 units	$ 9,725
Material B—1,800 units	5,635

	Material A	Material B
Materials requisitions:		
Issued from stores:		
Standard quantity	8,400 units	3,200 units
Over standard	400 units	150 units
Returned to stores	75 units	none
Direct labor hours:		
Standard		9,600 hours
Actual		10,000 hours

Wages paid:	Expenses:
500 hours @ $6.10	Manufacturing $20,125
8,000 hours @ 6.00	Selling 3,250
1,500 hours @ 5.90	Administrative 6,460

Required:

1. Make general journal entries to record operations for the month of March. Show computations of the amounts used in each journal entry. Materials purchases are recorded at standard.

2. Prepare an income statement for the month supported by an analysis of variations.

(AICPA adapted)

Cost Analysis for Management Decision Making

The features that distinguish cost accounting from managerial accounting are not easy to detect. To a degree, the differences between the two areas are subjective. Most cost accounting textbooks (including this one) give considerable attention to the managerial uses of cost data by interweaving the data uses and management needs with the discussions of cost systems. Most managerial accounting textbooks include some discussion of cost systems and the accumulation and processing of cost data. However, a more comprehensive coverage of cost accounting systems (job-order, process, and standard), which are the major thrust of cost accounting texts, increases an individual's analytical ability to resolve the special problems encountered internally by manufacturing firms.

Many studies that generate special reports for management use the regularly accumulated cost data; however, often the system's regularly compliled data must be altered and enhanced to create additional reports because of economic occurrences that were not predicted. These reports, which are prepared for internal use and are not distributed to external parties, require that the user understand terminology not commonly used in operational cost accounting systems. In this chapter, several new terms relating to the special-purpose reports for internal management decision making are introduced and defined.

DIRECT COSTING AND ABSORPTION COSTING

LEARNING OBJECTIVE
Recognize the difference between the direct costing and absorption costing methods of accounting for manufacturing costs

Under the **direct costing method,** the cost of a manufactured product includes only the costs that vary directly with volume: direct materials, direct labor, and variable factory overhead. This method is also referred to as **variable costing,** because only variable manufacturing costs are assigned to the product, while fixed factory overhead is classified as a period cost and charged totally to the period in which the fixed costs were incurred.

The alternative to direct costing is the **absorption costing** or **full cost method** (the method used in the preceding nine chapters). Under this method, both fixed and variable manufacturing costs are assigned to the product and no particular attention is given to classifying the costs as either fixed or variable.

PRODUCT COSTS VERSUS PERIOD COSTS

All costs, both manufacturing and nonmanufacturing, can be classified as either product costs or period costs. As discussed in previous chapters, a **product cost** (or inventory cost) is assigned to Work in Process and subsequently to Finished Goods. When inventory is sold, product costs are recognized as expense (cost of goods sold) and matched with the related revenues. In contrast, **period costs** are not assigned to the product but are recognized as expenses, totally in the period incurred. All nonmanufacturing costs are period costs. These include selling expenses and general and administrative expenses.

The only difference between direct costing and absorption costing is the classification of fixed factory overhead. Under the direct costing method, fixed overhead costs are classified as period costs. Under the absorption costing method, they are treated as product costs.

ILLUSTRATION OF DIRECT AND ABSORPTION COSTING METHODS

To illustrate the differences between direct costing and absorption costing, assume the following conditions for a 3-month period:

Selling price per unit	$11

Variable cost per unit:

Direct cost—materials	$ 2
—labor	2
Indirect cost—variable factory overhead	1
Variable cost per unit	$ 5

Fixed cost per unit:

Fixed factory overhead for the year	$108,000
Normal production for the year in units	36,000
Fixed cost per unit—($108,000 ÷ 36,000)	$3

	Units Produced	Units Sold
January	3,000	1,500
February	500	2,000
March	4,000	2,000

January has no beginning inventories.

The comparative production report in Figure 10-1 shows the costs charged to the product under each costing method. Note that under the absorption costing method, the goods manufactured in January are charged with the standard costs of the direct materials, direct labor, and

FIGURE 10-1   Comparison of Manufacturing Costs for Absorption and Direct Costing Methods

Comparative Production Report

	January (3,000 units)		February (500 units)		March (4,000 units)	
	Absorption Costing	Direct Costing	Absorption Costing	Direct Costing	Absorption Costing	Direct Costing
Direct materials	$ 6,000	$ 6,000	$1,000	$1,000	$ 8,000	$ 8,000
Direct labor	6,000	6,000	1,000	1,000	8,000	8,000
Variable factory overhead	3,000	3,000	500	500	4,000	4,000
Fixed factory overhead	9,000	—	1,500	—	12,000	—
Total cost	$24,000	$15,000	$4,000	$2,500	$32,000	$20,000
Unit cost	$8	$5	$8	$5	$8	$5

both fixed and variable factory overhead, totaling $8 per unit. Under the direct costing method, the fixed factory overhead is not charged to the product, resulting in a unit cost of $5.

Figure 10-2 uses the absorption method to compare the average fixed factory overhead of $9,000 ($108,000 ÷ 12) per month with the amount applied to production. In January, 3,000 units are manufactured, and the manufacturing costs under absorption costing include $9,000 ($3 × 3,000) in fixed factory overhead. February manufacturing costs covering the 500 units produced include fixed factory overhead of $1,500, and the manufacturing costs for March include $12,000. As a result of the overhead charges, in February $7,500 of fixed expense is not included in manufacturing costs; but in March, the fixed overhead is overapplied by $3,000. These variances of underapplied and overapplied factory overhead are reflected in the income statements for February and March as an addition to and a deduction from cost of goods sold, respectively. Under the direct costing method, no fixed factory overhead expenses are charged to production in any month. These fixed costs appear as an expense on each month's income statement.

Figure 10-3 compares the effects on income of the direct and absorption methods. Each month, cost of goods sold reflects a cost of $8 per unit under the absorption method compared to $5 per unit under the direct method. Under the absorption method, the difference between sales revenue and cost of goods sold is termed the **gross margin** or **gross profit**. The term commonly used in direct costing to designate the difference between sales and cost of goods sold is **contribution margin**. Because cost of goods sold determined under the absorption method includes both fixed and variable overhead, but includes only variable overhead under the direct method, the gross margin under absorption costing is always lower than the contribution margin under direct costing.

Under the absorption method, selling and administrative expenses are deducted from the gross margin to determine net income or loss. In

FIGURE 10-2   Schedule of Fixed Overhead Applied under Absorption Cost Method

Fixed Overhead Applied—Absorption Costing

	January	February	March
Monthly fixed factory overhead	$9,000	$9,000	$ 9,000
Fixed factory overhead applied	9,000	1,500	12,000
Under- (over-) applied overhead	-0-	$7,500	$ (3,000)

FIGURE 10-3   Comparison of Net Income for Absorption and Direct Costing Methods

COMPARATIVE INCOME STATEMENTS
For Three Months Ended March 31, 19—

	January (1,500 units sold)		February (2,000 units sold)		March (2,000 units sold)	
	Absorption Costing	Direct Costing	Absorption Costing	Direct Costing	Absorption Costing	Direct Costing
Sales	$16,500	$16,500	$22,000	$22,000	$22,000	$22,000
Cost of goods sold	(12,000)	(7,500)	(16,000)	(10,000)	(16,000)	(10,000)
(Under-)/overapplied factory overhead	—	—	(7,500)	—	3,000	—
Gross margin (loss)	$ 4,500		$ (1,500)		$ 9,000	
Contribution margin		$ 9,000		$12,000		$12,000
Less:						
Fixed factory overhead		(9,000)		(9,000)		(9,000)
Selling and administrative						
expenses	(2,000)	(2,000)	(2,000)	(2,000)	(2,000)	(2,000)
Net income (loss)	$ 2,500	$ (2,000)	$ (3,500)	$ 1,000	$ 7,000	$ 1,000

COMPARATIVE SCHEDULE OF COST OF GOODS SOLD
For Three Months Ended March 31, 19—

Finished goods inventory, January 1 .	—	—	$12,000	$ 7,500	—	—
Cost of goods manufactured	$24,000	$15,000	4,000	2,500	$32,000	$20,000
Goods available for sale	$24,000	$15,000	$16,000	$10,000	$32,000	$20,000
Less finished goods inventory,						
March 31	12,000	7,500	—	—	16,000	$10,000
Cost of goods sold	$12,000	$ 7,500	$16,000	$10,000	$16,000	$10,000

the illustration, these costs are assumed to be $2,000 each month. Under the direct method, the total amount of monthly fixed overhead is deducted from the contribution margin along with selling and administrative expenses. Thus, $9,000 of fixed overhead costs are charged against revenue each month regardless of the number of units produced or sold.

An examination of the comparative income statements in Figure 10-3 reveals the effect that fluctuating production has on reported income under the absorption costing method. Although February sales exceed January sales, the net income decreased from $2,500 in January to a net loss of $3,500 in February under the absorption method. This decrease is caused in part by adding $7,500 of underapplied overhead at the end of February to the cost of goods sold.

March sales are the same as February sales, but reported net income increased from a $3,500 net loss in February to a $7,000 net income in March. This increase is due to the increased production that caused more of the fixed factory overhead to be applied to production in March than in February. In fact, overhead is overapplied in March, and this overapplication is shown as a decrease in cost of goods sold on the March statement.

A study of the income statement under the direct costing method shows that as sales increase in February, income also increases. When sales remain the same in March as they were in February, income does not change.

With the absorption costing method, inventories have a higher cost than under the direct costing method because fixed costs are included in the cost of inventory in the absorption system. This element of fixed cost will not be reported as a charge against revenue until the goods are sold. Under the direct costing method, fixed costs are not included in inventory; they are charged against revenue in the period they are incurred.

MERITS AND LIMITATIONS OF DIRECT COSTING

The merits of direct costing may be viewed in terms of the usefulness of the data provided by its application. Some company managers believe that the direct costing method furnishes more understandable data regarding costs, volumes, revenues, and profits to members of management who are not formally trained in the field of accounting. It presents cost data in a manner that highlights the relationship between sales and variable production costs, which move in the same direction as sales. Furthermore, they believe direct costing helps management planning, because it presents a clearer picture of how changes in production volume affect costs and income. From the direct costing portion of the production report on page 442, management can determine that units produced and sold above normal production will cost only $5 each in out-of-pocket expenditures for variable costs, because the fixed manufacturing costs have been completely absorbed by the expected normal production. Therefore, the additional units will produce a marginal income of $6 each at a selling price of $11. Assume that a plant's capacity is not fully utilized and management has the opportunity to fill a special order at a selling price of $7 each. If management incorrectly used the absorption cost of $8 per unit in Figure 10-1, it would reject the special order. If it correctly compared the selling price of $7 to the additional variable costs of $5 to produce each unit, management would accept the special order and earn additional income of $2 per unit because the fixed overhead cost of $3 per unit had already been absorbed by the normal production and therefore should not be considered in making the decision. Only the additional variable costs should be the determinant.

Although direct costing may provide useful information for internal decision making, it is not a generally accepted method of inventory costing for external reporting purposes. The measurement of income, in traditional accounting theory, is based on the matching of revenues with associated costs. Under absorption costing, product costs include all variable and fixed manufacturing costs. These costs are matched with the sales revenue in the period in which the goods are sold. The direct cost method, however, matches only the variable manufacturing costs with revenue. The absorption method must be used for income tax purposes as well as for external financial statements. Regulations of the Internal Revenue Service specifically prohibit the direct costing method in computing taxable income.

Direct costing has other limitations and criticisms. Even when sophisticated statistical techniques are used to separate costs into variable and fixed components, the results may lead to erroneous conclusions. The procedures often use historical trends and data adjusted for future expectations in order to establish the components; but unforeseen occurrences may have a significant effect on such established cost categories. To avoid overlooking significant changes in cost behavior patterns, a systematic review of the costs and the statistical techniques should be included in the system. Any unexpected event related to previously established plans should trigger an analysis to determine its effect on the designated categories of costs so that faulty data is not used in decision making.

Direct costing is also criticized because no fixed factory overhead cost is included in work in process or finished goods inventories. In the opinion of direct costing opponents, both fixed and variable costs are incurred in manufacturing products. Because the inventory figures do not reflect the total cost of production, they do not present a realistic cost valuation.

Adjustments can be made to the inventory figures to reflect absorption cost on published financial reports while retaining the benefits of direct costing internally for income analysis purposes. In the example given, the unit cost was $5 under the direct costing method and $8 under the absorption method. The absorption method reflects 60% more cost than the direct costing method; therefore, inventories could be adjusted as follows:

	Ending Inventory Under the Direct Costing Method	Absorption-Direct Cost Ratio ($8 ÷ $5)	Ending Inventory Under the Absorption Costing Method
January	$ 7,500	× 160%	$12,000
February	None		None
March	$10,000	× 160%	$16,000

You should now be able to work the following: Exercises 1, 2, 3 and Problem 1.

SEGMENT REPORTING FOR PROFITABILITY ANALYSIS

Segment reporting provides data that management can use to evaluate the operations and profitability of individual segments within a company. A **segment** may be a division, a product line, a sales territory, or other identifiable organizational unit.

The results of a segment profitability analysis may be questioned as to its validity if it is based on absorption costing data. This is due to the fact that the measure of each company segment's profitability may be distorted by arbitrarily assigning indirect costs to the segments being examined. The contribution margin approach (as used in direct costing), which separates the fixed and variable elements that comprise cost, is often used to overcome these objections.

Segment profitability analysis requires that all costs be classified into one of two categories: direct or indirect. A **direct (traceable) cost** is a cost that can be traced to the segment being analyzed. Direct costs include both variable and fixed costs directly identifiable with a specific segment. An **indirect (nontraceable) cost** is a cost that cannot be identified directly with a specific segment. This cost is often referred to in segment analysis as a **common cost.** Under the contribution margin approach, only those costs directly traceable to a segment are assigned to the segment. The excess of segment revenue over direct costs assigned to the segment is called the **segment margin.** Common costs are excluded from the computation of the segment margin.

Although common costs cannot be directly identified with a specific segment, they are identifiable as common to all segments at a particular level of an organization. Often the differences between direct and common costs are not markedly distinctive; however, the costs that will disappear when the company eliminates the segment should be classified as direct costs. Costs difficult to classify should not be assigned without a careful evaluation.

The more refinement and sophistication attempted in segment reporting, the larger the amount of costs that will become common costs. For instance, if a company consists of two divisions, each division manager's salary would be a direct cost to the division. However, if each division manufactured two products, each division's product segment report would classify the manager's salary as a common cost. Arbitrarily allocating the manager's salary to a product would distort the profitability shown for each product.

The following table shows two segment reports, one listed by divisions and the other listed by products for one of the divisions. The company is divided into two divisions, and each division manufactures two products.

	Segment Report by Divisions			Segment Report by Product —Division One		
	Total Company	Division One	Division Two	Total Division One	Product A	Product B
Sales	$1,000,000	$750,000	$250,000	$750,000	$500,000	$250,000
Less variable costs	800,000	675,000	125,000	675,000	450,000	225,000
Contribution margin	$ 200,000	$ 75,000	$125,000	$ 75,000	$ 50,000	$ 25,000
Less direct fixed costs:						
Production	$ 50,000	$ 25,000	$ 25,000	$ 20,000	$ 10,000	$ 10,000
Administration	75,000	40,000	35,000	15,000	10,000	5,000
Total direct fixed costs . . .	$ 125,000	$ 65,000	$ 60,000	$ 35,000	$ 20,000	$ 15,000
Segment margin	$ 75,000	$ 10,000	$ 65,000	$ 40,000	$ 30,000	$ 10,000
Less common fixed costs:						
Selling	$ 30,000					
Production				$ 5,000		
Administration	20,000			25,000		
Total common fixed costs .	$ 50,000			$ 30,000		
Segment margin				$ 10,000		
Net income	$ 25,000					

An analysis of the segment report by divisions reveals that the division segment margin was $75,000 for the total company. Division One contributed $10,000 to the margin and Division Two, $65,000. The direct fixed costs chargeable to the divisions totaled $125,000, and the nonallocated common fixed costs totaled $50,000.

When Division One is isolated and analyzed to determine how each product contributed to the segment margin of $10,000, the direct fixed costs chargeable to the individual products amount to $35,000. Product A is charged $20,000 and Product B, $15,000. Division One has nonallocated common fixed costs of $30,000, not directly chargeable to either product. For example, the $25,000 for Administration listed under common fixed costs may represent the salary of the manager of Division One who oversees the production of both products. These reports reveal how costs shift from one category to another depending on the segment under scrutiny. Each segment report prepared for a company isolates those costs, variable and fixed, that can be charged directly to the segment elements. As different segments are analyzed, these costs may be direct costs in one segment and indirect (common) costs in another segment.

The divisions' contribution margins are determined by subtracting the variable costs from the sales. The contribution margin can be used as a guide in making management decisions in regard to short-run problems such as pricing of special orders.

The direct fixed costs chargeable to each segment are subtracted from the contribution margin to determine the segment margin. The segment margin can be used as a guide relating to the segment's long-run profitability. In other words, it measures the ability of the division or product to recover not only the assigned variable costs but also the direct fixed costs that must be recovered to keep the company solvent in the long run. In the short run, if a segment margin is positive, the segment should be retained even if the company as a whole is operating at a loss. Because the common fixed costs will usually remain at the same level even if a segment is eliminated, deleting a segment with a positive segment margin will only increase the amount of the company's net loss. The remaining revenue, after direct variable and fixed costs have been deducted, is the amount left to be applied toward the unallocated common costs and the net income of the company as a whole. The segment margin analysis is particularly beneficial as an aid to making decisions that relate to a company's long-run requirements and performance, such as changing production capacities, product pricing policies, decisions to retain or eliminate specific segments, analyses of segment managers' performance, and selecting a segment's expected return on investment.

COST-VOLUME-PROFIT ANALYSIS

LEARNING OBJECTIVE
Recognize the uses and limitations of cost-volume-profit analysis in management decision making

A company's net income is a measure of management's success in attaining its goals. In planning, management must anticipate how selling prices, costs, expenses, and profits will react to changes in activity when the activity is measured in terms of capacity or volume. When the degree of variability in costs is known, the effect of volume changes can be predicted.

Cost-volume-profit (CVP) analysis is a technique that uses the degrees of cost variability to measure the effect of changes in volume on resulting profits. Such analysis assumes that the plant assets of the firm will remain the same in the short run; therefore, the established level of fixed cost will also remain unchanged during the period being studied.

BREAK-EVEN ANALYSIS

The usual starting point in C-V-P analysis is the determination of a firm's break-even point. The break-even point can be defined as the point at which sales revenue is adequate to cover all costs to manufacture and sell the product but no profit is earned. The equation can be stated as follows:

Sales revenue (to break even) = Cost to manufacture + Cost to sell

Break-even analysis relies on segregating costs according to their degree of variability. The established groupings are usually classed as variable and fixed (or nonvariable) costs, and the break-even equation is rewritten as follows:

Sales revenue (to break even) = Fixed costs + Variable costs

The annual income statement for the Mongo Manufacturing Company in condensed form follows.

Mongo Manufacturing Company
Income Statement
For the Year Ended December 31, 19—

Net sales (10,000 units at $10)		$100,000
Cost of goods sold:		
Materials	$20,000	
Labor	25,000	
Factory overhead	15,000	60,000
Gross margin on sales		$ 40,000
Operating expenses:		
Selling expense	$15,000	
Administrative expense	10,000	25,000
Net income		$ 15,000

The costs and expenses of the Mongo Manufacturing Company were analyzed and classified as follows:

Items	Total	Variable Costs	Fixed Costs
Materials	$20,000	$20,000	
Labor	25,000	25,000	
Factory overhead	15,000	10,000	$ 5,000
Selling expense	15,000	10,000	5,000
Administrative expense	10,000	5,000	5,000
	$85,000	$70,000	$15,000

The analysis shows that variable costs are 70% of net sales ($70,000 ÷ $100,000).

The break-even equation in mathematical terms is as follows:

$$\text{Break-even sales volume} = \frac{\text{Total fixed costs}}{1 - (\text{Total variable costs} \div \text{Total sales volume})}$$

Using this equation, the break-even point for the Mongo Manufacturing Company would be as follows:

$$\text{Break-even sales volume} = \frac{\$15,000}{1 - (\$70,000 \div \$100,000)}$$

$$= \frac{\$15,000}{1 - .70}$$

$$= \frac{\$15,000}{.30}$$

$$= \$50,000$$

The break-even point can also be calculated in terms of units by using the following equation:

$$\text{Break-even sales volume} = \frac{\text{Total fixed cost}}{\text{Sales price per unit} - \text{Variable cost per unit}}$$

Using this equation, the break-even point for the Mongo Manufacturing Company would be as follows:

$$\text{Break-even sales volume} = \frac{\$15,000}{\$10 - \$7}$$

$$= \frac{\$15,000}{\$3}$$

$$= 5,000 \text{ units}$$

Note that 5,000 units multiplied by a selling price of $10 per unit equals the $50,000 break-even sales volume computed previously.

The break-even point can be rechecked, if desired, as follows:

Sales at break-even point	$50,000
Less variable costs at break-even point (70% × $50,000)	35,000
Margin available for fixed costs	$15,000
Less fixed costs	15,000
Net income (loss)	-0-

Break-Even Chart. The break-even point can also be graphically depicted by a break-even chart as in Figure 10-4. The break-even chart is constructed and interpreted as follows:

1. A horizontal line, the x-axis, is drawn and divided into equal distances to represent the sales volume in dollars.

FIGURE 10-4   Break-Even Chart

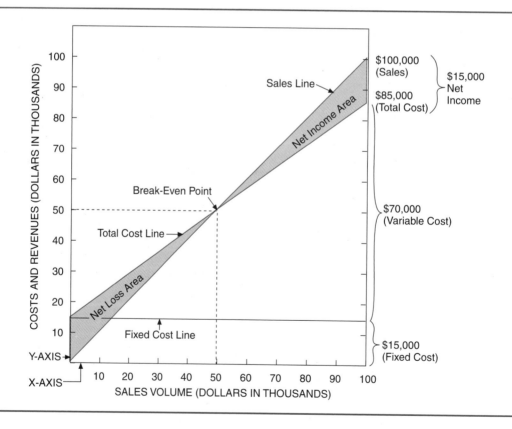

2. A vertical line, the y-axis, is drawn and spaced into equal parts representing costs and revenues in dollars.

3. A fixed cost line is drawn parallel to the x-axis at the $15,000 point on the y-axis.

4. A total cost line is drawn from the $15,000 fixed cost point on the left side of the y-axis to the $85,000 total cost point on the right side of the y-axis.

5. A sales line is drawn from the intersection of the x-axis and y-axis to the $100,000 total sales point on the right side of the y-axis.

6. The sales line intersects the total cost line at the break-even point, representing $50,000 of sales.

7. The shaded area to the left of the break-even point is the net loss area and the shaded area to the right of the break-even point is the net income area.

Break-Even Analysis for Management Decisions. Break-even analysis can be used to help management select an action when several alternatives exist. This analysis is based on the conditions that variable costs will vary in constant proportion to the sales volume and that fixed costs will be fixed over a prescribed or relevant range of activity. If management, therefore, wishes to test new proposals that will change the percentage of variable costs to sales volume, or the total amount of fixed costs, or even a combination of these changes, it can use the basic break-even equation to calculate the results.

For example, assume the Mongo Manufacturing Company has established its break-even point in sales volume at $50,000 and now wishes to determine the point at which an $18,000 net income can be expected. The $18,000 net income is viewed as a nonvariable factor, and the sales volume would be calculated as follows, using a modified equation:

$$\text{Sales volume} = \frac{\text{Total fixed costs} + \text{Net income}}{1 - (\text{Total variable costs} \div \text{Total sales volume})}$$

$$= \frac{\$15,000 + \$18,000}{1 - (\$70,000 \div \$100,000)}$$

$$= \frac{\$33,000}{1 - .70}$$

$$= \frac{\$33,000}{.30}$$

$$= \$110,000$$

The new conditions can be checked, in income statement form, as follows:

Sales	$110,000
Less variable costs (70% × $110,000)	77,000
Margin available for nonvariable factors	$ 33,000
Less fixed costs	15,000
Net income	$ 18,000

Further assume the management of Mongo Manufacturing Company, fearing that changing economic conditions may make it difficult for the company to attain its present sales volume, wants to analyze the effect on the break-even point if it increases the percentage of variable costs to sales and lowers fixed costs. Management believes that fixed costs can be reduced to $5,000, with a corresponding increase in the percentage of variable costs to 80%.

The break-even sales volume calculated with these conditions is as follows:

$$\text{Break-even sales volume} = \frac{\$5,000}{1 - .80}$$

$$= \frac{\$5,000}{.20}$$

$$= \$25,000$$

If the proposed shift from fixed costs to variable costs is accomplished, the break-even point is reduced from $50,000 to $25,000. The higher the variable costs, the smaller the risk of not attaining the expected break-even point. On the other hand, if the sales volume exceeds expectations, a large portion of the sales revenue will be used to cover the variable costs. Therefore, a smaller net income must be anticipated.

To illustrate, assume the Mongo Manufacturing Company achieves a sales volume of $200,000. With a variable cost percentage of 70%, the net income would amount to $45,000. If the fixed costs were reduced to $5,000 and the variable cost percentage increased to 80%, the profit would be only $35,000, a reduction of $10,000 at the same sales volume.

	Variable Cost Rate 70%	80%
Sales	$200,000	$200,000
Variable costs	140,000	160,000
Margin available for nonvariable factors	$ 60,000	$ 40,000
Fixed costs	15,000	5,000
Net income	$ 45,000	$ 35,000

CONTRIBUTION MARGIN RATIO AND MARGIN OF SAFETY

Two terms frequently used in cost-volume-profit relationships are *contribution margin* and *margin of safety*. The contribution margin, introduced in the discussion of direct costing, is the difference between sales revenue and total variable costs and expenses. When an income statement depicts the contribution margin, management can use it as a tool for studying the effects of changes in sales volume. The **contribution margin ratio**, also referred to as the **marginal income ratio**, is the relationship of contribution margin to sales.

The **margin of safety** indicates the amount that sales can decrease before the company will suffer a loss. The **margin of safety ratio** is a relationship computed by dividing the difference between the total sales and the break-even point sales by the total sales.

Sales (10,000 units @ $100)	$1,000,000	100%
Variable costs	600,000	60
Contribution margin	$ 400,000	40%
Fixed costs	300,000	30
Net income	$ 100,000	10%

The contribution margin is $400,000. The contribution margin ratio is calculated as follows:

$$\text{Contribution margin ratio} = \frac{\text{Total sales} - \text{Variable costs}}{\text{Total sales}}$$

$$= \frac{\$1,000,000 - \$600,000}{\$1,000,000}$$

$$= \frac{\$400,000}{\$1,000,000}$$

$$= 40\%$$

Using the contribution margin ratio of 40%, the break-even point can be calculated as follows:

$$\text{Break-even sales volume} = \frac{\text{Fixed costs}}{\text{Contribution margin ratio}}$$

$$= \frac{\$300,000}{.40}$$

$$= \$750,000$$

The margin of safety ratio (M/S) is calculated as follows:

$$\text{Margin of safety ratio} = \frac{\text{Total sales} - \text{Break-even sales volume}}{\text{Total sales}}$$

$$= \frac{\$1,000,000 - \$750,000}{\$1,000,000}$$

$$= \frac{\$250,000}{\$1,000,000}$$

$$= 25\%$$

Using the previous data, the margin of safety is 25% of the total sales, or $250,000. If the break-even sales equal $750,000 but the total expected sales are $1,000,000, the M/S ratio shows that the $1,000,000 in sales can decline by 25% before it reaches the firm's break-even level.

Because the margin of safety is directly related to net income, the M/S ratio can be used to calculate net income as a percentage of sales and vice versa.

Net income percentage = Contribution margin ratio × Margin of safety ratio
= 40% × 25%
= 10% (*Note:* This figure agrees with the net income as a percent of sales as shown in the contribution income statement on page 455.)

$$\text{Margin of safety ratio} = \frac{\text{Net income percentage}}{\text{Contribution margin ratio}}$$

$$= \frac{.10}{.40}$$

$$= 25\%$$

COST-VOLUME-PROFIT LIMITATIONS

Cost-volume-profit analysis assumes that all factors used in the analysis except volume will remain constant (unchanged) for a given period of time. It is unrealistic to assume that the established relationship between sales and production will remain as forecast, or even that the sales mix, as established, will remain constant for any long period. Even price changes that have not been predicted can occur, and the outcome will be substantially affected. If a fairly stable set of relationships cannot be established, a series of analyses should be prepared that recognizes the changing sets of circumstances and their related outcomes.

DIFFERENTIAL COST ANALYSIS

All management requirements cannot be satisfied by one concept or combination of cost data. The designated purpose for which a cost measurement is made needs to be studied carefully to determine what items should be included in the cost analysis. This study should then provide a series of alternative solutions based on the comparison of the different sets of relevant cost data. A study that highlights the significant cost data of alternatives is referred to as **differential cost analysis**.

Assume a company, now operating at 80% capacity, has been asked by a one-time purchaser to sell additional units at less than its established sales price. The company would make a study to determine the difference in costs at the two volume levels.

The company produces 30,000 units at 80% of its total capacity. Its fixed factory overhead costs are $20,000, and it sells each unit for $10. A new customer wishes to purchase 7,500 units for $4 per unit. Should the company agree to the terms or reject the offer?

The variable production costs per unit are as follows:

Direct materials	$2.00
Direct labor	1.00
Variable overhead	.75
Total variable cost per unit	$3.75

At the present level of operations, the total production cost per unit is $4.42 ([(30,000 units × $3.75) + $20,000] ÷ 30,000 units). If the additional units are produced, the total cost per unit would be $4.28 ([(37,500 units × $3.75) + $20,000] ÷ 37,500 units). Because the new customer is offering only $4 per unit, the company apparently should not accept such an offer.

However, when the total fixed factory overhead cost of $20,000 is not affected by producing the additional units, only the differential cost (or variable cost) will increase. Thus, each additional unit produced, and sold at $4, will increase the contribution margin by $.25 ($4 selling price − $3.75 variable cost per unit). If the company accepts the offer, its total increase in the contribution margin would be $1,875 (7,500 units × $.25). Because the fixed cost will not change, the gross margin would also increase by $1,875, shown as follows:

	Accept Order	Reject Order
Sales:		
30,000 units @ $10	$300,000	$300,000
7,500 units @ $ 4	30,000	-0-
Total revenues	$330,000	$300,000
Variable costs	140,625*	112,500**
Contribution margin	$189,375	$187,500
Fixed overhead costs	20,000	20,000
Gross margin on sales	$169,375	$167,500

*37,500 units × $3.75 (variable cost) $140,625
**30,000 units × $3.75 (variable cost) $112,500

The differential cost concept is applicable only when excess capacity exists that can be utilized at little or no increase in fixed cost. Also, in accepting additional orders at selling prices below the usual price levels, care should be exercised so that legislation barring sales to different customers at different prices is not violated or that regular customers will not expect the same price treatment for their purchases.

MAKE OR BUY DECISIONS

A company may buy a finished part that could perhaps be more economically manufactured in its own plant. For example, assume that 40,000 parts are purchased each month at a unit price of $1 per part. All the tools and necessary skills required for manufacturing this part are available in Dept. A of the company.

Dept. A has a total potential capacity of 30,000 direct labor hours per month. The present capacity is 24,000 direct labor hours, or 80%. Analyses of its factory overhead costs include the following:

	Budgeted (80%) 24,000 Hours		Normal (100%) 30,000 Hours	
	Total Costs	Per Hour Costs	Total Costs	Per Hour Costs
Fixed costs	$ 72,000	$3.00	$ 72,000	$2.40
Variable costs	48,000	2.00	60,000	2.00
Total	$120,000	$5.00	$132,000	$4.40
Differential cost			$ 12,000	$ .60

The costs to manufacture 40,000 parts include the following:

Materials	$ 2,000
Labor, 6,000 hours @ $4	24,000
Total	$26,000
Add differential overhead cost of 6,000 labor hours	12,000
Total cost to manufacture parts	$38,000
Cost per unit, $38,000 ÷ 40,000	$ .95

Because Dept. A is presently operating at 80% of its total capacity, the company can save $2,000 ($40,000, purchased cost – $38,000, cost to make) by making the 40,000 parts rather than buying them. If the 80% capacity level in Dept. A is a short-run condition, this factor must be considered before the final decision is made. The estimated savings may not be realized if the excess capacity of the department will soon be required for the company's regularly manufactured products.

DISTRIBUTION COSTS

LEARNING OBJECTIVE
Identify the appropriate techniques to analyze and control the distribution costs incurred in selling and delivering products

Cost accounting is frequently thought of as a method of accounting only for the costs of manufacturing; however, "cost," as a general term, covers more than merely manufacturing costs; it should include all of the costs of doing business. In other words, efficient control of all costs should cover both the production costs and the distribution costs. Distribution costs include the costs incurred to sell and deliver the product.

In recent years, state and federal laws prohibiting discriminatory sale prices and increasing competition have forced accountants to devote more time to the study of distribution costs. An attempt is being made to determine, by means of close and careful analysis, the answers to a variety of questions:

1. How much of the selling and administrative expense is allocable to each type of product sold?
2. How much of the selling and administrative expense is allocable to each particular sales office?
3. How much of the selling and administrative expense is allocable to each salesperson?
4. How much of the selling and administrative expense is allocable to each order sold?

ALLOCATING DISTRIBUTION COSTS

To illustrate some of the difficulties encountered, assume a company that sells bakery products also operates a fleet of delivery trucks to distribute the finished items. Each driver is a salesperson; therefore, each truck is a combination sales and delivery truck. At each stop, the driver takes an order from the store manager for bread, cakes, cookies, and other bakery products carried on the truck and then stocks the shelves. In one store, fifteen minutes may be spent selling four dozen loaves of bread, two dozen breakfast rolls, and a dozen boxes of doughnuts; while in another store, the salesperson may need forty-five minutes to sell only a dozen loaves of bread. Suppose the daily costs of the operation are $50 for the salesperson-driver's salary, $30 for truck depreciation, $15 for gasoline and oil, and $5 for miscellaneous operating expenses.

How much of the total truck expense is chargeable to each sale? Should it be allocated on the basis of the number of sales made? Should it be allocated on the basis of the time spent at each stop by the driver? What is the cost of selling a loaf of bread, a dozen doughnuts, or a package of breakfast rolls?

These questions are not academic, and businesses devote a considerable amount of time attempting to arrive at meaningful answers to such questions. The following example will show the usefulness of distribution cost studies.

Assume that a company is making three products, A, B, and C. The manufacturing cost per unit follows:

A	$10
B	15
C	5

During one month, 1,000 units of each product are sold at $15, $18, and $6 each, respectively. The gross margin for the month would be $9,000 ($39,000 – $30,000). If the selling and administrative expense for the month is $4,000, the net income for the month would be $5,000, a result that management would probably regard as satisfactory.

Now assume that study indicates that the distribution cost per product as follows:

Expense	A	B	C	Total
Selling expenses:				
Salaries	$ 300	$200	$ 300	$ 800
Commissions			500	500
Advertising	600	200	200	1,000
Telephone and telegraph	40		60	100
Sales manager's salary	133	133	134	400
Miscellaneous selling expense . . .	127	17	56	200
Total selling expense	$1,200	$550	$1,250	$3,000
Administrative expense	300	350	350	1,000
Total	$1,500	$900	$1,600	$4,000
Cost per unit	$1.50	$.90	$1.60	

To arrive at these figures, the company needed to make a study of the prevailing conditions and to allocate the various expenses to the products on some reasonable basis. For example, sales salaries might be allocated to the products on the basis of time reports showing the amount of time devoted to selling each product. Advertising might be allocated on the basis of the number of square inches of advertising space purchased for advertising each product. The sales manager's salary might be allocated evenly among the products. Miscellaneous selling expense might be allocated on the basis of the number of orders received for each product or the value of each product sold. No standard basis for allocating such expenses exist, but every effort should be made to use a reasonable basis for allocating each type of expense to the various products.

Using the preceding cost and sales data, it becomes apparent that a profit is actually being made only on products A and B. Product C is being sold at a loss. The following table, based on the sales for the month, shows the extent of the gain and loss:

Product	Cost to Make	Cost to Sell	Total Cost	Selling Price	Profit (Loss)
A	$10,000	$1,500	$11,500	$15,000	$3,500
B	15,000	900	15,900	18,000	2,100
C	5,000	1,600	6,600	6,000	(600)
Total	$30,000	$4,000	$34,000	$39,000	$5,000

As a result of the analysis of distribution costs, management determines that the company might make more money by selling less. If the sale of product C were discontinued, the profit would be greater by the amount of the loss being sustained on C. However, if a more intensive study were undertaken, it may show that products A and B could not sustain their profit margins if the inescapable costs charged to product C, such as the sales manager's salary, had to be charged to A and B. Also, the intangible benefits derived from continuing to carry product C must be considered. Frequently, the intangible factors play a major role in determining whether one action or another is more justified. The overall effect on the company usually determines such decisions.

DETERMINING THE OPTIMUM SIZE OF THE SALES FORCE

Another distribution cost problem may be determining the optimum size of a company's sales force. To resolve this problem, management should review the marginal income that could result from hiring additional salespeople. The sales saturation point is reached when the marginal revenue from sales generated by one additional salesperson is less than the marginal costs that apply to that person.

Suppose three salespeople are used in a regional area where the following sales have been made during the past three years:

Salesperson	19X1	19X2	19X3
1	$128,000	$132,000	$135,000
2	94,000	98,000	100,000
3	90,000	95,000	95,000
	$312,000	$325,000	$330,000

The sales record of the three salespeople indicates that a dramatic increase in sales should not be expected, although sales have improved a small amount in total each year.

Management analyzes the company's total costs and classifies them into fixed and variable categories. The costs directly related to selling activities are then summarized to determine whether an increase or decrease in the number of salespeople would be justified. The analysis, which uses only variable factors, follows:

Variable Costs

Number of Sales-people	Estimated Potential Sales	Variable Factory Costs	Sales Commis-sions	Other Variable Costs	Total Vari-able Costs	Mar-ginal Sales	Mar-ginal Costs	Marginal Profit or (Loss)
1	$135*	$ 65	$20.25	$ 25.90	$111.15	$135	$111.15	$23.85
2	235	120	35.25	45.20	200.45	100	89.30	10.70
3	330	170	47.25	73.40	290.65	95	90.20	4.80
4	410	225	57.00	97.60	379.60	80	88.95	(8.95)
5	480	270	66.00	127.30	463.30	70	83.70	(13.70)

*All figures are in thousands of dollars.

Each of the three salespeople employed by the company produces a marginal profit that ranges from $23,850 to $4,800. An additional salesperson should not be added because that person's marginal contribution would be a loss of $8,950. Although the marginal costs will decline by increasing the volume, the sales dollars generated at the higher production levels are not adequate to improve the company's profitability. The fifth salesperson, for example, would add $70,000 to sales; but the additional costs of using the fifth person would be $83,700.

The preceding illustration shows how the size of a sales force can be determined. Often, however, this problem is resolved incorrectly through intuition rather than by analysis of quantitative data, even though the issue is very significant for most businesses.

MEASURING COSTS IN A SERVICE BUSINESS

In a service business, the major resource is people. An article in *Management Accounting* discusses how to measure productivity and determine costs in a service business.

How do we go about determining productivity and measuring costs in the service sector? Because service businesses are labor intensive, we will need to go back to the source—people, and develop new managerial strategies and methods to define and measure the utilization of human capital. For the most part, this is already being done in manufacturing for the production of goods.

Almost from the beginning of the Industrial Revolution, cost analysis has been applied and fine-tuned in the industrial sector but only infrequently applied in the service area. Herein lies the opportunity for the modern manager.

We suggest here what may be a useful approach to the determination and measurement of productive costs in a service firm. This approach is similar to the standard cost method employed in many manufacturing companies, whether direct or full cost systems. The standard costing process facilitates management's evaluation as to whether or not the economic activity of the enterprise is being carried on efficiently. By providing a bench mark or a yardstick of performance, it allows management to take action when necessary to correct a problem or inefficiency.

Richard W. Possett, "Measuring Productive Costs in the Service Sector," *Management Accounting* (October 1980), pp. 16–24.

K E Y   T E R M S

Absorption costing, p. 441
Break-even analysis, p. 450
Break-even point, p. 450
Common cost, p. 447
Contribution margin, p. 443
Contribution margin ratio, p. 455
Cost-volume-profit (CVP) analysis, p. 450
Differential cost analysis, p. 457
Direct costing, p. 441
Direct traceable cost, p. 447
Distribution costs, p. 459
Full cost method, p. 441

Gross margin, p. 443
Gross profit, p. 443
Indirect nontraceable costs, p. 447
Marginal income ratio, p. 455
Margin of safety, p. 455
Margin of safety ratio, p. 455
Period cost, p. 441
Product cost, p. 441
Segment, p. 447
Segment margin, p. 447
Variable costing, p. 441

QUESTIONS

1. What is the difference between absorption costing and direct costing?

2. What effect will applying of the direct costing method have on the income statement and the balance sheet?

3. What are the advantages and disadvantages of using the direct costing method?

4. Why are there objections to using absorption costing when segment reports of profitability are being prepared?

5. What are common costs?

6. How is a contribution margin determined and why is it important to management?

7. What are considered direct costs in segment analysis?

8. What is cost-volume-profit analysis?

9. What is the break-even point?

10. What steps are required in constructing a break-even chart?

11. What is the difference between contribution margin and the margin of safety ratio?

12. What is differential cost analysis?

13. What is the importance of make-or-buy studies for a company?

14. What are distribution costs?

15. What is the purpose of the analysis of distribution costs?

16. In cost analysis, what governs which costs are to be included in the study?

EXERCISES

E10-1
Computing unit cost and cost of inventory-direct and absorption costing
Learning Objective 1

Southland Products Company uses a process cost system and applies actual factory overhead to work in process at the end of the month. The following data came from the records for the month of March:

Direct materials	$200,000
Direct labor	$100,000
Variable factory overhead	$ 80,000
Fixed factory overhead	$ 60,000
Selling and administrative expenses	$ 40,000
Units produced	25,000
Units sold	20,000
Selling price per unit	$ 25

There were no beginning inventories and no work in process at the end of the month.

From the information presented, compute the following:

1. Unit cost of production
2. Cost of the ending inventory under
   a. the absorption costing method
   b. the direct costing method

E10-2
Using direct costing and absorption costing
Learning Objective 1

The chief executive officer of the Metals Corporation attended a conference in which one of the sessions was devoted to direct costing. The CEO was impressed by the presentation and has asked that the following data of the Metals Corporation be used to prepare comparative statements using the direct costing method and the company's absorption costing method. The data follow:

Direct material	$ 90,000
Direct labor	120,000
Variable factory overhead	60,000
Fixed factory overhead	150,000
Fixed marketing and administrative expense	180,000

The factory produced 75,000 units during the period and 60,000 units were sold for $600,000.

1. Prepare an income statement using direct costing.
2. Prepare an income statement using absorption costing.
3. Convert the direct costing income determined in part 1 to an absorption costing income.

E10-3
Comparative income statements—direct and absorption costing
Learning Objective 1

Using the information presented in E10-1, prepare comparative income statements for March (a) under absorption costing and (b) under direct costing.

E10-4
Using direct and absorption costing

The following production data came from the records of the Kno-core Company for the year ended, December 31, 19—:

Materials	$480,000
Labor	260,000
Variable factory overhead	44,000
Fixed factory overhead	36,800

During the year, 40,000 units were manufactured but only 35,000 units were sold. If the company adopts the direct costing method, what effect would the adoption have on inventory valuation?
  Compute the following:

1. Total inventoriable costs and the cost of the 5,000 units in the ending inventory, using the direct costing method
2. Cost of the 35,000 units sold and of the 5,000 units in the ending inventory, using the absorption cost method

E10-5
Determining income by absorption costing
Learning Objective 1

A company had income of $50,000 using direct costing for a given period. Beginning and ending inventories for the period were 18,000 units and 13,000 units, respectively. If the fixed overhead application rate was $2 per unit, what was the income using absorption costing?

E10-6
Adjusting direct cost income to absorption net income
Learning Objective 1

The fixed overhead budgeted for the Othero Company at an expected capacity of 500,000 units is $2,500,000. A direct costing system is used internally and the net income is adjusted to an absorption costing net income at year-end. Data collected over the last three years show the following:

	First Year	Second Year	Third Year
Units produced	502,000	498,000	495,000
Units sold	496,000	503,000	495,000
Net income—(direct cost)	$500,000	$521,000	$497,000

Determine the adjustment each year to convert the direct costing income to an absorption costing net income. Compute the absorption costing net income for each year.

E10-7
Using CVP analysis
Learning Objective 3

Omega Company plans to produce two products, X and Y, and to sell 100,000 units of X at $8 a unit and 200,000 units of Y at $6 a unit. Variable costs are 70% of sales for X and 80% of sales for Y. What must the total fixed costs be to realize a total profit of $75,000?

E10-8
Computing break-even and margin of safety
Learning Objective 3

Esso Company has a sales price per unit for its only product at $13. The variable cost per units is $5. In year 19A, the company sold 80,000 units, which was 5,000 units above the break-even point.
    Compute the following:

1. Total fixed expenses
2. Total variable expense at the break-even volume
3. Earnings if in year 19B the margin of safety ratio is 20%

E10-9
Computing break-even plus net income
Learning Objective 3

Fabrix Company sells its only product for $50 per unit. Fixed costs total $600,000 per year. Variable expenses are $1,120,000 when 40,000 units are sold. Fabrix anticipates that its variable expenses will increase 15% per unit in the next year due to material price and labor cost increases.
    How many units must be sold to make a net income of $40,000?

E10-10
Determining units to be sold to exceed a budgeted amount

A department of the Cosee Company has the following data available:

Actual total overhead (fixed plus variable) . .	$198,000
Budget formula	$110,000 plus $ .50 per hour
Total overhead application rate	$1.50 per hour
Controllable variance	$ 8,000 (unfav)
Volume variance	$ 5,000 (fav)

If each unit takes 5 hours to manufacture, and the selling price is $4.50 per unit, use the overhead budget formula to determine how many units must be sold to generate $30,000 more than the total budgeted overhead costs.

E10-11
Using break-even analysis
Learning Objective 3

A company has prepared the following statistics regarding its production and sales at different capacity levels.

Capacity level	60%	80%	100%	120%
Units	60,000	80,000	100,000	120,000
Sales	$240,000	$320,000	$400,000	$480,000
Total costs:				
Variable	$120,000	$160,000	$200,000	$240,000
Fixed	150,000	150,000	150,000	150,000
Total costs	$270,000	$310,000	$350,000	$390,000
Net profit (loss)	$ (30,000)	$ 10,000	$ 50,000	$ 90,000

1. At what point is break-even reached in sales? In capacity?
2. If the company is operating at 60% capacity, should it accept an offer from a customer to buy 10,000 units at $3 per unit?

E10-12
Using CVP analysis
Learning Objective 3

A company has sales of $1,000,000, variable costs of $400,000, and fixed costs of $300,000. Compute the following:

1. Contribution margin ratio
2. Break-even sales volume
3. Margin of safety ratio
4. Net income as a percentage of sales

E10-13
Using break-even analysis

A new product is expected to have sales of $100,000, variable costs of 60% of sales, and fixed costs of $20,000.

1. Using graph paper, construct a break-even chart and label the sales line, total cost line, fixed cost line, break-even point, and net income and net loss areas.
2. From the chart, identify the break-even point and the amount of income or loss if sales are $100,000.

E10-14
Using differential cost analysis—special customer order

Maryann Company manufactures basketballs. The company's forecasted income statement for the year before any special orders follows:

	Amount	Per Unit
Sales	$8,000,000	$10.00
Manufacturing cost of goods sold	6,400,000	8.00
Gross profit	$1,600,000	$ 2.00
Selling expenses	600,000	.75
Operating income	$1,000,000	$ 1.25

Fixed costs included in the forecasted income statement are $4,000,000 in manufacturing cost of goods sold and $400,000 in selling expenses.

A new client placed a special order with Maryann, offering to buy 50,000 basketballs for $5.00 each. The company will incur no additional selling expenses if it accepts the special order. Assuming Maryann has sufficient capacity to manufacture 50,000 more basketballs, by what amount would operating income be increased or decreased as a result of accepting the special order?

(AICPA adapted)

E10-15
Deciding to make or buy

Reid Company needs 20,000 units of a certain part to use in its production cycle. The following information is available:

Cost to Reid to make the part:	
Direct materials	$ 4
Direct labor	16
Variable factory overhead	12
Fixed factory overhead applied	6
Total	$38
Cost to buy the part from the Coldwater Company	$36

If Reid buys the part from Coldwater instead of making it, Reid could not use the released facilities in another manufacturing activity. Seventy percent of the fixed factory overhead applied will continue regardless of what decision is Reid makes.

1. In deciding whether to make or buy the part, what are the total relevant costs to make the part?
2. What decision should Reid make?

(AICPA adapted)

E10-16
Using comparative net income analysis

Ladder Manufacturing Company wishes to determine the profitability of its products and asks the cost accountant to make a comparative analysis of sales, cost of sales, and distribution costs of each product for the year. The accountant gathers the following information, which will be useful in preparing the analysis:

	Product X	Product Y	Product Z
Number of units sold	30,000	20,000	20,000
Number of orders received	5,000	2,500	1,000
Selling price per unit	$50	$75	$100
Cost per unit	$30	$50	$ 75

Advertising expenses total $600,000 for the year, an equal amount being expended to advertise each product. The sales representative's commission is based on the selling price of each unit and is 8% for product X, 12% for product Y, and 16% for product Z. The sales manager's salary of $75,000 per year is allocated evenly to each product. Other miscellaneous selling and administrative expenses are estimated to be $15 per order received.

Prepare an analysis for the Ladder Manufacturing Company that will show in comparative form the net income derived from the sale of each product for the year.

PROBLEMS

P10-1
Absorption and direct costing income statements
Learning Objective 1

Ballast Manufacturing Company has determined the cost of manufacturing a unit of product as follows, based on normal production of 100,000 units per year:

Direct materials	$ 5
Direct labor	4
Variable factory overhead	3
Fixed factory overhead	3
	$15

Operating statistics for the months of March and April include the following:

	March	April
Units produced	12,000	6,000
Units sold	6,000	10,000
Selling and administrative expenses	$12,000	$12,000

The selling price is $18 per unit. There were no inventories on March 1, and there is no work in process on April 30.

Required:

Prepare comparative income statements for each month under each of the following:

1. The absorption costing method
2. The direct costing method

P10-2
Segmented income statement
Learning Objective 2

Greenwood Manufacturing Company manufactures two products, Alpha and Beta, which are sold in two territories designated by the company as East Territory and West Territory. The income statement prepared for the company shows the product-line segments.

Greenwood Manufacturing Company
Income Statement

	Total Sales	Product Lines Alpha		Beta	
Sales	$1,000,000	$600,000	100%	$400,000	100%
Less variable expenses	600,000	420,000	70	180,000	45
Contribution margin . .	$ 400,000	$180,000	30%	$220,000	55%
Less direct fixed costs	200,000	50,000		150,000	
Segment margin . . .	$ 200,000	$130,000		$ 70,000	
Less common fixed costs	120,000				
Net income	$ 80,000				

The territorial product sales are as follows:

	East	West
Alpha	$400,000	$200,000
Beta	200,000	200,000
Total	$600,000	$400,000

The common fixed costs are partially identifiable with East Territory, West Territory, and the general administration as follows:

East Territory	$ 54,000
West Territory	36,000
General administration	30,000
Total common fixed costs	$120,000

Required:

1. Prepare a segmented income statement by territories. The direct fixed costs of the product lines should be treated as common fixed costs on the segmented statement being prepared.
2. What is the significance of this analysis?

P10-3
Segment Reporting
Learning Objective 2

Sew Manufacturing Company has two product lines. The income statement for the year ended December 31 shows the following:

Sew Manufacturing Company
Product Line and Company Income Statement
For the year ended, December 31, 19—

	Product Lines		
	Zig	Zag	Total
Sales	$40,000	$60,000	$100,000
Less variable expenses	16,000	24,000	40,000
Contribution margin	$24,000	$36,000	$ 60,000
Less direct fixed expenses	16,000	14,000	30,000
Product margin	$ 8,000	$22,000	$ 30,000
Less common fixed expenses			12,000
Net income			$ 18,000

The products, Zig and Zag, are sold in two territories, East and West, as follows:

	East	West
Zig sales	$24,000	$16,000
Zag sales	18,000	42,000
Total sales	$42,000	$58,000

The common fixed expenses are traceable to each territory as follows:

East fixed expenses	$ 4,000
West fixed expenses	6,000
Home office administrative fixed expenses	2,000
Total common fixed expenses	$12,000

The direct expenses of Zig, $16,000, and of Zag, $14,000, are not identifiable with either of the two territories.

Required:

1. Prepare income statements segmented by territory for the year that includes a column for the entire company.
2. Why are direct expenses of one type of segment report not direct expenses of another type of segment report?

P10-4
Segment Reporting
Learning Objective 2

Sewell Publishing Company prepares income statements segmented by divisions but the chief operating officer is not certain about how the company is actually performing. Financial data for the year follows:

Segments

	Textbook Division	Professional Division	Total Company
Sales	$360,000	$820,000	$1,180,000
Less variable expenses:			
Manufacturing	$ 64,000	$410,000	$ 474,000
Selling and administrative . . .	8,000	41,000	49,000
Total	$ 72,000	$451,000	$ 523,000
Contribution margin	$288,000	$369,000	$ 657,000
Less direct fixed expenses	30,000	440,000	470,000
Net income	$258,000	$ (71,000)	$ 187,000

The Professional Division appears to be floundering and the CEO believes a closer look should be taken concerning its operating effectiveness. Additional data regarding this division follow:

	Accounting	Executive	Management
Sales	$280,000	$280,000	$260,000
Variable manufacturing expenses as a percentage of sales	60%	40%	50%
Other variable expenses as a percentage of sales	5%	5%	5%
Direct fixed expenses	$100,000	$150,000	$100,000

The Professional Division's accounting books are sold to auditors and controllers. The current data on these two markets follow:

	Sales Market	
	Auditors	Controllers
Sales	$60,000	$110,000
Variable manufacturing expenses as a percentage of sales	60%	60%
Other variable expenses as a percentage of sales	16%	2%
Direct fixed expenses	$40,000	$ 50,000

Required:

1. Prepare an income statement segmented by products of the Professional Division, including a column for the division as a whole.
2. Prepare an income statement segmented by markets of the accounting books of the Professiona Division.
3. Evaluate the accounting books of the Professional Division. Should all books be kept or should some books be discontinued?

P10-5
Break-even analysis
Learning Objective 3

The production of a new product required the Lanier Manufacturing Company to lease additional plant facilities. Based on studies, the following data have been made available:

Estimated annual sales—24,000 units

Estimated costs:	Amount	Per Unit
Materials	$ 96,000	$4.00
Direct labor	14,400	.60
Factory overhead	24,000	1.00
Administrative expense	28,800	1.20
Total	$163,200	$6.80

Selling expenses are expected to be 20% of sales and net income is to amount to $1.20 per unit.

Required:

1. Calculate the selling price per unit.
2. Prepare an income statement for the year.
3. Calculate the break-even point expressed in dollars and in units assuming that administrative expense and overhead are fixed but other costs are fully variable.

(AICPA adapted)

P10-6
Break-even point:
absorption and direct
cost analysis
Learning Objective 3

Williams Company has a maximum productive capacity of 210,000 units per year. Normal capacity is 180,000 units per year. Standard variable manufacturing costs are $10 per unit. Fixed factory overhead is $360,000 per year. Variable selling expense is $5 per unit and fixed selling expense is $252,000 per year. The unit sales price is $20.

The operating results for the year are as follows: sales, 150,000 units; production, 160,000 units; beginning inventory, 10,000 units; and the net unfavorable variance for standard variable manufacturing costs, $40,000. All variances are written off as additions to (or deductions from) the standard cost of sales.

Required:

1. What is the break-even point expressed in dollar sales?
2. How many units must be sold to earn a net income of $100,000 per year?
3. How many units must be sold to earn a net income of 15% on sales?
4. Prepare a formal income statement for the year under the following:
   a. Absorption costing (*Hint*: Don't forget to compute the volume variance.)
   b. Direct costing
5. Explain briefly the difference in net income between the two income statements.

(AICPA adapted)

P10-7
Calculating a sales price and break-even point
Learning Objective 3

Hondona Company is considering building a manufacturing plant in Mexico. Predicting sales of 100,000 units, Hondona estimates the following expenses:

	Total Annual Expenses	Percent of Total Annual Expenses That Are Fixed
Material	$19,000	10%
Labor	26,000	20%
Overhead	40,000	40%
Marketing and administration	14,000	60%
	$99,000	

A Mexican firm that specializes in marketing will be engaged to sell the manufactued product and will receive a commission of 10% of the sales price. None of the U.S. home office expense will be allocated to the Mexican facility.

Required:

1. Compute the sales price per unit that will cover all total annual expenses for the Mexican plant.
2. If unit sales price is $2, how many units must be sold to break even?

P10-8
Contribution margin and break-even analysis
Learning Objective 3

Palmer, Inc., produces and sells a product with a price of $100 per unit. The following cost data have been prepared for its estimated upper and lower limits of activity:

	Lower Limit	Upper Limit
Production (units)	4,000	6,000
Production costs:		
Direct materials	$ 60,000	$ 90,000
Direct labor	80,000	120,000
Overhead:		
Indirect materials	25,000	37,500
Indirect labor	40,000	50,000
Depreciation	20,000	20,000
Selling and administrative expenses:		
Sales salaries	50,000	65,000
Office salaries	30,000	30,000
Advertising	45,000	45,000
Other	15,000	20,000
Total	$365,000	$477,500

Required:

1. Classify each cost element as either variable, fixed, or semivariable.
2. Calculate the break-even point in units and dollars.
3. Prepare a break-even chart.
4. Prepare a contribution income statement, similar in format to the statement appearing at the top of page 454, assuming sales of 5,000 units.
5. Recompute the break-even point in units and dollars, assuming that variable costs increase by 20% and fixed costs are reduced by $50,000.

P10-9
Make or buy

Repel Corporation produces and sells a line of insect repellants that are sold usually in the summer months. Recently, the chief operating officer has become interested in possibly manufacturing a repellant that can prevent a person from being attacked if sprayed by a "pepper" repellant. The appeal of this product is that it would have year-around sales and would help stabilize the income of the company.

The product, however, must be sold in a specially designed spray can that will be safe from accidently being discharged. The product will be sold in cartons that hold 24 cans of the repellant. The sale price will be $96 per carton. The plant is now operating at only 65% of its total capacity, so no additional fixed costs will be incurred. However, a $100,000 fixed charge will be allocated to the new product from the company's present total of fixed costs.

Using the current estimates for 100,000 cartons of "Pepper" as a standard volume, the following costs were developed for each carton:

Direct materials	$12
Direct labor	6
Overhead	4
Total cost per carton	$22

Repel Corporation has requested a bid from a manufacturer of speciality dispensers for a purchase price of an empty can that could be used for the new product. The speciality company offered a price of $4 for a carton of cans. If the proposal is accepted, Repel estimates that direct labor and variable overhead costs would be reduced by 10% and direct materials would be reduced by 20%.

Required:

1. Should the Repel Corporation make or buy the special cans?
2. What would be the maximum purchase price acceptable to Repel Corporation for the cans?

P10-10
Expanding a market with a special order

Harold Manufacturing, Inc., is presently operating at 50% of practical capacity, producing annually about 50,000 units of a patented surgical component. Harold recently received an offer from a company in Yokohama, Japan, to purchase 30,000 components at $6 per unit, FOB Harold's plant. Harold has not previously sold components in Japan. Budgeted production costs for 50,000 and 80,000 units of output follow:

	50,000	80,000
Units		

Costs:		
Direct materials	$ 75,000	$120,000
Direct labor	75,000	120,000
Factory overhead	200,000	260,000
Total cost	$350,000	$500,000
Cost per unit	$7.00	$6.25

The sales manager thinks the order should be accepted, even if it results in a loss of $1 per unit, because the sales may build up future markets. The production manager does not wish to have the order accepted, primarily because the order would show a loss of $.25 per unit when computed on the new average unit cost. The treasurer made a quick computation indicating that accepting the order will actually increase gross margin.

Required:

1. Explain what apparently caused the drop in cost from $7 per unit to $6.25 per unit when budgeted production increased from 50,000 to 80,000 units. Show supporting computations.
2. Explain the following:
   a. Whether (either or both) the production manager or the treasurer is correct.
   b. Why the conclusions of the production manager and treasurer differ. Assuming that this order is a one time occurrence, whose conclusion would you support?
3. Explain why each of the following may affect the decision to accept or reject the special order:
   a. The likelihood of repeat special sales and/or all sales to be made at $6 per unit.
   b. Whether the sales are made to customers operating in two separate, isolated markets or whether the sales are made to customers competing in the same market.

P10-11
Differential costs analysis

Arhor Company manufactures household products such as windows, light fixtures, ladders, and work tables. During the year it produced 10,000 Model 10X windows but only sold 5,000 units at $40 each. The remaining units cannot be sold through normal channels. Cost for inventory purposes on December 31 included the following data on the unsold units:

Materials	$10.00
Labor	5.00
Variable overhead	3.00
Fixed overhead	2.00
Total cost per window	$20.00

Arhor can sell the 5,000 windows at a liquidation price of $10.00 per window, but it will incur a packaging and shipping charge of $6.00 per window.

Required:

1. Identify the relevant costs and revenues for the liquidation sale alternative.
2. Assume that the Model 10X can be reprocessed to another size window, Model 20X, which also costs $20 to produce but sells for only $25. Determine the most profitable course of action.

P10-12
Distribution cost
analysis
Learning Objective 4

Vega Corporation's actual and standard distribution cost data for the month of January follow:

	Budget at Standard Cost	Actual Operations
Sales	$750,000	$750,000
Direct distribution costs:		
Selling	$ 12,000	$ 15,000
Shipping salaries	7,000	9,450
Indirect distribution costs:		
Order-filling	17,250	21,500
Other	2,100	2,500
Total costs	$ 38,350	$ 48,450

Additional data:
a. Vega Corporation sells a single product for $10 per unit.
b. Shipping salaries and indirect distribution costs are allocated on the basis of shipping hours.
c. Data on January shipping hours follow:

	Shipping Hours
Budgeted	3,500
Standard operating level	4,400
Actual	4,500

d. Order-filling costs are allocated on the basis of sales and are comprised of freight, packing, and warehousing costs. An analysis of the amount of these standard costs by unit order-size follows:

Unit-Volume Classifications	Order-Filling Standard Costs Classified by Unit Order-Size			
	1–15	16–50	More than 50	Total
Freight	$ 1,200	$ 1,440	$ 2,250	$ 4,890
Packing	2,400	3,240	4,500	10,140
Warehousing	600	720	900	2,220
Total	$ 4,200	$ 5,400	$ 7,650	$17,250
Units sold	12,000	18,000	45,000	75,000

Required:

1. Compute rate and efficiency variances from standard cost for the following. (The analyses should compare actual costs and standard costs at the standard operating level.)

a. Shipping salaries
b. Indirect distribution costs—other

2. Management realizes that the distribution cost per unit decreases with an increase in the size of the order and, hence, wants to revise its unit sales prices upward or downward on the basis of the quantity ordered to reflect the allocated freight, packing, and warehousing standard costs. Management assumes that the revised unit prices will require no changes in standards for sales volume, the number of units sold in each order-size classification, and the profit per unit sold.

    a. For each unit-volume classification, prepare a schedule computing the standard cost per unit for each order-filling cost: freight, packing, and warehousing. Use the format shown in part d above.

    b. Prepare a schedule computing the revised unit sales prices for each unit-volume classification that would enable total sales revenue to remain at $750,000. (*Hint:* let x = the unit sales price of 1–15 units.)

(AICPA adapted)

P10-13
Optimum size of sales force
Learning Objective 4

A new company has completed a study showing that if five salespeople are hired, the sales to be made by each salesperson would be as follows:

Salesperson	Sales
1	$200,000
2	180,000
3	160,000
4	140,000
5	120,000
	$800,000

An analysis of the total costs of the company shows that variable costs associated with the different levels of sales are as follows:

Sales	Variable Costs
$200,000	$105,000
380,000	217,500
540,000	337,500
680,000	465,000
800,000	592,500

Additionally, each salesperson will be paid a commission of 10% on total sales.

Required:

Determine the number of salespeople the company should hire. Show computations.

GLOSSARY

A

Abnormal losses. Units lost in production due to circumstances not inherent in the manufacturing process. Such losses are not expected under normal, efficient operating conditions and are accounted for as period costs.

Absorption costing. A method of accounting for manufacturing costs that charges both fixed and variable costs to the product; also referred to as the "full cost" method.

Accounting information system. A set of procedures designed to provide the financial information needed within a business organization.

Activity-based costing (ABC). A method of applying overhead to products that considers new volume-related activities that create overhead costs as well as volume-related activities.

Adjusted sales value. A basis for allocating joint costs which takes into consideration the cost of processing after split-off.

Adjusted unit cost. The unit cost of a product after adjustment for units lost in the manufacturing process.

Algebraic distribution method. A method for allocating service department costs to production departments using algebraic techniques. While this method may provide the most accurate distribution of costs, it is more complicated than the other methods and the results obtained may not justify the additional effort involved.

Applied Factory Overhead. The account credited when applying estimated overhead to production; the debit is to Work in Process. Use of a separate "applied" account avoids confusion with actual overhead costs charged to Factory Overhead, the control account in the general ledger.

Attainable standard. A performance criterion that recognizes inefficiencies that are likely to result form such factors as lost time, spoilage, or waste.

Average cost method. A commonly used procedure for assigning costs to the ending inventories under a process cost accounting system. Under this method, ending inventories are valued using an average unit cost, computed as follows: (cost of beginning work in process + current period production costs) divided by the total equivalent production for the period.

B

Backflush costing. The name for the accounting system used with JIT manufacturing. Costs are not "flushed out" of the accounting system until goods are completed and sold.

Bar codes. These are symbols that can be processed electronically to identify numbers, letters, or special characters.

Bonus pay. An amount paid to employees in addition to regular earnings for outstanding performance, as a result of higher-than-usual company profits, or for a variety of other reasons.

Break-even analysis. An analytical technique based on the determination of a break-even point expressed in terms of sales revenue or sales volume.

Break-even point. The point at which sales revenue adequately covers all costs to manufacture and sell the product but no profit is earned.

Budget. Management's operating plan expressed in quantitative terms, such as units of production and related costs.

Budgeted income statement. A summary of anticipated revenues and expenses for the coming year based on budgets for sales, manufacturing costs, and nonmanufacturing expenses (selling, administrative, and other).

Budget for manufacturing costs. Budget of the costs of materials, labor, and factory overhead for each month (or shorter period) of the coming year.

Budget for receivables. Shows when cash can be expected from the turnover of inventory and receivables.

Budgets for administrative, selling, and other expenses. Individual budgets showing anticipated expenses for administrative, selling, and other nonmanufacturing activities; prepared after the level of activity for sales and production have been determined.

Budget variance—(two-variance method). The difference between budgeted factory overhead at the capacity attained and the actual factory overhead incurred.

By-products. Secondary products with relatively little value that are obtained in the process of manufacturing the primary product.

C

Capital additions budget. A plan for the timing of acquisitions of buildings, equipment, and other operating assets during the year.

Carrying costs. The costs incurred as a result of maintaining (carrying) inventories. These costs generally include: materials storage and handling costs; interest, insurance, and taxes; losses from theft, deterioration, or obsolescence; and recordkeeping and supplies.

Cash budget. Budget showing the anticipated flow of cash and the timing of receipts and disbursements based on projected sales, manufacturing costs, and other expenses.

Clock card. A preprinted card used to record the total amount of time spent in the factory by an employee.

Common cost. The term used in segment analysis to describe a cost that cannot be traced to, or specifically identified with, a particular business segment.

Contribution margin. The difference between sales revenue and variable manufacturing costs.

Contribution margin ratio. The relationship of contribution margin to sales.

Control. The process of monitoring the company's operations and determining whether the objectives identified in the planning process are being accomplished.

Controllable variance. The amount of the actual factory overhead costs differ from the standard overhead costs for the attained level of production.

Conversion cost. The combined cost of direct labor and factory overhead, which are necessary to convert the direct materials into finished goods.

Cost accounting. The branch of accounting that focuses on providing the detailed cost data that management needs in controlling current operations and planning for the future.

Cost accounting system. A set of methods and procedures used by a manufacturing organization to accumulate detailed cost data relating to the manufacturing process.

Cost and production report. A summary of cost and production data for a particular cost center.

Cost behavior. The determination of whether costs are fixed or variable.

Cost center. A unit of activity, such as a department, within the factory to which costs may be practically and equitably assigned.

Cost driven. The basis used to allocate each of the activities in activity-based costing such as number of setups and number of design changes.

Cost of production summary. A report that summarizes production costs for a period for each department and provides the information necessary for inventory valuation.

Cost-volume-profit analysis. An analytical technique that uses the degrees of cost variability for measuring the effect of changes in volume on resulting profits.

D

Debit-credit memorandum. A document used to notify the vendor that materials received do not correspond with materials ordered.

Defective units. Units of product with imperfections that are considered correctable because the market value of the corrected unit will be greater than the total cost incurred for the unit.

Department-type analysis sheet. One form of factory overhead analysis sheet; a separate analysis sheet is maintained for each department, with individual amount columns for each type of overhead expense.

Differential cost analysis. A study that highlights the significant cost data of alternatives.

Differential costs. The costs that are highlighted from a series of alternative solutions that compare different sets of relevant cost data.

Direct charge. A charge that can be exactly measured and charged to a specific department.

Direct (traceable) cost. The term used in segment analysis to describe a cost that can be traced to a specific business segment.

Direct costing. A method of accounting for manufacturing costs that charges the product with only the costs that vary directly with volume-direct materials, direct labor, and variable factory overhead. This method is also referred to as "variable costing."

Direct distribution method. A method for allocating service department costs to production departments. No attempt is made to determine the extent to which service departments provide services to each other; instead, all service department costs are distributed directly to the production departments.

Direct labor. The cost of labor for employees who work directly on the product being manufactured.

Direct labor cost method. A method of applying factory overhead to production based on the amount of direct labor cost incurred for a job or process.

Direct labor hour method. A method of applying factory overhead to production based on the number of direct labor hours worked on a job or process.

Direct materials. Materials which become part of the product being manufactured and which can be readily identified with a certain product.

Distribution costs. Costs incurred to sell and deliver a product.

E

Economic order quantity. The optimal (most economical) quantity of materials that should be ordered at one time; represents the order size which minimizes total order and carrying costs.

Efficiency variance. The difference between overhead applied (standard hours at the standard rate) and the actual hours worked multiplied by the standard rate; indicates the effect on fixed and variable overhead costs when actual hours worked are more or less than standard hours allowed for the production volume.

Employee earnings record. A form prepared for each employee showing the employee's earnings each pay period and cumulative earnings for each quarter and for the year.

Equivalent production. The number of units that could have been completed during a period using the total production costs for the period.

Expense-type analysis sheet. One form of factory overhead analysis sheet; a separate analysis sheet is used for each type of overhead expense with individual amount columns for each department.

F

Factory ledger. A separate ledger containing all the accounts relating to manufacturing, including the inventory accounts; it is maintained at the factory and tied to the general ledger through a special account.

Factory overhead. All costs related to the manufacturing of a product except direct materials and direct labor; these costs include indirect materials, indirect labor, and other manufacturing expenses such as depreciation, supplies, utilities, maintenance, insurance, and taxes.

Factory overhead analysis sheets. A subsidiary record of factory overhead expenses; replaces a subsidiary factory overhead ledger. Analysis sheets are commonly used by larger enterprises with several departments and many different types of overhead expenses.

Factory overhead ledger. A subsidiary ledger containing the individual factory overhead accounts; the total of the individual account balances in the subsidiary ledger should equal the balance in the control account, Factory Overhead, in the general ledger.

Favorable variance. The difference between actual and standard costs when actual costs are less than standard costs.

Federal Insurance Contributions Act (FICA). Federal legislation requiring both employers and employees to pay social security taxes on wages and salaries.

Federal Unemployment Tax Act (FUTA). Federal legislation requiring employers to pay an established rate of tax on wages and salaries to provide for compensation to employees if they are laid off from their regular employment.

Financial accounting. The branch of accounting that focuses on the gathering of information to be used in the preparation of external financial statements; i.e., balance sheet, income statement, and statement of cash flows.

Finished goods. The inventory account that represents the total cost incurred in manufacturing goods that are complete but still on hand at the end of the accounting period.

First-in, first-out. An inventory costing method based on the assumption that materials issued are taken from the oldest materials in stock. Thus, materials issued are costed at the earliest prices paid for materials in stock and ending inventories are costed at the most recent purchase prices.

Fixed costs. Manufacturing costs that remain constant when production levels increase or decrease; examples include straight-line depreciation, periodic rent payments, insurance, and salaries paid to production executives.

Flexible budget. A budget that shows expected costs at different production levels.

Flow of costs. The order in which materials are actually issued for use in the factory.

Flow of materials. The order in which unit costs are assigned to materials issued.

Forecast of sales. A budget of projected sales expressed in both units and dollars; serves as a basis for preparation of all other budgets.

For-profit service businesses. These are businesses that sell services rather than products such as airlines and accountants.

Four-variance method. The analysis of fixed and variable factory overhead costs based on the computation of a spending variance and an efficiency variance for variable costs and a budget variance and a volume variance for fixed costs.

Full cost method. See Absorption costing.

G

General factory overhead expenses. Overhead expenses that cannot be identified with a specific department and must be charged to departments by a process of allocation.

Gross margin. The difference between sales revenue and cost of goods sold; also referred to as "gross profit."

Gross profit. See Gross margin.

Gross profit percentage (or mark-on percentage). A percentage of manufacturing cost per unit; the percentage is applied to manufacturing cost to determine the gross profit which, in turn, is added to manufacturing cost to determine selling price.

Guaranteed annual wage (GAW). An amount to be paid to employees over a specified period of time in the event of a layoff or plant shutdown.

H

High-low method. A method used to isolate the fixed and variable elements of a semivariable cost; involves comparison of a high volume and its related cost with a low volume and its related cost to determine the variable amount per unit and the fixed element.

Holiday pay. An amount paid to employees for designated holidays on which the employee is not required to work.

Hourly-rate plan. A wage plan under which an employee is paid an established rate per hour for each hour worked.

I

Ideal standard. A performance criterion that reflects maximum efficiency, with no allowance for lost time, waste, or spoilage.

Incentive wage. A feature included in some modified wage plans to increase worker productivity by paying a bonus rate per hour when an employee meets or exceeds established production quotas.

Indirect (nontraceable) cost. See Common cost.

Indirect labor. The wages and salaries of employees who are required for the manufacturing process but who do not work directly on the units being produced; examples include department heads, inspectors, materials handlers, and maintenance personnel.

Indirect materials. Materials and supplies necessary for the manufacturing process that cannot be readily identified with any particular product manufactured or whose relative cost is too insignificant to measure.

Individual production report. A daily report prepared for each employee when labor costs are calculated on a piece-rate basis. The report shows the employee's work assignment and the number of units completed.

Inventory report. A form prepared when making a physical count of inventory on hand and used to reconcile differences between recorded inventory and the inventory quantities determined by physical count.

J

Job cost ledger. A subsidiary ledger that consists of the individual job cost sheet.

Job cost sheet. A form used to accumulate costs applicable to each job under a job order cost accounting system.

Job order cost system. A method or system of cost accounting that is appropriate for manufacturing operations that produce custom-made or special-order goods. Manufacturing costs are accumulated separately for each job and recorded on a job cost sheet.

Joint costs. The costs of materials, labor, and overhead incurred during the production of joint products.

Joint products. Two or more products that are obtained from the same manufacturing process and are the primary objectives of the process.

Just-in-time inventory system. A system that significantly reduces inventory carrying costs by requiring that raw materials be delivered by suppliers to the factory at the exact time that they are needed for production.

L

Labor cost standard. A predetermined estimate of the direct labor cost required for a unit of product.

Labor cost summary. A form showing the allocation of total payroll to Work in Process and Factory Overhead.

Labor efficiency (usage) variance. The difference between the actual number of direct labor hours worked and the standard hours for the actual level of production at the standard price.

Labor rate (price) variance. The difference between the average hourly direct labor rate actually paid and the standard hourly rate, multiplied by the number of hours worked.

Last-in, first-out. An inventory costing method based on the assumption that materials issued are the most recently purchased materials. Thus, materials issued are costed at the most recent purchase prices and ending inventories are costed at the prices paid for the earliest purchases.

Lead time. The estimated time interval between the placement of an order and the receipt of materials.

Liabilities budget. Shows how the cash position will be affected by payment of liabilities.

M

Machine hour method. A method of applying factory overhead to production based on the number of machine hours used for a job or process.

Make-up guarantee. An amount paid to employees under a modified wage plan when established production quotas are not met during a work period. The make-up guarantee is charged to the factory overhead account.

Manufacturing (or production) costs. All costs incurred in the manufacturing process; the costs are classified into three basic elements: direct materials, direct labor, and factory overhead.

Manufacturing process. The activities involved in converting raw materials into finished goods through the application of labor and incurrence of various factory expenses.

Marginal income ratio. See Contribution margin ratio.

Margin of safety. The amount that sales can decrease before the company will suffer a loss.

Margin of safety ratio. A relationship computed by dividing the difference between the total sales and the break-even point sales by total sales.

Mark-on percentage. A percentage of the manufacturing cost per unit.

Materials. The inventory account that represents the cost of all materials purchased and on hand to be used in the manufacturing process, including raw materials, prefabricated parts, and supplies.

Materials control. Procedures incorporated in the system of internal control that are designed to physically protect or safeguard materials (physical control) and to maintain the proper balance of materials on hand (control of the investment in materials).

Materials cost standard. A predetermined estimate of the cost of the direct materials required for a unit of product.

Materials ledger. See Stores ledger.

Materials price variance. The difference between the actual unit cost of direct materials and the standard unit cost, multiplied by the actual quantity of materials used.

Materials quantity (usage) variance. The difference between the actual quantity of direct materials used and the standard quantity for the actual level of production at standard price.

Materials (or stores) requisition. A form, prepared by authorized factory personnel and usually approved by the production department supervisor, to request materials from the storeroom; represents authorization for the storeroom keeper to issue materials for use in production.

Merchandisers. Wholesalers or retailers who purchase finished goods for resale.

Mix. The proportion or ratio of each material to the other materials required in the production process.

Mix variance. The change in cost that results from changing the proportions of materials added to the production mix; measures the effect of using a different combination of materials.

Modified wage plan. A wage plan that combines certain features of the hourly-rate and piece-rate plans.

Moving average. An inventory costing method based on the assumption that materials issued at any time are withdrawn from a mixed group of like materials, and no attempt is made to identify materials as being from the earliest or most recent purchases. Under this method, an average unit price is computed each time a new lot of materials is received and the new unit price is used to cost all issues of materials until another lot is received and a new unit price is computed.

N

Nonvalue added activities. Operations that include costs but do not add value to the product, such as moving, storing, and inspecting.

Normal capacity. The level of production that will meet the normal requirements of ordinary sales demand over a period of time; frequently used for budget development because it represents a logical balance between maximum capacity and the capacity demanded by actual sales volume.

Normal losses. Units lost due to the nature of the manufacturing process. Such losses are unavoidable and represent a necessary cost of producing goods.

Not-for-profit service agencies. These include charities, governmental units, and some health care facilities that provide services at little or no cost to the user.

O

Observation method. A technique used to classify a semivariable cost as either fixed or variable; involves examination and analysis of past relationships between the expense and production volume. Based on the observed pattern of cost behavior, a decision is made to classify the expense as either a fixed or variable cost, depending on which it more closely resembles.

Optical scanners. Devices that read bar coded material, such as employee identification badges

Order costs. The costs incurred as a result of ordering materials; includes salaries and wages of employees involved in purchasing, receiving, and inspecting materials; communications costs such as telephone, postage, and forms; and recordkeeping costs.

Order point. The point at which an item of inventory should be ordered; occurs when a predetermined minimum level of inventory on hand is reached. Determining an order point requires consideration of usage, lead time, and safety stock.

Outliers. Nonrepresentative data points that may be wrongly selected when using the High-low method.

Overapplied (or overabsorbed) factory overhead. The amount by which applied factory overhead exceeds actual factory overhead expenses incurred; represented by a remaining credit balance in Factory Overhead.

Overtime pay. The amount earned by employees at the regular hourly rate for hours worked in excess of the regularly scheduled time.

Overtime premium. An additional pay rate added to the employee's regular rate for hours worked in excess of the regularly scheduled time.

P

Payroll department. The department responsible for maintaining payroll records and determining each employee's gross and net earnings.

Payroll record. A form prepared each pay period showing the earnings of each employee for the period.

Pension costs. The costs incurred by an employer to provide retirement benefits to employees.

Performance report. A periodic summary of cost and production data that are controllable by the manager of a particular cost center.

Period costs. All costs that are not assigned to the product, but are recognized as expense and charged against revenue in the period incurred.

Periodic inventory system. A method of accounting for inventory that requires estimating inventory during the year for interim statements and shutting down operations to count all inventory items at the end of the year.

Perpetual inventory system. A method of accounting for inventory which provides a continuous record of purchases, issues, and balances of all goods in stock.

Physical unit of measure. A basis for allocating joint costs. Each product is assumed to have received similar benefits from the production process and therefore is charged with a proportionate share of the total processing costs.

Piece-rate plan. A wage plan under which an employee is paid a specified rate for each unit or "piece" completed.

Planning. The process of establishing objectives or goals for the organization and determining the means by which the objectives will be attained.

Practical capacity. The level of production that provides complete utilization of all facilities and personnel, but allows for some idle capacity due to operating interruptions such as machinery breakdowns, idle time, and other inefficiencies.

Predetermined factory overhead rate. A percentage or amount determined by dividing budgeted factory overhead cost by budgeted production; budgeted production may be expressed in terms of machine hours, direct labor hours, direct labor cost, or units. The predetermined rate is an estimate used in applying factory overhead to production.

Price. In the context of variance analysis, refers to the cost of materials or the hourly wage rate for direct labor.

Prime cost. The combined costs of direct materials and direct labor incurred in manufacturing a product.

Process costing. The act of assigning costs to a unit of activity within the factory.

Process cost system. A method or system of cost accounting that is appropriate for manufacturing operations that produce continuous output of homogeneous products. Manufacturing costs are accumulated separately for each department and are recorded on a cost of production report.

Product costs. Costs that are included as part of inventory costs and expensed when goods are sold.

Production department. A department in which actual manufacturing operations are performed, and the units being produced are physically changed.

Production department supervisor. The employee who is responsible for supervising the operational functions of a production department.

Production report. A report, used in a process cost accounting system and prepared by the department head, showing: beginning units in process; number of units completed during the period; ending units in process and their estimated stage of completion.

Production work teams. A recent concept where output is dependent upon contributions made by all members of the work crew.

Purchase order. A form, prepared by the purchasing agent and addressed to the chosen vendor, that describes the materials ordered, credit terms and prices, and the date and method of delivery; represents the vendor's authorization to ship goods.

Purchasing agent. The individual(s) in the organization who is responsible for the purchasing function.

Purchase price variance. The difference between the actual cost of materials and the standard cost.

Purchase requisition. A form, usually prepared by the storeroom keeper or employee with similar responsibility, that is used to notify the purchasing agent that additional materials are needed; represents the agent's authority to purchase materials.

Purchasing agent. The employee who is responsible for purchasing the materials needed for production.

R

Receiving clerk. The employee who is responsible for supervising incoming shipments of materials and making sure that all incoming materials are checked as to quantity and quality.

Receiving report. A form prepared by the receiving clerk for each incoming shipment of materials. The clerk identifies the materials, determines the quantity received, and records this information on the receiving report as well as the name of the shipper, date of receipt, and the number of the purchase order identifying the shipment.

Relative sales value. A basis for allocating joint costs proportionally based on the respective selling prices of the separate products.

Responsibility accounting. The assignment of accountability for costs or production results to those individuals who have the authority to influence costs or production.

Returned materials report. A form prepared to accompany materials being returned to the storeroom that had been previously requisitioned but were not used in production.

Return shipping order. A form prepared by the purchasing agent when goods are to be returned to the vendor.

S

Safety shock. The estimated minimum level of inventory needed to protect against stockouts.

Scatter graph method. A method that estimates a straight line along which the semivariable costs will fall by drawing the line by visual inspection through the data points plotted on the graph.

Schedule of fixed costs. A listing of fixed overhead costs, such as depreciation, insurance, and property taxes; provides the source from which fixed costs can be allocated to the various departments. Since fixed costs are assumed not to vary in amount from month to month, a schedule can be prepared in advance for several periods; at the end of a period, a journal entry can be prepared to record total fixed costs from the information provided in the schedule.

Scrap materials. By-products that are generated in the manufacturing process; usually, such materials have some value and their costs and revenues are accounted for separately.

Segment. A division, a product line, a sales territory, or other organizational unit that can be separately identified for reporting purposes and profitability analysis.

Segment margin. The term used in segment analysis for the excess of segment revenue over direct costs assigned to the segment; common costs are excluded in computing segment margin.

Semifixed costs. Costs that tend to remain the same in dollar amount over a certain range of activity but increase when production exceeds certain limits.

Semivariable costs. Manufacturing costs that are somewhat responsive to changes in production, but do not change proportionally with increases or decreases in volume; examples include indirect materials, indirect labor, repairs and maintenance, and power.

Sequential distribution method. A method for allocating service department costs to production departments, recognizing the interrelationship of the service departments. Costs are first allocated, sequentially, to other service departments and then to production departments. The sequence may begin by distributing the costs of the service department that renders the greatest amount of service to all other departments. Alternatively, the costs of the service department with the largest total overhead can be distributed first.

Service department. A department within the factory that does not work directly on the product but provides needed services to other departments; examples include a department that generates power for the factory; a maintenance department that maintains and repairs buildings and equipment; and a cost accounting department that maintains factory accounting records.

Shift premium. An additional rate of pay added to an employee's regular rate as compensation for working an evening or night shift.

Spending variance. See Budget variance. The difference between the actual factory overhead for variable costs and the actual hours × standard variable rate.

Split-off point. The point where joint products become separately identifiable; may occur during, or at the end of, the manufacturing process.

Spoiled units. Units of product with imperfections that cannot be economically corrected; they are sold as items of inferior quality or "seconds."

Stage of completion. The fraction or percentage of materials, labor, and overhead costs of a completed unit that have been applied during the period to goods that have not been completed.

Standard. A norm or criterion against which performance can be measured.

Standard cost accounting. See Standard cost accounting system.

Standard cost accounting system. A method of accounting for manufacturing costs that can be used in conjunction with either a job order system or process cost system. Standard costing makes it possible to determine what a product should have cost as well as what the product actually cost.

Standard costs. The costs that would be incurred under efficient operating conditions and are forecast before the manufacturing process begins. The predetermined standard costs are compared with actual manufacturing costs incurred and used by management as a basis for evaluating operating efficiency and taking corrective action when necessary.

Standard production. The volume on which the initial calculation of standard costs is based.

Standard unit cost for factory overhead. The act of estimating factory overhead cost at the standard, or normal, level of production, considering historical data and future changes and trends.

Step costs. See Semifixed costs.

Stockout. Running out of an item of inventory; may occur due to inaccurate estimates of usage or lead time or other unforeseen events, such as the receipt of damaged or inferior materials from a supplier.

Storeroom keeper. The employee who is responsible for the storing and maintaining of materials inventories.

Stores (or materials) ledger. A subsidiary ledger supporting the Materials control account in the general ledger. The individual accounts in the stores ledger are used to record receipts and issues of materials and show the quantity and cost of materials on hand.

Stores requisition. See Materials requisition.

Summary of factory overhead. A schedule of all factory overhead expenses incurred during a period; prepared from the factory overhead analysis sheets, the schedule shows each item of overhead expense by department and in total.

Summary of materials issued and returned. A form used to record all issuances of materials to the factory, returns of materials previously requisitioned, and returns of materials to the vendors (sellers). The summary, when completed at the end of a period, provides the information needed to record the cost of materials for the period.

T

Theoretical capacity. The maximum number of units that can be produced with the completely efficient use of all available facilities and personnel.

Three-variance method. The analysis of factory overhead costs based on the computation of efficiency, capacity, and budget (spending) variances.

Throughput time. The time that it takes a unit to make it through the production process.

Timekeeping department. The department responsible for determining the number of hours that employees should be paid for and the type of work performed by employees.

Time ticket. A document used to record the time spent by an employee on specific assignments. The time ticket is the basis for allocating the cost of factory labor to jobs or departments.

Transferred-in costs. The portion of a department's total costs that were incurred by and transferred from a prior production department.

Two-variance method. The analysis of factory overhead costs based on the computation of the volume variance and the budget variance.

U

Under- and Overapplied Factory Overhead. An account used to accumulate differences from period to period between actual and applied factory overhead. At the end of the year, the balance in this account may be closed to Cost of Goods Sold (if the amount is relatively small) or allocated on a prorata basis to Work in Process, Finished Goods, and Cost of Goods Sold (if the amount is material).

Underapplied (or underabsorbed) factory overhead. The amount by which actual factory overhead exceeds applied factory overhead; represented by a remaining debit balance in Factory Overhead.

Unfavorable variance. The difference between actual and standard costs when actual costs exceed standard costs.

Unit cost. The cost of manufacturing one unit of product.

Usage. The quantity of materials used or the number of direct labor hours worked.

V

Vacation pay. An amount paid to employees during their vacation periods as part of the employees' compensation for services to the employer.

Variable costing. See Direct costing.

Variable costs. Manufacturing costs which vary in proportion to changes in production volume; includes direct labor, direct materials, and some types of factory overhead.

Variance. The difference, during an accounting period, between the actual and standard or budgeted costs of materials, labor, and overhead.

Velocity. The speed with which units are produced in a manufacturing system. It is the inverse of the throughput time.

Vendor's invoice. A form, usually received from the vendor before goods are delivered, confirming a purchase of materials and representing a "bill" for the ordered goods. The purchasing agent should compare the invoice with the related purchase order to verify the description of materials, price, terms of payment, method of shipment, and delivery date.

Volume variance. The difference between budgeted fixed overhead and the fixed overhead applied to work in process; the result of operating at a level of production different from the standard, or normal, level.

Voucher system. A system for recording purchases in a voucher register that is widely used by manufacturing enterprises because it is more efficient than the alternative approach of using a purchases journal.

W

Waste materials. See Scrap materials.

Work in Process. The inventory account that includes all the manufacturing costs incurred to date for goods that are in various stages of production but are not yet completed.

Work shift. A regularly scheduled work period for a designated number of hours.

Y

Yield. The number of units produced from a standard amount of materials introduced in the production process.

Yield variance. Measures whether a change in materials mix affected the yield (output) and shows the difference in cost that results if the actual yield varies from the standard yield determined for a given input of materials.

Index